AULD GREEKIE

AULD GREEKIE

EDINBURGH
AS
THE ATHENS OF THE NORTH

Iain Gordon Brown

FONTHILL

www.fonthillmedia.com
office@fonthillmedia.com

First published in the United Kingdom
and the United States of America 2022

British Library Cataloguing in Publication Data:
A catalogue record for this book is available from the British Library

ISBN 978-1-78155-892-8

Typeset in 10pt on13pt Sabon
Printed and bound in England

For
PATRICIA

and also for four addresses in Georgian Edinburgh
32, 46, 1, 4
all with at least some 'Grecian' features, however modest

CONTENTS

'By the Second Athens, is meant "The Intellectual City",
a name that might afford the ground-work of a Tome.'

James Aikman, *The Cenotaph* (Edinburgh 1821)

PREFACE AND ACKNOWLEDGEMENTS

My interest in the subject of 'The Athens of the North' goes back a very long way. Though born abroad, I grew up in Edinburgh, and was conscious from a young age of its soubriquet. Those stark columns on Calton Hill fascinated me. Why were they there? What did they mean? Who had built them, and why? And why was it that what seemed to be part of a temple was either ruined or incomplete and, though looking old, yet also seemed, in a way, to be pristine? Ruined temples belonged in Italy or Greece, not in Scotland. I had been to Rome, and had seen similar fragmentary structures there—though clearly this one was built in a different order of architecture. It was neither florid Corinthian, nor slim Ionic with those curly volutes. My mother (who knew about such things) informed me it was Doric, *Greek* Doric, and that it had been intended as a copy of the Parthenon in Athens. My grandmother, who had been born in Edinburgh only sixty years after the first stones of this northern 'Parthenon' were laid, told me the story of the unfinished National Monument and was the first to introduce me to the opprobrious names of 'Edinburgh's disgrace' and 'Scotland's folly'.

At school I was extremely interested in the classical world and in the archaeology of Mediterranean lands. I started ancient Greek at the age of thirteen. When I was fourteen, my parents took me to Greece for the first time. My father had an introduction to an elderly gentleman in Athens who had been a liaison officer with British forces during the Second World War. We spent some time with Sidney Constantinidis, either strolling round the sites of the modern city (though he was not a boulevardier, his pace was frustratingly leisurely: I wanted to see more!) or in the National Museum. The rougher ground of the ancient sites he allowed us to tackle on our own, as indeed we wished to do, *Blue Guide* in hand. He entertained us in his elegant house, where he had an extensive library. I remember him being fascinated, maybe even surprised (for he had not, I think, ever been to Scotland) when we told him that Edinburgh was called 'The Athens of the North'. We sent him afterwards a copy of Ian G. Lindsay's *Georgian Edinburgh*.

In that admirable little book, our Greek friend would have read of the archetypal twentieth-century Edinburgh citizen who daily 'walks the pavements of the Modern Athens', and of the visitor from overseas who views 'the Athenian squares and terraces'. Although Lindsay's apparent suggestion was that 'Georgian Edinburgh' is synonymous with the much more amorphous concept of 'Modern Athens' or 'the Athens of the North', he nonetheless employed some telling phrases that might almost set the scene or act as a sort of epigraph for the pages that follow. My own book will attempt to demonstrate the complexities of the idea, and to indicate that the 'Athenian' phase of Edinburgh was set within the wider history of the city's Georgian development, both architectural and social. Most significant of all was Lindsay's choice of a single word: 'illusion'. By the early years of the nineteenth century, he wrote, Edinburgh had

> begun to see herself as a northern reflection of ancient Athens and took the illusion pretty seriously. To the Modern Athenians, the Calton Hill seemed to be an admirable Acropolis. That this was so there could be little doubt, for all travellers who had been to Greece told them so; in fact the Calton was a bit higher, and quite probably finer than the original ... This Grecian ardour was not ... to be confined to the rocks of the Calton, and all over the town porticos, pilasters and pediments sprang up. Almost every street was adorned with Greek detail of some kind ...

I distinctly recall going to a meeting of the Edinburgh Schools' Classical Society when the speaker—his name, however, long forgotten—lectured on the influence of ancient Greek architecture on the buildings of Edinburgh. He had lots of tired old black-and-white glass slides of the Parthenon and the Royal Scottish Academy, of the Choragic Monument of Lysikrates and the Dugald Stewart Monument, and so on. I gave the vote of thanks. In doing so, I remember making a plea that, somehow, someone might find the nerve and the authority to remove the vast statue of Queen Victoria from the pediment of the RSA building. Even then it seemed to offend my young eye—as still it does—and to render this Scottish Parthenon (yes, another one!) less authentically 'Greek'.

Later, at the University of Edinburgh, I took a senior honours course on 'Culture and Society in Scotland in the Eighteenth and Early Nineteenth Centuries', taught by the charismatic Dr Nicholas Phillipson. This was a formative experience, underpinning much of my subsequent scholarly existence. Then, later still, at Cambridge, I was fortunate to attend lectures in the History of Art department. A course on British architectural history of the same period fielded all the most distinguished scholars working in that area: John Harris, Marcus Binney, Dr Alistair Rowan, John Wilton-Ely, Dr Joseph Mordaunt Crook and Dr David Watkin; Dr Robin Middleton dealt with the European context. The Greek Revival was covered as part of the wider neoclassical movement. These classes complemented the more formal teaching I received from the inimitable Dr Hugh Plommer in the principles of Greek architecture as part of a course in Classical Archaeology. Soon, though not strictly speaking an architectural historian myself, I was committed to the serious study of architectural history as an aspect of a wider concern with British cultural history of the mid-seventeenth century to the mid-nineteenth.

Back in Edinburgh again, and now on the staff of the National Library of Scotland, in 1978 I mounted with a colleague, Alastair Cherry, a major exhibition entitled 'Scottish Architects at Home and Abroad'. This brought together, and exploited—in many cases for the first time—a remarkably wide range of printed and manuscript sources. It is gratifying that the catalogue is, apparently, still regarded as a work of reference. In it I wrote several substantial and wide-ranging entries discussing a number of key sources, some of which are revisited here, all these years later. Outstanding is the significant volume of letters and documents (NLS, MS. 638) relating to the history of the National Monument on Calton Hill: that would-be facsimile Parthenon, of which but twelve columns and their epistyle ever got built—and then only after most astonishingly convoluted debate, a paper war conducted in the pages of the periodical literature of the day, subsequent delay, and yet further prevarication. Ultimate failure to achieve the complete building could have been foretold from the outset. Reading over the exhibition catalogue entries headed, for example, 'The Making of Classical Edinburgh', 'The National Monument' or 'Modern Athenians', makes me realise that there is a prehistory of sorts to the present book.

Looking back, I was then actually rather ahead of the game in dealing with some of these sources and the issues behind them. But other work, and a host of different scholarly priorities, diverted me for many years from pursuing old interests in matters broadly connected with Edinburgh as the Modern Athens. Several younger scholars have followed where, perhaps, I had once played some small part in showing the way. They have, collectively, published on aspects of the wider topic at large, or have discussed discrete elements of it. Almost everything they have written has been relevant to my recent research.

Opportunity has now been offered to revisit these far-off fields; and, thus, I have returned to a fascinating era in the history of Edinburgh, and to some most intriguing problems. The relevance of these, long apparent to me, was thrown into relief only a few days ago when a visitor from Eastern Europe stopped me as I happened to be walking past the gates of the former High School below the slopes of Calton Hill. He wanted to know how he might ascend to what he called 'the Acropolis'. The vision of an 'Athenian' Edinburgh endures.

*   *   *   *   *

The references cited throughout this book will indicate the scholarship to which I am in one way or another indebted, and it is unnecessary to mention here all the writers of works I have found invaluable or merely helpful. But some names should be singled out.

First and foremost, there is the late Professor Charles McKean, with whom I discussed many of the issues long before I ever thought I might actually revisit the topic in a serious way. His few pages on Edinburgh as Athens of the North in his luminous *Edinburgh: Portrait of a City* (1991) are wonderfully stimulating and appealing, even if they also contain some eccentric theorising with which I take issue in my own text that follows. I also benefited from discussion with the late Dr Andrew Fraser, whose knowledge of Edinburgh history was so extensive and so willingly shared.

Those scholars and friends to whose work on Greek Edinburgh in its architectural manifestations I owe most are Professor David Walker, Professor Alistair Rowan and John Lowrey for their excellent general over-views of place and period; Dr James Macaulay (who died as this book was being completed), Dr Joe Rock, Dr Margaret Stewart, Dr Anthony Lewis, Helen Smailes and David Black for more specific knowledge of individual characters or topics; and Ian Gow, especially, not just for his admirable and stylish writings on William Henry Playfair and his world, but for his comprehensive knowledge of place and period. All have provided either inspiration or information over the years. A recent acquaintance, Ian McHaffie—author of a remarkable book entitled *Greek Secrets Revealed*, nominally on Greek inscriptions in Edinburgh but, additionally, full of quirky details on much else Hellenic—has been equally helpful. The relevant works of Professor Joseph Mordaunt Crook on the Greek Revival excited me long ago, as still they do. And whenever I reach for his great *Biographical Dictionary of British Architects* (two successive editions of which I had the honour to review) I remember with particular pleasure many years of 'information exchange' with the late Sir Howard Colvin.

By her kind invitation to give a lecture at the British Embassy in Athens, my friend Kate Smith CMG, lately British Ambassador to the Hellenic Republic, allowed me to gather thoughts on this topic some time before I imagined they might ever expand into the present work. That lecture commemorated the bicentenary of the first serious calls for a 'reproduction', 'reconstruction', 'facsimile' or 'transfer'— all these terms will be encountered and explored in the pages that follow—of the Parthenon of Athens in, or to, Edinburgh. Some of those ideas were first committed to paper in my article published in *The Book of the Old Edinburgh Club*, new series volume 15 (2019), which appeared in 2020. I am indebted to the editor of *BOEC*, Dr Wilson Smith, for permission to incorporate material from the original article in the Prologue and elsewhere in the first chapters of this present book.

In practical matters connected with access to material in collections both public and private, and permissions for their use or reproduction, I am grateful to the following, among others: Hazel Stewart and Alison Metcalfe of the National Library of Scotland; Dr Daryl Green, Stephen Willis and Paul Fleming of the Centre for Research Collections, Edinburgh University Library; Clare Padgett of Edinbugh City Libraries and Capital Collections; Sandy Wood of the Royal Scottish Academy; Dr Claire Pannell, Collections Officer, East Lothian Council; Air Commodore J. E. Linter, Secretary of the New Club; Thomas Barnes, Aviva Archives; the Image Request staff, RISD Museum, Providence, Rhode Island, USA; Elizabeth Bray, British Museum; James Hamilton of the Society of Writers to H. M. Signet; Karin Weber, Bayerische Verwaltung der staatlichen Schlösser, Gärten und Seen; Lauren Bufferd and Bonnie Seymour of The Parthenon, Nashville, Tennessee; Dr Nick Haynes; Karen Stevenson, Royal Incorporation of Architects in Scotland and Joe Waterfield, Historic Environment Scotland; Ian McHaffie; Marion Mackintosh; Dr Wilson Smith; David McClay; and John Stewart.

Professor Stephen Brown, of Trent University, Ontario, Canada—whose vast knowledge of the intellectual and cultural history of late eighteenth- and early nineteenth-century Edinburgh has always been generously put at the disposal of fellow scholars—convinced me that my proposed approach to the topic displayed originality, and that what I was planning to do and say was indeed worthwhile. He very kindly read the manuscript in its near-final form. Dr Murray Simpson, close friend and colleague for many years, has listened sympathetically (as often he does, and as only he can) while my thoughts developed. He has given time willingly to reading successive drafts of the text, and has made helpful suggestions for its improvement. The interest of my even older friend John Stewart provided welcome encouragement to continue.

It is a pleasure to be published once more by the remarkable Alan Sutton. I am most grateful to him, and to his colleagues at Fonthill, Jasper Hadman and George Kalchev, for bringing their experience and professionalism to bear in the production of a book as demanding as this.

* * * * *

The writing of *Auld Greekie* has been my personal contribution to the wider commemoration of the bicentenary of the start of the Greek Revolution. It is important to record this fact given that Edinburgh, which saw itself as the 'Modern Athens', played its part in promoting the cause of Greek freedom, and also manifested a concern for the fate of the monuments of ancient Athens during the course of the war of liberation.

Conversations with Dr Alasdair Grant were stimulating and enjoyable as he gathered materials and ideas for the 'Edina/Athena' exhibition (mounted by the University of Edinburgh in 2021 to mark the bicentenary) and as I commented on the labels and text panels in the role of an official academic adviser. This exhibition complemented the international 12th A. G. Leventis Conference on the theme of 'The Greek Revolution of 1821: Contexts, Scottish Connections, the Classical Tradition' held in the setting of Playfair's superb neoclassical library in the Old College of the University of Edinburgh. This was a most appropriate location, given the room's status as one of the greatest architectural set-pieces of the Athens of the North. Not wholly a purely 'Greek Revival' interior, but not yet a clearly Roman one either, it well illustrates the imprecision of style then current in the Northern Athens, a city in love with 'the antique' in whatever form it happened to find convenient, or to its taste, at the time. My own paper at the conference—on Sir Walter Scott, Greek, Greece and the Greeks—will appear in due course in the Leventis Studies volume resulting from the conference, to be published by Edinburgh University Press. Professors Niels Gaul and Douglas Cairns of the University of Edinburgh, and Professor Roderick Beaton of King's College, London (and Visiting Leventis Professor at Edinburgh in 2021) endorsed the project which now comes to fruition in this book, and I thank them warmly for their confidence.

Publication coincides with several notable and relevant bicentenaries which fall in 2022. These range from the initial promotion of the Philhellenic cause in Edinburgh, and the publication of Percy Bysshe Shelley's *Hellas*, to the completion of the decoration and the effective inauguration of the glorious room now known as the Upper Signet Library, and the commencement of Playfair's Royal Institution building. Two other 1822 bicentenaries stand out, themselves interconnected. One is the famous visit of King George IV, the first such visit to Edinburgh, or indeed to Scotland, by a reigning monarch for more than 170 years. The 'King's Jaunt' did much to focus public attention on the city as a place of topographical excitement and wild romance, as well as of intellectual eminence and self-satisfied smugness. The other is the laying of the foundation stone of the National Monument, which had become—in its preferred, though still putative 'Parthenon' form—the ultimate status-symbol of Edinburgh's claim to be another Athens.

*   *   *   *   *

My wife, Dr Patricia Andrew, has kept me sane and loved as I wrote *Auld Greekie*. She has supported me in every possible way through an intense period of work. She has read and re-read versions of the manuscript at various stages, and has made a great many immensely helpful suggestions and comments. I owe her more than I can say; the dedication is wholly inadequate to express my debt. But at least *this* Edinburgh structure 'in the Greek taste' has been completed; I can only hope it may not prove either a 'disgrace' or a 'folly'.

IAIN GORDON BROWN
Auld Reekie / New Athens
15 August 2022

ABBREVIATIONS
AND EXPLANATIONS OF SOME BIBLIOGRAPHICAL CURIOSITIES ENCOUNTERED IN THE SOURCES

Alison 1819 A: [Anon., but Archibald Alison], 'On the Proposed National Monument at Edinburgh', *Blackwood's Edinburgh Magazine*, V, no. xxviii (July 1819), pp. 377-87.

Alison 1819 B: [Anon., but Archibald Alison], 'Restoration of the Parthenon in the National Monument', *Blackwood's Edinburgh Magazine*, VI, no xxxii (November 1819), pp. 137-48.

Alison 1823: [Anon., but Archibald Alison], Art. VI, *The Edinburgh Review*, XXXVII, no. lxxv (February 1823), pp. 126-44. Under cover of a supposed 'review' of George, Earl of Aberdeen, *An Enquiry into the Principles of Beauty in Grecian Architecture; with an Historical View of the Rise and Progress of the Art in Greece* (1822), this is actually a lengthy essay clearly entitled—as the printed running head states—'Restoration of the Parthenon'.

Alison, *Autobiography*: Sir Archibald Alison, *Some Account of my Life and Writings. An Autobiography*, edited by his daughter-in-law, Lady [Jane R.] Alison, two vols (Edinburgh 1883).

B o S Edinburgh: John Gifford, Colin McWilliam and David Walker, *The Buildings of Scotland. Edinburgh*, reprinted with corrections (New Haven and London 2003).

Capital Collections: Collections of the City of Edinburgh Libraries, Museums and Galleries.

Cleghorn 1: [Anon., but George Cleghorn], *Remarks on the Intended Restoration of the Parthenon of Athens as the National Monument of Scotland* (Edinburgh 1824).

Cleghorn 2: 'An Amateur' [George Cleghorn], *Remarks on Ancient and Modern Art, in a Series of Essays By An Amateur* (Edinburgh 1837). This includes, at pp. 263-326, an essay entitled 'Restoration of the Parthenon as the National Monument of Scotland' which, Cleghorn explains (Preface, p. v), is partly a republication of the treatise of 1824 but 'condensed and remodelled'. The book, as a whole, is a notable discussion of western architecture; and it includes a very judicious but overlooked and unremarked survey of Scottish architecture, culminating in that of the 'Athenian' age of Edinburgh.

Cleghorn 3: George Cleghorn, *The Restoration of the Parthenon of Athens as the National Monument of Scotland* (Edinburgh 1846).

Cleghorn 4: George Cleghorn, *Ancient and Modern Art, Historical and Critical*, second edition [*sic*] corrected and enlarged, two vols (Edinburgh 1848). This is, in fact, a much revised and greatly expanded version of **Cleghorn 2**. The author explains (Preface, p. vi) that his remarks on the restoration of the Parthenon were omitted from the work due to the appearance of his second independent publication on the topic (as Cleghorn 3, above).

Cleghorn 5: George Cleghorn, 'Essay on the National Monument of Scotland', *Transactions of the Architectural Institute of Scotland*, 2 (1851-2), pp. 81-120.

Cohen: [Anon., but Francis Cohen, later Sir Francis Palgrave], Art. II, *The Quarterly Review*, XXVII, no. liv (July 1822, though not in fact published until 23 October 1822), pp. 308-37. This is nominally a review of Lewis Cottingham, *Plans, Elevations, Sections, Details and Views of the Magnificent Chapel of King Henry the Seventh, at Westminster Abbey Church; with the History of its Foundation, and Authentic Account of its Restoration* (1822). Neither this information, nor the *Quarterly*'s printed running head of 'Application of the Various Styles of Architecture', prepares the reader for what the article actually is, namely a polemical and very substantial essay on the National Monument of Scotland. Attribution of authorship to Cohen was established by Hill Shine and Helen Chadwick Shine, *The Quarterly Review Under Gifford: Identification of Contributors* (Chapel Hill, NC, 1949), p. 79. See also Jonathan Cutmore, *Contributors to the Quarterly Review, 1809-25* (London 2008), p. 170.

Colvin: Howard Colvin, *A Biographical Dictionary of British Architects 1600-1840*, fourth edition (New Haven and London 2008).

Edina / Athena: *Edina / Athena 1821-2021 The Greek Revolution & The Athens of the North*, exhibition catalogue by Alasdair Grant, Niels Gaul, Iain Gordon Brown and Roderick Beaton, University of Edinburgh (Edinburgh 2021).

'Edinburgh as Athens': Iain Gordon Brown, 'Edinburgh as Athens: New Evidence to Support a Topographical and Intellectual Idea Current in the Early Nineteenth Century', *The Book of the Old Edinburgh Club*, New Series, 15 (2019), pp. 1-12.

EUL: Edinburgh University Library.

Gifford: John Gifford, 'The National Monument of Scotland', *Architectural Heritage*, XXV (2014), pp. 43-83.

McKean: Charles McKean, *Edinburgh: Portrait of a City* (London 1991).

Mitchell: William Mitchell, *The National Monument to be Completed for the Scottish National Gallery on the Model of the Parthenon at Athens. An Appeal to the Scottish People* (London 1907). From a bibliographic point of view, Michell's work is curious, having variant title-pages and two apparently different titles. Published by A. & C. Black, it was also issued by Bernard Quaritch in some six different states of luxury, and could be had in two different 'enclosing cases'. A long, violet silk ribbon or 'streamer' is emblazoned with an image of the completed Parthenon after a now-lost model by Peter Slater.

Modern Athens!: *Modern Athens! Displayed in a Series of Views: or, Edinburgh in the Nineteenth Century* (London 1829). Images by Thomas Hosmer Shepherd; text by John Britton.

NER: [Anon.], '"Lectures on Architecture …". By James Elmes', *The New Edinburgh Review*, VIII (April 1823), Art. XV, pp. 554-603. This article makes no pretence to be what it is supposed to be, namely a review of James Elmes, *Lectures on Architecture* (1821; second edition 1823). Elmes's book is blatantly ignored, and the 'review' is in fact an extended diatribe on a wholly different topic, immediately turning into an extremely long but brilliant essay on the 'Athenian' pretensions of Edinburgh, its Greek Revival buildings, etc. The printed running head is simply 'Architecture'. Charles McKean, apparently alone among earlier scholars, knew of this article, citing it in his *Edinburgh. Portrait of a City* (1991), pp. 151-52. Nevertheless, he was uncertain of the date, circumstances and even place of publication, confusing the upstart *New Edinburgh Review* with its celebrated, older and more established near namesake, *The Edinburgh Review*. He also believed, without evidence (but presumably on the basis of this error) that the article was by Francis Jeffrey, though he subsequently suggested to me in private correspondence that it was by Henry Cockburn. Both attributions must remain a matter of conjecture. We simply do not know—just as influential people in the Edinburgh of the day had no idea either.

NLS: National Library of Scotland.

NRS: National Records of Scotland.

ODNB: *Oxford Dictionary of National Biography.*

'OROP': [Anon.], 'On the Restoration of the Parthenon', *The Edinburgh Magazine, and Literary Miscellany; A New Series of the Scots Magazine*, VI (April 1820), pp. 304-12.

'RPNM': [Anon., but 'R'], 'Restoration of the Parthenon for the National Monument', *Blackwood's Edinburgh Magazine*, V, no. xxix (August 1819), pp. 509-12. No authorship is attributed in Alan Lang Strout, *A Bibliography of Articles in Blackwood's Magazine*, 1817-1825 (Lubbock, Texas, 1959). But the 'R' as signature may possibly signify Andrew Robertson.

RSA: Royal Scottish Academy.

SAHA: *Scottish Architects at Home and Abroad*, exhibition catalogue by Alastair Cherry and Iain Gordon Brown, National Library of Scotland (Edinburgh 1978).

SNG: Scottish National Gallery.

'Traveller': Letter signed 'A Traveller', and headed 'Restoration of the Parthenon. To the Right Honourable the Lord Advocate of Scotland, Convener of the Committee on the National Monument', *The Edinburgh Magazine, and Literary Miscellany: A New Series of the Scots Magazine*, VI (February 1820), pp. 99-105. (This long 'letter' was subsequently reprinted as an independent pamphlet, of which a copy is in NLS, MS. 638, ff. 5-8.)

Williams, *Travels*: Hugh William Williams, *Travels in Italy, Greece, and the Ionian Islands. In a Series of Letters Descriptive of Manners, Scenery, and the Fine Arts*, two vols (Edinburgh 1820).

WS: post-nominal abbreviation for a member of the Society of Writers to Her Majesty's Signet.

PROLOGUE

'GILDED BY
THE RAYS OF AN ATHENIAN SUN'

In 1815, as the Napoleonic Wars ended, George Sibbald, from Edinburgh, was appointed to the Royal Navy frigate *Myrmidon* in the rank of Assistant Surgeon. Between 1816 and 1818, this warship bearing a name from Homer was deployed in the Eastern Mediterranean. Sibbald evidently kept a journal of his travels, and notes on the places he had seen in Egypt and the Levant, in the Aegean and Ionian islands, and in mainland Greece.

On his return to Britain, Sibbald wrote up his record in more complete form, giving the narrative of his adventures something of the character of a guide to the sites and cities he had come to know. His resulting manuscript, entitled 'Observations on Egypt, Syria and Greece', is undated. From a pencil note on the title-page we know only the period of Sibbald's Mediterranean voyage. His account is worthily pedestrian, and relatively unoriginal—expect in one particular aspect. He launches into a laboured but nonetheless remarkable comparison of the topography of Athens with that of Edinburgh. These passages are extremely interesting on account of the contribution they make to the historiography of the contemporary notion of Edinburgh as the 'Modern Athens', or 'the Athens of the North'—the former epithet tends to have chronological priority in terms of use; the latter seems to be a relatively later coining—and at a time when its citizens were regarded (more often than not by themselves) as 'Modern Athenians'.

Sibbald's manuscript is now in the National Library of Scotland.[1] Its discovery and acquisition, and the thoughts this stimulated, have been directly responsible for the investigation set out in the pages that follow. My book will demonstrate how the various terms indicating some degree of parallel and identification between ancient Athens and modern Edinburgh, and the notions behind them—all too frequently far-fetched and nugatory, but yet not entirely fanciful and thus potent nonetheless—were invented, developed and generally accepted; how they gave much pleasure and satisfaction to some, but also how they rebounded, and were ridiculed or resented by others.

Clearly the result of much labour over the years after the end of his posting in *Myrmidon,* Sibbald's account may or may not have been intended for publication. He was, however, neither an especially well-educated man, nor one blessed with great descriptive or analytical powers, and no amount of self-conscious classical reference or transfusion of English literary quotation can really mask these facts. The Greek part of the text, for example, is heavy with quotations from celebrated verses by Lord Byron. This is unsurprising given the tremendous influence the poet had in rendering Greece under Ottoman domination, and the romantic cause of the modern Greeks in their nascent struggle for independence, fashionable concerns among the 'Philhellenes' of Europe. Sibbald was evidently rather smitten by Byron's eponymous 'Maid of Athens' herself, Teresa Macri, whom the officers of *Myrmidon* met (with her family, being that of the late, Greek-born British Vice-Consul) at a *soirée* in the town.

Sibbald's manuscript is on the whole derivative of and dependent on contemporary travel literature and standard classical sources. He refers to published sources he must have consulted after returning home. In writing up the Athenian section of his travels he mentions works such as Edward Dodwell's *A Classical and Topographical Tour through Greece*, published in 1819. Internal evidence indicates that he must also have consulted works published in 1822 and 1823, this last being William Rae Wilson's *Travels in Egypt and the Holy Land*—so Sibbald's extended manuscript account has to post-date the appearance of this work. It is worth bearing in mind, as we examine Sibbald's comparison of Athens and Edinburgh, a marked tendency of Rae Wilson for insinuating Edinburgh and its buildings into the picture when discussing sites and structures that could only ever spring to the mind of the most ardent 'Edinaphile'. These parochial proclivities were pointed out by a writer in *The Edinburgh Review*, who found himself smiling at Rae Wilson's 'homely manner of bringing objects within the comprehension of his Scotch friends'.[2] The vanity of Edinburgh people in all matters concerning their own city was at times innocently endearing, and (to outsiders at least) occasionally puzzling or downright infuriating. This proves to be a constant factor in the complex story of how Edinburgh—long and affectionately known, from its polluted atmosphere and distinctive pall of smoke hanging above the city, as 'Auld Reekie' ('Old Smoky')—came to be compared with Athens.

*   *   *   *   *

Sibbald's comparison of the townscapes of Edinburgh and Athens makes an important point, and it highlights a general truth about the world of nuanced thinking on the topic of the New or the Northern Athens—these being other epithets in contemporary use. The very fact that he was a comparatively ordinary man in the Edinburgh street (just as he had occupied a relatively junior place in the wardroom of HMS *Myrmidon*) and *not* a classicist, a profound thinker or an accomplished writer, makes his opinion particularly illustrative of the concern with an issue of the day that was widely felt and earnestly debated. In a sense, George Sibbald acted the part of a cultural 'myrmidon': he followed the lead of others, and though he held his own views these were largely reflective of those of the leaders of taste and society.

The comparison between the two cities was a dual one: in the realm of the mind, and in physical terms. Two places regarded as exercising a like cultural and intellectual hegemony—the one in classical antiquity, the other in the age of the later Enlightenment—were also perceived as possessing a striking similarity in their topography: in their distinctive landscape features, and in a corresponding relationship to sea, coast and surrounding hills. (Figs 1-3; 6-8) Both led to Edinburgh's seeking to add to the *jumelage*, or imagined conjunction, the additional enhancement that a series of neo-Greek buildings would afford. Greek Revival Edinburgh of the period stretching very roughly from 1810 to 1850 was also thought to reflect the Athens of antiquity. In the Haldane Institute lectures given at Glasgow School of Art the year before his death, Alexander 'Greek' Thomson, the great Glasgow architect of the mid-nineteenth century, reserved unexpectedly laudatory words for the rival city of Edinburgh in earlier decades. Having described what he termed the 'nine Muses' of Athenian building-types most influential in the Greek Revival architecture of his own city, Thomson went on to state the following, which neatly unites ideas of cultural leadership evident in 'Athenian' terminology with the architectural expression of that ideal:

> Nevertheless, the buildings which constitute the glory of Edinburgh, and which entitle it to be called the modern Athens, were the fruits of this movement and of the concentrated intelligence of British society, which at the time had its seat in our northern capital.[3]

Here Alexander Thomson was returning to ideas he had first voiced five years previously in another Glasgow lecture in which he had spoken the following words in the context of an assessment of the progress of the Greek Revival in Europe, most notably in Germany and in Edinburgh. This had been an age

> when Edinburgh was distinguished above other cities for whatever was profound in philosophy, and elegant in literature, she adopted this style as the

fittest expression of the high degree of refinement to which she had attained, and found amongst her own sons, men well qualified to fulfil her desires, and the works which grew up under their hands constitute the chief charm of that beautiful city, and win for it the designation of which she is so justly proud, 'The Modern Athens'.[4]

Only Edinburgh's precarious financial position in the later 1820s had clipped the wings of its civic and architectural ambition. Thomson suggested that had not circumstances 'exhausted its energies, and left it prostrate for the succeeding thirty years, there is no saying what the talent of its architects and the influence of its intelligence might have accomplished throughout the country.'[5] Carrying on from Thomson's statement, it might be suggested that Edinburgh's 'winged Victory' had become its own now wingless *Niké Apteros*.

*   *   *   *   *

The relevant portion of Sibbald's extended musings can be placed within the literature of a particularly interesting period in the history of Edinburgh, its architectural development (both actual and projected) and the evolving idea of the city's conception of itself. Ideas about a Greek Edinburgh, about Edinburgh as another Athens, had a political dimension. In the eighteenth century, Scots had striven to sublimate their nationhood—lost in some measure, but by no means entirely, in 1707 with the Union of the Parliaments of England and Scotland—by scaling the slopes of Helicon. During the intellectual ferment of the Scottish Enlightenment, they seem to have thought about everything, and to have invented a great deal. Edinburgh was famously called by Tobias Smollett, in *The Expedition of Humphry Clinker* (1771), 'a hotbed of genius'.[6] Eighteenth-century Scots also saw political, economic and social opportunities in the new Union. London beckoned; ambitious Scots tended to go south. They laid claim to a disproportionate share of the responsibility for, and the profits from, the expanding British Empire through political activity at home, or military or East India Company service abroad. But, in the new world order, those who remained behind—notably men at the Scottish Bar—wanted to see Edinburgh find a unique place both within the Union and the Empire.

In the first decades of the nineteenth century, but especially shortly after the conclusion of the French wars, Edinburgh was exercising its civic soul on the question of its identity. Could it legitimately view itself as something greater than a mere provincial metropolis, the capital of a small country bound to some greater or lesser extent to be inferior to, or dependent on, its dominant partner within the wider United Kingdom of Great Britain and Ireland (as that had now become)? Lacking real political power, or overwhelming commercial and industrial weight, could not Edinburgh aim to be generally regarded, instead and more fittingly, as a city of the intellect: as a place unique in Britain, in the Empire, and in the world at large? The 'northern metropolis of science and art', was what one commentator hoped Edinburgh might become.[7] In 1821 the Swiss geologist Louis Albert Necker de Saussure ranked the city as 'not unworthy of the titles of *the Athens of the North*, and *the Capital of Mind*', thus employing two highly significant epithets within a single sentence—an early use (by a European writer) of the one, and perhaps the first (by anyone) of the other.[8]

London was obviously and unquestionably the 'Rome' of the Union and of the Empire. In the text of his *Metropolitan Improvements* of 1827 (written to accompany an extensive series of engraved plates by Thomas Hosmer Shepherd), James Elmes described London 'as the ROME of modern history', and lauded its greatness in what he called 'the Augustan Age of George IV'.[9] But, in these crucial years, Edinburgh appeared to have evolved, or to be turning itself into the 'Athens' of the British world, queen of its own cultural and intellectual realm.[10] It followed that the architectural expression of this new 'Athenian' identity should be sought and found in a style that was derived more purely and overtly from ancient Greek models.[11] A sequel to *Metropolitan Improvements* was published in 1829: bearing the title *Modern Athens! Displayed in a Series of Views: or, Edinburgh in the Nineteenth Century*, this was an equally complimentary volume, also with plates by Shepherd, and with descriptive text by John Britton. But matters are not quite so clear-cut as simply the notion of London's (and indeed England's) Rome to Edinburgh's (and Scotland's) Athens and Greece. London and England had also—and rather earlier—aspired to emulate Greece, and to inherit its cultural and intellectual traditions, not least by the collecting of classical Greek sculpture so as to 'transplant' (as Henry Peacham had charmingly put it) 'old Greece into *England*'. The Arundel Marbles were the precursors in the seventeenth century of much subsequent accumulation, culminating in the acquisition by Lord Elgin of the Parthenon sculptures. In a letter printed in the *Annals of the Fine Arts* for 1817, James Elmes had actually referred to Britain, as a whole, as 'a country that has not inaptly been called the Modern Greece'.[12] And in *Metropolitan Improvements*, he also appeared to compare the cultural and architectural flowering of London as akin to that of Athens under Pericles.[13] Moreover, Great Britain as a whole, victor in the Napoleonic Wars, entertained a distinct sense of itself—England just as much as Scotland, Edinburgh as completely as London—being heir to the freedom-loving and freedom-defending spirit of Athens during and after the Persian Wars.[14]

However, before Elmes had his say, Edinburgh's 'Athenianism' had been stirring. In an article of seminal importance published anonymously in the July 1819 number of *Blackwood's Edinburgh Magazine*, Archibald Alison the younger—a busy advocate also dabbling in journalism—described both the mood and the age in which Auld Reekie was to be transmogrified into something else. Determined not to see Edinburgh, 'the ancient metropolis ... degenerate into a provincial town', where 'in time, at least, a corresponding *decay* may take place in its literary and philosophic acquirements', Alison preferred to imagine the glorious moment when '... the city whose genius has already procured for it the name of the Modern Athens, might hope to vie with its immortal predecessor in the fine arts.' He continued:

> And thus while London is the Rome of the Empire, to which the young, and the ambitious and the gay, resort in pursuit of pleasure, of fortune, or of ambition, Edinburgh might become another Athens, in which the arts and sciences flourished, under the shade of her ancient fame, and established a dominion over the minds of men more permanent than even that which the Roman arms were able to effect.[15]

Archibald Alison will feature prominently in our story. (Fig. 17) A junior at the Scottish bar in 1819, he would later become an Advocate Depute, then Sheriff of Lanarkshire and, later still, Lord Rector of Glasgow University and a baronet. He was also famous as the expansive historian of Europe in the age of the French Revolution. With an eye to the buildings 'standing on the rock of the Acropolis' which inspired emulation in Edinburgh, Alison liked to imagine a future Edinburgh being (as he expressed it lyrically) 'gilded by the rays of an Athenian sun'.[16]

Like several of his legal contemporaries, Alison was motivated by the notion of a Scotland that might still find its distinctive voice within the United Kingdom. Such men, both Tory (like Alison himself) and Whig, might be described as patriotic Scottish nationalists but most certainly not as early proponents of Scottish independence. Their allegiance to the Union was solid. But Alison did look back wistfully to a pre-Union Scotland, and wished to see its ancient institutions preserved in all their erstwhile vigour. He lamented any diminution of the fundamental characteristics of Scottish society, or the independent legal system and financial structures of the country.[17] These beliefs led him to favour the romantic concept of Scotland—even just Edinburgh—as some sort of modern-day equivalent of a small, independent ancient Greek city-state. Hence the appeal of the idea of Edinburgh as the 'Modern Athens'.

*   *   *   *   *

August 1822 saw King George IV's celebrated visit to Edinburgh. As never before the city was viewed, and written of, as a place of striking beauty that some might term 'sublime' and 'picturesque'. A developing wealth of architectural splendour and refinement enhanced an incomparable natural setting to create a

dramatic Romantic-Classic landscape of immense distinction.[18] Equally, people
were (not surprisingly) interested in a city that had produced so many great
minds. It was perceived as a centre of intellectual brilliance where the fire of its
own eighteenth-century Enlightenment had been kindled, the embers of which
were still very much aglow.

The year 1822 was otherwise notable for the irrevocable decision to build,
on Calton Hill, the proposed National Monument as a memorial to the
Scottish dead of the French Revolutionary and Napoleonic Wars, and to build
it in the form of a replica of the Parthenon of Athens. (Figs 62-64) After much
uncertainly and prolonged debate on purpose, form, style and location, its
future construction was ensured by the high-profile ceremony of the laying of
the foundation stone during the 'King's jaunt'—albeit in the absence of the King
himself.[19] The royal visit, though important in the wider view, merely hastened
the project already largely decided upon. Calton Hill had become the focus of
Edinburgh's 'Athenian' ambitions. For it to become the 'Acropolis' of the New
Athens, the hill needed a Parthenon.

The resolution to build the National Monument on the 'model' of the
Parthenon had actually been agreed at a meeting of the Subscribers on 18 June
1821, the sixth anniversary of the Battle of Waterloo. 'The EDIFICE', it would
be affirmed at the end of that year,

> is the noblest that Architectural Genius ever planned; and the Calton Hill of
> Edinburgh, where it is proposed to place it, has so remarkable a similarity to
> the spot where the original Temple stands, that every Scotsman may be proud
> of an opportunity of completing the resemblance between the Metropolis of
> his native country and the principal city of ancient Greece.[20]

Various earlier schemes for commemorative monuments to the war effort,
and eventual victory in 1815, had come and gone. There was, for example,
a triumphal arch of clearly Roman inspiration, designed by James Gillespie
[later Gillespie Graham] in 1816 for the western end of Princes Street. (Fig.
15) A slightly later map actually shows an arch of different design spanning
the eastern end of Waterloo Place, just where the building-line gives way to the
open slopes of Calton Hill.[21] In this position, it would have formed an entry to
the city from the London Road. Neither arch was built.

The most grandiloquently preposterous of these schemes, by Archibald Elliot,
was for a hugely inflated 'Pantheon', in some ways more like that of Paris than its
ultimate, glorious original in Rome, though the stepped and saucer-shaped dome
clearly aspired to echo the latter. (Fig. 14) Behind an enormous hexastyle portico
and an encircling colonnade, and with another superimposed circular colonnade
rising above (both in a giant Corinthian order), Elliot's leviathan combined a vast
circular domed saloon or 'Inscription Hall' with a rectangular, basilica-like church

projecting to the rear in satisfaction of the early requirement that the Monument have some ecclesiastical function.[22] The engraving which accompanies the proposal for its erection gives no accurate sense of where the building was to stand. However, its site was to be at the southern (upper) end of the earthen Mound connecting the Old and New Towns. In that position, it would have been a grotesquely inappropriate intrusion into the cityscape at a particularly sensitive location. This megalomaniac idea was fairly rapidly dismissed.

Protracted and convoluted debate was then conducted at inordinate length in the periodical press. Liberties were taken by one or another author with what various writers had actually said for or against whatever kind of building was most suited for purpose and location. As a result of a change in taste and aesthetics, Greek ideas prevailed over Roman.[23] The would-be 'Athenian' soul of Edinburgh was asserting itself.

George Cleghorn, who would write so much in favour of the Parthenon scheme, summarised succinctly what happened between 1819 and 1821 and immediately before and after that period. 'It occurred at length to a few public-spirited individuals of more refined taste that a restoration of the Parthenon of Athens would be more eligible.'[24] The Edinburgh Parthenon was conceived initially as an elitist project which gradually captured the imagination of a wider demographic base. London might have the Parthenon sculptures in the form of the so-called Elgin Marbles, bought for the nation and housed in the British Museum. But Edinburgh would get the temple from which those sculptures came, in the form of a facsimile of the Parthenon itself.

Edinburgh was actually appropriating an idea first proposed for London. In 1816, Andrew Robertson, an Aberdeen-born miniature-painter who lived and worked in London, had advocated a war-memorial monument in the form of a copy of the Parthenon, and suggested that it be erected on Primrose Hill. He explained to a friend in Aberdeen that such a building—in effect, a reconstruction of the ancient original—would be highly appropriate, 'since we have now in this country its most valuable remains.' The reference was, of course, to the Elgin Marbles. 'It will be', continued Robertson, 'more beautiful than anything produced for 2000 years.'[25] The cost of a 'Parthenon' built in Aberdeen granite was estimated at £200,000, but a mere £160,000 if in Portland stone. Inferior freestone would be £130,000. Not unnaturally, the idea fell on deaf metropolitan ears. As he later recorded, Robertson had even made a detailed scale model, complete with tiny, specially cast bronze sculptures, and metopes half an inch square.[26] Indeed, he envisaged the production of several models for sale to collectors. His pride at the time was evident when he described how he intended to 'carry the finishing to the utmost degree of minuteness and delicacy'.[27]

Undeterred by failure in 1816 to secure a building and a site in London, and uncompromised by Edinburgh's subsequent adoption of the general notion of the Parthenon as an appropriate model for a war-memorial national monument, Robertson would revive his idea in 1838. By this date, Edinburgh's project had been stalled for nine years, if it had not ground to a complete and probably permanent halt. This time Trafalgar Square was to be the suggested site: the building was to stand right across the front of the National Gallery. Here, as Robertson was to state, 'it would dwell with us, and be constantly before our eyes.' It is somehow symbolic of the various notions and confused stylistic ideas flitting about in London, and thus not just in Edinburgh, that Robertson thought the Trafalgar Square site, with the addition of this Greek behemoth surrounded by much supporting sculpture on a vast terrace, might 'become, as were, our *Roman* Forum [my italics]'.[28]

The mixture of ideas of what early nineteenth-century Edinburgh was, or wanted to be, is demonstrated by some remarks by George Cleghorn, though expressed anonymously. In discussing the idea, 'voted by the nobility and aristocracy of Scotland', that the visit of George IV be commemorated by an equestrian statue of the king to stand in front of the western portico of the proposed National Monument 'in unison with the taste and decoration of the Athenian Acropolis', Cleghorn reveals that this work was actually to have been modelled on the statue of the emperor Marcus Aurelius on the Capitol in Rome. 'Had the Calton Hill', Cleghorn mused,

> in addition to the restoration of the Parthenon, possessed this interesting accession of dignity and classic art, it might, without prescription, have claimed some faint resemblance in character and association of objects, to the Athenian Acropolis and the Roman Campidoglio.[29]

This uneasy pairing of the notional 'Greek' site, and the Roman-inspired sculpture to be placed within its curtilage, is compounded by a further remark of the Edinburgh-trained doctor, travel writer and man of letters William Beattie. In 1838 Beattie described 'the architectural magnificence of the Calton-hill, which has been styled the Capitoline—or according to others, the Acropolis—of the North ...'.[30] No one else, beyond Cleghorn and (presumably following him) Beattie, ever called it the former, though the latter epithet had by then occurred to many people.

In the resolution of 1821, the Parthenon was cited simply as the 'model' for what might adorn Calton Hill. But even before this, it was being said that the ancient Greek temple might be 'imitated' or 'adapted'. After this, it became customary to speak of the Parthenon being 'restored' in the National Monument; better still, that the National Monument was to be a 'classic restoration' of the original. And then Edinburgh was to have what was called a 'facsimile' of the prototype.[31] A wish to identify with another (? better) place at another (? better) time is perhaps a fairly common human emotion. David

Lowenthal categorises one kind of 'transformation of relics' as 'indirect': how they are 'seen, explained, illustrated and appreciated'. 'Relics inspire copies, replicas, models, emulations, depictions; monuments and re-enactments commemorate people and events. Action of these kinds converted Edinburgh into "the Athens of the North"...'[32]

Little by little, and step by step, the Parthenon as the most desirable symbol of Edinburgh's would-be status began to dominate Modern Athenian thinking. Most radically of all, Archibald Alison had written in July 1819 of the Parthenon as being somehow 'transferred' to the Modern Athens—the word was used with deliberate vagueness but, conversely, with utter confidence and without a trace of embarrassment at the peculiarity of the notion.[33] The spirit, as it were, of a single iconic building would imbue the successor city with all the ancient virtue and timeless glory of the prime original. As Alison went on to suggest in his next article, to 'transfer' the building would somehow have the effect of 'transferring to the inhabitants [of Edinburgh] the taste which grew up in Athens'.[34] As we shall see, almost everything about the general amorphous conceit of Edinburgh as the Athens of the North is hedged about with oddity, contradiction and paradox.

It seems likely that George Sibbald had kept abreast of some, at least, of the extensive writings on the subject of the projected Edinburgh Parthenon and its siting that had, since 1819, appeared in various journals and pamphlets. It is also quite possible that he was aware of the printed circular letters of 25 December 1821 and 24 January 1822 in which groups of influential men—various surviving copies bear different combinations of signatures that are sometimes autograph, sometimes engraved in manuscript facsimile, and sometimes typeset—had attempted to persuade their fellow Scots, both at home and furth of the realm, that the projected National Monument should be in the purest Greek Doric taste.[35] They had argued that the proposed monument should not just emulate the Parthenon but copy it exactly. The repeated lapidary phrases 'restoration', 'facsimile' and the like were now an inalienable part of the rubric. However, although it was to be a 'copy' of the 'Temple of Minerva', it was to be a replica without its sculpture. It does seem extraordinary that those who wrote so fully and forcefully of 'restoration', 'facsimile' and even (most remarkably) of 'transfer', did not adequately recognise from the outset the irony that the chief glory of the original was not to be replicated in Edinburgh, or even imitated in a modern sculptural idiom. This glaring anomaly being set aside, however, they had—most significantly—sought support for the proposal that the new structure should crown a rocky eminence which was regarded not just as a superb site for present and future monumental building development, but (however improbably) as a finer location even than the Acropolis of Athens. Sibbald's acceptance that the Calton Hill should unequivocally be regarded as Edinburgh's answer to the Athenian acropolis is significant. Only a few years previously, Edinburgh Castle would—not unnaturally—have been widely regarded as the 'acropolis' of the city: yet now the Calton Hill held sway, giving the Northern Athens a second such distinctive topographical landmark.

*   *   *   *   *

One of the enduring oddities of the entire story of Edinburgh as Athens of the North is the obsession with the Calton Hill as this alternative 'acropolis'. As the ancient, fortified, hill-top citadel looming over Edinburgh, the Castle on its rock should never have been usurped by anything else. There was nothing wrong with it, either as ancient symbol of national strength or as romantic backdrop enhancing the view southwards from the New Town. It was visible from miles around and dominated approaches to the city from all directions. (Fig. 6) It is interesting to read the unequivocal opinion of a twentieth-century authority, the then Keeper of Greek and Roman Antiquities in the British Museum, who, in seeking a comparison for the Athenian Acropolis, should instinctively have suggested the castle-rock of Edinburgh.[36] It is of equal interest to note the views of a near contemporary of George Sibbald and one, indeed, of his own profession. Another Scottish Assistant Surgeon in the Royal Navy found himself in Athens a dozen or so years after Sibbald had been there. He reported that 'the Acropolis Rock rises somewhat like Edinburgh Castle, but not quite so high nor so steep, though the road that leads up to it is more so.' Perhaps significantly, he made no further high-flown topographical or other comparisons with Edinburgh, and he certainly insinuated no reference to a Northern or Modern Athens. Evidently less impressionable than Sibbald, he went on to admit that 'The Parthenon, even with its multitude of pillars, did not strike me much...'. [37]

Looking back to the early nineteenth century, we may legitimately wonder how, indeed, the Castle on its rock came to be almost disregarded by the Modern Athenians in their quest to make their city something it was not, and could never truly be. Yet, from almost every angle, the Castle Rock stole the topographical and picturesque show. The text accompanying an album of engraved views of Edinburgh published in 1825 referred to the King's visit, and to how His Majesty, on entering Princes Street in the course of his first progress through the city, would have seen two contrasting towns. On the one hand was 'the picturesque irregularity of the Old Town, surmounted by its venerable and majestic Acropolis'; on the other 'the elegance and splendour of the New Town, with the Calton Hill in front ...'.[38] There was no doubt in the mind of this writer, James Browne, that, in its Castle, Edinburgh had its Acropolis (with a capital 'A'). Calton Hill was accorded no such honours. However, the Calton was effectively an almost bare and largely undeveloped platform on which the dreams of ambitious men might be played out. Their vision was of an 'Athenian' Edinburgh, and the Calton Hill came to serve their needs.

It is certain that Sibbald will have read the work of one of the protagonists in the story of an 'Athenian' Edinburgh: Hugh William 'Grecian' Williams, the artist and traveller, who was such a significant figure in the identification of the two cities. (Figs 18-19) There are sufficient similarities between the gist of what Williams wrote in his celebrated *Travels* of 1820, and what Sibbald attempted to say in his manuscript, to infer the influence of the one upon the other. Williams paired Greece and Scotland in general terms, and in doing so displayed some of the tendency to topographical distortion and far-fetched supposition that colours Sibbald's account: 'Suppose the lakes of Scotland were plains, I know no country so like illustrious Greece ...'[39] Sibbald, nevertheless, with noted single-mindedness of purpose, went further and more forcefully down this road of topographical comparison: in his account it really becomes bizarre.

Between 1819 and the time Sibbald was working on his laboured travelogue, it had been argued, constantly and repeatedly, that Edinburgh was capable of becoming a re-born Athens. Its citizens were increasingly captivated by the beauties of the 'Grecian' style in architecture, and alive to the possibilities of imaginative town-planning that would give full rein to the picturesque. The cerebral and topographical similarity was distinct and widely accepted. The congruity might, so the 'Modern Athenians' believed, lead in time to actual superiority for their city, and Edinburgh might even come to enjoy an ascendancy over the prototype on every level. That pre-eminence would be due, in the first place, to what many believed was the finer and even more picturesque natural setting enjoyed by the Northern Athens. It would be compounded once Edinburgh was enhanced by greater architectural achievement, especially if that were to be focused on a range of archaeologically accurate 'Greek Revival' buildings. This architectural pre-eminence would be achieved, structurally, by the ready availability of superb-quality, fine-grained Craigleith sandstone and the unrivalled local skill to work it. The notion would be made incarnate by an enlightened and artistically educated populace, fully equipped to appreciate the glories of architecture and architectural sculpture. The inhabitants of the Modern Athens might thrive in a political climate conducive to progress and supportive of the values of civic and national pride. It would be nurtured in an urban environment without peer in a wider, united British state unchallenged in the power and prosperity won by arms, and increasingly to be secured by arts and science.[40] The Edinburgh of the early 1820s was thus truly poised to 'out-Athens' ancient Athens itself.

The 'Athenian' epithets, even if not entirely home-grown, were certainly (as we shall see) adopted and made their own by late-Georgian Edinburgh people. And as we shall also learn, the terms for the city as a 'modern', 'new' or 'northern' Athens soon came to have a much wider, international currency among those who visited the place or who admired it from afar. The expressions were celebrated: they were certainly in common—even hackneyed—use at the time, and have continued to be deployed, often unthinkingly, ever since. The phrase

'Athens of the North' is still regularly pressed into service, without clarification or explanation—on five occasions, at least, in *The Times* newspaper alone (in restaurant and hotel reviews, and in the context of civic issues) in the period when this book was being written—on the assumption that the term is both understood and effective in conveying an aspect of Edinburgh's present-day personality.

*   *   *   *   *

Sibbald's topographical comparison of the two cities in terms of the compass-points requires some measure of concentration, not to mention flexibility of mind and effort of imagination, in orientating oneself.

> Athens has been so often & so minutely described by various authors, that we shall merely content ourselves with noticing some of its most remarkable places. We shall, however, more particularly describe the Parthenon, or temple of Minerva, not only because it has been the admiration of all ages, but because also it has furnished a model for the national monument, intended to be built in our metropolis of Scotland. And we think that Edinburgh has received the appellation of Modern Athens, with so much justice, not merely for her superiority in the arts & sciences, but also for her general appearance & relative situation, that, pointing out her resemblance in these respects, may enable, we think, such of our readers as are acquainted with the capital of Scotland, the better to understand our description of the capital of Attica.
>
> It must be particularly observed, however, that the absolute situation of Edinburgh is quite the reverse from that of Athens, & that in pointing out the resemblance of her relative situation, we must suppose the east & west, the north & south to change, & take the place of the opposite quarters.
>
> Keeping this in remembrance, the Calton-hill will represent, with considerable exactness, the Acropolis or citadel of Athens, & the appointed spot for the national monument will precisely point out the corresponding situation of the Parthenon, which it is intended to represent. The circumstance also that the Parthenon in the ancient Athens was dedicated to Minerva, the goddess of war, which the monument to be built in the modern Athens is to commemorate the warlike actions of our illustrious countrymen, will be an additional proof of the striking resemblance.
>
> Nelson's Monument,[41] in its relative situation to the national Monument, exactly corresponds to the Erechtheion, which was also built upon the Acropolis; & we cannot but here also notice the resemblance that the latter was the temple of Neptune, the god of the sea, while the former was erected in commemoration of the naval victories gained by our celebrated Admiral on that god's watery empire.[42]

A little east from the Calton-hill may represent the situation of the Areopagus & a little farther to the east & north may point out the place of the Pynx [*sic*: the author means the Pnyx].[43] The Firth of Forth corresponds well with the Aegean sea, the hills of Fife with the hills of Peloponnesus, while the harbour of Leith will represent the Piraeus or harbour of Athens, from which it is distant between 3 or 4 miles. Inchkeith, if supposed to be five or six times farther distant, will point out the situation of the island Aegina, which was about 20 miles in circumference & 18 from the Piraeus.

Without the walls of Athens is the Temple of Theseus,[44] once king of Athens, corresponding in its situation to the Palace of Holyroodhouse, and the ruins of the Temple of Jupiter Olympius corresponding in like manner to the Register House;[45] while Mount Anchesmus is remarkably similar in situation & appearance to the Castle-hill.[46]

The Water of Leith also may bear some resemblance to the river Ilissus, only this was nearer the Acropolis than that is to the Calton-hill.[47] And if we are not censured for having already carried this resemblance too far, we may mention that to the north-west of Athens are two rocky insulated hills, the larger of which is called the Colonus Hippius or the Equestrian Hill[48] & is distant from the other about 200 yards; & recollecting to make the same change as before, north-west will become north-east,[49] & then these hills will be strikingly contrasted by Arthur's Seat & Salisbury Craigs.

It is interesting to note that Sibbald, loyal in this (as in all things) to Edinburgh, seems to express a preference for the aesthetic qualities of those examples of Athenian stone which had, through time, been subjected to similar weathering as that of the buildings of his own city. In a passage essentially reflecting the observations of Edward Dodwell and also those of Hugh Williams, but with the addition of a sailor's concern for the elements, Sibbald wrote thus of the masonry of the Parthenon:

Very little of the marble of the Parthenon, which was originally white, retains its pure natural colour. From exposure to the air & weather, the different parts have been more or less affected. Thus, the south side of the building retains somewhat of its original whiteness, & is altogether of a lighter colour than the other sides; & we may perhaps find a sufficient reason for the difference in the south winds at Athens being less accompanied with rain than what blow from other quarters. The west side has received a fine rich yellow tint from the setting sun. The north, exposed to more storms, & receiving fewer rays from the sun, is of a cold dark green colour; while the east side, coloured with a yellowish red of different hue & mixed with a dusky black, produced by the smoke of some neighbouring chimneys, has been rendered extremely picturesque.[50]

Admiration of the effects upon the ancient temple of an almost Scottish mixture of severe weathering through wind and rain, and distinct discolouration by soot and smoke, thus made Athens appear as a kind of 'Auld Reekie' of the south.

Sibbald's assessment of the damage done to the Parthenon by modern antiquity-hunters (the most infamous of whom, of course, was a Scotsman, Thomas Bruce, seventh Earl of Elgin) was severely critical. His comments on 'depredations' in Athens, and particularly on the Acropolis, were clearly much influenced by the published remarks by Dodwell, whose forthright but reasoned views he quotes approvingly. Dodwell had also written eloquently of the 'dilapidating mania' that had, elsewhere in Athens, so much affected the Choragic Monument of Lysikrates, a building shortly to be the ultimate inspiration for two of the Calton Hill memorials (those to Dugald Stewart and Robert Burns), and in condemnation of the 'tasteless cupidity' and 'selfish rapacity of amateurs' who had wanted to carry off the whole building.[51] When considering the despoiling of the Parthenon itself of so much of its sculpture, which he had actually witnessed taking place in 1801, Dodwell had written forcefully of what he called the 'unhallowed violations' and the 'devastating outrage' perpetrated at a 'scene of havoc and destruction' through the action of 'insensate barbarism'.[52] For his part, Sibbald refrains from naming and shaming Lord Elgin—who was, after all, playing an influential role in the campaign for the National Monument in Edinburgh—though he makes clear his disapproval of Elgin's past actions.

> It must always be a subject of great regret, that this splendid aedifice [the Parthenon] has been pillaged by the curious & the learned; & that, even now, comparatively little remains but ruins, to point out its former situation & extent, & the structure & elegance of the building.

Although he does not actually cite him as a source, Sibbald quite probably had in mind the comments recently made by Williams on the Greek depredations, which had contributed so greatly to what he saw as the diminution of the very 'identity of Athens'.[53] One can only hope that Sibbald and his shipmates were not guilty of a crime such as that condemned by Williams, who had drawn attention to the handiwork of some British sailors (apparently Scotsmen at that) in besmirching the architrave of the temple at Cape Sounion with names written in pitch in letters two feet high. Williams added censoriously the injunction: 'I advise our Scottish youths to reflect a little, before they again proceed to such wantonness.' And he continued with just a hint that somehow the mantle of ancient Greece had descended, above all, upon Scottish shoulders, and that even boisterous young midshipmen and junior naval officers—such as Sibbald, in fact—were Modern Athenians in the making: 'They, of all others, should be grateful for the stream of light which has flowed from Greece, and accordingly should respect her few remains.'[54]

*   *   *   *   *

George Sibbald had been infected by the architectural and more general cultural fervour of Edinburgh in its New Athenian persona. As a commentator observed in 1820:

> No one can have lived in Edinburgh last winter, and mingled in its society, without perceiving that the subject of the restoration of the Parthenon engaged a very large share of public attention and more particularly was espoused by those whose rank, talents, or acquirements qualified them to take a lead in forming the public opinion.[55]

Sibbald's writings of around this time reflect his earnest desire to belong to that elite tier of Edinburgh society. All his reading of the literature of the campaign for, and against, a National Monument in the Greek taste, will have had the cumulative effect of turning the ship's assistant surgeon into an apparent authority on the matter, when he was not really one at all. His manuscript comparison of Athens and Edinburgh marks a general truth. As such, it is a valuable preface to an investigation of the world of differing and subtly shaded thoughts on the whole question of the Northern Athens. For Sibbald represents exactly the sort of specious character adduced by the anonymous writer in *The New Edinburgh Review* in 1823 as a product of the times.

> It has been the misfortune of these popular and wordy discussions, to have made every man imagine himself an architect and a man of taste; and it is the misfortune of the age that, by skimming the surface of pamphlets, and newspapers, and reviews, it has acquired a scum and skin of all learning, which it mistakes for solidity and reality. It is an age of vast superficies, of paint, and tinsel, and gilding … There are few, very few, who have ever seen a Doric temple; and not one in thousands, of those who have heated themselves even to smoke and obscurity on the subjects before us, who knows more of ancient classical architecture … Even that much was scarcely known twelve months ago, to those who can now talk of the Parthenon, and of peristyles, and cells, and intercolumniations, and pediments, with all the familiarity of household words.[56]

*   *   *   *   *

In this book, topics and questions that suggest themselves include the following.

When, why, by whom and with what lasting consequences (for good or ill) was Edinburgh given the 'Athenian' accolade? In what lay the city's imagined 'Greekness'?

If Edinburgh was thought to be Athenian, in the years around 1820, was that the result of feelings that had developed in the eighteenth century or even earlier, and which came to maturity after 1800, or perhaps before that date?

Was the identification of modern Edinburgh with ancient Athens due first, or largely, to topographical circumstances and architectural developments, or because the city's supposed similarity to Periclean Athens lay much more in the cerebral realm of philosophy, the arts, science, medicine, and cultural prowess in general?

In physical terms, what came first? Was Edinburgh the Athens of the North because it chanced, in the second and third decades of the nineteenth century, to begin to be adorned with Greek Revival buildings—which is very probably what 'the man on the Princes Street omnibus' still imagines today? Or were the neo-Greek buildings erected there because the city was already discerned as the Modern Athens, some northern equivalent of the ancient seat of culture and the intellect? These points are important, because the secondary literature is often confused and contradictory. Britain's leading historian of the Greek Revival, for instance, states at one moment that it was 'the remarkable expansion of public and private building which turned early 19th-century Edinburgh into the "Athens of the North"'; at another, he implies that Edinburgh, being 'the Athens of the North'—presumably because it looked like Athens, or because it already had acquired, or assumed, cultural, 'Athenian' airs—was an ideal scene for building 'Greek' on the grandest of scales.[57]

Was it essentially a matter of cultural identification or parallelism between the 'primary' Athens and the 'secondary' one? What part did topography, townscape and architecture play? Does the answer in fact lie somewhere in between: the cerebral identification joined with the notion of physical similarity? It is extremely difficult, as we shall see in the chapters that follow, to separate the various strands: the topographical slides into the mental; the cerebral elides with the architectural; the structural shades off into the sentimental; and so on.

Who in particular might be deemed 'Athenian', and why? Could some even feel 'Athenian' at one moment and in one context, but not the next? And what accounted, more than anything else did, for that feeling of being 'Athenian'?

As they came into initial use, and on their subsequent general acceptance, did the 'Athenian' epithets imply unqualified praise, or were they tinged with opprobrium—or does an answer lie somewhere between these poles?

Did the creation of the Calton Hill 'acropolis' really transform 'Auld Reekie', actually or spiritually, into 'The Athens of the North'—or was the result not, more probably, just that the city became some curious physical, spiritual, cultural and architectural hybrid that we may conveniently call 'Auld Greekie'?

THE NORTHERN ATHENS IN THE EYE

'ONE SPLENDID WHOLE ... ONE GLORIOUS SCENE'

John Brown Patterson, a precocious classicist and recent Divinity graduate of the University of Edinburgh, published *On the National Character of the Athenians* in 1828. His long and learned essay had won him a prestigious prize the previous year. For a brilliant young scholar working in Edinburgh at this particular time, parallels with another place and age were obvious. 'Athens', Patterson wrote,

> has become a sort of proverb to the nations, expressive of all genius and all beauty ... A modern city, if distinguished by beauty of situation, by elegance of structure, or by literary refinement, straightway assumes the title of the Modern Athens.[1]

Patterson here neatly epitomised the three essential strands of perceived parallelism between modern Edinburgh and ancient Athens. Like the Serpent Column of Delphi, which in antiquity commemorated the allied Greek victory over the Persians at Plataea in 479 BC, these writhen strands are intertwined. There are other strands, too, to be examined later. But the physical factors—what Patterson termed 'situation' and 'structure' (which must include the architecture that enhances the landscape, or benefits from the geographical setting) and 'literary refinement'—the cerebral component—together constitute the first three elements to be discussed.

* * * * *

Topographical parallels between places are easy to assert, and they have been made frequently. One sees what one wants to see. Amsterdam and St Petersburg have both been called the Venice of the North—though Venice is not usually denominated the Amsterdam or St Petersburg of the Adriatic. Absurdity can creep in. St Petersburg has also been christened the Palmyra of the North. Henry Matthews called Zurich 'the Athens of Switzerland', though in this case he was surely thinking in terms of literary eminence or social refinement.[2] John Galt, a novelist loyal to his west of Scotland roots, and a man whom we shall have reason to look to again in the debate on the 'Athenian' nature of contemporary Edinburgh, was delighted to allude to Glasgow, with its river, its shipping, its docks, its ship-building tradition and its prosperous merchants, in humorous self-aggrandizement as 'the northern Venice'.[3] In 1751, Berlin under Frederick I of Prussia was called the Athens of the North; then a second Sparta under Frederick William.[4] Moving forward in time, it is not uncommon to hear of Berlin in the age of Karl Friedrich Schinkel—where and when a profusion of Greek Revival buildings help in the would-be identification—referred to as 'the Athens on the Spree'. Schinkel himself, however, visited Edinburgh in 1826 but refrained from saying anything about its being likened to Athens, and never wrote of it as such.[5] John Britton, in his text for the explicitly but oddly titled *Modern Athens! Displayed in a Series of Views: or Edinburgh in the Nineteenth Century,* never actually compared Edinburgh with Athens in topographical terms, but did say that the layout of its New Town resembled 'the famed city of Washington, in America'.[6]

   Edinburgh has been said to resemble, for reasons mostly topographical rather than anything more intangible, Stockholm, Lisbon, Genoa, Naples, Palermo and Constantinople. In the journal of his visit to the city in 1813, the widely travelled Sir Nathaniel Wraxall drew most of these parallels, and added Prague and Bath for good measure; but Lisbon and Naples, he considered, seemed the places most readily identifiable with Edinburgh—though he considered that she outdid them both.[7] Naples sprang most readily to the mind of a commentator in 1822, beholding the prospect of Edinburgh in its setting on the Firth of Forth, in which the island of Inchkeith made its Capri and Arthur's Seat its Vesuvius, an impression heightened by the gun-salutes, fireworks and illuminations surrounding and surmounting the mountain as part of the royal visit festivities.[8] Lord Byron inexplicably called Edinburgh 'the Caledonian Cremona': here was a man who could have called it 'Athens', but who, significantly, did not.[9] Sir Robert Gardiner, a soldier who had served in Sicily, compared Edinburgh to Palermo, with parallels ranging from Arthur's Seat as Monte Pellegrino to the Forth estuary as the Sicilian city's setting on its glorious Conca d'Oro bay.[10]

   A salutary corrective to the kind of topographical distortion or false identification in terms of imaginative—not to say bizarre—shifting of the compass-points so evident in George Sibbald's strained comparison of Athens with Edinburgh, is supplied by some remarks made by William Beattie. In 1838 Beattie (as we have noted, an Edinburgh medical graduate) published the

letterpress description for a series of images of Scottish scenery. With regard
to views from the Castle or Calton Hill, Beattie observed that the prospects
had been compared to those of the Bay of Naples from the Castel Sant' Elmo.
In a note, he tabulated which points in Edinburgh and its environs should be
paired with which Neapolitan landmarks or natural features. But Beattie wisely
cautioned that 'here the resemblance fails', admitting that because

> the one view is sufficiently like to remind us of the other, the spectator will
> readily observe, that the respective features of resemblance are *reversed*, and
> that the objects to the *right* hand in the Scottish view, correspond only with
> those on the *left* in the Neapolitan.[11]

Noting that William Gilpin had compared North Bridge—when seen from
a distance—to a Roman aqueduct, and that Gilpin had drawn it as such, John
Stoddart had written of what he termed the 'forced assimilation' of this kind.[12]
It was Stoddart, a lawyer and *littérateur* later in life to become Chief Justice
of Malta, who seems to have been the first actually to express the Athenian
topographic parallel.

> The Lanerk [sic] road affords a view of Edinburgh, interesting not only in
> itself, but from its similitude to ancient Athens. One might almost believe,
> that a landscape of the latter place, exhibited a few years since by Mr [Henry]
> Tresham, had been taken from this spot; so similar is the citadel [the Acropolis
> of Athens] to Edinburgh Castle, and the sea, with its islands, to the Firth of
> Forth, which here forms a most beautiful back-ground.[13]

Stoddart, who published this in 1801, having made his observations in the
previous two years, was closely followed by the lawyer and travel writer Sir
John Carr. 'The classical eye', Carr wrote, after using his own eye in 1807, 'has
discovered some resemblance between Edinburgh and Athens; the castle has
been compared with the acropolis, Arthur's Seat with Mons Hymettus, and
Leith and Leith-walk with the piraeus [sic].'[14]

When Walter Scott selected views to include in his collection of images
published as parts of his *The Provincial Antiquities and Picturesque Scenery of
Scotland* (issued as a series between 1819 and 1826, and then as a two-volume
collected edition in 1826) he chose two that are of particular significance for
our understanding of what he thought about the Edinburgh-Athens parallel—
or, more accurately, what he did *not* think about such a matter. The view of
Edinburgh from Corstorphine Hill, engraved after the oil painting by the Revd
John Thomson of Duddingston and issued on 20 December 1819, is described
by Scott in his accompanying commentary in these terms: '... The prospect
abounds also with objects of curiosity, both to the antiquary, the philosopher,

and the man of taste.'[15] But despite these 'Athenian' intimations, Scott made no mention of any perceived topographical similarity to Athens. He wrote, of course, before Hugh William Williams had directed public attention towards the topic. The view of Edinburgh from the Glasgow road, after the oil painting by Alexander Nasmyth and issued on 1 July 1821, is described in rather different terms. (Fig. 6) Its most prominent feature, the Castle rock, is given the accolade of 'that ancient and martial acropolis of Caledonia'. When this plate was published, Williams's travelogue with its comparisons between Athens and Edinburgh had appeared, and indeed Scott had received a copy from the publisher, Archibald Constable, who hoped that Scott would review it. He did not in fact do so; but the ideas of Edinburgh's 'Athenian' nature had evidently struck even a man such as Scott, who lacked much classical interest. In his commentary on the view, Scott went on to write of 'the number of excellent architects who have lately arisen in this country'. He was referring to the men who would build the Modern Athens.[16]

In the year of Scott's death, Lieutenant Colonel Robert Batty—an intriguing man who, after taking a medical degree at Cambridge had become an officer in the 1st Foot Guards, then turned to art, and who was later elected a Fellow of the Royal Society—published his *Select Views of Some of the Principal Cities of Europe* (1832). Batty contrived to squeeze Edinburgh in with Oporto, Gibraltar, Lisbon, Rotterdam, Amsterdam, Brussels and Antwerp, this rather strange selection reflecting mostly the military service he had seen in the Iberian Peninsula and in the Waterloo campaign in Belgium. Edinburgh is represented by six plates engraved after Batty's own paintings. His commentary on the first of these drew attention to the city's 'commanding and picturesque appearance'; that on the third—of the Calton Hill, with the Nelson and National Monuments featuring—pointed to the city's 'boasted title of the Modern Athens'. The view of what was arguably not just the best designed and most effectively sited building but also the most 'Athenian' structure in the city, is accompanied by the statement that 'Amidst the various fine edifices which have of late years risen, as if by magic, in this interesting capital, none is more deserving of notice than the new High School.'[17]

John Stoddart had written of the contrast between the two towns of Edinburgh, so noticeable at 'first sight': the New Town's regularity, and the Old Town's constricted natural setting, giving its cityscape the air of a 'confusion ... piled together in a chaotic mass' of 'scattered parts' with 'no uniting principle ... so entirely out of all rule.' Admittedly, the Old Town had lost a great deal by the departure of nobility and court, its grand old houses in decay and now inhabited very largely by the poor. It remained, however, a picturesque draw for visitors throughout the period discussed in this book: the era of the Modern Athens, the physical setting and the architectural manifestations of which were not the only aspects that brought the tourists to Edinburgh in the age of romanticism.

Yet much about the Old Town promoted feelings of disquiet, disgust even, due to the palpable decay. But the New Town, to which gentility had flown, was distinguished by its own distinct sense of disappointment to the visitor: despite handsome, regular planning and some fine classical public buildings, there was a noteworthy want of liveliness due to the unequal distribution of the social classes. There were few shops; grass grew in the streets.[18]

Stoddart was not alone in pointing up the contrasts between the two Edinburghs. In 1792 the Revd John Lettice had commented rather more favourably on both, writing of the 'air of antiquity and uncouth grandeur' of the Old Town.

> The castle on its naked rock, from its bold and exalted situation, its vastness, domineering aspect and picturesque irregularity of parts, its battlements and towers, &c. first seizes the traveller's sight, and, for some moments, rivets his attention ...[19]

Lettice matched this with his praise of the 'great taste in architecture' displayed in the New Town. He found less to detract from the distinction of its 'magnificent suite of parallelograms', where '[O]ver the whole prevails an air of lightness, elegance and splendour, probably not to be surpassed, if equalled, in any other city in Europe.' If Edinburgh's physical size necessarily rendered it 'only among capitals of the second order', it was nevertheless, as a local capital, a 'brilliant' city.[20]

Visitors such as Lettice and Stoddart began the tradition of appreciation of the grand prospect of the Picturesque that came to characterise Edinburgh as a whole, comprehending both the 'Auld Reekie' and the 'Modern Athens' sides of its Janus face. Those visitors, and Edinburgh citizens themselves, would comment on the unique qualities of the city for as long as the Athenian epithet was in common use, or while it still seemed to mean something. James Grant, writing in the very early 1880s, described the Old Town as 'strikingly picturesque in its broken masses and the disorder of its architecture'; the New as 'so symmetrical and almost severe in the Grecian and Tuscan beauty of its streets and squares' which, perhaps, 'combined with its natural situation quite as much as its literary character, may have won for it the fanciful name of "the Modern Athens."'[21] Grant, indeed, equated the New Town with the Modern Athens that Edinburgh had become, and still remained to his day—in imagination if not in substance.

*   *   *   *   *

Several modern writers have stated that the comparison of Edinburgh with Athens was first made by James 'Athenian' Stuart, the architect and decorator, in his celebrated *Antiquities of Athens*,[22] the first volume of which (actually a joint production with Nicholas Revett) appeared in 1762-63.[23] This is not, in fact, the case: Stuart and Revett said no such thing anywhere in their great work. The error—regularly repeated, and still enduring—can be traced, very probably, to Francis Groome,[24] and before that to the compiler of A. & C. Black's *Picturesque Tourist of Scotland*,[25] both of whom were themselves evidently borrowing from Robert Chambers. And Chambers incorrectly credits the observation first to Stuart ('the Athenian' as he calls him), then to Dr [Edward Daniel] Clarke and finally to Hugh William Williams.[26]

Edward Daniel Clarke, travelling tutor, clergyman and Professor of Mineralogy at Cambridge, knew both Scotland and Greece. In 1797 he had compared the scenery of the Sound of Mull to prospects such as 'one would witness in the Aegean'.[27] (A few years later John Galt was put in mind of the Firth of Clyde viewed from Bishopton Hill when he looked back down the Gulf of Corinth towards Patras.)[28] But one cannot say that Clarke's letters from Greece hammer home any definite Edinburgh comparison, for none is ever mentioned; indeed Clarke specifically states that he had never seen anything like Athens, 'which exceeds all that has ever been written or painted from it. I know not how to give an idea of it …'. The only mention of Scotland in Clarke's Greek correspondence is in the context of Lord Elgin's depredations, when he condemns the 'pulling down temples that have withstood the injuries of time and war, and barbarism for ages, to adorn a miserable Scotch villa.'[29] The Earl of Elgin and Kincardine's seat of Broomhall, Fife, where some of the sculpture removed by his famous forebear indeed remains to this day, hardly merits such a splenetic and demeaning description.

It is, however, true that, when Clarke published his *Travels in Various Countries*, he did indeed compare the topographical relationship of the Piraeus to ancient Athens with that of Leith to modern Edinburgh. The ancient Long Walls and their surviving traces formed a sort of corridor somewhat akin to Leith Walk, the western of Edinburgh's two historic main routes to its port. But the Edinburgh-Athens comparison is relegated to a mere brief footnote: '*Edinburgh* exhibits a very correct model of a *Grecian city*: and with its *Acropolis, Town*, and *Harbour*, it bears some resemblance to *Athens* and the *Piraeus*.'[30] Nowhere in the relevant Greek portions of Clarke's eight-volume discursive travel memoirs does he state, as Archibald Alison and others asserted Clarke had done, that all Edinburgh wanted to make complete the resemblance to Athens was 'a temple of great dimensions placed on the Calton Hill'.[31] What Clarke does write is that Greek temples were designed to be seen from afar, and he continues in this vein:

> It is to this cause that the *Doric*, in buildings of so much vastness, owes its superiority over all the other orders of architecture—to that *simplicity* which is the very soul of grandeur; where nothing that is *little* can be tolerated for an

instant. Excessive minuteness of design, and of execution, may suit the puny imitations of *Grecian* architecture seen in the buildings of modern cities ...[32]

Clarke would certainly have approved of the monumentality of the conception of the Parthenon, 'transferred' to and 'restored' in 'facsimile' upon Calton Hill, as being worthy of both specific site and wider setting, and faithful to the Greek conception of highly visible Doric grandeur. But Clarke does not actually call Edinburgh 'the Athens of the North'.

What of Hugh William 'Grecian' Williams—a man granted the enduring epithet despite having himself spent less than two months in Greece? Walter Scott referred to Williams as 'the Grecian' even in an artistic context wholly concerned with the recording of Scottish Border antiquities.[33] Scott wrote that Williams had 'stolen the whole country of Attica and brought [it] to Britain in pencil'.[34] Williams had at least *been* to Greece. None of the Scottish-born architects of 'Modern Athens' had travelled there; and, indeed, most of them had not even visited the Continent. Archibald Alison and his fellow agitators for a 'Greek' Edinburgh had not been to Greece either. In his autobiography, Alison implies by his book-derived description—and so would have us believe—that he had been to Constantinople, Mount Athos and 'the islands of the Archipelago'; but, in fact, he had not, though he had at least seen the Greek temples at Paestum, south of Naples.[35]

But Alison was perhaps the second to draw attention to and to praise 'the beautiful drawings which Mr Williams has brought home of Grecian scenery'.[36] The first to laud Williams was John Gibson Lockhart, in *Peter's Letters to his Kinsfolk* (1819). He did so in almost idolatrous terms. According to Lockhart's fictional character (but effective alter ego) the Welsh visitor Dr Peter Morris, Williams had

> gazed upon the majestic face of Nature in lands, where her majesty borrows a holier and a sublimer influence from the memory of men and actions, in comparison with which the greatest of modern men, and the most brilliant of modern actions, must be contended to appear as dim and pigmy ... It was reserved for the desolate beauty of Greece, to breathe into this fine spirit such a sense of the melancholy splendour of Nature, in climes where she was once no less gay than splendid ...

Lockhart has Morris continue in this hyperbolic vein to extol yet further Williams's artistic vision:

> ... besides, the scenes of Greece, and the desolation of Greece, are things to my mind of yet nobler power than any of which even Claude had command ... it is there, that the footsteps of men appear to have stamped a grander sanctity

even on the most magnificent forms of nature ... has thrown such a breadth
of yellow radiance around the crumbling monuments of wisdom and valour
... and you gaze with your hand over your eyes upon the golden decline of
Athens with the same unquestioning earnestness, as if you were transported
all at once to one of the sunny slopes of Hymettus.[37]

Williams was a crucial figure in the promotion of the idea of topographical
similarities between Athens and Edinburgh. His role has been given full credit
by Mordaunt Crook, who goes so far as to say that the title of Edinburgh as 'the
Athens of the North' was 'invented' by Williams.[38] This is not quite accurate,
as we shall see; but it is certainly getting on that way, and it serves to indicate
Williams's importance in the wider story, and on account of what else Williams
did with both pen and paintbrush to establish a public predisposition to see
parallels between the cities. It is however, quite erroneous to suggest, as has
rather surprisingly been done, that Williams was called 'Grecian' because of
'the neo-classical buildings he designed in Edinburgh'.[39] He was not, and never
had been, an architect, despite a confident modern statement to that effect and
the gratuitous information that he 'helped to turn the New Town of Edinburgh
into a proud neo-classical city'.[40] Proud of Edinburgh Williams certainly was;
but his real importance lay in the ways that he taught his contemporaries to
think of topographical parallels with Athens, and so promote the general idea
of Edinburgh as an Athens of the North.

It does appear that, both in his observation of a topographical similarity,
and of a parallel pre-eminence on an intellectual level, Williams's comparisons
of Edinburgh and Athens are seminal. Ancient Athens had been 'the light
of the world ... where genius, wisdom, and taste, had reached their highest
perfection'.[41] A spiritual identification between Athens and Edinburgh was
manifest, and was clearly intended to be understood. However, in purely
topographical terms, it was not actually Edinburgh but Stirling that had sprung
to Williams's mind when he and his Scottish travelling companion, William
Douglas of Orchardton, first saw Athens from the Sacred Way leading east
from Eleusis. There was, from this direction, a 'considerable likeness' between
Athens and Stirling in its distinctive, hilly landscape.[42] John Galt had, in fact,
already entertained similar thoughts. In one of his *Letters from the Levant*,
Galt had written of how 'The distant appearance of the Acropolis [of Athens]
somewhat resembles that of Stirling Castle, but it is inferior in altitude and
general effect.'[43] Unsurprisingly, in the eye of a Scottish traveller, the Scottish
scene enjoyed more picturesque power than the foreign one, even if that scene
were of Athens itself. But Williams, conscious that most of his Scottish readers
of a book produced in Edinburgh would be Edinburgh people, not Stirling
'heads', continued in his own published letters: 'From every other point it
[Athens] bears a striking resemblance to Edinburgh, especially as seen from the

Braid and Ravelston Hills.'[44] From yet another direction, Athens ('the Queen of Greece') stirred memories of home: 'this distant view of Athens from the sea is extremely like that of Edinburgh from the Firth of Forth, though certainly the latter is considerably superior.' (Fig. 4) Williams and Douglas may have taken off their hats to Athens (literally: they were, as Williams put it archly, 'too well bred to pass without uncovering'), but already the idea that Auld Reekie was the finer place had begun to take hold.[45] Moved, for instance, by the temple of Poseidon at Cape Sounion (then supposed to be dedicated to Athena), he had expressed the sincere wish that the 'exquisite' Doric capitals might be 'adopted in some of our public buildings in good old Edinburgh'.[46]

* * * * *

One of the oddest features of the story of Edinburgh's early nineteenth-century assumption of a 'Modern Athenian' identity is that there was, of course, already a real 'modern Athens': the contemporary town where modern Greeks, and their Ottoman overlords, lived cheek by jowl with the ruins of the Athens of antiquity. But it was only this earlier Athens with which the citizens of Edinburgh readily identified. They were not much interested in the small and poor Greek town that now occupied the same geographical site, and which certainly did not lay claim to the spiritual resonances of the great cultural and intellectual city of the past. And when the people of Edinburgh claimed to be 'Athenian' and to live in 'the Modern Athens', that other modern Athens was left out of the equation, if not discounted entirely. They were much more attracted by the romanticised, idealised and picturesque vision of Greece, such as Williams conveyed to them, than by anything that might illustrate the reality of a poor little town on the fringe of Europe, sunk (as they saw it) in servitude both to Turk and to past time.

A traveller such as John Galt, who actually visited contemporary Athens, was dismissive of its appearance, from its 'paralytic gates' to its surrounding countryside:

> I cannot describe the modern city of Athens in fewer words, than by saying, that it looks as if two or three ill-built villages had been rudely swept together at the foot of the north side of the Acropolis, and enclosed by a garden wall … As a fortress, it is incapable at present of resisting any rational attack; the Turks, however, consider it a mighty redoubtable place; nay, for that matter, they even think frail old Athens herself capable of assuming a warlike attitude.[47]

Intellectually, too, Athens of the 1800s was not what it had once been. As Galt put it sarcastically, 'literary honours are no longer known at Athens'. A once-famous seat of learning was reduced to 'two pitiful colleges' where 'classic Greek is professedly taught'. But Galt recognised, too, that for many Britons the dream of ancient Athens would never die, even if the actuality of the present disappointed:

> To the mere antiquary, this celebrated city cannot but long continue interesting; and to the classic enthusiast just liberated from the cloisters of his college, the scenery and ruins may often awaken admiration, and inspire delight. Philosophy may here point the moral apophthegm with stronger emphasis; Virtue receive new incitements to perseverance, by reflecting on the honour which still attends the memory of the ancient Great; ... but to the traveller who rests for recreation, or who seeks a solace for misfortune, how wretched, how solitary, how empty is Athens![48]

*   *   *   *   *

Edinburgh was changing. Looking back only eighteen years from 1833, a writer fixed 1815 as the inauguration of 'the era of true taste in Edinburgh. The pure Grecian architecture was now beginning to be studied in its best models ...'[49] In fact, 1817 may be taken as a year especially indicative of urban renewal, and altered aesthetic and historical priorities. In that year, Archibald's Elliot's County Hall became the first 'Greek' interloper in the fabric of the Old Town. (Fig. 39) This was a fine neoclassical building in Parliament Square West, with a massive and distinctive portico in the Ionic order of the Erechtheion, and a side elevation in the same order facing onto the High Street. Opposite its site was the Old Tolbooth, famous as 'the Heart of Mid-Lothian' of Sir Walter Scott's great novel. This building still had its special, and very visible, platform and other appurtenances for public executions. The Tolbooth was demolished the same year that the new County Hall went up: 'Greek' conquered 'Gothic'. Patrick Gibson could not resist showing both buildings together, elegant Greek columns facing gruesome gibbet mechanism and the rest, in an etching published in 1818: a view that was by then actually impossible as the Tolbooth was now gone. (Fig. 40) Gibson made sure that his readers knew about the place of public execution that was no more.[50] The Old Town thereafter descended into a picturesque and antiquarian quarter where the mood among the Edinburgh elite was one of sentimental nostalgia mixed with unease and disgust at the degradation that enveloped the former centre of their city.

Waterloo Place was being developed at around the same time. As the scheme for the street evolved, with its flanking pavilions at the Princes Street end, and with the proposed 'Wellington Bridge' (which became the Regent Bridge) incorporated in its length, the style of the monumental thoroughfare reflected elements of both Greece and Rome, but in time the Greek predominated. The architect Richard Crichton's proposal for the entrance to the street, illustrated in an aquatint plate by Robert Scott after Crichton's drawing, published in 1814, was for twin pavilions in an unfluted Ionic order. (Fig. 16) In each, distyle convex or inverted quadrants framed a flat centrepiece, itself articulated by paired, Ionic columns: the whole was surmounted by balustraded attics, lunette windows and trophies of arms. In contrast with these almost baroque terminations, the street behind appears relatively plain, though the cornices are topped by balustrades and the attic storeys by large urns. At the far end, below the slope of Calton Hill, was to be a large saucer-domed edifice, with a substantial pedimented portico, the whole redolent of Rome. A commentary on the plate suggests that this 'may represent the Court-house and Public Offices, intended there to be erected'.[51]

In the end, Archibald Elliot was the preferred architect, beginning work on a street conceived with a 'Grecian' triumphal bridge 'commenced', as the inscription tablet on the north arch states, 'in the ever memorable year 1815'. (Figs 45-47) In two interesting etchings Patrick Gibson recorded the early stages of building. These prints show work in progress, with various different stages compressed or collapsed into the same perspective view, both accompanied by informed descriptions. One plate shows how the processional street would be 'decorated with columns of the Ionic and Corinthian orders': these were 'exhibited in their unfinished state' in Gibson's images. (Figs 42-43) But if this illustrates the impending triumph of Greece over Rome, full respect is still given, in Plate II, to 'the *chef d'oeuvre* of Mr [Robert] Adam', namely the Register House, the first notable building to be shown from the artist's vantage point in the evolving Waterloo Place. This was an architectural triumph 'certainly still unequalled in this city, notwithstanding the many expensive buildings that have been erected since that period.' The plate telescopes the view, so that the arches of the new Regent Bridge appear much nearer to Register House than in fact was ever the case. Greece meets Rome with no perceptible stylistic disjunction.[52]

On his return to Scotland, Hugh William Williams appended to his Mediterranean travelogue a note (he called it a 'Conclusion') on developments in Edinburgh which helped further to clinch his view of its actual—or certainly potential—superiority to Athens. A man who had seen the ancient buildings of Athens and Attica for himself felt no unease about referring to the new structures gracing the Edinburgh townscape: the elegant and daring Regent Bridge spanning a ravine below the very 'Grecian' buildings of Waterloo Place, and the Greek Ionic County Hall (all designed by Elliot); the 'exquisite and classical building the Observatory' on Calton Hill (designed by William Henry Playfair); and so on. More 'magnificent works' and 'superior designs' were in contemplation, 'with the view of giving a classical air to modern Athens!'[53] (It should be noted that Williams did not write 'Athens of the North'.) Edinburgh was already an Athens in the eye: more, and better, Greek-style buildings would reinforce the conceit.

The idea of Edinburgh as the 'Modern Athens', already advanced by Alison and others, was now compounded by Williams. From this time onwards, the duality was so widely accepted that no explanation was deemed necessary when drawing the parallel or stating the case as fact. Edinburgh *was* the Modern Athens. Her new identity might be yet further confirmed or enhanced if a 'fac-simile, or a restoration of the Temple of Minerva' should come to crown the Calton Hill as a monument not just to the military glory won by Scottish soldiers and Scottish sailors in the campaigns against Napoleon, but also of 'the pure taste which distinguishes our country in the present'.[54] It was Williams who originated the term 'fac-simile' in connection with the idea of a 'Parthenon' national monument in Edinburgh. Within a very short time, indeed, as 'a gentleman whose reputation in this city stands deservedly high; and whose authority is of importance in this discussion, since he is well known as an artist, a traveller, and an amateur', Williams was being credited with the introduction of the idea.[55] 'Is it too much to expect', wrote Williams in bringing his case to an end, 'that an enlightened patronage may call up genius, kindred to that of ancient times, and may direct our native talents to efforts, similar to those which gave splendour to the age of Pericles?'[56]

Williams published this in 1820. Subsequently, he furnished Robert Chambers with a note that would form a coda to Chambers's *Walks in Edinburgh* (1825). Williams's authorship of this appendix to such an influential guide has tended to be overlooked; his contribution was placed within a special section headed simply 'Edinburgh and Athens'.[57] Here Williams supplied a 'brief comparison of the two cities', as if visitors (or residents) were to be invited to reflect on these similarities as they perambulated the New Town or ascended the soon-to-be Parthenon-crowned 'acropolis' of Calton Hill.

In stating his case, Williams declared that the epithets 'Northern Athens' and 'Modern Athens' had frequently been applied to Edinburgh. He (and, following him, George Sibbald) knew the word on the street in a way that we cannot do. It seems, in all probability, that the terms were indeed in comparatively common use, and that therefore the ideas that had given rise to them were current for some time prior to the moment when Williams and Chambers actually set them down on the page in something as commonplace as a popular guidebook. It is also the fact that people must genuinely have regarded the townscape of the one city as if they were, at any rate in their dreams, looking at that of its sunnier, southern counterpart. 'The mind', Williams noted,

> unconsciously yields to the allusion awakened by these terms [the 'Northern' and 'Modern' Athenian epithets] and imagines that the resemblance between these cities must extend from the natural localities, and the public buildings, to the streets and private edifices.

But to think thus was wholly mistaken; indeed, the very reverse was the case, for Athens was actually the runner-up in this beauty parade. 'Athens, even in her best days, could not have coped with the capital of Scotland.'[58] And, in modern times, Plaka, with its mean houses, was no Old Town of Edinburgh, let alone the newer districts being in any way equal to the splendid New Town. 'Athens—as it now exists, independent of its ruins, and deprived of the charm of association,—is contemptible: its houses are mean, and its streets scarcely deserve the name.' But Williams summoned up reserves of charity which concealed a certain patronizing attitude: the modern city still 'appears almost worthy of the Acropolis ...'.[59]

The true comparison between the cities lay neither in the domestic buildings nor in the streets: in these there was no contest or parallel. The essential likeness lay in the landforms and in the distant views. Williams described, especially, that of Edinburgh from Torphin and Colinton. There 'the landscape is exactly that of the vicinity of Athens, as viewed from the bottom of Mount Anchesmus [the outcrops of the so-called Tourkovounia range, culminating in Mount Lykabettos]'. From that point, in Athens, Mons Brilessus (that is Pentelikon, north-east of Athens) resembled the Braid Hills. Mixing the topography of both cities in a series of confusing pairings, Williams declared that Edinburgh Castle on its rock took on the character of the Athenian Acropolis—'In the abrupt and dark mass of the Castle, rises the Acropolis ...' was his explicit statement—and the Calton Hill, most improbably, assumed that of Lykabettos coupled with the Areopagos. Beyond, the widening Forth estuary seemed as if it were the Saronic Gulf, with Inchkeith the island of Aegina; the hills of Fife resembled those of the distant Peloponnese.[60] 'It is, indeed, most remarkable and astonishing', Williams concluded in his piece for Chambers, 'that two cities, placed at such a distance from each other, and so different in every political and artificial circumstance, should *naturally* be so alike.'[61]

The classical scholar William Mure of Caldwell published his *Journal of a Tour in Greece* in Edinburgh in 1842, four years after his visit. He discussed briefly 'the Hill of St George' explaining that this distinctive feature, once known to scholarship as Mount 'Anchesmus' but now as 'Lycabettus', is 'to Athens what Vesuvius is to Naples, or Arthur's Seat to Edinburgh'. Later on in his book, Mure stated that the Choragic Monument of Lysikrates had been 'imitated' in the Burns Monument on Calton Hill. Here is a case of a Scotsman in Athens suggesting, in the first instance, topographical parallels with home and (in the second) noting the result in Edinburgh architecture of the influence of an ancient Greek building.[62] But Mure never allowed himself—as, in the circumstances, he might so easily have done—to lapse into use of the 'Modern Athens' soubriquet. Nor, significantly, did he mention Edinburgh's own 'Parthenon'.

Nor would John Stuart Blackie do so either. Both were West of Scotland men, Mure coming from Renfrewshire and Blackie being Glasgow-born. Blackie, however, had not long been appointed to the chair of Greek at Edinburgh when he, too, travelled in Greece for the first time. In letters to his wife Eliza (for whom he had a charming Greek pet-name) he made no mention by its soubriquet of 'the Athens of the North' he had left, nor of the National Monument even when he looked at the Parthenon. His descriptions of the primary Athens may perhaps suggest that he preferred it to Edinburgh on several counts. In May 1853 Blackie wrote to his wife:

> To-morrow we make another expedition to Mount Pentelicus, out of whose womb came all the marble on which Phidias and Praxiteles stamped their souls ... I was amused when I found myself living in University Street, as if the shop could never leave me ... From this window ... I have a view open to the pillared range of the Parthenon ... to my left rises honeyed Hymettus. Behind the house there is a garden, which will soon be richly shaded with the quiet-spreading foliage of the vines, and this garden looks out on the famous mountain Lycabettus, which overhangs Athens as Arthur [*sic*] Seat does Edinburgh ... in my immediate neighbourhood are the streets of Hippocrates and Aristides, Sophocles and Euripides, and you may imagine that to a classical man no strange lodging could be more familiar. I am both at home here and not at home in a manner that considerably disturbs me, so that as yet I scarcely know where I am nor how to feel, and am habitually overpowered by a pleasant sort of discomfort ...[63]

Blackie described the dress, demeanour, features and facial expressions of the Greeks as giving a 'living idea of a Homeric Agamemnon or Ajax'; some 'noble and kingly', others 'dark, scowling, and savage ... ferocious, cutthroat faces...'. How telling was the remark: 'To a person just stept from the leading-strings of cold Edinburgh proprieties and etiquettes, the sensation of strange, rich naturalness was magical.' On a lengthy expedition through Boeotia, and then to and around Delphi and Mount Parnassus, which he ascended on mule-back, he observed lakes not nearly as good as Scottish lochs, but streams 'leaping down with a fine Scottish vigour'; and he asked rhetorically of his wife in Edinburgh, 'how shall our mightiest Bens look when contrasted with this classic Parnassó[s] ...'.[64]

* * * * *

Williams's topographical identification of Edinburgh with Athens became an enduringly popular conceit. The Victorian tourists' vade mecum, John Murray's *Handbook for Travellers in Scotland*, could still state in the 1870s that Edinburgh's 'appellation of "The Modern Athens" is not merely a general comparison', but the result of careful study of the similarity of landscape.

Williams continued to be quoted on all the points of view which had led to his conclusion. The index to Murray's *Handbook* is typographically interesting, for under 'Edinburgh' appear the conjoint lines

> {General Description}
> {Modern Athens}[65]

Later still, William Mitchell, the Edinburgh solicitor who in the first years of the twentieth century would spearhead a campaign to complete and re-purpose the unfinished National Monument, and who had been to Athens and who was of a generation still conditioned by what Williams had long before suggested, would state categorically that

> our good town of Edinburgh need not fear comparison with the renowned capital of Greece. I have approached both cities from the sea, and was surprised, I confess, to find the view of Modern Athens, rising from the Forth towards the Castle on the right, and the Calton on the left, backed by the lion of Arthur [*sic*] Seat and the Salisbury Crags, and the ranges of the Braids and of the Pentlands, blue in the distance, infinitely more picturesque than the Ancient City.[66]

It is a fact that, in his perfervid search for congruity and parallel, Williams had actually become confused as to where the Edinburgh 'acropolis' most appropriately lay. In his *Travels* (1820) he had declared unequivocally for Calton Hill, crowned as he hoped it would be by a new Parthenon. But in his note for Chambers's *Walks* (1825) he envisioned the National Monument taking the place of the 'present Barracks in the Castle'.[67] If the Monument were to be located in the latter situation, 'an important additional feature of resemblance would be conferred ...; that being the corresponding position of the Parthenon in the Acropolis.' So, by 1825, Edinburgh actually had not one putative acropolis but two, in the Castle Rock and the Calton Hill. With the coming of the National Monument in its Parthenon guise, and later Thomas Hamilton's superb High School on the hill's southern flank to fulfil the role of the Propylaea, only one site would win out. If Calton Hill was imagined as the Acropolis of the Modern Athens, the Castle was relegated, in Modern Athenian eyes, to the superannuated status of what Robert Burns, in his 'Address to Edinburgh', had described as

> Like some bold Vet'ran, gray in arms
> And mark'd with many a seamy scar—

Alternatively, it could be said that the Castle remained the acropolis of Auld Reekie, while the Calton Hill became that of the New Town, otherwise known as

New Edinburgh, or the 'Modern Athens'. For his part, however, George Sibbald was to admit to no such confusion or want of sharp focus, and went all-out for transforming Calton Hill into the Acropolis of the Athens of the North.[68]

Although Stuart and Revett wrote of no similarity between Athens and Edinburgh, one image in their first volume does make a most effective pictorial comparison, and one much heightened when certain views were produced in Edinburgh in the mid-1820s.[69] Stuart's perspective view of the Acropolis with the Tower of the Winds in the foreground—it is the specific subject of discussion—finds a remarkable foil in J. W. Ewbank's view of Edinburgh Castle and The Mound from the north-east. This appears, engraved by W. H. Lizars, in *Picturesque Views of Edinburgh* of 1825 (with text by James Browne) and in *Edinburgh Delineated* of 1832. Strikingly, the circular Panorama house on The Mound appears in more or less the same place in relation to the battlemented profile of the Castle Rock as does the Tower of the Winds to the fortified rock of the Acropolis. (Figs 10-12)

*   *   *   *   *

In his brief text prefacing Williams's 'Edinburgh and Athens' appendix to the *Walks*, Chambers advertised the fact that it was Williams's intention to issue a pair of engravings 'representing the Ancient and the Modern Athens, as seen from the points where their resemblance is most conspicuous'.[70] Williams had already contrived to produce views of Athens which—in their general feeling for the topography and the way that the townscape, with its citadel upon its craggy rock, relates to adjacent hill, mountain, plain and sea—really do appear to resemble the setting and environs of Edinburgh, thus adding visual imagery to the 'mental' idea of similitude. [71] (Figs 1 and 3)

In 1822 and 1826 Williams mounted two influential exhibitions of his watercolour paintings in which Greek and Scottish views were mixed promiscuously. Furthermore, from 1823 he issued, in parts, engravings of many of his most effective Greek scenes, several of which were strongly romanticised and idealized re-imaginings of celebrated sites such as Plato's academy, or 'the Academic Grove'. [72] (Fig. 33) These views were then brought together in 1829 in a two-volume collection, *Select Views in Greece with Classical Illustrations*.[73]

The catalogues of both exhibitions bear almost exactly the same title. These catalogues, and the later volumes of plates, are replete with, and indeed are given additional scholarly substance by, a remarkable range of quotations from classical authors translated by the young prodigy John Patterson. The initials 'J.P.' attached to these selections and translations are his, and are not, as has been assumed, those of the printer of the catalogues, John Pillans (brother of James Pillans, formerly Rector of the High School and Professor of Humanity in the University of Edinburgh).[74]

Admission to the exhibitions was a hefty two shillings, though, to catch Modern Athenians at an impressionable age, 'young ladies and gentlemen under fifteen' were admitted at half price.[75] Williams's oeuvre was received with great acclaim. On the walls of the Calton Convening Rooms at the east end of Waterloo Place, just below the site earmarked for the Edinburgh Parthenon (Fig. 36), 'Hellenophiles'—'Philhellenes' is a term carrying specific contemporary political and emotional meaning—were transported to Greece through the medium of Williams's views. A reviewer suggested that the exhibition was 'emblematic of the progress of taste in Scotland', noting also the 'enchanting glow' that the Greek views appeared to radiate, conveying as they did so 'the magic of classical association'.[76] Scottish patriots, at any rate of a certain rank in society, were confirmed in their belief that they, too, lived in a sort of Arcadia, as Williams captured Caledonian scenery in similar manner with similar tonalities in a comparable palette.

William Hazlitt reviewed the first exhibition for *The London Magazine* in richly glowing, even luscious, terms. He suggested that the display of the paintings and 'the attention they have excited' did as much credit to 'the taste of the northern capital' as it did to the landscape of Greece itself. It was clear that there was some almost indefinable parallelism between Greece, Scotland as a whole, and Edinburgh in particular. There seemed, also, to be a certain sympathy between subjects and viewers, even if Scotland (in Hazlitt's view, which was in contradiction to what Williams himself had suggested in the first instance) appeared to be outclassed in both the potency of the landscape itself and in the power to provoke appreciation of that landscape. Williams had

stretched out under the far-famed Calton Hill, and in the eye of Arthur's Seat, fairy visions of the fair land of Greece, that Edinburgh belles and beaux repair to see with cautious wonder and well-regulated delight. It is really a most agreeable novelty ... to see the beauty of the North, the radiant beauty of the North, enveloped in such an atmosphere, and set off by such a back-ground. Oriental skies pour their molten lustre on Caledonian charms ... There played the NINE [muses] on immortal lyres, and here sit the critical but admiring Scottish fair, with the catalogue in their hands, reading the quotations from Lord Byron's verses with liquid eyes and lovely vermilion lips—would that they spoke English, or any thing but Scotch!—Poor is this irony! Vain the attempt to reconcile Scottish figures with Attic scenery! What land can rival Greece? What earthly flowers can compare with the colours in the sky? What living beauty can recall the dead? For that word, GREECE, there breathe three thousand years of fame that has no date to come! Over that land hovers a light, brighter than that of suns, softer than that which vernal skies shed on halcyon seas, the light that rises from the tomb of virtue, genius, liberty!... Thou that art a Goddess, and we thy worshippers, say dost thou not smile for ever on this land of Greece, and shed thy purple light over it ... But here (in the Calton Convening Room, in Waterloo place, close under the Melville Monument—strange contradiction!) another Greece grows on the walls— other skies are to be seen, ancient temples rise, and modern Greek ladies walk ... We have at once an impressive and satisfactory idea of the country of which we have heard so much; and wish to visit places which, it seems from this representation of them, would not bely all that we have heard. Some splenetic travellers have pretended that Attica was dry, flat, and barren. But it is not so in Mr Williams's authentic draughts; and we thank him for restoring to us our old, and, as it appears, true allusion—for crowning that Elysium of our school-boy fancies, with majestic hills ... and scooping it into lovely winding valleys once more ...

Hazlitt ended his piece with the rather bathetic note that 'There are a number of very interesting sketches interspersed, and some very pleasing *home* views, which seems to show that nature is everywhere herself.'[77]

However, though the Modern Athenians may have looked, they did not buy, certainly first time around. Many if not most of the works hanging in 1826 had been in the show of 1822. But this did not stop Robert Chambers indulging in the hyperbole of describing Williams's watercolours, in their totality as a collection, as 'by far the most exquisite specimen of the arts ever produced in Scotland'.[78]

Two pictures from the first of Williams's exhibitions stand out in importance. Number 7, 'The Remains of the Parthenon, or Temple of Minerva, at Athens' has the catalogue note that follows below. The wording suggests that the ruined Parthenon was to be (first) transported in some magic way to its future Edinburgh location, and (second) that it was there to be re-assembled by some skilled engineering and architectural intervention, thus reversing the progress of devouring time.

> This is the Edifice proposed to be erected on the Calton Hill of Edinburgh, as the National Monument of Scotland. That hill bears a striking resemblance to the Acropolis, on which the Temple stands; and whether the grandeur of the Edifice, or the peculiarity of the situation, be considered, the restoration of this temple would give to Scotland the noblest and most classical building that modern Europe can boast of. The length of the Temple is two hundred and twenty-seven feet, the width one hundred and one, the height, from the ground to the top of the pediment sixty-five feet six inches.[79]

Number 39 in the first exhibition was a 'View of Athens from the foot of Mount Anchesmus': it was shown again in 1826 as number 5. The long description of the topography of ancient Athens ends with a separate paragraph, isolated for effect, which states: 'This is the point of view in which the resemblance between Edinburgh and Athens, so often mentioned, is perhaps the most conspicuous.'[80] The second catalogue includes lines from Milton's *Paradise Regained*.

> ... on the Aegean shore a city stands
> Built nobly, pure the air, and light the soil;
> Athens, the eye of Greece, mother of arts
> And eloquence; native of famous wits ...

By extension, Edinburgh was here implied, both in Williams's (or perhaps Patterson's) choice of the quotation and in his definitive statement that the specific viewpoint in the painting evoked Edinburgh.

When discussing the influence on 'Athenian' taste in Edinburgh of picturesque topographical views of Greek buildings and locations, notably those by Williams, it is important to correct the misapprehension that William Henry Playfair, the architect par excellence of the Modern Athens, owned a large number of Williams's works. The catalogue of Playfair's sale has been misinterpreted, and the impression given that he was imbued with more Hellenophile passion that he really had.[81] Playfair in fact owned only three specifically Greek views out of a total of nine watercolour paintings by Williams. The auction in question was actually that of the collections of two people, not of a single individual; one was Playfair, the other was Aeneas MacBean, WS.[82] A prosperous lawyer with a house and office at 11 Charlotte Square (on the smart, north side), MacBean had been Williams's executor in 1829. He also happened to act for Lord Elgin. MacBean was the greatest collector by far of Williams's Greek views. It is likely that he acquired most or all from Williams's estate. He owned forty framed and glazed pictures of Greek subjects, all of which had been engraved for the *Select Views in Greece*. All these were lotted separately. Then, in addition to a miniature portrait of the artist himself, the MacBean sale catalogue records a total of sixty-five further Williams entries, ranging from fine finished watercolours to a variety of drawings, sketches and sketchbooks. Many of the lots were substantial, containing numerous individual sheets. Of these, at least eight can be identified as wholly 'Greek' in theme or subject. With his almost obsessional interest in Greek landscape as depicted by its great Edinburgh interpreter, Aeneas MacBean really *was* a consummate Modern Athenian.

THE MODERN ATHENS IN THE MIND

'The sun that shines on Athens looks bright alike on us'

The developing notion of Edinburgh as another Athens in natural rock and hewn stone was itself paralleled by that of the cerebral 'twinning' of the cities. Here the idea may actually go back rather further than the perceived topographical similarity. The origins may perhaps be traced to the earlier days of the Scottish Enlightenment, and to the recognition by the Scots literati of their own worth. David Daiches remarked concisely that the Edinburgh literati called their city '"the Athens of the North" and consciously practised civilization'.[1] Both these statements are true; but *when* they said the former has never been entirely clear.

Daiches was thinking of the later eighteenth century. Before that, however, in 1616, an inscription in Greek was erected over the door to the library of the Town's College of Edinburgh.[2] The University, as it would later be known, was long controlled by the city. The Greek inscription was accompanied, in 1617, by a Latin one stating, in translation, that 'the Senate and People of Edinburgh have taken care to construct this house [or hall: in other words, these buildings] for Christ and the Muses.'[3] By this is meant 'for the promotion of the Christian religion and the Arts', a neat amalgamation of pagan classical and Christian ideology, as the Muses espoused many of the arts and sciences. Above the Latin text is a delightfully naïve representation of the city's arms, and the fingers of a bas-relief sculptured hand, point (equally naïvely) towards the words.

The Greek inscription is the earliest known to have been erected anywhere in Edinburgh.[4] Greek was taught in the Town's College because of its significance in philosophy and, above all, for its importance as a necessary prerequisite for theology and New Testament studies. The tablet is flanked on either side by Scottish heraldic lions rampant. It reads: ΔΙΠΛΟΥΝ ΟΡΩΣΙΝ ΟΙ / ΜΑΘΟΝΤΕΣ ΓΡΑΜΜΑΤΑ. 'Double they see, those having learned letters' is the literal translation. 'Those who are educated have double insight', is what the text really means; or we could say that 'people who can read and absorb what they learn see twice as much as those without such ability'. Menander, the dramatist of the later fourth to early third century BC, is the source of the apophthegm. It is highly appropriate to an academic library. (The suggestion that the text, with its allusion to 'seeing double', implies one can get drunk with learning is an amusing example of modern facetiousness.)[5] Perhaps it may not be a case of additional facetiousness to suggest that 'seeing double' may have come to assume a supplementary significance in the late eighteenth and earlier nineteenth centuries: in the way that Edinburgh looked inward and outward at the same time, and saw itself not just as the city of Edinburgh, capital of Scotland, but as something else: itself as the Athens of the North.

The stone, which has occupied several positions in the Old Quad of the University of Edinburgh, has recently found a new location in the vestibule of the Law School library. It is thus conveniently adjacent to an early nineteenth-century room designed by William Henry Playfair, which is one of Edinburgh's most distinctive (not to say eccentric) Greek interiors. Playfair's striking room and the Menander text together constitute a little corner of Greek—if not quite purely 'Athenian'—Edinburgh, city of the mind.

*   *   *   *   *

Sir George Mackenzie of Rosehaugh, the King's Advocate and also Dean of the Faculty of Advocates, formally inaugurated the Faculty's library in 1689. The institution developed rapidly into the national library of Scotland in all but name; its transfer to the nation by the Faculty of Advocates some 235 years later was to make it such in actuality. Mackenzie described his creation as 'this Parnassus and bosom of the Muses', perhaps the most eloquent statement made in Edinburgh by that time of a wished-for identification with the culture of ancient Greece. In the early nineteenth century, a superbly elegant, emblematic design was chosen to embellish the bindings of the Advocates' Library's books. The handsome stamp features Medusa's head, as if on the boss of the shield of Athena, within a wreath of laurel. (Fig. 35) The implication is clear: the motif symbolises the Faculty of Advocates' championship of scholarship through its great Library, at that period one of the major institutions of learning in what was, by then, 'the Modern Athens'.[6]

Early eighteenth-century uses of 'Athens' or 'Athenian' should be treated with circumspection. They carry by no means the same weight as similar terms employed a century later, generally being used as self-conscious synonyms for 'learned' or 'intellectual'. In 1720s Edinburgh there was a certain amount of what one might call 'playful Athenianism'. (In the 1820s, by contrast, everything was much more intense.) The female members of the bluestocking 'Fair Intellectual-Club', in existence by at least 1720, indulged in some flirtatious literary banter with the 'Brethren' of 'an Athenian Society in Town' which flourished between about 1717 and 1723.[7] One 'J.C.' addresses 'the Masters in the University of Edinburgh'—'On whom Minerva and the Muses smile'—with the rhetorical question 'But, who, ATHENIANS, merit more than you?' There is even an implication of intellectual and cultural rivalry with London, with the suggestion that Edinburgh does not come off worst:

> *Edina* yields not to *Augusta* yet
> For Learning, Sense, Integrity and Wit.[8]

All this, despite the near-contemporary remarks by the antiquary Alexander Gordon who saw London very much as 'Apollo's favourite residence'. Though an ardent Scottish patriot, Gordon was nevertheless disenchanted by lack of what we might term 'Athenian' feeling in Scotland.[9] There appeared to him all too little evidence in Edinburgh, and still less in his native Aberdeen, to suggest a city or a country poised to assume 'Athenian' airs.

The poet Allan Ramsay's proto-'Athenianism' was even less precise or well-defined. If his Edinburgh was not exactly an Athens, Ramsay certainly inhabited a world where a blithe spirit of pastoral classicism pervaded his poetry and his cultural ideas. Men might shine in Edina's

> ... witty clubs of minds that move at large,
> With ev'ry glass can some great thought discharge ...

They might shine also in the legal profession in the city, at the College, in artistic and musical circles, or in preparing to play a part in political or military affairs at home and abroad. The ladies, meanwhile,

> Shall in bright order fill the dazzling ring:
> From Venus, Pallas, and the spouse of Jove,
> They'd gain the prize, judg'd by the god of love ...

Arthur's Seat was Ramsay's Parnassus; but he delighted in notions of Helicon, too, and Pegasus pranced about among his gentle shepherds in engravings by Richard Cooper; his aristocratic friends in the Royal Company of Archers were like 'Grecian Chiefs ... before old Troy'.[10] In the Preface to his first quarto volume of poems (1721), Ramsay confessed his almost total ignorance of Greek but, nevertheless, his admiration for the third-century BC Sicilian pastoral poet Theocritus. And, indeed, Ramsay himself would come to be regarded as a 'Scottish Theocritus'. Of his own verses Ramsay wrote:

The *Scotticisms* [sic], which perhaps may offend some over-nice Ear, give new
Life and Grace to the Poetry, and become their Place as well, as the Doric
Dialect of *Theocritus*, so much admired by the best Judges. When I mention
that Tongue, I bewail my own little Knowledge of it, since I meet with so many
Words and Phrases so expressive of the Ideas they are intended to represent.

Classical literature, and 'a small Acquaintance with that language [Greek]',
should inspire emulation in verse written in Ramsay's native Scots dialect, and
so convince readers of his pastorals that it was possible to 'spend too much
Time in looking abroad for trifling Delicacies, when we may be treated at
home with a more substantial, or as well as a more elegant Entertainment.'[11]
Perhaps Edinburgh did not need to be another 'Athens' at all. But, in the 1730s,
Ramsay built for himself a quaint octagonal *rus in urbe* retreat on the Castle
Hill, known to his circle as 'the House of the Muses'. Here he liked to imagine
himself living in a kind of sub-classical retirement. In the nineteenth century,
visitors to Edinburgh still sought out this villa, a 'Parnassus north the Castle
hill', somehow emblematic of early ideas of association between the capital of
Scotland, by then generally known as the Modern Athens, and the fringes of the
world of Greek antiquity.[12] (Fig. 11)

Allan Ramsay was among the founders, in 1729, of the short-lived but
significant Academy of St Luke, the earliest of Scotland's art academies.
Drawing from casts of classical sculpture was part of the curriculum pursued
in premises the use of which was granted by the Town's College. William
Adam, *paterfamilias* of the great architectural dynasty, also signed the St Luke's
foundation document or 'indenture', as did the younger Allan Ramsay, then a
promising prodigy as both draughtsman and portrait-painter.[13]

Looking back to the 1720s and to the 'Fair Intellectual Club, a society of
female literati', Alexander Campbell saw it (albeit somewhat patronisingly) as
'a proof that the ladies of the Scotish [sic] capital had made great progress
in the improvement of the mind ...'.[14] More generally, and progressing in his
survey more nearly to his own day, Campbell wrote of how the 'middling and
superior ranks of the inhabitants of Edinburgh were now advancing in that
refinement and high polish of society which ... became so conspicuous and
manifest.' Campbell's assessment of what he thought had occurred after the
failure of the Jacobite rising of 1745-46 is worth quoting at length.

And, now, the tide of opinion gliding smoothly along in one direction;
liberality of sentiment expanding daily; the pulpit, the bar, and the bench,
filled with persons of moderation and talents; the university rearing in its
bosom the future ornaments of the civil and ecclesiastical departments, and
the distinguished luminaries of the Scotish [sic] literati; all, all concurred in
hastening the happy era, when a state of civil society, in refined and polished

manners second to none in any section of Europe, should eventually obtain, and diffuse its influence in every direction.

By the mid-eighteenth century, Campbell believed,

> the way to wealth and distinction lay open to all whose talents and industry were excited by the hope of reward, honour, and celebrity … their mental resources contained a mine of inexhaustible knowledge; and, as knowledge is power, so, in the proper exercise of that power, the rock on which the temple of Fame stood, though seen afar, was to be climbed and a seat secured in that sacred fane to which all eyes are eagerly directed.[15]

Literature, 'whose lustre, like the diamond, the more it is handled the brighter it sparkles', became a fashionable pursuit. And, like the precious stone, 'still the more brilliant will its native beauties appear to the discerning eye of true taste and judgment.' Campbell went on the trace a sort of line of succession of the literary and philosophical societies of Edinburgh from that formed by Thomas Ruddiman in 1718 to the Royal Society of Edinburgh, effectively Scotland's national academy, in 1783.[16]

Robert Adam, an early Fellow, designed an emblematic device to ornament the title-pages of the first volumes of the *Transactions* of the Royal Society of Edinburgh; this was engraved by John Beugo.[17] (Fig. 31) The composition, of medallion form, shows a muse, or the personification of learning, in Grecian drapery; probably she is also intended to embody the spirit of either 'Scotia' or 'Edina', as she holds a sprig of thistle in her left hand. The setting is clearly Edinburgh, the Castle looming above the Nor' [North] Loch which mysteriously appears as a stretch of water allowing shipping to pass, and thus trade to flow in. The figure is in the process of inscribing a shield, in Latin, with factual details of the Society's establishment. Below, on a pedestal supporting two columns (perhaps emblematic of the arts and the sciences) with the Scottish heraldic unicorn between them, there is a Greek inscription. Although unattributed, it is in fact taken from a passage in the celebrated Funeral Oration delivered by Pericles and given by Thucydides in his history of the Peloponnesian War, Book II. 40. In translation this reads: 'Our love of what is beautiful does not lead to extravagance; and we cultivate the mind without loss of manliness.' Thus, sentiments characteristic of native Scottish restraint and economy are matched by the high-flown philosophy of fifth-century Athens, the whole being adapted to the spirit of Edinburgh in the earliest phases of its Modern Athenian age. Had that plinth been large enough, Adam (or whoever among his scholarly Edinburgh friends pointed out the lapidary text to him) might have expanded the inscription to comprehend an earlier passage in the speech, where Pericles had alluded to the elegance and good taste displayed in Athenian private houses, and the greatness of the city as a lodestone for the world.

*   *   *   *   *

The lawyer Sir Gilbert Elliot, who took the title of Lord Minto on being raised
to the Scottish bench, wrote an important pamphlet in 1752. This is a key
document envisaging a future direction for Edinburgh, for in it proposals for
the city's social and economic as well as physical development are outlined.
Elliot argued that the 'situation, conveniency and beauty' of the capital of a
nation might lead it to become 'the centre of trade and commerce, of learning
and the arts, of politeness, and of refinement of every kind.'[18] Edinburgh might,
by this reckoning, become another Athens in all but name. But to do so, it
had to break the bonds of confinement upon the narrow ridge where the Old
Town—a place, as Elliot described it, of 'so many unavoidable nuisances'—had
developed in higgledy-piggledy fashion. The Old Town itself had to be reformed,
certainly, with various new public buildings, offices and facilities; but it was
the regrettable fact that few people of rank still lived in Edinburgh at all, and
that the city, being a place where 'narrow notions, inconsistent with polished
manners' were still 'obstinately retained', was 'rarely visited by strangers'.
It was obvious that 'an attempt to enlarge and beautify' the metropolis was
necessary.[19] Accordingly, Elliot looked to the establishment of a New Town, to
be built in an extended civic 'royalty' on open ground across the Nor' Loch; but
he warned, in doing so, that the example of comparable 'new towns' in Europe
tended to produce districts not only of 'spacious streets and large buildings' but
also a sort of cultural and social desert lacking vibrancy.[20] With these strictures
in mind, the citizens of Edinburgh were soon to embark upon their own New
Town project.[21] The new city they built, from the last years of the 1760s, was to
be the true setting of the 'Modern Athens'.

In 1757, David Hume expressed, to the same Sir Gilbert Elliot of Minto,
his pleasure—mixed with surprise—at the state of Scotland's eminence in the
republic of letters:

> ... really it is admirable how many Men of Genius this Country produces
> at present. Is it not strange that, at a time when we have lost our Princes,
> our Parliaments, our independent Government, even the Presence of our chief
> Nobility, are unhappy, in our Accent & Pronunciation, speak a very corrupt
> Dialect or the Tongue which we make use of; is it not strange, I say, that, in
> these Circumstances, we shou'd really be the People most distinguish'd for
> Literature in Europe.[22]

Writing earlier to Elliot, Hume had listed some celebrated seats of learning,
including 'Rome, antient & modern, Athens ...'.[23] This fragment of evidence
must be handled carefully for, if the wrong text is used, Hume might well be

thought to be referring here to Edinburgh, otherwise the 'Modern Athens'. In his edition of Dugald Stewart's philosophical works (1854), Sir William Hamilton misprinted this phrase of Hume's (quoted by Stewart in his *Dissertation: Exhibiting the Progress of Metaphysical, Ethical, and Political Philosophy since the Revival of Letters in Europe*, first published in 1821) as 'ancient and modern Athens', thus distorting the sense of Hume's comment as he had made it in his original letter to Elliot.[24] Had Hume actually written what Hamilton printed, it would indeed have implied the Athens of classical antiquity *and* the contemporary Edinburgh of Hume's own day: a misplaced comma makes all the difference. Hamilton, a product of 'Athenian' Edinburgh, was—perhaps quite unconsciously—seduced by the language and terminology of his own time when looking at the language and ideas of the past.

Hume's comment on the number of Edinburgh's intellectual prodigies finds an echo in the celebrated anecdote related by the printer William Smellie, who recounted the observation of John Amyat, the King's Chemist: 'Here stand I at what is called the *Cross of Edinburgh*, and can in a few minutes take fifty men of genius and learning by the hand.'[25]

The earliest occasion on which Edinburgh was compared directly with Athens on the cultural level may be in 1761, in a letter of the Revd Alexander Carlyle to Sir Gilbert Elliot. Carlyle describes how the public lectures of the Irish elocutionist Thomas Sheridan, aimed at the improvement of the language of the Scottish literati, had been taken up enthusiastically by the luminaries of the Select Society, itself transformed into an 'Academy for the English Tongue'.

> Instead of Manufactures, we are now to set about emproving our Language ... Elocution in all its branches. The *Fervidum Ingenium Scotorum* was never more apparent. Sheridan has told us that Edinburgh is the Athens of Great Brittain, & we believe him ...[26]

A further letter, rather similar in sentiment, was printed in the London *St James's Chronicle*: this purported to have been written from Edinburgh on 31 August 1761. Also describing the success of Thomas Sheridan's lectures, it concludes: 'You may soon therefore expect to find Scotland the standard of elocution and of the English tongue: And while Britain is to be the Greece of Europe, *Scotland* is to be the Athens of Britain.' The letter was subsequently reprinted in the *Edinburgh Evening Courant* of 23 September 1761.[27] Thus, the notion of an Athenian Edinburgh, percolating to London, was re-exported back to the place of its origin.

Then, in 1762, the Hon. Andrew Erskine, a friend of James Boswell, contributed 'An Epistle' to the printer Alexander Donaldson's second *Collection of Original Poems by Scotch Gentlemen*, referring both to Sheridan's lectures and to what the Irishman had said about a future Edinburgh.

> The time shall come, by prophets old
> And Mr Sheridan foretold,
> When fair Edina shall become
> A second Athens, or a Rome.[28]

The element of equivocation between the two great cities of antiquity adds its own interest.

The Select Society was the brainchild of Allan Ramsay the younger, by then not just one of the leading portrait painters in Britain but a man of letters of some distinction. From its foundation in 1754, it rapidly developed as a major *agora* for 'Athenian' debate.[29] Ramsay himself made a significant allusion to Edinburgh as another Athens. In 1762 he suggested to his friend Sir Alexander Dick of Prestonfield that the increasing number of institutions, intellectual and cultural, established in the city and focused upon the propagation of 'usefull knowledge and ... liberal accomplishments' might rapidly make Edinburgh 'the Athens of Britain', and thus render it superior even to London, for all its apparent metropolitan advantages. Included among those institutions regarded as socially desirable for the promotion of *bon ton* was the riding academy. This might seem a strange establishment for Ramsay to single out; but in a proto-Northern Athenian context, it appears almost like a facility directed to the needs of the equivalents of the *hippeis* or aristocratic cavalry of the ancient city. Writing from London, Ramsay took pleasure in affirming that 'The people at this end of the Island are forced to confess the great superiority of their Northern neighbours in almost every art they engage.'[30] His use of the 'Athenian' nomenclature for Edinburgh is intriguing, but his exact words must be noted. He wrote of Edinburgh as 'the Athens of Britain', not of the city as 'the Athens of the North'. Nice distinction it may be, but the historian who seeks to trace the adoption of the second epithet must not become confused by the other soubriquet, as has recently been the case.[31]

In his letter to Sir Alexander Dick, Ramsay mentioned his re-issue of his *Dialogue on Taste*, originally published in 1755 and republished in 1762 (with the title *On Taste*) as one of four essays constituting his *The Investigator*. In the pamphlet, Ramsay stressed the superiority of Greek civilisation and culture in all its aspects, not least in architecture, over that of Rome.[32] With his interest in classical archaeology, history and ancient art and architecture, Ramsay will certainly have taken full notice of Stuart and Revett's *Antiquities of Athens* on its appearance in January 1763: there is every possibility that Ramsay will have known something of its contents in advance of publication. And as a son of Edinburgh, who had already declared his native city to be 'the Athens of Britain', did he perhaps imagine an intellectual parallelism between Athens and Edinburgh when he read what Stuart and Revett had to say about the standing of ancient Athens? For that was a place whose citizens—like, indeed, the men of the Scottish Enlightenment—'distinguished themselves by a pre-eminence and universality of Genius, unknown to other Ages and Nations.'[33]

James Craig's engraved plan for the New Town of Edinburgh of 1766-67 is, in all its various forms and states, embellished with a cartouche or tablet enclosing lines from a poem surely familiar to all who looked at these designs. The poem is *Liberty* (1735-36), by Craig's uncle, James Thomson. The specific quotation used as this epigraph is taken and slightly adapted by Craig (who almost literally worshipped Thomson), from Part V, 'The Prospect [of Britain]'. In Thomson's 'poetical vision', Liberty has flown from Greece, via Italy, to Britain. And it is in Britain that there is the freedom, good government, wealth and taste to promote science, arts and public works. The line 'Lo! stately Streets, lo! *Squares* that court the breeze!' was seen as especially applicable to Craig's prospect of, and for, Edinburgh, where Thomson himself had once been a student. If Britain was now the throne of Liberty, and if Edinburgh was on the verge of re-inventing itself as a great new city planned on rational lines with an elegance never before seen in Scotland and perhaps not even in England, might not those who read the verse on Craig's plans have reflected on still other lines from an earlier part of Thomson's poem? Part II of *Liberty* is entitled 'Greece'. There Thomson had described Athens, spreading 'with bright marbles big, and future pomp' beneath the slopes of Hymettus with its bees and honey, and between the twin rivers Ilissos and Kephissos:

> This hive of science, shedding sweets divine,
> Of active arts, and animated arms ...

and how, there

> A quick, refined, a delicate, humane.
> Enlighten'd people reign'd ...
> In Attic bounds hence heroes, sages, wits,
> Shone thick as stars, the milky way of Greece!

The *literati* of Edinburgh must surely have felt that Auld Reekie itself might well be poised to assume the spear, shield and aegis of Athena and step forth as the Athens of the day.[34] As in antiquity Isocrates had tried to encapsulate what it was that made Athens so distinctive a force in creating an Hellenic 'intelligence', a way of thinking, so in the later Scottish Enlightenment the literati must have looked to Greek precedent. As Isocrates had put it, '... so far has our city distanced the rest of mankind in thought and in speech that her pupils have become the teachers of the rest of the world'. Athens had 'either invented or stamped with her approval' so many of the arts, 'and has presented them to the rest of the world to enjoy.'[35] In like manner, Edinburgh came to assume national and international intellectual leadership.

John Gillies's influential *History of Ancient Greece* was published in 1786. The author would later become Historiographer Royal for Scotland and indeed, at one point in his book, Athenian possessions are compared with Scotland in the matter of extent of territory.[36] Gillies's assessment of the greatness of Periclean Athens may have stirred emulation in the breasts of Edinburgh's literary establishment as well as those of her civic leaders, who carried on the vision, first entertained by the great Lord Provost George Drummond, of what the city might become.

> But it is the peculiar glory of the Athenians that ... they cultivated, with a generous enthusiasm, the arts which adorn peace as well as war, and carried them all to a perfection which few nations have been able to imitate, and none have found it possible to surpass. During the administration of a single man, more works of elegance and splendour, more magnificent temples, theatres and porticoes were erected within the walls of Athens, than could be raised during many centuries in Rome, though mistress of the world ... In the same period of time sculpture attained a sublimity ... and a republic hitherto inferior in works of invention and genius to several of her neighbours ... produced, in the single lifetime of Pericles, those inestimable models of poetry, eloquence and philosophy, which, in every succeeding age, the enlightened portion of mankind hath invariably regarded as the best standards, not merely of composition and style, but of taste and reason. The name of Greek seemed thenceforth to be sunk in that of Athenian ...

As if this passage did not contain enough inspiration, Gillies compounded the desire, in physical terms, for anyone in Edinburgh who cared to think about beautifying the city even more, now that the New Town was established and expanding:

> The Athenians began the laborious task of rebuilding their ... city ... with uncommon magnificence, and which the acquaintance gained ... with the graceful forms of Ionic and Doric architecture, might enable them to adorn with more beauty and elegance than had yet been displayed in Europe.[37]

*   *   *   *   *

In 1785 the geographical writer John Knox published a 'greatly enlarged' edition of his strangely titled and oddly themed *View of the British Empire, More Especially Scotland ...*, a work which actually concentrates on Highlands and islands fisheries, but which nevertheless includes an interesting assessment of Edinburgh as 'a rising city'. The many 'allurements' of the place are described, in a way that would have stuck a chord with Allan Ramsay. Lords Provost George Drummond and (Sir) James Hunter Blair were praised for their foresight in creating 'a great and splendid city, which, from the advantages of nature, and a due regard to the embellishments of art, may eclipse in beauty, any city in Europe, those of Italy excepted.' But, in excepting Italy, Knox looked to a place even more seminal in terms of culture, and the evocation of learning; for Edinburgh was even now

> considered as the modern Athens, in politeness, science and literature. The writings of its professors, divines, and lawyers, are every where read and admired. In the healing art it hath been long and justly celebrated. A seminary thus qualified will consequently draw thither many students from various parts of Europe and America ...[38]

This may be the first time that the precise epithet 'the modern Athens' is used of Edinburgh.

The first English writer to display similar sentiments appears to be the Hon. John St John. In his tragedy *Mary, Queen of Scots*, performed at Drury Lane and published in 1789, St John wrote of what might have been, had his heroine lived

> in more enlighten'd times,
> When graces were not sins, nor talents crimes,
> Admiring nations had confess'd her worth;
> And SCOTLAND shone the ATHENS of the NORTH.[39]

Though St John wrote of the sixteenth century, one cannot but believe that Edinburgh in its golden age was here informing his retrospective and imaginative view. His use of the epithet 'the Athens of the North' appears to be the first, though, strictly speaking, it comprehends a whole country rather than just its capital city.

That a Scotsman might feel this way is much more understandable. *Edinburgh: a Poem, in Two Parts* by Robert Alves also appeared in 1789. This is heavy with strained allusions to the classical air of the city of the Enlightenment, apparently peopled by the nymphs and swains of Arcadia, if not exactly ancient Athens. But the poem suggests that the attitudes of the inhabitants of Edinburgh were 'Athenian' nonetheless, as were their buildings—if, that is, Alves knew what Greek architecture really looked like. There was the University, even though the foundation stone of Robert Adam's new building was laid only that same year, and nothing other than the architect's drawings could as yet have suggested much in the way of neoclassical elegance or grandeur and, even then, a splendour very much of a Roman idiom:

> Hail, for they various learning known,
> *Athens' Lyceum*, all thine own!
> Thy *Alma's* willing sons appear,
> From eastern, western hemisphere ...

With the addition of the Register House, also by Robert Adam—'Oh wondrous proof of *Graecian* art'—Edinburgh was Athenian in all but name:

> For Science, Wit and Learning known,
> And all thy polish'd arts thine own!

Classical buildings helped; but the notion of a place of learning was there first. The Midlothian countryside, too, was endowed with a quality of Tyrrhenian and Aegean romance:

> Like *Paestum's* flowery banks of yore,
> Or watery *Baia's* tepid shore;
> Or *Graecian Tempe's* groves and rills,
> *Eurota's* banks, or *Hybla's* hills ...

Robert Heron took the example of the building of Adam's University and Register House as developments 'through which Edinburgh might be distinguished by the architecture no less than by the Science of Athens.'[40] The entrance front of Adam's University, with its huge monolithic columns, triumphal arch centrepiece and Piranesian-vaulted vestibule, was very obviously the essence of Roman grandeur on an heroic scale. (Fig. 13) But the fact that it was being built at all nevertheless suggested some 'Athenian' spirit at work in the city. This, together with a reading of the Comte de Choiseul-Gouffier's magnificent folio *Voyage Pittoresque de la Grèce* (1782), to which Heron makes reference in a note, caused him to indulge in a whimsical aside on the prospect some future age might entertain of classical Edinburgh in ruin.

> And, if, amidst the vicissitudes of Human Things, barbarism should ever again spread ruin and desolation through those regions; levelling our palaces and public buildings with the temples and porticoes of *Athens* and *Palmyra* ... Then shall the enthusiastic votary of Taste and Science repair hither in devout pilgrimage, from the Wilds of Siberia perhaps, or from the remotest corners of North America, and weep over the broken columns, and kneel to kiss the thresholds of the dismantled and desolated temple which the Citizens of Edinburgh now fondly rear to Learning.[41]

If Heron could muse thus on Edinburgh, as he knew it in the 1790s—without a single neo-Greek building to its credit—what might he have dreamed of the city in the 1820s and after, complete as that would be with a Parthenon in 'pre-fabricated' ruin?

* * * * *

Visiting Edinburgh in 1793, R. Legge Willis evidently accommodated himself well to the heady ancient air of the incipient Modern Athens, even as Alves and Heron inhaled it. Some 'classical hours' spent in the company of Henry Mackenzie was time described as 'the feast of Reason', and as constituting 'an Attic evening'—in the sense of one both refined and elegant.[42]

The French geologist Barthélemy Faujas de Saint-Fond acknowledged the 'Greekness' of Edinburgh. He enumerated its various scholarly institutions, and observed that 'the arts, the sciences, and the Belles-lettres are cultivated and esteemed in this city'. Edinburgh was the nursery of many great men of learning, and host to many students drawn from all over the world, in part owing to 'its situation and its tranquillity'. Faujas concluded with an acknowledgement of putative ancient Greek inspiration: 'From time immemorial the muses have chosen to reside on the top of a hill near a solitary fountain.'[43]

The London printer Joseph Mawman visited Edinburgh in 1805. He was impressed with its setting: 'a succession of scenery, the most singular and romantic imaginable, filling the mind with sublime impressions of the peculiarity, the vastness, and grandeur of the city.' However, although he described at some length what he termed Edinburgh's 'revived claims to national fame' in philosophy, criticism, history, science and medicine—being very conscious of the flowering of the intellect in the preceding thirty or so years—and wrote much about the riches of the Advocates' Library, he was not actually disposed to use any Athenian simile. This was a city of the mind, certainly; but not necessarily another 'Athens'.[44]

Town Fashions, or Modern Manners Delineated, A Satirical Dialogue is attributed to Hector MacNeill. Published in 1810, it purports to analyse what the author describes as 'a sudden and unexampled change of Manners' in Edinburgh, 'a general system of ostentatious shew and Imitation which has pervaded all ranks and descriptions of society.' An exile returns—or perhaps it is a visitor who arrives: it is not clear which. What is plain is that something has happened to Edinburgh to make it 'our *very* Fashionable Capital'. A sense of 'Athenianism' is abroad. The newcomer speaks as one

> ... hither drawn by rumours of renown
> That Britain's Athens is your polish'd Town.

A footnote explains: 'Our good Southern Neighbours have now denominated Edinburgh the Athens of Britain.' This notion is taken up later in MacNeill's publication in a series of consequential 'Remarks' in prose, these being inspired by the poem itself. Of life in the metropolis the author states: 'We are certainly not *Athenians*, but in philosophical patience and indifference under trials, we surpass them as much as they surpassed all others in elegance, taste and simplicity.'[45]

Louis Simond, whom Walter Scott described as a clever if rather conceited 'American Frenchman', considered that Edinburgh was 'in a great degree, the Geneva of Britain'.[46] By this he implied a city of elegance and intellect rather than suggesting any topographical or physical comparison. But then, homing in on Edinburgh's role as a centre of learning, Simond declared it to be 'the Birmingham of literature;—a new place which has its fortune to make'. He contrasted the city and its university with Oxford and Cambridge: the two ancient English seats of learning 'repose themselves under their laurels, while Edinburgh cultivates hers'.[47] Expressive though the notion is of a city, where so much printing and publishing was carried on, as an intellectual 'workshop of the world'—in the way the muck-and-brass Birmingham analogy suggests—Simond's words rather diminish the refined pretensions of the Northern Athens.

In precisely the same year, 1815, the young John Gibson Lockhart, newly arrived in Edinburgh to read for the Scottish Bar, put it all rather more elegantly and appealingly.

I have been for a fortnight in *this our Athens*. Certainly if the name Athens had been derived from the Goddess of Printing—not from the Goddess of Wisdom—no city in the world could with greater justice lay claim to the appellation. An author elsewhere is a being *somewhat* at least out of the common run ... Every other body you jostle is the father of at least an octavo, or two, and it is odds if you ever sit down to dinner in a company of a dozen, without having to count three or four quarto makers in the circle. Poets as plenty as blackberries—indeed much more so unless blackberries mean sloes.

The slight barb of equivocation is that Lockhart does not necessarily imply that all the rivers of ink and mountains of paper consumed by, and issued from, the presses of Edinburgh—and ultimately from the brains of Modern Athenians—were of a uniformly 'Athenian' standard.[48]

No such ambivalence is detectable in the opinions of Louis Albert Necker de Saussure who (as we have seen) declared, in 1821, that Edinburgh 'is not unworthy of the titles of *the Athens of the North*, and *the Capital of Mind ...*'. He did so on account of 'its Institutions', 'the manner of life of its inhabitants', and because of his belief that information

was more generally diffused in Edinburgh than in any other city, in proportion to the population: there naturally results from this, that learning, knowledge, and literary merit, are also more appreciated, and enjoy here a consideration altogether peculiar. From the above spirit, reciprocal advantages are derived for men of letters, who find continual encouragement in good society by the esteem which is evinced for them, and for society itself, which being capable of appreciating the talents of men of letters, invites them to join its circle, and is thereby enriched with the talents which it calls forth and develops. Thus there are few cities where so many men of genius and talent are united as in Edinburgh.[49]

Necker was in no doubt that, as a whole, 'Scotland has contributed largely to the progress of the human mind' in a 'prodigious flight towards every thing that is distinguished', in which movement it appeared 'not less astonishing to find that the Scottish nation has not purchased the benefits of an advanced civilization by the sacrifice of virtue.'[50]

*   *   *   *   *

It is, perhaps, odd—and worthy of remark—that Edinburgh never had, in its 'Athenian' age, an institution called an Athenaeum. There were many comparatively small clubs with miscellaneous intellectual, convivial, social or political purposes. We have already encountered the Select Society. The Speculative Society, established in 1764 and based in the University, where it was granted special accommodation early on, encouraged debate and public speaking; Playfair designed opulent rooms for the Society in 1818 as part of his master-plan for the University, and there the 'Spec' still flourishes. The New Club, the city's premier club on the London West End or St James's pattern, was founded in 1787, and thus is older than all but three London clubs of a similar nature. The Society of Antiquaries of Scotland was established in 1780; the Royal Society of Edinburgh, which came to regard itself and to be recognised as Scotland's national academy, was founded in 1783 and had developed out of the distinguished Philosophical Society itself founded in 1737. In the earlier nineteenth century, a number of historical and literary 'book clubs' arose with the aim of printing and publishing texts and source materials. The men who formed these were convivial as well as scholarly. But there was no actual 'Athenaeum' in the Athens of the North. The London club of that name was founded in 1824, at the height of what James Elmes had thought of the 'Augustan age' of London. But Liverpool had its Athenaeum by 1797, its principal function being to provide a library and newsroom for its membership. Plymouth had an Athenaeum by 1819, this boasting a very 'Greek' interior adorned with casts of some of the Parthenon marbles. Manchester established an Athenaeum in the mid-1830s as a centre for the city's literary life. In Scotland, Stirling, which John Galt and Hugh William Williams had first imagined as having a close physical resemblance to Athens, had an Athenaeum in 1816, again as a library and meeting rooms. Aberdeen followed in 1819 with a fine neo-classical building by the architect Archibald Simpson, an excellent 'Grecian'. Glasgow brought up the rear with an educational establishment named an Athenaeum in 1847.

So why not Edinburgh? The answer can only lie in the city's soubriquet. The Modern Athens did not need another institution in order to emphasise the original inspiration of its claim to contemporary cultural eminence. Also, the so-called Royal Institution at the northern end of The Mound was a remarkable building housing several different bodies including the Society of Antiquaries, the Royal Society and the so-called Trustees' drawing academy. (Figs 59-60) Were it not for the (Royal) Institution for the Encouragement of the Fine Arts exercising a sort of overall leadership in this single building, and its fortunate achievement in associating its name with the one structure in which other organisations had their collections, libraries, museums and meeting rooms, then that building might well have been termed the 'Athenaeum'. The fact that the Trustees' Academy sculpture gallery, which occupied its east side, contained a large assemblage of casts of the Elgin Marbles, added to the general 'Athenian' ethos of the whole building. By 1838, this collection had been augmented through the acquisition of a run of casts of both the greater part of the Parthenon friezes, together with some of its pedimental sculpture, to form the best cast collection then extant in Great Britain. A drawing of 1832 by William Henry Playfair for the north elevation of 'The Building for the Societies'—in its second, much enlarged and elaborated form—shows an allegorical female figure enthroned on the attic behind the acroterion at the apex of the pediment, very much in the position that John Steell's statue of Queen Victoria would actually assume in 1844.[51] Playfair's figure is an amalgam of Athena and Britannia, but neither wholly one nor the other. She wears no aegis and carries no spear. Although her crested helmet lies at her feet, she has neither trident nor shield. To her left is a lion couchant. Behind, to her right, a *fasces* is incongruously propped, connoting an element of Roma, too. She holds a book, which neither Athena nor Britannia ever normally does. It is clear that the iconography is a curious blend of classical and British symbolism. But the suggestion of a warlike yet beneficent patron goddess of learning and the arts is clearly intended. This is her building, an *Athenaeum Britannicum*.

Somewhat earlier, Athena had been imagined as the presiding genius of classical learning in an interesting image by David Allan, appointed Master of the Trustees' Academy in Edinburgh 1786. Two years later Allan drew and engraved for his friend James Tassie, the great modeller of gems, a deeply emblematic image that Tassie was to use to illustrate the catalogue of his collection of casts after antique and modern originals, both cameo and intaglio, published in 1791 with text by Rudolf Erich Raspe.[52] (Fig. 32) Allan's image shows Athena, her helmet crowned by a rather fetching owl, her gorgon shield beside her, in the splendid setting of a neoclassical saloon that might have been designed by Robert Adam. Seated on a Greek *klismos* chair, of the kind that was on the very point of becoming fashionable among advanced neoclassical artists, the goddess opens the door of a magnificent collector's cabinet that could have been designed by James 'Athenian' Stuart. This is itself symbolic of the culture of virtuoso collecting of ancient coins, medals and gems. Some notable assemblages of this kind existed in the Edinburgh of the day, and the Faculty of Advocates had acquired, only a few years before, a princely medal cabinet. Allan captures well the ethos of a world conscious of Greek culture, and anxious to emulate it.

*　*　*　*　*

George Galloway, 'An Old British Tar' as his title-page informs us (he was presumably a former naval rating, and therefore one of those unusual voices emanating from the lower decks of the fleet), published the third edition of his *The Loyal Albany Museum...* in 1817. Included in this miscellany of Galloway's songs and verses was one poem entitled 'The Calton Hill'. It is strangely prescient. Galloway, unquestionably a Freemason, looked forward to a time when the Calton would be the focus of extensive building development, and Masonry would

> ... plan the street, square, pillar, and the arch,
> Whereon to ride, to run, to walk, or march; ...

Patriotic monuments would cover the hill's flanks and even summit, and the city as a whole would be developed for industry, trade and the common good.

> Thus Rome and Lisbon shines on several hills,
> Like Constantinople that our wonder fills;
> So Edinburgh be the Athens of the hour,
> In learning, and in genius looms her power;
> The masons shine in spacious buildings skill,
> Health, wealth, to adorn the aspiring Calton Hill.[53]

Certainly, the most significant building that would come to adorn the 'aspiring' hill, and which would embody the 'Athenian' aspirations of Edinburgh in the realm of learning, was the High School. (Figs 67-68) This ancient institution was to move from its site in Infirmary Street near the University to a magnificent position on the southern flank of the Calton Hill, and to a building of unparalleled splendour and sophistication designed by Thomas Hamilton and constructed between 1825 and 1829. Before this move, however, other sites for the school had been suggested, including a very central one near the junction of Princes Street and The Mound which was advocated by a pamphleteer writing under the pseudonym 'Scotus'.[54] In the face of a body of influential citizens who wanted to establish a new, separate and private school in the New Town near Canonmills—the foundation of which, as the Edinburgh Academy, was feared to be potentially divisive on both social and educational grounds—another clique defending the ethos and democratic tradition of the High School rose in support of its teaching. They advanced its credentials as a truly 'classical' establishment, admirably suited to the civic ideals of the Modern Athens. The school was said now to be 'avowedly Classical', with Greek to be taken from the fourth year and the teaching of the language much improved under the Rector, James Pillans.[55]

The Town Council made a strong and appealing case to the citizens of the New Athens: one focusing on the democratic virtues of the High School, for which such splendid accommodation was even then under construction, or soon to be built. 'The mingling of all ranks of life in its classes', their *Address ... on the Subject of the New Buildings for the High School* stated,

> with no recognised preference or distinction whatever, save that which is earned by talent and virtue; thus teaching the high that, without intellectual exertion, rank and wealth are an empty name, and practically holding out to the humblest individual, who there enters the lists of literary competition, the fame and respectability to be attained by persevering mental labour, and industry.[56]

In pursuit of his own ideal of educational democracy, 'Scotus' had earlier resorted to some architectural analogies. He alluded to the 'Corinthian Capital', giving his readers to understand that by this he meant 'the aristocracy of the empire'. But he was at pains also to stress, with reference of this most elaborate of metaphorical column capitals, that he had 'no wish to break off the most trivial even of its ornaments'. His moral purpose was, however, best served by adducing what he termed 'the Doric order of the people'. This was 'majestic in its simplicity, and is, equally with its more florid companion, the attribute of a strong and noble pillar of the Commonwealth.'[57] The High School on its site on the flank of the Calton Hill was designed in the Doric order. (Fig. 78) But so was the new Edinburgh Academy. Interestingly, this new, more socially elevated school, with its higher fees and its New Town upper-middle and professional-class catchment, was built in an even more uncompromisingly austere and 'primitive' Doric style. (Fig. 92)[58]

Percy Bysshe Shelley composed his 'Lyrical Drama' *Hellas* in 1821, and it was published in 1822. The dates coincide, first, with Edinburgh's decision to take the Parthenon as model for the National Monument and, second, the laying of the foundation stone. It is difficult to believe that the Modern Athenians were unmoved by the resonances they must surely have found in Shelley's chorus, which is recited by enslaved Greek women.

> The world's great age begins anew,
> The golden years return, ...
>
> A brighter Hellas rears its mountains
> From waves serener far; ...
>
> Another Athens shall arise,
> And to remoter time
> Bequeath, like sunset to the skies,
> The splendour of its prime; ...

One of the most distinguished classicists in Edinburgh's academic history, and one of its most kenspeckle characters, was John Stuart Blackie, already mentioned above. In 1852 he was translated from the chair of Humanity (Latin) at Marischal College, Aberdeen, to the chair of Greek at Edinburgh. Blackie had earlier studied at the University of Edinburgh, and he had returned to the city to read for the Scottish Bar, being admitted to the Faculty of Advocates in 1834. Of this period, and of his life 'at one of Edinburgh's most brilliant social epochs', Blackie's first biographer wrote perceptively of the city at a time

> when its claims to be called the Modern Athens rested far more on its attitude towards art and literature, on the oratory of its platforms and the sparkling talk of its dinner-tables, than on the buildings which imitate remotely the perfect structures of the ancient capital of Greece ...[59]

In Athens in 1853 Blackie met George Finlay, the Scottish philhellene who became a leading historian of Greece in several of its eras, and also of the Greek Revolution in which he himself had played a distinguished part. Most of Finlay's works were published in Edinburgh by William Blackwood, and Finlay (who had settled in Athens and lived there until his death in 1875) returned to Scotland occasionally, both on family and literary business. As Blackie's biographer put it, Dr Finlay 'appeared in the Modern Athens from time to time, laden with the woes of its old and eponymous metropolis'—that is the *real* modern, Greek Athens. He once communicated news to Blackie of current events in Athens, writing to the northern sister city from what he called 'the headquarters of marble monuments and marble dust'.[60] On a later visit to Athens, Blackie—long interested in the matter of ancient Greek pronunciation—is recorded as having tried to discover whether or not Homer was intelligible to the modern Greeks. A pleasing scene unfolded in the market place of the city, where Blackie declaimed to the crowd:

one of the embodiments of a Modern Athenian spirit was carrying the spirit of ancient Greece back to its source. So little was he understood that a local is said to have exclaimed: 'It's only a crazy old Scotchman saying his prayers.'[61]

In the text of *Scotland Illustrated,* William Beattie made several significant allusions to the 'Athenian' status of Edinburgh. He wrote, in 1838, of the University, which had in modern times 'accumulated strength, wisdom, and honour—shone preeminent in all the departments of literature and science, and justified its proud title as the throne of an intellectual city—"Urbs addicta Minervae"'. The University possessed a 'magnificent and richly stored museum', and a superb library. Its buildings were now completed 'in a noble and classic style of architecture'. In short, it was 'one of the most sumptuous temples of learning in Europe'.[62] Beattie continued:

> But in this 'Modern Athens'—a name given to it not more from its external than its intellectual resemblance to the ancient capital of Attica—not a street could be pointed out in which learning has not established her sanctuary, however humble or obscure.[63]

And there was more. The city and its university (and equally, one might add, the High School, in its palatial yet publicly endowed new buildings) were a nursery of what would later be called 'the democratic intellect'.[64] Beattie expanded on this, suggesting that what the University of Edinburgh had become was a metaphor for a changed, pacified and 'improved' Scotland as a whole:

> The claymore and the dirk have long been converted into the ploughshare and sickle—the plaid and feather into the cap and gown—while the masculine intellect that either lay uncultivated, or was only roused into activity by feuds, *raids,* and rebellions, is now directed to mighty exertions in the cause of literature, art, and science, which flow from these rugged rocks in all directions, and fertilize every land from the rising to the setting sun. Those who bask in the sunny bowers of Minerva, on the banks of the Cam and the Isis, may affect to contemn [*sic*] the peripatetic and uncloistered philosophy of a Caledonian university; but they who have wandered over the world, explored the busy haunts of man, and permeated the various grades of society, can well appreciate the extended and powerful influence of that practical information which is zealously inculcated and imbibed in these humbler *emporia* of knowledge.[65]

Beattie then turned his attention to the Calton Hill, there to ponder a site where the columns of the National Monument, 'rising in splendid gradation, crown the eminence, as permanent records of the nation's prosperity.' The nation, or at any rate its metropolis, was in fact then in dire financial straits, and the Edinburgh

Parthenon had come to a halt, certainly for the time being and (as most perceptive observers must surely have realised) in all probability for good. But Beattie was not to be deterred. He wrote of the Robert Burns Monument by Thomas Hamilton, architect also of the great 'Grecian Doric' High School, observing that, in its position below the 'Parthenon', it was nevertheless 'still sufficiently conspicuous for him [Burns] who, having a temple in every Scottish heart, can afford to have his monument even in a corner'. (Fig. 69) Beattie continued: 'In this respect, indeed, the Calton-hill may be considered as the common pedestal to a series of trophies—opera haud ignara Minervae.'[66] The tag is from Virgil's *Aeneid*, V. 284, though 'opera' should actually read 'operum'. But the sense is valid enough. Edinburgh's Calton 'Acropolis' was the talisman of a city that saw itself as the Modern Athens, and so was 'not unskilled in the works—or tasks—of Minerva': the arts of peaceful industry and, in particular, the ponderings of the mind.

Those 'arts of peaceful industry' were very much the concern of a body founded by David Brewster in 1821: one that laid claim to the iconography of Athena (Minerva) herself. What became the Royal Scottish Society of Arts in 1841 was established as 'The Society for the Encouragement of the Useful Arts in Scotland'—its interests being technology, mechanics, engineering and science in general, with specific application to 'manufactures'. A clear distinction was thus made between these 'useful arts', and the fine arts, traditionally regarded as more socially and intellectually elevated. Both aspects of the ancient mythological concerns of a patron goddess were, however, perceived to flourish in the Modern Athens. The bust of Athena, with her 'Corinthian' helmet, was early adopted as the Society's device, appearing on the title-page of its *Transactions*. The Society obtained a grant of arms in 1978, the head of Athena being fixed upon as crest, and the shield adorned with, among other charges, two owl masks.

*   *   *   *   *

By the time that Archibald Alison wrote the first of his influential articles in July 1819, primarily to promote the building of a replica Parthenon, he had in view a general renaissance of metropolitan civic taste, and thus Scottish national taste at large. Edinburgh was already the Modern Athens in the mind. It could also be an Athens of the North in stone.

> If the PARTHENON of ATHENS were transferred to Edinburgh, the public taste would be formed on the finest model which exists in the world, and to the perfection of which the experience of two thousand years has borne testimony. The taste which sprung up round the work of Phidias might then be transferred to our northern regions; and the city whose genius has already procured for it the name of the Modern Athens, might hope to vie with its immortal predecessor in the fine arts.[67]

In 1819, too, the Institution for the Encouragement of the Fine Arts in Scotland was founded. Paradoxically, a body with this high-sounding name did not actually permit practising artists to participate in its management: that was for its aristocratic members. It collected pictures, as if for the nation. It also held loan exhibitions, at first purely of Old Master paintings but then of contemporary works by living artists. But its attitude alienated the Scottish artists of the day, a good many of whom transferred their allegiance to another new body, the Scottish Academy, established in 1826. Both Institution and Academy obtained royal charters. It would be the Institution that pulled sufficient rank to arrogate its name to Playfair's 'temple' of the arts and learning built at The Mound between 1822 and 1826; it would be the Academy that fought for exhibition space within the temple; but it would be the Academy that survived as an autonomous body and which ultimately, many years later, would be able, finally, to attach its name to that same, though subsequently greatly enlarged building. In 1826 one of the artists—who may have been Patrick Gibson, but who employed the pseudonym 'Roger Roundrobin'—delivered a pamphlet attack on the Institution. Looking back seven years, he recalled how the artists had entertained hopes of 'the bright morning ... that was to dawn on the Arts of their country: at the return of the age of PERICLES, of AUGUSTUS, and of LEO; about to bless our northern regions,—our Northern Athens.'[68]

Hugh William Williams was, as we have seen, instrumental in first perceiving and then fixing in the Edinburgh mind a visual connection between the city and Athens, and indeed between Scotland and Greece in a more generalised artistic way. But Williams is not without significance in the context of the development of a cerebral link. Many, certainly, sensed and appreciated this; others sensed it, but could go only part-way with him. Anne Grant of Laggan received from Williams a wreath of ivy from the supposed tomb of Virgil at Posillipo, near Naples, and also 'a chaplet prettily formed and bound up of the Attic olive, from a tree growing by the ruin or site of the Delphian temple'. These, Mrs Grant confessed, 'have their own value in their own way', but added the rider that 'compared to my coins, [they] are but fable compared to history.'[69]

For Williams himself, Scotland and Greece were like the Dioscuri, star-crowned twins. In his *Travels*, Williams recounts his actions at Delphi.

> ... I made an excavation, in which I placed a bottle hermetically sealed, containing separate lists of our Scotish [*sic*] poets, poetesses, and learned men, my personal friends, and every one I could think of, who has contributed to enlighten our dear Scotland; especially Edinburgh, 'the queen of the north,'— the fairest among modern cities.[70]

THE ATHENS OF
THE NORTH IN STONE
'TO TRY THEIR SKILL IN PEDIMENT AND PILLAR'

When Alexander Carlyle and Allan Ramsay were writing, in 1761-62, of Edinburgh as the Athens of Britain, they can only have been thinking of the city as an Athens of the mind. There was, as yet, no architecture in a revived Greek style to warrant such comparison.[1] James Craig's plan for the New Town, with its grid of stately streets and squares, was still five years in the future; George Square, lying to the south of the old city centre, would not be laid out until 1766. Some of the grander houses there, of the 1770s, were to have classical-columned door-pieces. But even these structures and developments, as was the case with a few other residential enclaves and institutional buildings in this southern quarter, had not a hint of genuine, archaeologically correct Greek revivalism.

With the exception of some pockets of development, mainly on the south side, the Edinburgh of the early 1760s was almost wholly confined to the Old Town on its ridge, in which the only 'modern', classical building was John Adam's Royal Exchange, completed in 1761. Alexander Campbell described this as 'a goodly earnest of the elegance and accommodation which awaited the inhabitants...'.[2] There were, however, miscellaneous instances of the use of a vernacular form of the language of classicism. Greyfriars Kirkyard contains many examples of classical forms and details on tombs and funerary monuments dating from the seventeenth and eighteenth centuries. Elsewhere, there were isolated examples of early classicism dating from the sixteenth century. John Knox's House in the High Street, for example, displays self-conscious Doric pilasters, urns, garlands and even one of Edinburgh's five inscriptions in Greek dating from before 1825. But the ΘΕΟΣ of the High Street was no unknown 'Athenian' God, and the city was, in architectural terms, no unknown and unremarked Athens in the making.

An essay by David Steuart Erskine, eleventh Earl of Buchan, on building during the Roman Empire, which may perhaps have been intended for publication in the Edinburgh periodical *The Bee*, contains the following passage lamenting the fate of Greek architecture even in, and certainly after, the Augustan age.

> ... that composite Taste in Architecture was adopted which has gradually spoilt and fritted away the noble simplicity of Grecian Architecture introducing Domes, pilasters, overcharged Pediments, friezes, Capitals & Architraves which have in our days altogether corrupted and debased the Taste of the Publick. If therefore we are to contemplate the chaste, noble and Natural Stile of Architecture we must either study the ruins of Athens or those constructed on the same model, and if we wish to restore a Taste which will continue to charm Posterity for ever we must either implicitly copy the Greeks or Study the same Originals from which they drew their ideas.[3]

Buchan's views on a 'Greek Revival' style are interesting. He suggests that buildings admirably suited to one climate and people may be inappropriate constructions for and in another; and he notes 'the absurdity of fashioning a northern Portico in Britain to tell us that we are at Athens'.[4] Buchan (whom we shall encounter again in the next chapter) was a noted eccentric, remembered today largely for his many quirks of character. But he was also a man capable of entertaining perfectly sensible notions when it came to architecture and the picturesque.

The construction of neo-Greek buildings in Edinburgh enhanced the physical and mental parallel with Athens, and gave material form to the Greek idea. The conjunction of eye and mind led quite naturally to expression in stone. However, 'Classical Edinburgh' is not the same thing as 'Greek Revival' Edinburgh, though of course the one subsumes the other. 'Greek' Edinburgh is a special dish on the menu of Edinburgh classicism. It has quite properly been questioned whether, when Edinburgh began to assume its new identity as 'the Athens of the North', the architecture of the city could justify a physical claim corresponding to the legitimate one to be found in the intellectual sphere. It has been observed that 'at the time Edinburgh began to develop its Hellenic pretensions, it had little architectural justification for doing so.'[5]

We have seen that the two most common 'Greek' epithets for Edinburgh were 'Modern Athens' and 'the Athens of the North'. Two centuries on, another appears to have been invented: one that has not been noted in any previous literature. This is 'Grey Athens of the North'. Significantly, the first (and perhaps only use of the soubriquet) has been by a geologist, presumably thinking in petrological rather than cultural terms of a city 'characterised by stone'.[6] Craigleith sandstone, the most celebrated and predominant building material of the New Town, certainly weathers from light buff to grey, aided (in former times at any rate) by atmospheric pollution. However, 'Grey Athens' was not an idea that would have occurred to Archibald Alison and those of his contemporaries who dreamed of Athenian sunshine gilding, caressing even, Edinburgh's neo-Greek façades and colonnades. Alison praised the quality of Edinburgh stone and, while alluding to the city's 'cloudy atmosphere', seemed to suggest that both could see off whatever is 'admirable in Grecian marble ... under an Athenian sun'.[7]

Even if there had been 'Greek' buildings, few observers would have been able to recognise them as such, and to make the necessary distinction between what was purely Greek or anything else that was loosely 'classical'. In the Edinburgh of the late eighteenth and early nineteenth centuries there was simply no precision in describing Classical architecture. Whatever was truly Greek Revival (in varying degrees of archaeological purity), Roman, or merely builders' pattern-book 'antique', might be described as 'Grecian'. A writer in *The Bee* proposed:

> It will not ... be denied by any person that a stately fabric, surrounded with a regular colonnade of majestic columns, in the purest simplicity of the Grecian style of architecture, is an object that strikes the mind with a sensation of dignity, and has a tendency to please.[8]

George Cleghorn, who actually knew more than most of his contemporaries about architectural history and stylistic developments, but whose knowledge has gone largely unremarked and unrecognised by recent scholarship, declared in 1837 that

> The term Grecian is frequently used in a very loose and inaccurate manner, being not only applied to the architecture strictly so designated, but to the Roman and Italian styles—to almost every kind of building that is not Gothic.[9]

Thinking, doubtless, of Holyroodhouse in its form acquired under Kings Charles II and James VII, with its courtyard dignified by classical pilasters superimposed in the correct sequence straight from a textbook, and its entrance flanked by massive coupled Roman Doric columns supporting a frieze with metopes emblematic of Scottish sovereignty, William Gilpin wrote of a palace designed by Sir William Bruce 'since the Grecian orders were introduced'.[10] We have seen that Robert Alves could define Robert Adam's elegant Register House, distinguished by a stepped saucer dome evidently derived from the Roman Pantheon, as 'Grecian'. Henry Skrine likewise described the same building as 'executed with all the elegance of a Grecian temple'.[11] Hugo Arnot wrote of Adam's David Hume mausoleum, a very 'Roman' structure indeed and one with intriguing ancient Roman sources, as being 'in the Greek taste'. Alexander Campbell followed, calling it 'a Grecian tower'. Others concurred that it was 'in the Grecian style'.[12] St Bernard's Well, clearly a 'Tivoli' temple but with a representation of a hefty Hygieia imprisoned within its circular colonnade, was regarded as 'a Grecian fane'. In this opinion Campbell followed Robert Heron and James Cririe, who had earlier classed it as such.[13]

Walter Scott saw nothing odd about, and indeed in quoting without demur, in 1826, the description of the twelfth-century Norman Dalmeny kirk, in West Lothian (Linlithgowshire), compiled by the minister, Thomas Robertson, in 1791. 'The parish church', Robertson had written, 'from the style of its architecture, which is Saxon, or a mixed species between the Greek and Gothic, seems to be between 7 or 8 hundred years old.' Robertson went on to describe the windows, which have 'a very elegant Grecian appearance; and were it not for the Gothic capitals of the columns, and the shafts being too thick for their height, the whole might be taken for Greek architecture.' The south door does indeed have 'volute' capitals. But neither Robertson in the original, nor Scott in the retailed description, were even approaching safe architectural ground in their use of the term 'Greek'.[14]

William Stark was an early and excellent exponent of the Greek Revival in Glasgow, where his Justiciary Court House, with its hexastyle Doric portico, was much admired. It ranks, in fact, as probably the second public building in Britain to be ornamented with a Greek Doric portico, and the second largest such at the time. But he also worked in a more general classical idiom, and observers clearly were not able to distinguish just what was what. Shortly before his death in Edinburgh in 1813, he had designed the opulent but in no way pure 'Greek' interior of the Upper Signet Library—that is the splendid first-floor room originally built for the Faculty of Advocates. (Fig. 57) This was considered admirable because of the architect's loyalty to the proportions observed 'in the best edifices of Greece. His designs have, therefore, a chaste and classical air', which, 'besides their intrinsic excellence, will recommend them to every man of improved taste.'[15]

St Andrew's Church and the Physicians' Hall (both in George Street) were, however, according to another source, merely 'Grecian', and 'in good taste': in other words, they were considered generically 'classical', with orders, porticoes and pediments, but lacking identifiable, text-book, ancient sources.[16] Necker de Saussure's analysis of classical architecture in Edinburgh makes for odd reading. For example, he states that in Robert Adam's use of the Venetian window ('of a mixture of Greek and Gothic') in the Register House and elsewhere, 'much of that noble simplicity, which agrees with the Greek style, is taken away'.[17] Robert Chambers drew attention to the 'exceedingly fine' prospect from the Botanic Garden in Leith Walk towards the quadruple-porticoed, but domed, Observatory on Calton Hill, which gave the view 'on the whole, if we may use the expression, quite a *Grecian air*'.[18]

One double-page opening of Shepherd and Britton's *Modern Athens!* describes two buildings both later demolished. One is the Merchant Maiden Hospital, by William Burn, of 1816-19. This had an Ionic tetrastyle portico derived from the Temple on the Ilissos in Athens as recorded by Stuart and Revett.[19] It is described by Britton as being 'of a Grecian character'. Opposite is a description of the Physicians' Hall in George Street, by James Craig, of 1776-78. Its portico was Corinthian, and the *piano nobile* windows had triangular pediments. Though very much a fragment of Rome in Edinburgh, it is nevertheless described as a 'handsome building of chaste Grecian architecture'.[20]

Sir John Carr, who in 1807 (whether from personal experience or hints) had noticed some topographical similarity between the settings of Athens and Edinburgh, was struck not so much by any perceived 'Greekness' in Edinburgh's architecture, but by an alarming tendency of the place to overreach itself in *grands projets*. These were too costly for the country's resources. The specific development he had in mind was the new University buildings, started in 1789 but unfinished and lying forlornly in that state for fifteen years past. But a greater truth was evident: 'infatuation' for things that could not be achieved.

> ... the shrewd and economical character of the Scotch, who know so well and so creditably, on all other occasions, to make the ends correspond with the means, seems to have been exchanged for the random and thoughtless generosity of their Irish brethren ... Thus a large sum of money, and much talent, toil, and time, have been consumed, in raising to the sight of the citizens of Edinburgh a pile, which, when tinted by 'the mellowing hand of Time', will afford them the melancholy but picturesque effect of a mighty ruin.[21]

Carr could not find enough 'Greekness' in Edinburgh itself. For hints of the Greek in Scottish architecture he had to look a little beyond the city, to the Earl of Abercorn's Duddingston House.[22] Designed by William Chambers in the early 1760s, this displays 'the first hint of the Greek revival in Scotland'.[23] But Carr also looked further afield, to the Earl of Elgin's 'magnificent seat' of Broomhall, across the River Forth in Fife. Carr, however, explaining that he had not actually been able to visit the house, proceeded to describe what he had been told by way of recent developments in its construction. Most notable was the fact that Broomhall now had a front

> on the exact model of the remaining examples of Grecian architecture brought by his Lordship from Greece, under the able and tasteful direction of Mr Porden ... Broom-hall is entitled to the rank of a highly classical building. The grand portico is exactly formed from the Temple of Minerva, at Athens; the two lateral porticoes are true copies of the Propylæa; the two others,

entrances to the offices, resemble the Agora [that is, presumably, the Theseion, sited above the ancient market-place]; and the grand hall is the exact model of the interior of the Ionic Temple [presumably that on the Ilissos] ...

Carr continued with praise for Lord Elgin and his work in bringing home 'several statues and precious fragments from the different temples of Athens ... which, with a noble liberality, he has opened to the public inspection.'[24] What Carr said of Elgin himself is the customary flattery of the day. What he said of Elgin's house is fascinating, because no such complete refashioning of Broomhall, beyond Thomas Harrison's south front of the late 1790s, had then taken place—Lord Elgin being astonishingly fickle in his demands, and notoriously changeable in his preference for one architect and one scheme after another. William Porden had merely carried out some internal work. Perhaps Carr's informant had seen Porden's drawings of 1807 when they were exhibited at the Royal Academy in London the next year.[25] In fact, Carr's description of the re-cast Broomhall makes it sound very like the designs of 1808 by William Stark, also not executed. Both architects had proposed severe hexastyle Doric porticoes, without pediments—so not 'exactly formed' from the octastyle, pedimented Parthenon. Robert Smirke would propose a 'Parthenon' portico for the house in 1810.[26] But perhaps the entire description published by Carr may have been conceived and conveyed to him by some unknown 'Modern Athenian' to reflect what the seat of such a central figure in the rise of Greek taste in Britain *should* look like. It is an interesting conceit.

An intriguing reference connects Lord Elgin with an early (but unachieved) venture in Edinburgh's architectural development of the Greek style. In 1812 Benjamin West, President of the Royal Academy, was asked to send to Edinburgh some drawings of the Theseion from Elgin's collection, presumably made at Elgin's request in Athens: this was 'with a view to the designs for the Observatory'.[27] The Edinburgh Astronomical Institution had been established the previous year. The Observatory building that stands on Calton Hill (in the end designed, as we have seen, by Playfair and completed in 1818) might earlier have assumed a character more purely Greek than the actual Roman Doric structure we see today. Indeed, it seems feasible that Elgin's drawings might have provided further inspiration in an Edinburgh newly fascinated by the Greek, thus enabling the city to have had a structure with porticoes modelled after, or at any rate influenced by, the Theseion. Might William Stark have designed this?[28] Perhaps so; but Stark died prematurely in 1813. Had he achieved an observatory in this style, it might have been one of the two earliest essays in Greek Doric in the city.

Writing in his travel journal in 1813, Sir Nathaniel Wraxall similarly saw nothing in Edinburgh that caused him to perceive any generally classical building even as 'Grecian' let alone as 'Greek'. He was not, in fact, disinclined to see structures as 'Grecian' when he considered them such: after all, he had just been looking at the Duke of Argyll's new house at Rosneath in Dunbartonshire, designed by Joseph Bonomi, which Wraxall described as 'a beautiful, elegant, & delicious Palace, such as Pericles might have designed or constructed on the finest model of Athenian Taste'.[29] Rosneath certainly boasted Ionic columns, but these were oddly arranged as porticoes of five and three columns each; the eccentricity was evident, too, in the capitals, which had strikingly flared volutes.[30] Nevertheless, thought Wraxall, the house contrasted favourably with the Duke's principal seat at Inveraray, which appeared, in its Gothic, castellated dress, 'barbarous ... just such a structure a child might have cut out of cards, for it has no pretension either to Taste or to Architecture'.[31] But when Wraxall arrived in Edinburgh, he visited many buildings and localities without assigning any 'Greek' qualities to them. Robert Adam's Register House was 'a magnificent Fabrick', but Wraxall did not venture to define it by any specific stylistic term. The David Hume mausoleum had, he noted, 'a handsome architrave of the Doric Order', but he specified neither Greek nor Roman sources. Nevertheless, it was 'the finest Monument ... erected in our Time, in Europe, to any Man of Speculative Genius & Letters'.[32]

Wraxall thought that some streets of Georgian houses—he was referring specifically to Buccleuch Place in Edinburgh's 'Southern Districts'—were 'exceedingly dull'. Nor was this terrace 'quite finished'. Adam's front of the new University building had a 'magnificent appearance'; but what struck Wraxall most—it could hardly not do so—was its incomplete state. It was

> a magnificent Monument of Folly, or least of Want of sound Calculation. It seems likely to continue many years longer, in its present State, for Want of Funds to complete it. In *Dublin*, this Circumstance would not so much have surprized me; but I gave the *Scots* credit for more Reflexion & for better digested Plans.[33]

In these remarks, Wraxall expanded on the similar if more mundane sentiments of Joseph Mawman, who had noted the 'imperfect state of the new buildings', and who had gone so far as to assert that they were 'not likely ever to be finished'.[34] John Stoddart had previously described the new University buildings, then in enforced suspended animation, as 'a melancholy memorial of ill-judged haste in the commencement', indicative of the 'mania' for speculative building that he noted as affecting the incipient Athens of the North.[35] Now, the incomplete state of much of the New Town greatly surprised Wraxall: many streets with gap-sites; even two sides of Charlotte Square unbuilt, with its large and prominently domed St George's Church likewise still unfinished; and so on.

> Indeed, nothing here seems to be completed. The University, the Monument to Nelson on the Calton Hill, the Observatory on the same; various other

Public Buildings remain half finished. The War now existing is assigned as the Reason for this Circumstance, but it seems to impugn the good Sense of the Magistrates or Inhabitants.[36]

What might Mawman, Stoddart, Carr and Wraxall—deliverers, all, of what may seem to us prophetic words—have made of the unfinished National Monument, had they been able to return to Edinburgh about 1830?

'The Scottish national character is vanity': so wrote John Stark in 1806. He called on Edinburgh's record of being unable to complete its public buildings to support his contention.

In no instance has this characteristic feature of the people discovered itself in a more striking manner than in the transactions of the citizens of Edinburgh ... Scottish vanity is most conspicuous in the public buildings. When forming the plans of many of these, it was on a scale of magnitude which the poverty of the country prevented them from executing. The Observatory on the Calton-hill [i.e. that predating Playfair's] stood for a number of years with only a small part built of the intended plan; and from poverty was at last finished in a very inferior style.[37]

Robert Adam's projects, in particular, had suffered. Register House was a great building but one suspended in a half-finished state; the plan for the Bridewell had been trimmed back; the University stood 'an immense ruin, a monument of vanity of which poverty has prevented the completion'.[38] Elsewhere, other buildings and monuments were incomplete, including the Nelson Monument, which had been noted by Wraxall as unfinished. It awaited a substantial, and visually vital, castellated structure around its base. Prospect of imminent completion would allow the tower to be 'no longer laughed at by strangers' (as was said in 1814) 'and regarded by others as a specimen of Modern Ruins'.[39]

This was the regrettable background against which, twenty years after John Stark highlighted the three deadly sins of vanity, poverty and irresolution affecting architectural achievement in the city, the Modern Athenians would undertake the most spectacularly risky project of all, and also—if they failed— the one that would be the most visibly demeaning to the city's self-esteem.

*   *   *   *   *

In *Peter's Letters to his Kinsfolk* (1819), John Gibson Lockhart has his fictional visitor, Dr Peter Morris, indulge in some pleasant Hellenic musings at the Observatory on Calton Hill.[40] These are complemented, in reality, by a detail in a perspective view by Playfair of his original proposal for the Observatory. (Fig. 52) This drawing is the very embodiment of the idea of Romantic Classicism in its

Edinburgh incarnation, even if it also symbolises the stylistic confusion in the minds of Modern Athenians. Playfair's building is shown in a much more elaborately eclectic style than that of the Roman Doric structure, with the small, high dome that was actually erected. In the drawing, the four hexastyle Corinthian porticoes of the Greek cross plan are surmounted by a shallower Pantheon saucer dome. The architect shows the proposed building set amid Roman-seeming ruins, heavy with vegetation, including (at the left) a structure perhaps influenced by drawings of the Arch of Hadrian at Athens, but reduced further to ruin. The Romantic concept of a splendid fragment of ancient Rome (surrounded by its own image in partial decay) upon an Edinburgh hilltop is made odder still by the figures which inhabit Playfair's view. These are, in fact, lifted directly from a plate in Stuart and Revett. The original image showed Stuart and Revett themselves in oriental costume, and Turkish types chatting, drinking coffee and smoking beside the Monument of Philopappos on the Hill of the Muses in Athens. (Fig. 53) Playfair translated the figures of Stuart and Revett to a position below the left-hand portico of the Observatory, and placed the Ottoman figures in the left foreground.[41]

The confusion and lack of precision in both style and source is amply demonstrated in the remarkable article in *The New Edinburgh Review* for April 1823, referred to above. The anonymous author states that he 'cannot perceive any violent incongruity, or any solecism, in placing a Greek building in Edinburgh, or any necessity for pulling down the monuments of Scottish antiquity by which it will become surrounded.' Then comes the highly controversial, if not wilfully perverse, suggestion that the city's 'predominant buildings derive from the architecture of Greece'. Holyroodhouse is cited, just as it had been by Gilpin, as Greek; but the Palace is now said to be 'as much Greek as Whitehall, or the Colisæum, if we except its turrets'.[42] The first part of this statement (that about Whitehall) is otiose, because we have no idea which classical building or buildings were in the author's mind—although it is likely to be the Banqueting House by Inigo Jones, of 1619-22, rather than, say, Robert Adam's Admiralty Screen of 1760; the second part (relating to the Colosseum) clearly absurd; the third part rather more an insouciant case of architectural amnesia than anything constructive. The New Town is then declared to be Greek 'throughout, whether in its public or its private buildings'.[43] Later on, the proposition is made that 'the leading architecture of our city is not Gothic, but Greek, derivative or direct.' Presumably this covers both the buildings constructed in a vaguely classical style, and those with some pretension to be archaeologically correct. Finally comes the strangest statement: 'Our earliest buildings were Roman, and therefore Greek.'[44] Confident, if highly misleading assertions such as these indicate just how little the pundits actually understood about architectural style and its precise definitions.

But, no matter how much precision might be lacking in the understanding of classicism, the tide of taste was running very much to architecture inspired by

classical antiquity. The Nelson Monument on Calton Hill, designed by Robert
Burn (1807 and 1814-16), can be seen as a sort of yardstick of taste. However
much its resemblance to a telescope may have been seen as suitably naval, and
thus perhaps fitting in some settings, it had been erected in the most conspicuous
position on a prominent hill in a city with grand ideas for itself as a new Athens.
This was, therefore, not the kind of sophisticated structure regarded as either
desirable or appropriate. It was widely condemned as an 'unaccountable departure
from the classic models of antiquity, so often complained of by every man of
correct taste. As we deviate from these admirable models, we stray from nature,
and loss [sic] sight of perfection.'[45] Hardly a single person involved in the debate
about buildings suitable for the Calton Hill's would-be 'Athenian' summit had any
time for the Nelson Monument. One commentator, praising the merits of the hill as
a fine feature having 'just that degree of abruptness which harmonizes with human
habitation, the medium between the rude and the tame,' noted ruefully that

> modern taste has perpetrated its usual exploits here, and on the verge of this
> hill is perched a column in honour of Nelson, and in contempt of all grace.
> The Town Dilettanti have at length discovered its resemblance to a chamber
> candlestick, and take comfort in the fortunate friability of the rock, which is
> already splitting, and must soon abolish the Nelson column.[46]

Most, however, were not prepared for geological time to take its interminable
course, and simply wanted to tear down the Nelson Monument forthwith.
Only George Sibbald—a naval man, after all, and as such perhaps more at ease
with the concept of a giant petrified spyglass—saw no problem with it, and
incorporated it (in the position of the Erechtheion) in his curious comparison of
the Calton Hill with the Athenian Acropolis.

*   *   *   *   *

By the end of the second decade of the nineteenth century there was a degree
of genuine appreciation of the distinction between authentic neo-Greek
architecture and architecture that was merely, and loosely, 'Grecian'—or what
James Elmes called in a derogatory way, when writing of the work of Robert
Adam, 'pseudo-Grecian'.[47] The former category owed its authority to its
derivation from ancient Greek models, as illustrated in the great archaeological
publications of J.-D. Le Roy (*Les Ruines des Plus Beaux Monuments de la
Grèce*, 1758); Stuart and Revett's *The Antiquities of Athens* (four volumes,
1762/63-1816); Stephen Riou's *The Grecian Orders of Architecture* (1768);
and the work of Richard Chandler, Nicholas Revett and William Pars, published
as the Society of Dilettanti's *Ionian Antiquities* (1769). The architects of 'Greek'
Edinburgh derived their knowledge from books such as these seminal works.

As has already been pointed out, none had been to Greece, or even to Sicily or southern Italy. But they had excellent libraries, and put their book-learning to good use.

The publication by Stuart and Revett was the key source for the creation of Athenian Edinburgh. James Elmes expressed so well the influence that *The Antiquities of Athens* had on the British imagination; also how profound was the effect of the actual architecture and decoration that Stuart—a man who 'received the honourable addition of "Athenian" prefixed to his name'—and his disciples produced, influenced by the images in the printed volumes which had themselves resulted from actual encounter with the ancient buildings of Athens. Elmes wrote of the epiphany experienced by 'the higher and learned classes' who

> duly appreciated the high taste of refinement and purity exhibited in this grand style now known to them for the first time. No event that ever occurred in the history of architecture in England ... produced so sudden, decided, and beneficial an effect ... It surprised and delighted the learned and admirers of art; the majestic grandeur and simplicity of form exhibited in the general outline of its beautiful temples, and the exquisite purity and elegance of detail ... fascinated the eye of taste. The natural form, in which everything was subservient to utility, proved how pure was the taste of the elegant Athenians ... Samuel Johnson, on finding a Greek quotation amidst some modern trash ... exclaimed 'So much Greek, so much gold.' So does the man of true taste on viewing the architecture and sculpture of the godlike Greeks.[48]

Archibald Elliot's County Hall, at the corner of the High Street and Parliament Square West, was rightly praised by a minority, Elliot having studied his ancient Greek sources assiduously. The story of the County Hall (demolished at the very end of the nineteenth century) offers another barometer of taste in the emerging Modern Athens. (Figs 39-41) As we have seen, Williams had singled it out for praise. Nothing symbolised more strikingly both the transition to Modern Athens in architectural terms, and the fervid debate around this topic, than the construction of the County Hall in 1817. It was an interloper, not just into the fabric of the Old Town, but into the world of the post-Adam classicism of Robert Reid's facades of the Advocates' and Signet Libraries, and of the Parliament House in its classical dress.

Interestingly, the County Hall had been subject to a late change of taste, but one still informed by archaeology. Sir William Rae, Sheriff of Edinburgh, had been in Paris and had seen there a model of the Erechtheion. It so took his fancy that, with some urgency

> he recommended it ...; and that eminent architect, Mr Archibald Elliot, who had previously furnished a design in the Grecian doric [sic] style, having

examined the fragments among the Elgin marbles, prepared a plan, in which he adhered most scrupulously to the proportions, and otherwise assumed as much of the ancient temple as could with propriety by introduced into a modern building intended for a different purpose ...[49]

Despite the bold inscription (visible in some photographs) 'Archibald Elliot Architect' on the topmost fascia of the architrave, a pseudonymous writer of 1825 insisted that Rae himself was 'generally understood to be the architect'. In view of the many criticisms the same writer had to make of the structure, this may, however, be a sort of back-handed compliment to amateur enthusiasm and, perhaps, acknowledgement of the presumption of unskilled design.[50]

The portico was a convincing borrowing of the Ionic order of the tetrastyle north porch of the Erechtheion on the Acropolis of Athens, its columns having the correct Attic bases (though the upper torus mounding lacked the guilloche enrichment of the originals); it also had the distinctive enrichment of the column neckings, and other appropriate refinements. The anta and pilaster capitals of the façade were somewhat less elaborate than the originals.

Patrick Gibson's discussion of the County Hall in 1818 raised many issues in a perceptive and intelligent way. His greatest criticism was that the County Hall's design was not 'assimilated ... to the style of the other buildings immediately adjoining'. Those other buildings—notably the two legal libraries—were themselves 'by no means objectionable in point of design'. Any new structure should really have been designed 'in a style of as perfect congruity with them ... to give the necessary degree of beauty to the whole.' As things were, the 'disproportion of parts is very conspicuous...'. Gibson was pleased to give credit where it was due: Elliot's portico—which Gibson did not illustrate in his album of etchings—was 'magnificent ... certainly the finest in the city'. But praise given was immediately taken away: the portico's 'massive character' and great height in comparison with the overall length of the building 'renders it in itself extremely objectionable, and is unsupported by any authority from the ancients'. Furthermore, the siting of the County Hall was wrong, for its north end projected into the High Street. This rather narrow façade—which Gibson illustrated in order to show its shortcomings all too clearly—was articulated by a pair of columns, with their associated antae, supporting the entablature. The columns appear inordinately tall in such a position on so comparatively narrow a side elevation.

The propriety of the decorations of this part is not so obvious, as this unmeaning arrangement neither accords with the simplicity of the Grecian style, nor is it warranted by any considerations of beauty or utility, as the recess between the antae is furnished with two windows for the admission of light, which must be obstructed by the columns at their side.[51]

It is remarkable how much this one building was criticised, quite unjustly it would seem, judging by prints and photographs which show an elegant essay in adapted, but nevertheless still largely archaeologically correct Greek Ionic. The 1820 edition of Stark's *The Picture of Edinburgh*, quoted above, supplies an early complimentary assessment, perhaps the first wholly approving judgment, of this controversial building. Here was a distinct fight-back for Greece against a publication such as the *New Picture of Edinburgh* of 1818, a presumptuous and opportunistic rejoinder to Stark's established *Picture of Edinburgh* guidebook. The *New Picture* had gone into much less detail about ancient sources, stating simplistically that the portico was of 'the Grecian order', and indulging in ill-informed criticism of a building assessed as 'very deficient in taste, after all the money that has been expended in erecting it'.[52] The implication was that to build in an affected Greek idiom was an expensive indulgence which failed to benefit the ordinary inhabitants of Auld Reekie.

In 1825, the writer designating himself 'A Builder' praised the County Hall as 'one of the most magnificent, as well as perhaps the chastest of our Modern Structures', offering the opinion that it would be improved if only a new front to the west could be added.[53] This was a desideratum that was entirely dependent on a long-running debate about access to Bank Street and The Mound from the south. Opportunity eventually arose with the laying out of George IV Bridge; but Elliot's County Hall never achieved a front to that street due to pre-existing buildings. Only the much inferior edifice that replaced it on the site in 1900-1905 (the Midlothian County Chambers) attained the double-fronted distinction of a public building linking Parliament Square West and George IV Bridge, facing and accessible from both.

For his part in the contretemps with the 'Builder', the writer known as the 'Plain Honest Man' riposted with the opinion that, save the 'magnificent' portico, the County Hall as a whole was

> one of the clumsiest, ill imagined masses of masonry we have, whether we consider its external form, its incongruity with the neighbouring structures, its site, its position in relation to the street, and the tastelessness displayed in the decorative parts of its interior, such as the lobby, staircase and court-room, not to mention the awkward public entrance to this latter apartment.[54]

The practicalities involved in adapting the Greek temple form to the needs of modern civic life and judicial requirements was a sobering one, likely to quench the enthusiasm of the most ardent Modern Athenians. Almost exactly fifty years after the 'Builder', the 'Plain Honest Man' and their contemporaries had crossed swords, Alexander Thomson, in his Glasgow lectures, would criticise the architects and patrons of the Modern Athens for their failure, 'not because of the scantiness of the [source] material, but because they could not see through the material into the laws upon which that architecture rested. They failed to master their style, and so became its slaves.'[55] Yet after the initial, controversial experiment of the County Hall, those same Athenian spirits went on to pray for a Parthenon.

George Cleghorn's view of the County Hall was ambiguous. The building was 'a handsome edifice'. But 'the anomaly of its architecture' (as Cleghorn put it) contrasted with its surroundings. It was really the anomaly of a classical building *in such a location* that Cleghorn should have pointed up. His actual words were as overblown as they were misleading: 'the preposterous absurdity of its site and position, its flank being turned to the High Street, below the level of which it is sunk several feet.'[56] Cleghorn moderated his language in a later publication.[57]

Many others condemned the building out of hand and on almost every level, from its style to its location. By 1833 its demolition had been discussed, and appeared practically in train; but three years later it was still being described as 'now intended to be removed.' (This was because it was then seen as an impediment to the laying out of what was to become George IV Bridge.)[58] Its case is actually a study in changing taste. It seems strange that the County Hall should have been almost universally damned by so many writers of the high 'Athenian' age of Edinburgh, only to be rather more appreciated once that era was past its zenith. In 1838 William Beattie described it as 'an edifice upon a Grecian model, and very appropriate to a public building.'[59] Fullarton's excellent *Gazetteer* of 1842 continues the encomium of a 'handsome structure', praised as exhibiting 'no common beauty', with its elegant portico and finely carved capitals.[60] Black's *Picturesque Tourist* praised its 'general plan' as one taken from the Erechtheion, and suggested that its principal entrance was derived from the Choragic Monument of Thrasyllos.[61] Murray's *Handbook for Travellers* rated it 'a handsome building'.[62] In 1882 James Grant thought that it possessed 'no uncommon beauty', praising its fine portico and its main entrance with their authoritative archaeological sources.[63] Taste changed once more, culminating in its regrettable demolition at the end of the nineteenth century, when it was replaced by an over-ornate and 'flabbily Palladian' successor.[64]

*   *   *   *   *

The National Monument was to be an imitation of the Parthenon. The Doric order was reckoned the most suitable for reproduction or replication: in the land of its birth, it seemed (as the traveller and, later, gentleman-amateur architect Charles Kelsall supposed) 'best calculated to triumph over the elements, earthquakes, the lapse of time, and the fury of barbarians'.[65] That should suffice for less dramatic Edinburgh conditions and circumstances, and every possible eventuality! Despite mention of Walter Scott in his verse, and Robert Burns in the notes to his poem, Kelsall cited no Scottish examples of the revived style, for he wrote his *Letter from Athens* just too early to have witnessed or heard about the first stirrings of the Scottish Greek Revival, and of buildings in North Britain 'conceived and executed in the true spirit of Greece … [reflecting] honour on the talents of the artists'.[66]

As far as Edinburgh was concerned, those 'artists' were confined to a handful of men: literally so, for they numbered five. There were, of course, other architects working in the city, some not without consequence; but the five leading players in 'Athenian' Edinburgh formed a principal quintet within the whole orchestra, and of this small band three made up an even more distinguished and exclusive trio.

The oldest of the five was Archibald Elliot (1761-1823). We have met him as designer of the Ionic County Hall, and the elegant Waterloo Place with its twin Erechtheion Ionic porticoes framing the view from Princes Street to Calton Hill, and with the delightful Regent Bridge half-way along. This most interesting and impressive street is further dignified by excellent recessed Ionic columnar porticoes (of subtly different forms) over the entries to the former Stamp Office and Post Office. The highly ornamented anta and pilaster capitals are derived from those of the Temple of Apollo at Didyma, in the territory of ancient Miletos in Asia Minor, which are of a distinctive, so-called 'sofa' type. Elliot evidently based his designs on those described and illustrated by Chandler, Revett and Pars in the Dilettanti Society's *Ionian Antiquities*.[67] The Regent Bridge has screens in an unfluted Ionic order and higher central arches with unfluted Corinthian columns, the capitals of which include elements— the elegant helices, and the palmettes on the abaci—taken from the Choragic Monument of Lysikrates, recorded by Stuart and Revett in their *Antiquities of Athens*.[68] (Figs. 45-51) The order changes to Doric towards the eastern end of Waterloo Place. Here there are fluted columns in door-pieces on the north side and, on both sides, aedicules with what have been described as unfluted and almost 'primitive' or archaic columns articulating the niched retaining screen walls of the Old Calton Burying Ground.[69] Whether or not the description 'primitive' is entirely accurate, the style of column chosen seems to do the job perfectly in this less sophisticated, more rural, part of the street. The pleasing and understated Calton Convening Rooms bring the processional way to a happy termination with a half-rounded hexastyle Doric colonnade. (Fig. 36)

Elliot could also design effectively in the Doric on a more monumental scale, as demonstrated by his Dr John Brown's Chapel (later Broughton Place Church, now Lyon & Turnbull's auction house). He proposed the 'Pantheon' design for a national monument at the head of The Mound, in the Corinthian order. There were those, like Lord Elgin, who wanted to see Elliot appointed architect of the National Monument on Calton Hill in its Parthenon guise. Death, however, removed him from competition; he had lived to be twenty years older than William Stark, whose own early death was, by common consent, a great loss to the Edinburgh architectural world. One senses that Elliot's demise, too, even though rather more understandable at sixty-two, still robbed the city of a talent that might have had even more to give.

Next in seniority was Robert Reid (1774-1856), principal official architect for Scotland, handling Government works with the title of 'King's Architect'. Reid was loyal to the Adam style, as in his wrap-around façades of 'ponderous Adamesque wallpaper' in Parliament Square.[70] But he was conscious of the coming wave of 'Grecian' taste, and accommodated himself to it with some success, designing buildings that were restrained yet had a monumental and sophisticated solidity. Correct Greek architecture, or at any rate elements of text-book correctness, first came to 'the Athens of the North' through its 'Piraeus', the sea-port of Leith. There, Reid's Customs House of 1810-12 is notable for its severe pair of Greek Doric columns: 'brutalist neo-classical' is one modern judgment.[71] Shepherd and Britton's *Modern Athens!* does not even name the architect, nor does it waste a word of text on the actual building or its new style, pointedly choosing to devote the section 'Custom-House, Leith' wholly to local dock developments.[72] The sombre building was to be 'softened' by additions by William Burn a dozen years later.

Reid achieved some real distinction in his layout of the Second, or Northern New Town—where so many influential Modern Athenians lived—and in the design of the palace-fronted elevations of its great streets, most notably Great King Street. What Reid attempted to do (1811-14) with Robert Adam's unexecuted plans for St George's Church in Charlotte Square has attracted perhaps unjustified criticism. In a move away from Adam's largely Roman classicism towards a slightly (but only very slightly) more Grecian idiom, and in a façade not accurately Greek in any real sense, Reid created a recessed loggia with four massive unfluted Ionic columns where Adam had offered a projecting portico. Reid's arrangement was kinder to church-going Modern Athenians, in providing shelter from the wind and rain. But as far as his work on his revision of Adam's scheme went, *Modern Athens!* piled on the criticism of a building 'found to be destitute of all architectural proportions, and an object of general disapprobation'. A letter of 1813 to the *Scots Magazine* was quoted with some evident glee:

> ... nothing but a mere mass of stone, and possessing no greater claims to admiration, than could be given with facility, and very little ingenuity, to the face of Craigleith quarry, by cutting it regularly, and excavating a small opening in the centre.[73]

Then comes Thomas Hamilton (1784-1858): with his great rival, W. H. Playfair, one of the real geniuses of Athenian Edinburgh.[74] Defeated by Playfair in the competition to complete the University in 1816, Hamilton again lost out to Playfair in the contest to design the National Gallery in 1849. His magnificent High School of 1825-29 is, however, one of the great creations of international neoclassicism. (Figs 67 68) It draws inspiration from the Theseion in Athens, but also plays the role of the Propylaea or entrance building of the Acropolis. Some contemporaries saw in it, too, elements of the Monument of Thrasyllos. But all were agreed that (in the words of one commentator) Hamilton's triumph in the building placed his 'professional character ... upon what we may term a fixed basis'.[75] Elsewhere, Hamilton made further great contributions to the fabric of the Modern Athens. His were the remarkable (and sadly demolished) Hopetoun Rooms in Queen Street, elegant scene of assemblies or 'routs'. These took place beneath a lantern carried on caryatids, multiplied to twice the number of the ancient originals that supported the Erechtheion porch, the maidens having made their way via the pages of Hamilton's source-books to the Northern Athens.

Hamilton's, also, is the opulent and unconventional Royal College of Physicians, at the other end of Queen Street, with its porch derived from the Tower of the Winds in Athens. William Blackwood's shop in George Street, with its elegant Ionic porticoes, attracted attention. The Burns Monument on the flank of Calton Hill, inspired by the Choragic Monument of Lysikrates but with hints, too, of the so-called Temple of the Sibyl at Tivoli, is a triumph of architectural design matched with an ideal physical location in the Romantic-Classic landscape. Hamilton claimed a wide familiarity with the published sources of classical architecture, complimenting himself, in 1819, on his 'acquaintance with all the most eminent authors'; in other words, his magisterial grasp of the archaeological literature on which he capitalised most successfully.[76] But yet, of a single authentic building in Greece, Sicily or Southern Italy, he had enjoyed not a personal glimpse.

William Burn (1789-1870) who, like W. H. Playfair, had trained in the London office of Robert Smirke, comes fourth in seniority.[77] Burn's remarkable North Leith Church, with a massive tetrastyle portico of the Ionic order derived from the Temple on the Ilissos, above which rises a steeple ornamented by other orders with similar archaeological sources, was a significant early contribution to the Greek Revival in the Modern Athens. Rivalry, amounting to open hostility, marked his relationship with Playfair. Burn and Hamilton were contemporary competitors in the realm of great Edinburgh school or educational institution design, with Burn achieving a thoroughly respectable if rather conventional three to Hamilton's inspired two. It has been most aptly said, with reference to Hamilton's High School, that 'Its design penetrates the essence of Greek architecture without anywhere appearing merely academic; and an analysis of Hamilton's terse and meaningful manipulation of its elements ... makes Burn appear facile and Greek only by sleight of hand.'[78] Burn was, perhaps, the least charismatic of the leading trio of Edinburgh 'Grecians': highly competent, certainly; prodigiously well-organised, undeniably, and with an almost factory-like production line, churning out able work of all sorts; but more derivative than the others of the great trio, and lacking something of true genius.[79]

Last in this parade of architectural talent is William Henry Playfair (1790-1857), a man who made his mark, as no one else, in his magnificent public buildings and monuments as much as in his handsome streets of terraced houses forming an 'orderly girdle of classicism round the knoll of the Calton Hill'.[80] More so, even than Hamilton, it was Playfair who gave embodiment in stone to the idea of the Northern Athens. Indeed, it has been well said that Edinburgh's 'soubriquet as the "modern Athens" now depends on the prominence of his distinguished buildings'.[81] (Fig. 22) Embedded from boyhood in the highest levels of Edinburgh's Whig intellectual society, Playfair became its prime candidate to design the buildings intended to house the city's learned bodies with which the members of that intellectual and social coterie were professionally connected: buildings for the law, for medicine, for academia, for the church, for the arts. Undoubtedly, he benefitted greatly from his connections, and his career was promoted by well-placed and influential supporters. He was given opportunities which he seized, and in which he succeeded through a combination of tremendous talent and powerful patronage. The latter fact cannot be underestimated. Playfair's progress was resented by his rivals, and by those who thought the active support he received from the Edinburgh elite misplaced. Grumblings were expressed by playing on his name: such-and-such a job was not won by 'fair-play', and 'foul-play' was suspected in the award of this or that commission. 'Oh! It is not playfair, but playfoul.'[82]

Playfair was the local executant of the London architect Charles Robert Cockerell's designs for the National Monument. (Fig. 63) But, as an independent practitioner, he had already masterminded the completion of the University. He had designed the Observatory that everyone called 'Greek', but which was really Roman Doric. He went on to plan and design the terraces of Grecian houses in (among others) Blenheim Place, Windsor Street, Hillside Crescent, Brunswick Street and Regent Terrace; to design the Doric Royal Institution, twice over (Figs. 59-61); the Ionic Surgeons' Hall (Fig. 90); and major parts of the Advocates' Library which, had circumstances been different, he could have completed in splendid Corinthian style and on an heroic scale. There were minor masterpieces in memorials with impeccable (if sometimes obscure) classical sources, including that to his own scientist uncle, perhaps derived from the so-called Tomb of Theron at Agrigento in Sicily.[83]

Playfair's lonely bachelor existence and his recurrent poor health were writ large in his correspondence with his fellow architect Cockerell, and with his great friends Andrew and Sophia Rutherfurd. 'Consolation was sought in the doubtful affections of "old Madam Architecture whose courtship, though sometime very fatiguing, frequently helps to wear though many a solitary hour."'[84] When Cockerell married Anna, daughter of the civil engineer John Rennie, Playfair compared Cockerell's good fortune with his own: 'I am a slave to the drawing board. And I find my present mistress, Architecture,'—he also referred archly to 'his fair goddess the lady Architecture'—'sufficiently coy. She bestows her favours only after a terrible long courtship.'[85] This image of domestic despair is compounded by the peculiarly Northern Athenian vision of Sophia Rutherfurd easing the architect's miserable lot by interviewing potential household servants: a task Playfair described quaintly, as if he were some elderly valetudinarian Greek, as 'the hiring of nymphs'.[86]

All these architects, and their supporters, waged an internecine war where personality, as much as scholarship and taste, was the fuel of dislike and dispute. In a fictional 'Noctes Ambrosianae' scene, set in the new saloon of William Blackwood, the publisher, in George Street, Blackwood himself is made to introduce Thomas De Quincey to Thomas Hamilton, the shop's designer. De Quincey has been waxing lyrical about Blackwood's new premises—'nothing, in the whole range of architecture, within the same bounds, so magnificent'— and now continues: 'The names of Hamilton, Burn, and Playfair have long been familiar to fame.'[87] This was published two years after a genuine epistolary exchange between Hugh William Williams and Cockerell, in which Williams had written:

Nothing but improvements going on here—new approaches and consequently new streets and public edifices. Edinburgh will really be a noble and beautiful place at no distant date. Playfair has his share, and Burn, and Hamilton, three clever fellows.[88]

It all sounded idyllic. Yet all three—and other, lesser men—were consumed by rivalry. Williams went on to ask Cockerell: 'What do you think of the Liverpool people employing Gillespie [James Gillespie Graham] after having seen the High School by Hamilton and the other public buildings by the other architects?'[89] Williams, however, was open and generous in his praise of both Playfair and Hamilton. Playfair's University Library 'has a most magnificent appearance', Williams told Cockerell, himself watching in the wings, so to speak, from London; and Hamilton's High School 'is certainly a very perfect specimen of architecture'.[90] But even Playfair could often ill-conceal his dislike of his contemporaries. Hamilton was 'full of intrigue and vulgar taste'; this said by Playfair when he feared that Hamilton might win the National Gallery competition for a site at The Mound that Playfair felt very much his own.[91] In Playfair's opinion, Burn was 'purse proud and ostentatious and overbearing', generally 'creating horrid blots in the landscape where ever he is employed … His utter want of genius is only to be equalled by his copious supply of impudence.'[92]

Archibald Alison praised what Elliot and Playfair had already designed in an idiom that was, in the one case, convincingly 'Greek', and, in the other, a style with sufficient 'ancient' elements to persuade the Modern Athenians that they were on the way to re-imagining Athens on Scottish soil. Rather unfairly, Alison ignored the excellent work of William Stark, though Stark's achievement was much praised by Playfair, and also by Walter Scott and Henry Cockburn.[93] It was Cockburn who recognised that Stark's mantle had descended on Playfair.[94] Stark had practised in Glasgow before moving to Edinburgh and establishing himself in the Modern Athens—though clearly not sufficiently for Alison to have recognised him as a pioneer 'Athenian'.

The Prussian architect Karl Friedrich Schinkel, having visited Edinburgh, concurred with many other observers in thinking Stark's interior of the Advocates' Library—that is the Upper Signet Library of today—good; but he did not choose to comment on any perceived loyalty to Greece. (Fig. 57) On the contrary, Schinkel singled out for mention the fact that, in Playfair's Natural History Museum in the University there was much 'detail derived from Greek monuments, but lacking a feeling for proportion and its practical application. Everything seems more of an experiment than well-organized endeavour ...' (Figs 55-56) Schinkel appeared happier in the knowledge that on Calton Hill, where the foundations were even then (in 1826) being dug, 'a faithful replica of the Parthenon' was to be built.[95] Here, there would be no room for eclectic borrowing from a variety of sources. Nor would there be any opportunity for improvising buildings that the architects of Edinburgh thought were accurately or at least convincingly 'Greek' simply because they were designed with reliance on a shelf-full of archaeological works to hand.

The generality of Edinburgh people may not have been able to determine readily and precisely just what was Greek and what was Roman, or Renaissance, or an example of Adamesque eclecticism, or to distinguish one 'style' from another. Most will probably have known only that they liked something that was vaguely classical or, as they quite possibly called it, 'Grecian'. But, around 1819, they came to know—or were led to believe—that what they most wanted, above everything, was an indisputably Greek 'Parthenon'. That really would mark them out as citizens of the Northern Athens.

*   *   *   *   *

It is not the intention here to deal in detail with the story of the actual building of the National Monument. (Figs 62-64) Rather, we shall be concerned with notions of taste, aesthetics and the 'Modern Athenianism' that informed the choice of the Parthenon as the model for the Monument. Several articles have discussed the episode at length and in detail.[96] A recent book has also placed the building in the general context of the development of Calton Hill.[97] The purpose of the pages that follow is to supplement existing literature by making some connections previously overlooked; by correcting several misunderstandings; and by offering information culled from a variety of manuscript and printed sources not previously examined to the full, especially one highly important, but neglected, periodical publication.

Archibald Alison has, rightly, assumed a position of importance, indeed of leadership, in the story of Edinburgh's assumption of an 'Athenian' identity. There was, he suggested, a great need to improve on what had previously been achieved, both in terms of public appreciation of authentic Greek buildings and in the emulation of those originals by the architectural profession.

> Now it has unfortunately happened that the Doric architecture, to which so much of the beauty of Greece and Italy is owing, has been hitherto little understood, and still less put in practice in this country. We meet with few persons who have not visited the remains of classical antiquity, who can conceive the matchless beauties of the temples of Minerva at Athens, or of Neptune at Pestum [*sic*]. And, indeed, if our conceptions of the Doric be taken from the few attempts at imitation of it which are here to be met with, they would fall very far short, indeed, of what the originals are fitted to excite.[98]

Now, however, a far grander gesture was called for, and it happened that opportunity offered a chance to build the Parthenon in replica. 'It is vain', Alison wrote, 'to expect that human genius can ever make any thing more beautiful than the Parthenon.' The temple's

> form and character is associated in every cultivated mind with the recollections of classical history; and it recalls the brilliant conceptions of national glory as they were received during the ardent and enthusiastic period of youth; while its stern and massy form befits an edifice destined to commemorate the severe virtues and manly character of war.

The Parthenon restored on Calton Hill 'will stand at once the monument of former greatness, and the pledge of future glory'.[99] It would provide a superb model for, and impetus to, yet further architectural and wider cultural improvement. Nature had already given Edinburgh a physical setting beyond compare, and 'the means of becoming the most *beautiful* town that exists in the world'. Translated thither, and specifically to the Calton Hill, 'the Parthenon of Athens would ultimately, in all probability, render this city the favourite residence of the fine arts'.[100] Choice of any other location than the hill would fail to do justice to the purity and splendour of the original design: witness earlier, tentative steps in the introduction of Greek Revival architecture to the city, notably in the Ionic portico of the County Hall, widely perceived to have been built in the wrong location and to be lost amid the unworthy surroundings of the insalubrious Old Town, where no one might 'conceive the beauty of the originals [that is, the Erechtheion north porch], standing on the rock of the Acropolis'. A processional Waterloo Place would lead the eye to the Calton Hill, and thus 'exhibit at the close of that beautiful Grecian Street the most splendid of Grecian triumphal edifices'.[101]

In his posthumously published autobiography (written in stages, and completed before 1862), Alison maintained that his articles in *Blackwood's Magazine* and elsewhere 'contributed much to produce the noble but unfinished structure which now adorns the Calton Hill'.[102] He expanded on this:

> ... after the usual amount of resistance by which every new project is assailed, public opinion in Edinburgh had come to be generally in favour of the plan I had so warmly advocated, of placing a fac-simile of the Parthenon of Athens on the Calton Hill ...

Alison explained that his committee had met every week for above two years, and that, with Sir William Rae (Lord Advocate, and former Sheriff of Edinburgh) and Michael Linning, Secretary of what had become the grandiloquently titled Royal Association of Contributors to the National Monument, he had signed the builder's contract for the first phase of the work. Here it was stipulated that

> every stone ... should be of the same dimensions as the corresponding one in the original—being well aware how much the effect of Doric architecture depends on the magnitude of the material employed. This was faithfully complied with under the direction of the able architects of the building ... and the effect thus secured forms one of the most striking features in that noble structure ...

Alison stated that the individual column drums weighed seven or eight tons; the blocks of the entablature some fifteen to eighteen tons. Twelve horses and a hundred men were needed to move the blocks on their special carriages from quarry to building site.[103] Contemporary accounts of the effort and expense involved in nineteenth-century Edinburgh echo the surviving records of the similar labour required in the quarrying and transportation of the materials for fifth-century BC Athenian temples.[104] 'This ambitious structure soon excited attention both in Scotland and among strangers who visited its metropolis', but it 'awakened jealousy among those artists who thought that the restoration of a monument of antiquity was an undeserved slight on modern genius.'[105] For his part, Cockerell claimed that the stones surpassed in size 'anything hitherto known in this country or in the modern world'.[106]

There was, unquestionably, a sense of satisfaction that the building-stone was locally sourced at Craigleith quarry, within sight of Calton Hill.[107] The parallel with Athens cannot easily be dismissed for, as John Boardman has pointed out, the marble quarries of Mount Pentelikon were within sight of the Acropolis and were the exclusive source of the material for the Parthenon.[108] The Craigleith sandstone beds were much nearer. The quarry was one of the sights of Edinburgh, much sketched by artists and appearing in illustrated publications. Indeed, it was something to proud of. By contrast, John Galt had considered that the famous quarries of Pentelikon, though they had 'become, it seems, one of the standing curiosities of Greece', were not actually much to look at, and he was actually quite rude about the place—'a large hole in the side of the hill … just like that of any other cavern.'[109]

Boardman has also expressed, in a memorable and dramatic essay on the conception and construction of the original monument, the effort involved in building the Parthenon.

> The creation of such a great temple, its sculptural decoration [and its cult statue] had been a project more complicated than any military operation, more costly and more time-consuming. It required money, men, skills and foresight in planning which could anticipate the effect of such a large and unusually proportioned building in its setting, and more than a touch of genius in design and execution.[110]

The Modern Athenians must surely have been aware, from their knowledge of Plutarch and other sources, just how amazingly quickly the original Parthenon had been built, with structural completion achieved in about nine years and the sculptural work being finished in about another five.[111] Robert Gourlay would later remind the Edinburgh public that 'in the days of Pericles, architecture was more advanced than now'.[112] This was very much the sentiment Alison and his acolytes entertained.

Andrew Robertson, who has already been mentioned, remains an under-recognised protagonist in this story. It is in the context of Robertson's published appeal for a national monument to be erected to the memory of Robert Burns that the origins of the Edinburgh Parthenon may first be identified. Robertson's brief paper serves as a sort of preface to a pamphlet entitled (on its wrapper) *National Monument to be Erected at Edinburgh, to the Memory of Robert Burns* and (on its title-page) *Festival in Commemoration of Robert Burns; and to Promote a Subscription to Erect a National Monument to his Memory at Edinburgh: Held at the Freemasons' Tavern, in London, on Saturday, June 5, 1819.*

Three key ideas were advanced: the concept of the 'restoration' of an appropriate ancient monument; the Calton Hill as its site; and the notion that the resulting structure might also assume, in due course, something of the character of a national 'Valhalla'. 'It is universally acknowledged', Robertson proposed,

> that since the works of the ancient Greeks have become more generally known … public taste in Architecture has been greatly improved … If such advantages have been derived from the contemplation of Ruins, and even from Prints representing them in their original perfect state, what may not be expected

from an actual restoration in this country, of some of these wonders of Art, whereby their principles might be shown, and their excellence displayed, in all variety of effect produced by light and shade? ... One such Building, placed on the Calton-hill, might lead to the erection of others, until it should become the Acropolis of the Northern Athens, and Edinburgh be called the City of Temples and of Taste.[113]

There had been a preliminary meeting on 24 April, likewise in the Freemasons' Tavern, at which Robertson had spoken. Readers in Auld Reekie were informed by *The Caledonian Mercury* of 29 April 1819 that he had reminded his London audience—consisting largely if not wholly of prominent London Scots—that 'Edinburgh had been called the Athens of Britain; and it was to be hoped that at some future day the Calton Hill might lay claim to the title of the Acropolis of Edinburgh.'

But there is actually another, and earlier, strand to this tale. There had been a proposal (as we have already seen) for a Parthenon monument, commemorating victory in the Napoleonic Wars, to be sited on Primrose Hill in London. This had originated in a letter to *The Times* by one 'B.'[114] Robertson appears to have stepped forward when nothing came of this suggestion, and eventually it was his revivification of the idea that led to Edinburgh's growing 'Athenianism' trumping London's reluctance to spend its 'Roman' riches on a monument of this or any kind. (Robertson would try again, as we have also seen, to foist a Parthenon on London, this time in Trafalgar Square.) It is not too difficult to believe that Alison elaborated on Robertson's initial suggestions and was prompted by them to make his own proposals for 'transfer' of the Parthenon to Edinburgh, and thus the establishment of 'the taste of Phidias' in 'our northern regions'.[115]

There is no foundation for Charles McKean's mischievous assertion that the Modern Athenians did not, from the outset, intend to build an entire replica of the Parthenon: that what was built was all that was ever projected, and thus that it was the 'intention from the very first to build only the small section that we can see. It is therefore a deliberate folly ...'[116] In his own word-portrait of Edinburgh (published three years later) Allan Massie, assuredly following McKean's lead, appears to half-accept, half-doubt his assertion, describing as 'convincing' the evidence of the drawings to which McKean makes reference (though Massie almost certainly never examined them), and himself stating 'one curious circumstance' relating to the Parthenon project. The National Monument, writes Massie, 'may never have been seriously intended to be more than a folly, a picturesque false ruin.' And yet, as if the Parthenon had been conceived and constructed by some Jekyll and Hyde characters, Massie displays dubiety on this same contentious point, admitting that 'if this was the intention, the secret was well kept; the result an example of Edinburgh's taste for duality.'[117]

The idea of playful neoclassical follies on Calton Hill cannot be squared with the rather humourless intensity of the Edinburgh Greeks. The dreams of Modern Athens were too powerful for the dreamers to have been satisfied with anything less than a complete temple of their own. All the evidence clearly points to this, and there is nothing whatsoever to suggest the contrary.[118] Any building has to start somewhere; and the contract drawings cited by McKean in support of his theory are merely those for the part of the National Monument to be built as the first stage of what was, from the outset, understood to be a long-term undertaking, dependent, of necessity, upon phased construction as resources permitted. In a letter to Cockerell, Playfair referred to 'the part of the Western portico' and to the 'portion' first contracted for, consisting of 'eight columns of the front' and two 'on each flank'.[119] (Fig. 63) Years later, Archibald Alison alluded to the contract he had signed as being 'for that part of the structure which we had funds to execute, and which has since been erected ... the funds subscribed (£15,000) would not do more ...'[120] When that initial contract came to an end (with the construction of the western octastyle portico, two further columns of each long side, and the appropriate epistyle or architrave) work ceased because there were insufficient funds to carry it on—*not* because it was the completion of what had ever, or only, been intended. Playfair said as much in his letter to Cockerell of 30 June 1829, stating that the builder [William] Wallace's contract was complete with respect to this specific part of the whole:

> Our Parthenon is come to a dead Halt. And is I am afraid likely to stand up a striking proof of the pride & poverty of the Scots. The masonry is as good as can be, & the Columns look like each of one stone. When the Sun shines & there is a pure Blue Sky behind them (a rare event you will say) they look most beautiful but surprisingly small. And the Architrave being the top line, gives the whole a hard ... appearance ... what is to be done next I know not. I suppose *Nothing*.[121]

*   *   *   *   *

The title given by *Blackwood's Magazine* to an article published in response to Alison's initial polemic is significant: 'Restoration of the Parthenon for the National Monument'.[122] That monument, when constructed, was expected to be Greek, in the Doric order, and to be a *restoration* of the Parthenon. Alison had written initially only of the Parthenon being 'imitated'. The new Blackwood author, 'R.', suggested that, just as Athens under Pericles was the climax of a slowly evolving civilisation, so Edinburgh, even in its Regency glory, was merely witnessing the very beginning of a similar cultural development which might, in due time, bear fruit:

... long ere the sun of Grecian taste had shed its meridian lustre on the Acropolis, there must have been many bright indications of the light which was to come ... How presumptuous were it then in us to hope, that, by the mere effort of our will, however powerfully seconded by talents and wealth, we can reach at once an excellence which it cost even the Greeks so many centuries to accomplish.[123]

Nevertheless, the writer stressed the advantages that Edinburgh possessed in having a situation for the proposed temple finer than could be offered by any other city, and strikingly similar, if not indeed fully equal (or perhaps rather superior) to that selected by 'Phidias himself'. The interesting suggestion was made that Scots in India would no doubt contribute handsomely to the costs of constructing such a building as 'the Parthenon of Athens ... restored ... in the capital of their native land'.[124] One thinks of 'tribute' paid by the cities and island communities of the ancient Delian League as that was transformed into the Athenian Empire with its funds retained in Athens as metropolis.

Alison's robust rejoinder showed him a doughty fighter for his beliefs, but as one who got too easily carried away on the tide of his own rhetoric. Given what he wrote and how he expressed it, he might as well have said of the ancient Athenians that, had they but had the choice, the original architects and stonemasons of the Parthenon would rather have been modern Scotsmen than ancient Greeks, and to have lived and worked in early nineteenth-century Edinburgh in preference to mid-fifth-century Athens.

Not content with making Edinburgh Athenian, Alison pointed out that there was room still for Rome, too: 'while the rock of Edinburgh would vie with the Acropolis in the matchless glories of its triumphal edifice, the level extent of the New Town would rival the plain of Rome'. Monumental columns might rise to Scottish heroes, such as Lord Melville. Modelled after those of Trajan or Marcus Aurelius, they would serve such commemorative purposes so much better than a feeble trifle like the non-classical and indeed nondescript Nelson Monument, 'a lasting blot ... a blemish upon the taste of a people': 'unworthy', a 'prominent deformity ... a disgrace'.[125]

In his next manifesto for a classical Edinburgh, Alison focused on the style and especially the siting of the proposed monument to Melville.[126] But his main contention was actually that the 'Athenian' character of Edinburgh would be made much more convincing by the massing of her monuments.

It is a matter, too, of the greatest moment, in arranging edifices for the present and future ornament of a city, to have them so combined as to form, if possible, *some one splendid whole*; the attractions of which may withdraw the attention from objects of subordinate or minor interest, and the magnificence of which may produce an indelible impression on the mind of the spectator.

The example of the single island of 'Greekness'—namely the unfortunate County Hall—in a surrounding sea of degradation was yet again cited.

> And if we require a confirmation of so obvious a truth, we have only to go
> to the High Street of Edinburgh, where even the beautiful pillars of Athenian
> Doric [*sic*: carried away, Alison actually meant Ionic] lose their effect under
> the chilling influence of the surrounding buildings.

Alison had no time for 'beauties lurking in some unseen spot', or the 'sequestered charms' of some hidden building:

> A feeling of disappointment is experienced when we find some beautiful edifice
> buried in an obscure situation, similar to what would be felt if a brilliant jewel,
> instead of adorning the brow of grace and beauty, were to be buried under the
> folds, or concealed by the least ornamental part of her drapery.

What he favoured, by contrast, was '*some one glorious scene*'. For Edinburgh, that should be the Calton Hill, with the monumental centre of the city laid out around it.

> No one has visited Athens without feeling the imposing effect which the
> combination of ruined magnificence on the Acropolis produces; an effect
> greater than any single edifice, however perfect, could possibly occasion; and,
> notwithstanding the stately buildings which adorn our own metropolis, it is
> certainly more to the happy nature of their situation, which bring them all
> into view at once from the Calton Hill, than to their intrinsic excellence, that
> its well known celebrity is to be ascribed.

Edinburgh would become most effectively Athenian by heeding this example:

> it is of the utmost moment to combine, as much as possible, the ornamental
> edifices of Edinburgh into one centre; and to aid the natural effect of its
> situation, by assembling, into one view, all that the public spirit of its citizens
> can produce of the beautiful in architectural design.[127]

The Parthenon, re-created on the summit of Calton Hill, for which Alison so earnestly wished and lobbied, should—and would—attract to itself a constellation of lesser monuments and buildings. He was supported by the pseudonymous 'Traveller', mentioned before, who argued that the Calton Hill was 'as well fitted for its reception [that is, of the proposed National Monument in Parthenon form] as the Acropolis was for the Temple of Minerva'.[128] The 'Traveller' concluded:

It has often been asked, If such be really the advantages of the Grecian architecture above that which is the growth of this country, why have we not imported it before now? The answer to which is, that we were, until very lately, almost entirely ignorant of the very existence of the fine buildings of Greece, or, to speak more correctly, we were ignorant of their extraordinary beauty, and of their effect in forming the taste and chastising the judgment in all matters connected with the science of architecture.

Seminal was the experience and knowledge of travellers such as himself. Under their influence, the 'Greekness' of Edinburgh would come to pervade all aspects of life.

There is no man of sense and education who has examined a temple of the pure Doric style without being strongly affected, or without being conscious of having thereby acquired an unexpected accession of correct taste, and sound judgment of architectural subjects. The impression left is never to be erased ...[129]

An interesting comment on the aesthetics of the choice, both of the architectural model and of the site, and of these coalescing in one place and one place only, is buried in the text of another long and anonymous contribution to the Edinburgh periodical press. In this, a further direct comparison between the ancient and the modern Athens is made in the context of the hoped-for decision to site the proposed Parthenon on Calton Hill.

No other edifice could possibly produce this imposing effect, or add to the embellishment of the city so much as this would ... The Calton Hill, in the opinion of those who have visited both, is a finer situation for the display of a Grecian temple than even the Acropolis of Athens; and precisely such an eminence as the Greeks everywhere chose for the site of their ornamental edifices, and which Claude and Poussin adopted for similar Grecian temples in their compositions of ideal beauty.[130]

Resort to the appeal of the picturesque in landscape is thus manifested by evoking the names of the two most venerated practitioners of the tradition of seventeenth-century classical landscape painting. This was a new addition to the Calton Hill Parthenon debate, and an important one, given the contemporary interest aroused by Hugh William Williams's evocative views of Greece.

Another telling passage criticises architectural ambition and achievement prior to the current age of new-kindled 'Athenian' consciousness.

Taste is but of recent growth in this city; and every one must recollect the period when, in place of feeling a pride, as at present, in the public spirit of its inhabitants, and the taste and judgment with which they are guided, it was a matter of universal regret amongst ourselves, and of continual reproach from strangers, that the unparalleled natural advantages of stone and situation were lost, from the indifference of the inhabitants to public undertakings, and the want of taste in those who formed them ... we cannot forget that many buildings exist in this city, intended for public ornament, which are a lasting blot on the taste and judgment of the age ...[131]

The writer went even further when he suggested that Scots in India might actually be *un*willing to subscribe to a National Monument out of sheer disbelief that anything worthy of the name could be erected in the Edinburgh they remembered from their youth, considering it a place where nothing of consequence ever got built or was worthily finished; when buildings were 'a disgrace rather than an ornament to their country'; when

the national taste was at a very low ebb, and when the public buildings of Edinburgh ... were as remarkable for their clumsiness, as those since erected are for their elegance and beauty. The rapid progress which a taste for architecture has made amongst us since that period, could not *a priori* have been anticipated, and certainly in India is almost wholly unknown.[132]

A fixed resolution to adopt the Parthenon scheme would allay all doubt in India, that 'region of profuse expenditure', and subscription money would flood home.[133] East India Company writers and collectors (that is, clerks and magistrates) would pay up to beautify the city they had left as Auld Reekie, but which was transforming itself into the Athens of the North.

* * * * *

Archibald Alison was never one to remain silent for long. In an article in *The Edinburgh Review* he set out to counter arguments made in *The Quarterly Review* (perversely, neither 'review' in either of the periodicals was really a book review as such). In what purported to be a critique of a work on a wholly different subject, the *Quarterly*'s anonymous writer—in fact Francis Cohen—had proceeded to question at great length the legitimacy of a National Monument of Scotland being constructed in an 'alien', Greek style.[134] According to Hugh William Williams, who wrote to Cockerell in bullish terms, this *Quarterly* article had made 'but a small impression here & certainly has not in any degree abated the enthusiasm of the admirers of the Parthenon ... In short you alone will be the Restorer of the Ancient Gem.'[135] But now, in his putative review of the antiquarian Earl of Aberdeen's *Inquiry into the Principles of Beauty in Grecian Architecture*, and as a direct riposte to Cohen,

Alison delivered the next round of his stentorian argument for an 'Athenian' Edinburgh. Without naming an author, David Brewster told Cockerell that the article in *The Edinburgh Review* was one of two rejoinders shortly to appear in answer to the *Quarterly*'s tirade.[136] (The other was that in *The New Edinburgh Review*, already referred to above.) The two greatest Reviews of the English-speaking world of the day—the *Edinburgh* and the *Quarterly*: Waugh and Innes's *New Edinburgh* was a short-lived interloper—were thus locked in combat on a single topic, namely the 'Greekness' of Edinburgh. The typography of this new article by Alison is significant. The running head is 'Restoration of the Parthenon'. The reader can be in no doubt as to the real subject of Alison's enthusiastic and elegant though interminable prose.[137] It was not for nothing that, in *Coningsby* (1844), Disraeli lampooned Alison—by then celebrated as author of an enormous history of modern Europe—as 'Mr Wordy'.[138]

Under the cloak of his 'review', Alison's actual topic is his vision of Edinburgh as a 'Grecian' city—certainly a city of the intellect and, increasingly, one of architectural statement. The climax of the transformation might (and, in his view, should be) the construction of the northern Parthenon. The moment for Edinburgh to become truly Athenian had arrived: architecture would be the agent of this ambition. Until then, architecture had lagged behind the flowering of other forms or expressions of genius in the city. Now Edinburgh displayed 'a very strong desire for architectural embellishment'. Some step was necessary that would 'render our people independent of foreign travelling, or of the borrowed aid of foreign edifices'. This might be done most effectually by re-creating Greece in Edinburgh. Alison notes that Lord Aberdeen had expressed the view that 'By a person writing on the subject of architecture, the name of Athens can scarcely be pronounced without emotion.' Alison took this idea further in suggesting that this emotion naturally led connoisseurs to wish to 'restore some one of the great models of antiquity in this country'. The opportunity beckoned in the National Monument scheme, to be carried into execution on the Calton Hill. Such an act would be transformative.

> By adopting the Doric temple, therefore, and by that measure *alone*, is it in the power of the Subscribers to compensate the disadvantages of a narrow kingdom and a barren soil; and, by placing the Temple of Athens on the Acropolis of Edinburgh, to confer a distinction on this city which no southern capital can boast ...[139]

The 'rocky eminence' on which to build the temple was 'precisely similar' to the Athenian Acropolis. And yet, because this was *Edinburgh*, it was one somehow offering 'a finer situation' even than the Acropolis itself (Alison was adopting— perhaps unconsciously, perhaps not—the words first used by the writer in *The Edinburgh Magazine, and Literary Miscellany* of April 1820). A combination of fortunate circumstances thus gave the Modern Athens, its architects and craftsmen, a distinct advantage over their ancient forerunners, especially if one could be deluded enough to rank fine-grained Craigleith sandstone over the purest Pentelic marble.[140]

Alison then turned to the architectural 'Greekness' of Edinburgh. In doing so, he betrayed an uncertainty or even confusion as to what precisely constituted a pure, Greek Revival style, and what distinguished it from the merely 'Grecian' or simply the 'classical'. The centre of the city, Alison suggested, 'already bears the Grecian character'. He was not the first to distort the architectural history of the city, and he would not be the last to take a blatantly biased view of what precisely constituted the style of which he wrote.

> The edifices with which the Calton Hill is surrounded, are in the *same style of architecture* as the Temple which it is now proposed to place on its summit ... The palace of Holyrood-house, the dome of St George's, the Melville monument, the University, St Andrew's Church, the Register house, and the Observatory ... are all in the Grecian style. The approach ... through Waterloo Place, is adorned by colonnades of remarkable beauty, copied from the temple of Erychtheus [*sic*] at Athens; and the new streets which are building on the northern and eastern sides of the Hill, are enriched by Doric columns of the finest proportions, and exhibit perhaps the most beautiful fronts in the Grecian style of which the Island can boast. The new and beautiful edifice about to be raised on the Mound for the public societies [Playfair's Royal Institution], is in the same order [Doric]; and the traveller, returning from Sicily or Athens, is astonished to find the Genuine Grecian architecture revived with a degree of spirit and fidelity in this metropolis ... Nor is it difficult to foresee that this order will continue to be the prevailing style in future times; the enormous expense of Gothic ornament rendering buildings of that description too costly for our age ... What, then, can be more appropriate than, in the centre of a city which already bears the Grecian character, to place the most superb monumental edifice of which ancient Greece can boast?[141]

As if this statement were not remarkable enough, Alison the Athenian enlisted even the verse of Walter Scott to his cause. But his quotation from *Marmion* was not the famous passage about the poet's 'own romantic town', with its 'ridgy back' heaving to the sky and ancient castle holding its state above the smoky Old Town 'piled deep and massy, close and high', but a later stanza (in fact one from the dedicatory epistle to Canto Five of the narrative poem, published in 1808). This Alison interpreted as Scott's paying tribute to a city 'O, how altered now'; a city 'Flinging ... its white arms to the sea', its bright lines of new classical building catching the rays of the setting sun. 'The long lines of light', Alison argued, 'which are here so beautifully described, accord perfectly with the features of the Grecian edifice.' He went further still in his Greek crusade, stating that it is 'a total mistake to imagine, that Edinburgh is a Gothic town ...', before pointing out how few such ancient Gothic structures could be seen from Calton Hill—precious little in that line that was genuinely *ancient,* and, of the *modern* 'Gothic' structures, only the two Episcopal chapels, both in York Place in the New Town, one recently built and the other dating from the 1790s. All else, Alison maintained, was 'Grecian'. 'To hold, that these insulated edifices should chain the architecture of this metropolis for ever to the Gothic style, is to debar men from all variety or improvement in their designs.'[142]

*   *   *   *   *

It is necessary to rehearse at some length how and why Archibald Alison was arguing for an 'Athenian' Edinburgh, with a Parthenon at its would-be Hellenic heart, because his views have been misinterpreted. In fact, it has been said that he was doing precisely the reverse. The entire thrust of Alison's clear and unambiguous case has been misunderstood.[143] It was not Alison, but rather Francis Cohen, in his anonymous article in *The Quarterly Review*, who advanced the anti-Greek view. In his *Edinburgh Review* article, Alison was taking Cohen to task for that very view. For his own part, Alison was most certainly not, as Marc Fehlmann has suggested, 'pleading for a National Monument constructed on vernacular Scottish principles', or arguing against 'all manners of imitating or emulating ancient models' in the belief that it was 'degrading to copy the architecture of another people ... that it is absurd for us to place a Grecian Temple on Calton Hill'.[144] Far from it! Alison was (as Robert Adam had put it in another context, referring to James 'Athenian' Stuart) 'Greek to the teeth'.[145]

The long and remarkable *New Edinburgh Review* article of 1823 with its running head of 'Architecture'—an essay almost wholly unknown to scholarship, and neglected as a source of great importance—is a fascinating manifesto for a Greek Edinburgh founded on what the author characterised as

> the simple principles and general purity of design or proportion, which belong to the architecture of Greece ... And this is one of the great arguments in favour of the Greek style of art, where the simplicity of the principles is such as not to admit of those wanton or ignorant violations; while a competent knowledge of them is also of comparatively easy acquisition.[146]

In the past, there had been 'the want of those daily obtruding models of beauty in architecture'. However, 'Though late, yet the taste has at length arisen, and is fast spreading.' There might still be lapses, and the writer drew attention to the castellated Gothic St George's Episcopal Chapel in York Place. Ironically, this had been designed by none other than James Adam. Even a good classic might fall from grace. But, generally speaking, a corner had been turned.[147]

> Every day which improves on our existing designs, or which adds new specimens from a pure source, raises a fresh barrier against the deterioration of the public taste ... We do not imagine it possible that such a work, for example, as the Tron Church, or Gillespie's Hospital, should ever again be erected; and we are quite sure, that the day which shall place the Parthenon on Calton Hill will remove the possibility to a more impracticable distance ... The cultivated taste ... will in chusing and dwelling on what is good, reject what is faulty. But such styles mislead the vulgar and uneducated, who are incapable of discriminating ...[148]

Taste was not 'an expensive commodity'. It was founded on and displayed in 'design and proportion; not in ornament, nor in bulk, nor in complication ... No power of fillagree [*sic*] will ever render an ill-designed building beautiful ...'[149]

In a moment of unexpected tolerance of what the past had bequeathed the present in the form of some Gothic 'horrors' both old and relatively new, the author did not want to see all destroyed. 'Far from it ... in this strangely wild and romantic city, architectural works not only admit, but demand variety.'[150] A few pages later he returned to this point: Edinburgh was fortunate in its

> romantic and fairy-like scenery and disposition ... Europe produces no situation so calculated for the display, and for the advantageous display, of every species of architecture ... We have ... the splendid advantages of an outline on the sky ... Our buildings form parts of our landscape ...

But henceforth the style was to be—or should be—Greek, with the Parthenon showing the way:

> ... we are confident, that after this building shall have been twenty years displayed, no architect, not even a stone mason, will repeat, even in Gothic architecture, such things as we now see every where risen, and, we fear, still rising about us.[151]

Uses, principal or subsidiary, for the National Monument were discussed, including its possible 'Pantheon' function as national shrine to greatness. Interestingly, the writer showed himself open to the use of glass in the building, either as windows or in glazed roofing. 'We may worship antiquity as we please ... But we are not called on to worship and copy its defects; to deprive ourselves of the advantages we have gained over the ancients ...'[152]

At approximately the mid-point of this fascinating essay the author caught his breath, taking a moment to remind both himself and his readers that, no matter how 'Athenian' they might wish to feel, they were still Scots.

> The self same sun that shines on Athens looks bright alike on us. The Acropolis, like the Calton Hill, has its days of darkness and of light, of brilliant suns and gloomy rains, of azure calm, and livid tempest ... yet what can Italy or Greece produce in natural scenery, which our own lovely country does not rival? Must we shut our eyes to the splendour and beauty of Loch Lomond, in its days of brightness, because its skies have not been dipped in the hues of Claude, because its azure is less blue than that of Attica, because every morning does not rise with the clearness of the diamond, and every evening does not set in crimson and gold?[153]

On this elegiac note, the writer returns to the Edinburgh Parthenon. If anything were to endure wind, water, the cycles of nature and even the march of geological time, this truly would last.

> If there be any class of refined architecture calculated for duration, assuredly it is the simple and steady Doric. How else has the Attic Parthenon itself withstood for so long the ravages of time and barbarism united; and whence Pæstum, still surviving to teach us what Greece could do? When all our Gothic temples shall have vanished into dust and thin air, the columns, even of our own Parthenon, shall rear their heads to the sky ...[154]

In copying the finest building of antiquity, the Modern Athenians would be able 'to place it in a situation more nearly corresponding to that of the original than could have been hoped for; a situation not to be paralleled in Britain.' The place that the Edinburgh Greeks had chosen for '[their] own copy' of the Parthenon was (as others had also said) very possibly superior to that of the original. Picturesque considerations were paramount. Edinburgh satisfied all desires, and every requirement.

> The Calton Hill is a splendid architectural landscape even now; and with the proposed addition, it will display a combination of natural and artificial forms, of dark rock, and cliff, and of buildings adapted to these several lines and masses ... It is the peculiar boast of Edinburgh, that ... nature has done every thing, has laid every foundation, and disposed of every line of its rocks and its hills, as if she had designed it for the display of architecture. It will also be the boast of our Parthenon, that while it is the eye and centre of one of the noblest architectural landscapes of Europe, it will be every where supported by forms which will give to it additional importance and additional picturesque effect

... Its character... will ever be the soul of the scene, that to which all bow ... it will still rise in virgin majesty and beauty, the queen of all ... and could but the spirits of Pericles and Phidias look down on us, they would hail the day, and rejoice in the taste and energy that has revived their works, and, from the dust and ashes of their falling monuments, raised another phœnix to prolong their memory and their fame to new and far distant centuries.[155]

It is a great pity that we do not know who among the Modern Athenians had time to write all this. When David Brewster told Cockerell that both the *Edinburgh Review* piece (by Alison, as we know) and this *New Edinburgh Review* article were to be out in a few days, he failed to name the author of either.[156] Presumably he himself was in the dark. Briefless advocate of literary inclination? Cultivated gentleman of private means? Scholarly clergyman in a comfortable parish? Sinecure-holder with time on his hands? For there was yet more to come. In the passage below, the Edinburgh Parthenon was eulogised as if it were already in glorious existence.

Again, if we look on the Parthenon as the prime and the fundamental feature of the great architectural landscape ... or general composition of our wild and wonderful city ... not another position could be found where its value would be so great ... If the splendid regularity of its noble colonnades gives the tone to that Grecian architecture which rises near to it, or which is indicated in the long lines of the New Town ... not less is its value, as embellishing, by contrast, the long and wild ridge as it sweeps up in one commanding and simple, yet varied line, from the palace ... to the solid and strong, yet picturesque mass of our *ancient* Acropolis [the Castle] ... Here also, like the Attic Temple, our own Parthenon looks down in proud majesty on the humbler crowd of our domestic buildings beneath, their guardian and their citadel ...[157]

This led on to the crucial question of what might happen if the great project failed to materialise or, having done so, then failed to progress to conclusion. The *New Edinburgh Review* author's words were prophetic. The 'leading and high reasons' for the choice of the Doric temple had been given. He was not now ashamed to speak of 'the sinews of architecture', namely 'money and stone'; for 'without these we may draw, dispute, and visit Athens, and invoke the genius of Greece in vain.' The danger was that, if the campaign for the National Monument were badly funded, or the building's ultimate purpose too multifarious, confused and complicated, then Edinburgh might well see again what had once been witnessed with the new University buildings: 'a premature ruin ... possibly [to] remain such for ever.'[158] With the simple proposal for a Parthenon replica, 'we are certain of attaining beauty, when the building is completed...'. With any other scheme, 'both events are uncertain'. Should the project fail, 'not only it cannot be repeated, but it will stand the eternal monument of our rashness and our ignorance'.[159]

It is, perhaps, worth remarking that in all the literature of the day, whether in print or unpublished personal communication, no one at the time thought to quote the New Testament. These were all people who knew and read their Scripture, and Alison, for one, was the son of an eminent divine. In the Gospel according to St Luke were to be found other prophetic words, apposite to the story of the National Monument:

> For which of you, intending to build a tower, sitteth not down first, and counteth the cost, whether he have sufficient to finish it? Lest haply, after he hath laid the foundation, and is not able to finish it, all that behold it begin to mock him, Saying, This man began to build, and was not able to finish.[160]

It was only the anonymous author of *Edinburgh Dissected*, published in 1857, who made allusion to this passage when he suggested that the unfinished National Monument stood 'as a practical commentary on Luke xiv, 28, 29, and 30...'.[161]

There never was, nor probably ever could have been, any serious intention 'to restore the sculptures of the Parthenon'. On this the *New Edinburgh Review* writer was adamant, adding (conveniently for the Edinburgh proponents of the building's 'transfer') that the sculptures of the original are 'incidental and supererogatory'.[162] The issue of the sculpture was a diversion from the essentials of structure and setting, though an interesting little aside is insinuated into the concluding passages of the article. Lord Elgin, of course, is the unnamed hero.

> It is to Scotland that London is now indebted for the possession of the inestimable sculptures of the Parthenon. A moment of activity, happily exerted by a much and unjustly calumniated individual, (himself, we are proud to add, one of the most strenuous friends to this restoration,) rescued from impending loss or destruction that which the entire world may never equal, and which nothing could replace. It remains for Scotland to complete its work by renewing what it cannot transport; and it will be to its eternal honour, that, by its own exertions, it has preserved all that could be preserved of a work that was the pride of Greece in its best of days ...[163]

Another anomaly was, of course, the materials to be used. The writer was curt in dismissing any protest on this score. 'To say that a sandstone temple is not a restoration of a work in marble, is a quibble which does not deserve notice.'[164] The fact is that, as we know, Greek temples in Magna Graecia—in Sicily and Southern Italy—had been built of local limestone because marble was not available; temples in Greece itself, before the earlier fifth century BC, had likewise been built of local stone.[165] Thus, for the Modern Athenians to have set out to erect a temple in Edinburgh using local sandstone of very high quality was not actually wholly inappropriate. The problem arises, however, when that temple is supposed to be a *facsimile* of the marble Parthenon. Then one would imagine that marble was the only possible material, and that not to use it would be an unacceptable solecism.

As his huge paper neared its conclusion, it seems appropriate that the writer should admit that it was all 'a war of words'. There was little more to add. 'A Greek temple in Edinburgh' might once have been 'as incongruous as a Greek sentence in an English oration'.

> We shall yet see the Parthenon on our own,—its own hill. As the smoke flies off before the blasts of our wonderful city, glorious in its romantic and various beauties, discovering even now architecture of which we may well be proud, so shall these objections, shapeless and bodyless as the breeze, and fuliginous as the dingy clouds, vanish and roll away; while the Doric temple shall shine out in proud contempt, lifting to the clear sky its virgin graces, unveiled in its original glory, guardian and queen of the fairest of cities.[166]

*   *   *   *   *

George Cleghorn, the author of a substantial pamphlet published anonymously in 1824, had two main aims. One was to argue for the adoption of the Parthenon scheme. The other was to oppose the suggestion (then enjoying some favour) that a National Monument, whether in classical or other dress, should take the form and assume the function of a Christian church, very possibly having 'catacombs' or burial vaults within its stylobate (supporting platform). The cause and the quibble were to remain in the forefront of Cleghorn's mind for the next twenty-five years, and through four subsequent publications. There were still those who favoured a church alone: one either with a non-Greek design, or else a facsimile Parthenon temple-monument adapted in some way to an ecclesiastical purpose. The building Cleghorn wanted was one uncompromised in its essential Greek purity, and he was vehement in his opposition to any debasement.[167] Indeed, he continued to voice his opposition to the Parthenon-cum-church idea—the essential stumbling block to any revivified scheme—when he brought out an equally substantial diatribe as another large pamphlet in 1846. Abandoning anonymity, he lent his name to this second publication.[168]

But, in 1824, Cleghorn raised objections to the idea that any windows of modern type, wholly alien to the tradition of classical Greek architecture, could be tolerated as a way of combining the ancient temple form with modern liturgical requirements.

> Double rows of capacious modern windows staring through the colonnade, would completely destroy the illusion of a building having any pretensions to a Grecian temple ... in a professed restoration of the purest and most splendid example of Athenian art in the age of Pericles, the exclusion seems absolutely imperative. Should, they, however, be admitted, in defiance of all consistency and good taste, it would be nearly as absurd to call it a *fac simile* of the Athenian Temple, as to proclaim St Andrew's Church, (George Street, Edinburgh) a restoration of the Pantheon of Rome, of which, indeed, it is a kind of ludicrous caricature.'[169]

Cleghorn would, presumably, have been displeased to see Playfair give his Royal Institution sash-and-case windows between the columns of the peristyle. These were certainly practical for a working, nineteenth-century building, and a sensible compromise between archaeological accuracy and modern utility; but they were hardly 'Parthenon-proper'.

C. R. Cockerell had written of the ancient Greek temple as 'a vast historical gallery recording every event which could flatter the recollection or stimulate emulation'.[170] (Fig. 62) He had disciples in Edinburgh who shared this view, but not very many, and even the most ardent of them recognised the financial impracticalities. Unlike some other contemporaries, Cleghorn was adamant that a vital element of the ancient temple 'facsimile' was missing. He wanted the Edinburgh Parthenon to bear sculpture—albeit sculpture in a modern idiom—that would accord with an integral part of its ancient prototype.

> Deprived of sculptural decoration, the National Monument might be a handsome Doric Temple—it could have no pretensions to be styled a restoration of the Athenian Parthenon. A body without a soul; it would be a mere model or framework, void of meaning or expression.[171]

In his next publication, Cleghorn would write of sculptural decoration as 'an essential attribute of the highest style of Grecian architecture'. For this 'splendid feature' the ancient Parthenon 'stood proudly pre-eminent'.[172] The Edinburgh 'restoration' must emulate the original in this respect.

A few years later Cleghorn would turn again to the question of sculpture, a taste for which was rapidly increasing in Scotland; a native school with many distinguished practitioners had emerged to satisfy the demand. But to have a theoretical and aesthetic taste for sculpture was easier than actually achieving tangible results. Cleghorn gave eloquent expression to the dilemma.

If our modern Athens do [*sic*] not soon rival her ancient prototype in monumental statuary, it is not for want of monument-voting meetings, speeches, resolutions, subscription lists, committees, and titled names to grace them. Novelty is the all-powerful ingredient in the patronage of the day. At a meeting for a new statue or monument, the speeches breathe nothing but fire and enthusiasm. The most magnanimous resolutions are passed by acclamation. Yet a little while, and all subsides into the most perfect indifference and imperturbable repose. No sooner is the first burst of excitement over, than the tide turns in the direction of some new object; and then, as well might we hope to bind the ocean with chains as attempt to lead the current back to its former channel.[173]

*   *   *   *   *

In his speech at the founding of the National Monument in 1822, the Duke of Hamilton, Grand Master Mason of Scotland, declared his hope and belief that the building might herald a new dawn made bright by emulation of ancient Athenian virtues. Edinburgh's temple was to be

similar to one raised at Athens in the pure age of Grecian refinement ... Worthy it is of Scotsmen to imitate such a model. The sons of Caledonia ... have ever possessed the patriotic valour of the ancient Greeks. Having rivalled them in the field, let them now emulate their eminence in the arts; and let this monument ... become the model of Scottish taste.[174]

The rash of pamphleteering and review-writing, for and against the construction of a Parthenon facsimile, was followed by two or three fallow years before any Doric column rose on Calton Hill. In the interim, the popular literature filled this temporal void, emphasising the similarity of the hill to the Acropolis of Athens and informing the reader that the Parthenon ('this boasted relic of ancient art') was to be restored or rather 'renewed' there. It was said that, along with Hugh William Williams's drawings of the original location, a model of the temple by 'Mr Reid, architect' (who had visited the original building) had 'probably contributed to infuse a taste for the Doric grandeur of the Grecian architecture'.[175]

As has been stated already, very few in Edinburgh—either professional architects or merely self-appointed leaders of taste—had actually seen a Greek temple. But interest was undoubtedly abroad in the city, or was shared by Scots in London. Many began to think themselves architects, or to consider that they could deal with architects almost on an equal footing. In the same month as he published his attack on the Greek pretensions of the Modern Athens, Francis Cohen wrote a remarkable letter of gratuitous advice to Cockerell, who was then emerging as front-runner for the commission to design the Edinburgh Parthenon. Both men were London-based. It is not clear whether Cohen ever visited Edinburgh; but Cockerell was just about to set out for an initial visit to the city to meet the proponents of the Monument and to discuss its style and location.

> ... with your knowledge of the spirit of Grecian architecture you cannot fail to convince 'the Committee' [for the building of the National Monument] of the inexpediency of this scheme ... act boldly—convince the committee that you know more about Grecian architecture than any man in Europe—and then—maul them—pound them—baste them—until they adopt your real opinions—Recollect that you have now an opportunity of rising far—above the puerile school of mere copyists and of showing that you are not Mr *** or Mr **** or Mr ***** or any of the other *portfolio* men—Do not compromise—you will neither gain solid pudding nor empty praises ...[176]

When Cockerell had been appointed joint architect (with Playfair) for the Edinburgh Parthenon, Captain Basil Hall, RN, wrote to him thus:

> This [letter] will be given to you by my brother Mr James Hall, who is very desirous of having the pleasure of your acquaintance. He has all along taken a great interest in our Great Parthenon question, & was one of those who rejoiced most sincerely at your first appointment with Mr Playfair... My brother has not been in Greece, but he has studied the magnificent edifices at Pæstum and in Sicily, & is naturally desirous of comparing notes with one so eminently qualified to furnish him with new matter as you are; & in order that he may not put you to such trouble without offering some return, I have recommended him to carry one or two of his sketchbooks with him.[177]

James Hall, a young advocate who became a gentleman painter, had indeed captured excellently, on the pages of his tiny sketchbooks, the huge temples of Paestum, Segesta, Selinunte and Agrigento.[178] (Figs 26-28) 'The sensation produced by seeing the Temple of Neptune [as he termed the so-called Temple of Poseidon at Paestum] is equal to the aggregate of all previous sensations produced by objects of the same sort.' This one temple, 'the noblest work of man', was 'literally worth all the buildings of Italy ... put together'. With a nod to the philosophers of the Scottish Enlightenment, he went on to write that 'It is a perfect union of beauty and grandeur which the metaphysicians pretend to separate as inconsistent.'[179] Even when he saw the temples of Selinunte and Segesta in Sicily, he still thought that those of Paestum remained the ideal: 'the first of human works ... unquestionably the finest objects I shall ever see on earth.'[180] To indicate the vast scale of buildings such as these, Hall drew one of his travelling companions, Adam Paterson, standing against a drum of an unfinished column the Sicilian quarry where it had been hewn, or sitting on a fragment of fluting from the top of a shattered column shaft at Agrigento; James Veitch was sketched lying full-length in a groove of a huge triglyph block of the Temple of Olympian Zeus at the same site.[181] (Figs 23-25) When Sir Walter Scott saw the temples of Paestum in 1832, he described them as

> pillars to which any that ever I saw are like pipe staples [clay tobacco pipe stems] in point of size and scarce any other wise imperfect than in being roofless ... nothing I have yet seen have so much reality about them.

He must have felt they mocked the all-too modest Greek Revival buildings of his own Athens of the North.[182]

* * * * *

Cockerell had spent some considerable time in Greece, and his familiarity with Greek architecture was unrivalled in his day. His eventual appointment as architect of the Edinburgh Parthenon—jointly with Playfair as local, executant colleague—was generally welcomed in the Modern Athens. Yet it was clear from an early stage that there was a predisposition in Edinburgh to see a 'Scotch architect' somehow involved.[183] Those effectively commissioning the National Monument, or otherwise interesting themselves in its progress, conveyed their hopes and expectations in a particularly interesting series of letters. Frequently, parallels between antiquity and the present, and between Athens and Edinburgh, were noted and exploited.

Sir Robert Liston had served in Constantinople as British minister-plenipotentiary to the Sublime Porte from 1811 to 1820, after an earlier period in that office in the 1790s. He had travelled widely in the Aegean, and visited Athens in 1815. In retirement he lived at Millburn Tower, near Gogar, to the west of Edinburgh. In due course, Liston became a Director of the Royal Association of Contributors to the National Monument. His excitement at what was proposed for the Calton Hill bubbled over in a letter to Cockerell.

> I hope to live to see the work begun, perhaps to watch the gradual rise of the edifice, and to receive frequent visits from the Superintendent General, who will wish to observe the effect of this beautiful erection at a distance, for you know the front [of the National Monument] points directly towards this cottage [Millburn Tower].[184]

Much concern had been shown by the Modern Athenians about the prominence the Calton Hill site would give their Parthenon, and much knowledge was exhibited about ancient Greek preferences for the placing of their temples in locations where the buildings could be seen and appreciated from a distance. Cockerell himself had used as an epigraph to his notes on Greek temples a passage from Xenophon's *Memorabilia*, where Socrates says that temples should be visible from afar, yet built in locations that were peaceful, untrodden and undefiled.[185] The Calton was just such a site, isolated from the smoke of the city, and still a place of comparative rural peace and solitude.

Dr Archibald Alison the elder, episcopalian clergyman father of the ardent Modern Athenian, was among the first to give his views to Cockerell. Alison was interested in aesthetics, and was author of the well-regarded *Essays on the Nature and Principles of Taste* which has appeared as long ago as 1790. Now he hoped for 'the cordial cooperation of the Genius both of England and Scotland in renovating a work which was originally formed by the united efforts of Grecian talents.' And he spoke thus for all his fellow supporters of the project:

> They know that the jealousies which occasionally subsist between Artists of an inferior class are unknown to those who are at the head of their profession; and they cannot anticipate from the Gentlemen in this Island who have attained that eminence, a less degree of unanimity than prevailed among the Architects of the age of Pericles.[186]

Basil Hall wrote to Cockerell the same day. He imagined Cockerell and Playfair 'like Phidias & Callicrates'. There could not be any doubt that

> with your extensive & accurate knowledge of all the details of this wonderful building, & with Mr Playfair's skill, taste, & talents, the work will be accomplished in a manner to immortalise both. This is the universal feeling in this City ... greater than anything which has occurred for many years ... all is confidence and hope, when there is no longer a shadow of doubt respecting the masterly manner in which this most magnificent work will be planned & executed.

In praising Playfair, Hall continued:

> He is well aware of the immense advantage which you possess over all other men in having lived so long within the atmosphere of the Acropolis of Athens & in having profitted [sic] by your opportunities to lay in a stock of knowledge which will enable the present generation to rival that of Pericles. He [Playfair] is a man of great taste, & has an intimate knowledge of Grecian Architecture—with the most devoted feeling towards this grand restoration. As a practical man he has no equal, & at this moment his building on the

Mound [the Royal Institution] is literally astonishing the Town, & I have remarked a very general feeling gradually rising even amongst moderately informed men, in favour of Grecian Architecture, in proportion as these Columns of Playfair's have risen—what will it not be when your united efforts shall have given regeneration to the Parthenon![187]

Playfair himself expressed to his new colleague his assurance that in

the Restoration of the Parthenon ... there would exist but one feeling between us; a feeling of anxiety to restore that noble work in all its purity, and to realize the great expectations which have been justly formed of the Beauty of its appearance ... The Directors wish to raise up an exact resemblance of the Parthenon of Athens ... and ... I in no instance shall interfere with the spirit and the meaning of the Original Building.[188]

Basil Hall was never shy of testifying to Playfair's abilities. It was impossible to believe, he assured Cockerell, that

the work could have fallen into better hands than his; for he is not only intimately versed with the Grecian Architecture, as an elegant study—but he has for some years been practically engaged in adapting it to the purposes of modern edifices ... No architect on the spot has so accurate a knowledge of all the details of building ... this noble work, which he is as well convinced as you, & all of us are, must be an exact fac-simile of the original—at least in all the external features, whatever internal arrangements may be agreed to. This earnest feeling about not improving on Phidias is no trifling consideration ...[189]

*   *   *   *   *

The area at the foot of The Mound (the erstwhile 'Earthen Mound', that massive, artificial ramp and causeway connecting the Old and New Towns) was also invested with a quasi-Greek identity. When the English visitor the Revd Dr Thomas Frognall Dibdin wrote, in 1838, of 'the Parthenon' in Edinburgh, he did not mean the unfinished temple upon Calton Hill. Rather it was the Royal Institution, or what he calls 'the *Museum* and *Academy of Painting*'. This was 'the Parthenon of Mr Playfair ... a stone building of remarkable brilliancy of component parts—encrusted with exterior ornaments ...'. Dibdin admired this, but thought it wrongly sited: 'It should not be at the bottom, but at the top, of a hill.'[190] Returning to this building again later, Dibdin commented further on its style and situation. It is ironic that Playfair's Royal Institution, built originally between 1822 and 1826, but greatly increased in size and splendour between 1831 and 1836, should have been so greatly lengthened just before Dibdin criticized it for being *too* long.

> In Grecian and Roman architecture, a love of taste, and yet more of truth, induces me to place Mr Playfair at the head, simply because he has not only had the *opportunity* of doing great things, but of doing them *well* ... His Academy of Painting, &c. is doubtless his masterpiece; but for just proportion it should lose one fourth of its length. Necessity alone compelled its elongation to the present extent. Placed upon Calton Hill, for picturesque effect, this building would kindle emotions as if we were contemplating another Parthenon.[191]

Dibdin had apparently discussed the Institution's siting with Playfair himself. The architect agreed that the building would be better and more effectively positioned if on an eminence; 'but the centrality of the situation', concluded Dibdin, 'was doubtless the chief inducement: or I could have wished it to occupy the "Place of Tombs"'—namely the Calton Hill.[192] Dibdin's opinion was shared by James Fergusson, the distinguished Victorian historian of architecture, and a former pupil of the High School of Edinburgh, who thought that the Royal Institution was too low-set. If sited on Calton Hill, it would be superb: 'one of the most faultless of modern buildings.'[193]

It is odd that Dibdin should make no reference to the National Monument. It is as if he were advocating not one but two Parthenons for the Athens of the North—just as there has been some doubt whether there was one 'acropolis' or two, depending on how the commentator viewed the Castle Rock vis-à-vis the Calton Hill. This would have given the city something of the character of, perhaps, ancient Akragas (Agrigento, in Sicily) with its many-templed temenos, or indeed Paestum, which had so impressed young James Hall and Sir Walter Scott. As things were, however, Dibdin's praise of what Playfair had achieved in his Royal Institution marks a shift in where the heart of 'Greek' Edinburgh was perceived to lie: a change of focus from Calton Hill to The Mound. The northern end of The Mound thus became, partly in the imagination of the Modern Athenians, but also in the reality of stone and lime, a rival centre of 'Greekness'. Perhaps it can be regarded as a sort of low-lying *agora* in contrast to the Calton *acropolis*.[194]

In 1822 the idea of building a new High School in this area of the city was advanced, in what the pamphleteer ('Scotus') called a 'centrical situation'. This proposed site was also at the lower end of The Mound, but extending eastwards from the junction of Hanover Street and Princes Street.[195] At the same time, and in the same connection, there was a fleeting idea that the National Monument itself, in its Parthenon guise—not yet even founded, of course—might occupy the site at the junction of The Mound with Princes Street, precisely where the Royal Institution was, in fact, to be constructed. The evidence is somewhat difficult to interpret and, it appears, easy to misinterpret.[196] The pseudonymous author's argument ran as follows.

A model of the Parthenon of Athens is the favoured plan of a monument to be a depository for memorials of departed genius and worth among our countrymen. Be it so. But let the fabric be connected with, and rendered beneficial to the youth of the country. With reference to any class of *men* among us, such a monument is an unmeaning bauble. The character of the present generation ... is fixed irrevocably by the events which have passed away [i.e., the late war]; and if the object of those who wish a national monument, be to stamp on their countrymen to remote posterity the most enduring impressions of patriotism, it is on those whose young spirits are still unmoulded and untarnished in the arena of life that the charm must operate. To combine the splendour of classic, with the glories of our own times, in the young and ardent associations of our sons, by converting the Parthenon of Athens into the great hall of our national academy [the High School]— adorned on every side with statues ... of... lights in the land, either gone or not yet faded away—would be an arrangement which ought to reconcile the views of all parties ... It is proposed, therefore, not as an indispensable part of any plan for removing the High School to the only open space in the midst of the city, but as a subject for consideration, that the great hall or National Monument be placed near the north end of the Earthen Mound ... In that situation it would be visible from a great many parts, and over a considerable extent of the Old and New Town: it ... would give, in the very bosom of the city, a character more truly Attic to our metropolis than any other edifice which it contains.[197]

The actual classrooms of the High School might be disposed to the south and east of the Parthenon-like centrepiece, the whole complex to be 'designed on the purest Grecian models'.[198]

It is a droll thought that a city Carr and Wraxall had said could never finish its buildings should have effectively built, and then a decade later *rebuilt*, the Royal Institution. As time went on, it would be paired with Playfair's National Gallery, erected on a site immediately to its south. The foundation stone of the National Gallery was laid in 1850 and the building was completed in 1854; this structure was in fact to accommodate both the new National Gallery and the Royal Scottish Academy, each organisation having one longitudinal suite of galleries and subordinate spaces, ingeniously and conveniently arranged. The design, as finally realised, was perhaps less convincingly 'Greek' than one of Playfair's earlier proposals. It pleased Henry Cockburn, however. Always a great admirer of Playfair, whose taste (he said) was 'the just pride of the city', Cockburn confessed he would really have preferred The Mound to have been left unencumbered, free of all building. But Playfair's 'beautiful design for a Gallery' was as good as it could be, both in itself and for its site. Having evidently had an early glimpse of an intermediate-stage drawing in the summer of 1849, the effervescent Cockburn wrote of how 'that long, low, elegant, colonade [*sic*] makes my very Middriff quiver with delight'.[199] Architecture in the Modern Athens had a visceral hold on its devotees!

The balustrades crowning the cornice of the finished National Gallery are, of course, wholly un-Greek, as are the high attics designed to conceal the skylights: these features alone are indicative of just how much the buildings of the Modern Athens are free translations—sometimes very free translations— of ancient forms and exemplars. Several other, even less-Greek elements and details were omitted or trimmed-back in an effort to cut costs to assuage a concerned Treasury, ironically thus rendering the finished building more austere and therefore *more* 'Greek' than the architect had actually intended.[200]

Playfair's elegant 1848 perspective view of his existing Royal Institution and his proposed new National Gallery to its south (the latter delineated in a form much more in keeping with the ethos of the Modern Athens) sets the two buildings in a landscape that could almost be in Greece. (Fig. 86) The colouring of the drawing helps greatly in this respect, for the tonality might well be that of a 'Grecian' Williams watercolour of twenty years earlier. The foreground, and the repoussoir on either hand, are occupied by mixed woodland, including cypress trees, giving a very Mediterranean or Ionian feeling to the scene. The proposed National Gallery is shown as a severely Doric stoa, much less elaborately and fussily ornamented than the Royal Institution. The treatment of the roof is convincingly Greek. The east elevation is starkly plain: paired pilasters set at fairly wide intervals provide the only relief on an otherwise long, blank wall. In later designs, enlivenment in the form of pedimented Doric porticoes, tetrastyle at north and south ends and hexastyle on the long east and west elevations, were introduced, breaking forward from the rectangular 'box'. Subsequently translated into Ionic, these were the features eventually agreed for the building. Playfair's initial idea would have provided a better foil for the Royal Institution even than his eventual design would do; and, of course, its order would have maintained a consistent Doric theme rather than exhibiting the slightly jarring change to Ionic that the National Gallery, as built, actually offers. This single drawing by Playfair is one of the most effective images of 'the Athens of the North' ever conceived.

Much more elaborate, but constituting a truly splendid potential contribution to the cultural 'temenos' at The Mound, was Thomas Hamilton's proposal of 1848 for the same site: a new National Gallery and a Royal Scottish Academy as twin buildings conceived as a pair of Doric stoas of highly elaborate form and exhibiting a profusion of freestanding sculptural ornament. (Fig. 87) They were to have north-facing hexastyle porticoes of the order of the Theseion, beyond which the vestibules were to have cupolas internally supported on eight caryatids. At the southern end of the eastmost of Hamilton's two stoas would have risen an octagonal structure, ultimately derived from the Tower of the Winds in Athens.[201] If one had looked south-west from a very low viewpoint beside the railway line in Princes Street gardens, over Hamilton's proposed galleries and up across The Mound towards the Castle, the prospect before one would have evoked in no small measure that of the perspective view in Stuart and Revett, showing the Acropolis with the Tower of the Winds in the foreground.[202] (Figs 89 and 10)

Hamilton was justly proud of his scheme, exhibiting the drawings in Paris.[203] He also published (in Edinburgh) full details of his proposed buildings as explanatory text to accompany a group of plans, elevations and most effective perspective views, both close and more distant, these being reproduced by the eminent lithographer Friedrich Schenck. (Fig. 88) To justify his approach to the project, Hamilton quoted C. R. Cockerell who (as he said) had observed: 'We are of Classic tutelage, and the style of Greece and Rome would best meet modern requirements.' Hamilton gave it as his own opinion that, in an art-gallery, 'the structure should embody the spirit of the actual times as well as that of antiquity.'[204] As a whole, Hamilton's scheme has been assessed as perhaps the most carefully developed and most complete architectural expression of the concept of a Modern Athens; the designs themselves described as Hamilton's 'stylophilous dreams', and as more rigorously Athenian than Playfair's actual achievements at The Mound.[205] Again, the tonalities of the exhibition watercolour are suggestive of Greece.

*   *   *   *   *

No major building in 'Greek' Edinburgh was actually, or perhaps could be, a direct copy of an ancient Greek original.[206] Cockerell recognised this even with respect to the so-called 'facsimile' of the Parthenon. William Burn had actually suggested to him a Parthenon 'on a reduced plan', or even some 'less expensive Greek edifice' as a 'model' for the National Monument.[207] Writing to Archibald Alison the elder in 1825, Cockerell confessed that the *model* of the Parthenon was all very well, but it had to be adapted for modern and specific purposes. Success depended upon 'the felicity of this adaptation' and that determined the very 'wisdom of the building'.[208] Keen though he was on a Parthenon exactly 'restored', even George Cleghorn admitted that some concessions might have to be made. In considering 'revived' Greek architecture in general terms, Cleghorn made the distinction between the 'pure Greek'—such as a 'restored' Parthenon would ideally represent—and what he termed 'mixed Greek … adapted to a certain degree to modern edifices'. In doing so, he gave the example of Hamilton's High School in Edinburgh and, rather further afield, of the Munich Glyptothek by Leo von Klenze, and the 'the Berlin Museum' (the Altes Museum) by Karl Friedrich Schinkel.[209] Cleghorn was a great admirer of contemporary architecture in Germany, and of the work of these two masters in particular.[210] The essence of his own Modern Athens in stone was the skill with which its

Scottish architects could devise free translations of admired originals, and so produce something strikingly new and original in their own way.

Cleghorn's two monographs, and a further long article, are important sources for the history of ideas about how the National Monument should have developed or might still be brought to fruition. But even more than his substantial pamphlets are Cleghorn's volumes of general essays on art and architecture significant in the wider story of the developing idea of a Greek Edinburgh. Cleghorn saw the city as a place with a distinctive architectural ethos distinguishing it from architectural developments in London, and as a centre displaying more in common with contemporary Europe. In an essay on Modern English Architecture, Cleghorn compared and contrasted developments in the revival of Greek architecture in England (by which he effectively meant London) with the 'modern and practical restoration' which he noted was happening in Europe and to some extent in Scotland.[211] 'The beauty and superiority of Grecian architecture', Cleghorn suggested in 1837, 'have formed the constant theme of all our modern English architects and writers on architecture.' He continued:

> It has been extolled—and not without reason—as the perfection of the art. With all this abstract taste for, and speculative admiration of pure unadulterated Grecian architecture, it might naturally have been expected that they [the architects of England] would make some attempts to imitate or restore its models, or at least to approximate as nearly as possible to their style and composition.[212]

Here Cleghorn insinuated a passage and a note that brought the reader face-to-face with the author's major and almost obsessional concern:

> One solitary case in Scotland excepted, [here the footnote indicates that this is 'The Restoration of the Parthenon of Athens as the National Monument of Scotland'] which has failed only for want of funds, no attempt worthy of the name has been made in Great Britain. The classic taste of our architects, dilettanti, and writers on the art, is confined to theory, books, and portfolio designs—evaporates in antiquarian research, hypercritical disquisition, barren eulogy, and empty declamation. Their Grecian practice extends no further than the substitution of the Grecian Doric and Ionic, for the Roman and Italian orders of the same name, in detached porticos, porches, and parasitical decoration. This far, and no farther, has their boasted Grecian style advanced.[213]

Cleghorn looked to and wrote of what was happening abroad; but in doing so he made it abundantly, if subtly (albeit repetitiously) clear that Scotland thought and built Greek in a purer and more authentic way than England:

What a contrast do all these afford to modern British architecture and British art! While our English architects, architectural writers, and their dilettanti patrons, have ... been indulging in abstract and barren speculations, on the perfection of and superiority of Grecian architecture, which they never dream of reducing to practice ... the great continental nations have been quietly and steadily improving their taste, and raising magnificent and lasting monuments of architecture ...[214]

In a later, revised version of this passage, Cleghorn strengthened his rhetoric in condemning architects for failing truly to emulate Greek prototypes 'except in detached portions and on a pitiful scale'.[215] Almost repeating himself once more, Cleghorn had written that:

The beauty and perfection of Grecian architecture are universally admitted, even by those who are opposed to its modern restoration ... In Scotland we have made the attempt, and, indeed, have partly succeeded. Nor can it be denied, that there exists among our architects, as well as amateurs, an earnest desire, as far as circumstances permit, to restore the Grecian in a few select public structures, not merely in its orders and component parts, as porticos, &c., but in its genuine purity of composition and massive construction. Let those who doubt the truth of this assertion view the classic works of Playfair, Hamilton, and Burns [*sic*].[216]

Whereas what he termed the 'Anglo-Greek' was in his judgment 'incapable of conveying even a glimpse' of this true, revived style and feeling, Scotland might build upon the foundations of taste and skill already laid:

Restorations of a few of the most celebrated temples of antiquity, executed in a style of national grandeur and magnificence in their exteriors and interiors, and decorated with statuary and painting, would call forth the admiration of all men of taste and refinement; and by enabling the community to appreciate the beauty and majesty of Grecian architecture ... would be the most powerful means of fixing and improving the national taste, and preparing the way for new and successful modifications of existing styles.[217]

Cleghorn greatly admired and commented favourably and perceptively on two buildings in particular of the Modern Athens. Writing first of the Royal Institution, he could not do otherwise than admit that it was unfortunately placed in 'a hollow' and thus overlooked from all quarters. But he also explained that it was to have formed part of a much larger and grander complex of buildings at The Mound, comprising shopping arcades and galleries almost like a modern 'mall'. Cleghorn actually called it a 'bazaar', and noted that it was to have a Doric screen thus linking it stylistically to the Institution.[218] From Playfair's drawings we can see how elegant this would have been.[219] With its double ranges of shops, contemporaries compared the idea to the Burlington Arcade, off Piccadilly in London.[220] It was one of several schemes for the development of The Mound, any or all of which would have made a great contribution to the area as an urban focus and as a linking complex of real and coherent architectural distinction between the Old and New Towns. Cleghorn was especially enthusiastic about Playfair's enlargement and recasting of his original Royal Institution building. 'Instead of being, as formerly, a heavy and anomalous imitation of a Greek temple, it is now, as if by magic, transformed into a rich and magnificent composition of Greek columnar architecture.' The projecting porticoes 'give the appearance of a continued peristyle to the flanks'. This successful modification reflected great credit on the architect: 'it will hence forth from one of the most striking and splendid architectural ornaments of our city.'[221] (Figs. 60-61)

Even greater praise was reserved for Hamilton's High School. Cleghorn's appreciation and understanding of the subtleties and 'Athenian' resonances of this magnificent building are notable. He considered it 'a fine specimen of classical taste, as well as original composition, affording a good illustration of the successful application of a modified Grecian to a modern structure.' The disparate elements were 'in perfect harmony with each other', and the whole was well adapted to the site. 'All the parts are so judiciously disposed as not to distract the eye, but to produce the effect of one united whole, varied in its picturesque grouping as the spectator changes his position.' In a telling comparison of the school buildings with the arrangement of the Propylaea in relation to the Parthenon and the rest of the Acropolis structures, Cleghorn perceptively teased out the essential subtleties of Hamilton's overall design: what he called 'picturesque variety in the grouping of the different members of the structure'. He also observed that the detached pavilions on the flanks are not at right angles to the body of the structure but rather 'face each other obliquely'.[222] (Fig. 69)

*   *   *   *   *

Completion of Robert Adam's University building had been Playfair's first great challenge and triumph. Interestingly, George Cleghorn, who was so much inclined to seek for and praise the Greek, saw in it only 'Roman and Italian' styles.[223] But Playfair was actually able to introduce some admirable Greek elements in his interiors. Adam's design had been a powerful exercise in a profoundly Roman idiom; Playfair remained loyal to Adam's Roman Doric in the east front of the court and to Adam's Ionic quadrants, but introduced a rich array of Corinthian engaged columns and pilasters on the long north and south sides. Thomas Frognall Dibdin reckoned that Adam's University entrance front to South Bridge, with its huge monolithic columns of utmost Roman splendour and ponderous solidity which 'has yet a noble air', was nevertheless 'put to a severe test by almost facing the most brilliant portico in the city, from the classical hand of Mr Playfair', namely Surgeons' Hall.[224]

Situated a few hundred yards south and across Nicolson Street, and described by Cleghorn as being designed 'in a bold and fine taste',[225] Surgeons' Hall is a bravura and adventurous design of which the most notable element is the hexastyle Ionic portico. (Fig. 90) Its fluted columns stand on an austere screen wall, and thus are 'thrust forward into view rather than set back on a flight of steps' in a rather similar way to the distyle porticoes of Adam's University entrance, likewise advanced on massive plinths and which 'deliberately obtrude into the perspective towards the bridge'.[226] The screen wall shuts the medical precinct off from the otherwise un-learned street, whence the distinguished surgeons of the Modern Athens might pass through the magnificently pedimented pedestrian gates to their College hall, lecture room, library and museum.

At the University, from 1817, Playfair experimented with some Greek forms and decoration. In the lower hall of the Natural History Museum, on the west side of the quadrangle, he first proposed 'two Grecian Doric Columns at each end which will communicate to it a certain degree of interest...'.[227] In actuality, he gave the room an internal Greek Doric colonnade (engaged along the sides, freestanding at the ends) supporting an entablature with a frieze of triglyphs and metopes, filled with wreaths of a more elegant form than he would use on the Royal Institution. Because of the width of the intercolumniations, there are two triglyphs between each of the columns on the long sides, except at the ends where the junction with the short sides is handled awkwardly, with the metopes and their wreaths shunted up against one another uncomfortably.[228] Because of a difficult problem of floor levels the columns have to stand on small plinths, and are thus completely out of accord with classical Greek architectural practice. Despite the possible qualms of some Modern Athenians over these solecisms, the whole forms a remarkable if eccentric room, pertinently described as 'a Greek Doric temple inside out'.[229] If one imagines a (sophisticated) child's rubber model of a temple which can be pressed inwards and back on itself, then one has some idea of the oddity of what Playfair conceived. (Fig. 54) Cockerell looked it over with a critical eye in 1822, and was none too flattering to architect and design.

> Saw Mr Playfair's Museum ... nonsense to put doric entablature wh. is the outside representation of beam ends, inside Ro[om]:; never done by ancients I believe—as usual the example is followed as far as it leads & then blank we can go no further. I would have shown the beams & so made an ornamental & reasoned ceiling as did the ancts ...[230]

It is something of a simplification to say that Playfair's use of the Doric order in the lower hall of the museum was his 'only obvious acknowledgement of the current Greek Revival fashions'.[231] In fact, in the upper museum, Playfair supplied, at either end, pairs of Ionic columns derived from the North Porch of the Erechtheion, these having correct bases, the enriched necking and capitals of the originals, and the appropriate antae.[232] (Figs 55-56) In the great room that now bears the name of the Playfair Library Hall, the architect introduced—though beneath a Roman coffered barrel vault—pairs of immensely tall and superbly enriched Ionic columns of authentic Greek character at either end, with a further pair for additional 'afforestation' in the vestibules, and a profusion of friezes with anthemion and palmette detail. Of the decoration, Dibdin wrote (with a sort of connoisseur's lasciviousness) that 'In such a magnificent interior you can hardly be too brave and saucy in the upper ornaments.'[233] (Fig. 58) 'Saucy' though the decoration indeed is, it is neither wholly and correctly Greek, nor yet is it exactly pure Roman; but its opulence has its own undoubted distinction, and it is symbolic of the relaxed attitude to classical style in the city, even at the height of its 'Athenian' phase. Playfair proposed column capitals for the Venetian windows of the upper museum derived from an unusual type—'palm' or 'water leaf', with superimposed but lower acanthus leaf—as illustrated by Stuart and Revett from the Tower of the Winds in Athens.[234] Due to its derivation, this particular order would seem rather appropriate for a windy city such as Edinburgh. Possibly the only other place where it can be found among the 'draughty parallelograms' of the Modern Athens is in Thomas Hamilton's porch for his Royal College of Physicians in Queen Street, of 1844. There, two Greek personifications of medicine, Asclepius and Hippocrates, surmount the Tower of the Winds portico, allowing the goddess Hygieia to queen it over them on the aedicule above.

*   *   *   *   *

Had the Parthenon been translated to the Calton Hill in anything like a finished form, it would never have borne, due to cost alone, the quantity of sculpture that the original possessed; and it is further obvious that there would have been major differences both in quality of material and craftsmanship. There never was any intention to replicate the sculpture on the original building in an antique style. Prior to its enlargement, Playfair's original Royal Institution had no sculptural decoration whatsoever, though he designed pylon-like plinths to support sculpture. These were built; but they never had to perform their projected duty. (Figs 59-60) In many ways, this austere, boxy temple of learning became less purely Greek with its rebuilding, when its pediments acquired their florid decoration. In its enlarged form, there is also a prominent frieze of anthemion and lotus, behind the peristyle and towards the top of the 'cella' walls, effectively in the position of the actual sculptured frieze on the Parthenon. The tympana of the pediments of both Doric and Ionic structures—Playfair's Royal Institution and his Surgeons' Hall—were filled by swirling fronds of vegetable-themed ornament, notably anthemion. As far as enrichment went, Playfair used foliate vegetable forms to decorate the friezes of his Ionic Surgeons' Hall, which has alternating stylised honeysuckle palmettes and lotus flowers. The tympana of the front and rear pediments of the Royal Institution have particularly robust and luxuriant honeysuckle stems, tendrils and flowers; the central ornamentation is in the form of large lotus flowers. The theme is repeated in the smaller tympana of the four corner porches. Handsome anthemion motifs are to be found on the soffits of the angles of the raking cornices on all the two principal and four subordinate Royal Institution porticoes: a feature derived from the Parthenon. (Fig. 79)

Hamilton and Playfair respected ancient convention and gave their Doric buildings (the High School and the Royal Institution) friezes with triglyphs, metopes and the requisite refinement of guttae and mutules. Burn designed his both with and without regular friezes (John Watson's Hospital and the Edinburgh Academy respectively). However, all three architects either left the metopes blank (as in Hamilton's twin stoa design for the Mound galleries, or Burn's John Watson's), or else filled the metopes with wreaths (as in Hamilton's High School or Playfair's Royal Institution). These latter details, though executed with a fine quality of carving, do become rather monotonous. Hamilton's wreaths are of a neater, more 'classical' type, with smaller leaves and a more elegant fillet binding the sprays. This feature evokes the frieze of the Choragic Monument of Thrasyllos in Athens: the irony is that the original was destroyed in 1826, during the Greek War of Independence, just while it was being emulated in the Athens of the North. (Figs 78, 80-81) Playfair's wreaths are altogether lumpier, though for source they do have the impeccable authority of a detail in Stuart and Revett.[235] (Figs 82, 85) In their Ionic buildings, Reid, Elliot and Playfair designed architraves with the three fasciae of the Erechtheion order, whereas Burn consistently preferred to design his with the plain architrave of the Temple on the Ilissos. Playfair's sphinxes on the Royal Institution are totally different from the full-breasted Adamesque creatures perched fetchingly on the top of the roof-line of Robert Reid's Parliament House frontages up in the Old Town. Down in the New Town, a later form of neoclassicism showed itself in the heavy-muscled, truculent male sphinxes with Egyptian Nemes headdresses which lour on pedestals over the projecting porches. (Fig. 82)

The Athenian Choragic Monument of Lysikrates was also influential. A number of Edinburgh architects either adapted it on a larger or smaller scale, or incorporated elements of its structure or decoration into buildings of their own, most notably Hamilton and Playfair respectively in their Burns and Dugald Stewart Monuments. Both are very free translations, in which the source is at once obvious but also cleverly adapted so as almost to conceal it under the Modern Athenian architects' veil of novelty. Archibald Elliot had incorporated two elements of the Corinthian column capitals of the Monument of Lysikrates—the distinctive and delicate helices, and the palmettes—in the capitals of the central features of his Regent Bridge in Waterloo Place. (Fig. 75) In the Dugald Stewart Monument, Playfair went very much further in his exercise of imitation and adaptation: although his version veers far from the ancient prototype, most notably in the design of an open peristyle and the absence of both lower and upper sculptural friezes (the latter being replaced by a frieze of Playfair's characteristic wreaths), the Corinthian order of the columns of that peristyle are quite closely derived from the source.[236] (Figs 73-74) The flutes have the same elegant and subtle termination in the form of upright leaves curving slightly, but perceptibly, outwards: doubtless much more expensive than normal standard fluting in terms of the masons' time, and requiring a high level of skill in stone-craft. The capitals reproduce to some degree those of the Lysikrates Monument, having the same helices but omitting the lowest of the three tiers of leaves, so that they start simply with the second row of acanthus present in the original. The palmette on each side of the abacus is present. All in all, the effect nearly reproduces the sophistication and richness of the ancient model. (Figs. 75-76) Yet some were less than enthusiastic. In 1833, the otherwise fair and perceptive commentator known to us only as 'C.' damned Playfair with faint praise, and hedged his or her remarks about with excessive and demeaning dubiety, in writing that it was 'understood to be somewhat after the manner of a Grecian building called the Lantern of Demosthenes'—by which name, indeed, the Monument of Lysikrates had long been known in the accounts of early travellers. But 'C.' was seduced by Hamilton's Burns Monument, and would brook no rival, thinking that Hamilton's would have been better sited had it taken the place of Playfair's Stewart Monument, the latter, in its elevated position, being 'too gracile' when seen from below.[237] (Fig. 69)

In 1854, towards the end of Edinburgh's 'Athenian' phase, the architectural firm of Peddie & Kinnear would contribute a new Corinthian porch to the original, but already much adapted, 1772 house at 22 St Andrew Square. Over-elaborate pediment and aedicular form apart, this porch reproduces the Lysikrates order at a much smaller scale than Playfair's columns on the Stewart Monument, but does so complete: the order has the sophisticated curved leaf-topped shaft, the full capital with all three rows of foliage, and the palmettes on the faces of the abacus. It is a last, but barely noted and hardly appreciated hurrah for the Athens of the North. Insensitive placing by the new Malmaison Hotel of over-sized, intrusive and unnecessary spotlights hard above the abaci has only very recently demeaned this little late-in-the-day manifestation of a more tasteful and scholarly age. (Fig. 77)

As in any city at any time, Edinburgh in its Athenian age saw many buildings designed but never built. A little-known example is Burn's design for the New Club of about 1822. This also demonstrates well the eclecticism and versatility of the architects of the Modern Athens when proposing buildings that would suggest an element of the new Greek taste, while respecting the earlier classicism of the streets and settings into which the new buildings were expected to fit. A rare, misidentified engraving of what is certainly this building (as the named rooms on the plans indicate), sited at the extreme east end of Princes Street, shows a pedimented Corinthian portico at *piano nobile* level set over a round-arched, channel-jointed ground storey. A Corinthian pilastrade along the return up Register Street politely acknowledges the order of Adam's Register House. The entrance is in the form of a small Ionic aedicular porch in uneasy juxtaposition, and the whole is a rather confused mixture of styles. Yet of this C. R. Cockerell wrote in praise, and did so as if the building had actually been erected. In his record of buildings seen in Edinburgh in August 1822 he mentioned no architect, but described the fluted portico as 'very agreeable' and 'in that proportion & size which may be called the precious'.[238] Although this proposal for the New Club came to nothing, William Burn did actually go on to design its very grand clubhouse on Princes Street just west of The Mound (and in close proximity to the Greek Doric Royal Institution) in 1834. It is, perhaps, indicative that, even by then, Edinburgh's high Athenian moment had passed, or was shortly to pass; for what Burn gave the New Club was an Italianate palazzo (later made even grander by David Bryce) that would have been by no means out of place in Pall Mall and at the heart of a 'Roman' London.

One of the least-known architects of classical Edinburgh, George Winton—a man who was really a mason-builder, but who claimed the title of 'architect' on his monument in St Cuthbert's Kirkyard—died in 1822, the year the foundation stone of the Calton Hill Parthenon was laid. Winton designed for himself one of the best small structures that link Edinburgh and Athens: at least, for want of other evidence, it must be presumed he was his own designer. (Fig. 70) His memorial is derived directly from the Choragic Monument of Thrasyllos.[239] (Fig. 80) Every distinctive element of the original is present: the frieze of eleven elegant olive wreaths with a continuous band of guttae below; the twin plinths forming the attic above, with a stepped and recessed centrepiece; antae defining the façade, and a single square pilaster dividing it. The whole Winton Monument is a most striking symbol of devotion to the Athenian idea. Indeed, it may be the earliest accurate reproduction of the Monument of Thrasyllos anywhere, though there is, in the MacVicar burial enclosure in the same kirkyard, an earlier but only partial derivation of the original. (Fig. 113)

In Greyfriars Kirkyard, against the southern wall, there is an anonymous monument in what might be termed a stripped-down Thrasyllos style and one now, additionally, stripped of the memorial tablets formerly affixed to its carcass. However, the monument of the former Lord Provost, William Trotter of Ballindean, the great Regency Edinburgh furniture-maker (which is to be found in the western extension of the graveyard) is complete, and exhibits some interesting variants of the Thrasyllos pattern. Trotter (died 1833) gave himself, or was given, a monument with several differences, but one that still preserves the idea of the Thrasyllos prototype: there are six wreaths on the frieze, with three more on the visible return; paired pilasters at the ends frame the square central one in approximation to the Athenian original. (Fig. 71) Thirty years later, a more remote variant of the Thrasyllos form can still be recognised in the monument in the Canongate Kirkyard to the portrait-painter Sir John Watson Gordon (died 1864), a man who had captured the likenesses of many a Modern Athenian, such as Archibald Alison and Henry Cockburn.

Also deriving from the Monument of Thrasyllos, and equally evocative of fealty to antique sources, is an elaborate twin door-piece to otherwise plain tenemental properties in Broughton Street, of 1810, which is undoubtedly influenced (although less obviously and faithfully) by the same Greek original. (Fig. 72) Four engaged Doric columns are substituted for the antae and central pilaster. However, the hallmark eleven olive wreaths—with one more on each return of the entablature, visible from both up and down the street and therefore adding a satisfactory additional element of sophistication to the composition—and the continuous moulding of guttae, indicate very clearly the specific source.[240]

There is even a superficial similarity between the Choragic Monument of Thrasyllos and the attractive device drawn and engraved by William Home Lizars for use as an ornamental heading on the policy documents of the Edinburgh Life Assurance Company, established in 1823.[241] (Fig. 37) A vignette, unacknowledged but in fact after Raphael's *Madonna della Sedia*, is the central allegorical feature of this masthead. This is, however, of much less interest to us than the decoration around and below the image. Luxuriant thistles surround the Raphael tondo and surmount a Greek Doric prostyle portico, emblematic of the Athens of the North; Edinburgh Castle looms in the background, symbol of Auld Reekie. Here were the twin identities of early nineteenth-century Edinburgh. But, in life as in death, many of its citizens wanted to show, most of all, that they were Modern Athenians.

'THE ATHENS' FROM WITHIN

'A CHARACTER MORE TRULY ATTIC TO OUR METROPOLIS'

The scene was the House of Lords, the date was 2 May 1844, and peers were debating a subject which, at first glance, seems to have little relevance to 'Athenian' Edinburgh. The issue was how there might be established in Edinburgh 'more effective sanatory regulations with respect to the dwellings of the lower classes'. Lord Campbell of St Andrews, formerly Solicitor General, Attorney General and sometime Member of Parliament for Edinburgh, was speaking. *The Times* newspaper reported proceedings. Lord Campbell said:

> That town had very deservedly obtained the name of the Modern Athens, both from the beauty of the buildings, and the intelligence of the inhabitants, but, unfortunately, it was very unhealthy, which might be remedied by good sanatory regulations.

In the chamber of the Upper House was Lord Brougham and Vaux, sometime Lord Chancellor: Edinburgh-born, educated at the High School and University, member of the Faculty of Advocates before being called to the English Bar, and once a regular contributor to *The Edinburgh Review*. Brougham started up from the woolsack (as *The Times* reported) to say that it was as well that his noble and learned friend Lord Campbell no longer represented Edinburgh in Parliament

> for, if he did, he would certainly not have the support of his worthy constituents for having mentioned a subject which was the most delicate and the most painful to an Edinburgh man that could be well conceived. (*Laughter.*)

But this delicate subject was not the shameful sanatory conditions of the Edinburgh poor. It was something much more important. The newspaper account continued:

> They [the constituents of the city] looked upon it as the next thing to insult to speak of Edinburgh as the Modern Athens. They regarded it as so exceedingly vain and presumptuous an assertion, which there was nothing in the slightest degree to authorize (*Continued laughter*) that they considered it one of the greatest gibes that could be thrown upon them. (*Laughter.*) He assured his noble friend, that when he was in Edinburgh he was taken to task for so speaking of it, and was told that the use of the term "Modern Athens" was a personal insult to every one in the place. (*Great laughter*).

Lord Campbell retorted: 'Well, all I can say is, that Edinburgh produced my noble and learned friend, who, in his own person, is Alcibiades, Pericles, and Demosthenes. (*Roars of laughter.*)'[1]

Within three years, a much-abbreviated version of this Parliamentary altercation featured in a footnote in the fifth edition of Black's *Picturesque Tourist of Scotland*. This states that Lord Brougham had said that 'the epithet "Modern Athens" was resented by the inhabitants of Edinburgh as a mockery or an insult'. Editor or publishers appended an aggrieved comment: 'So far as our own experience goes, we have never heard of any of our townsmen quarrelling with the epithet.'[2]

* * * * *

Henry Cockburn memorably assessed Edinburgh's social and intellectual standing in the years around the turn of the eighteenth and nineteenth centuries:

> The society of Edinburgh was not that of a provincial town, and cannot be judged of by any such standard ... It was metropolitan ... Over all this there was diffused the influence of a greater number of persons attached to literature and science ... than could be found, in proportion to the population, in any other city in the empire ... And all this was still a Scotch scene. The whole country had not begun to be absorbed in the ocean of London.[3]

Mrs Anne Grant of Laggan arrived in Edinburgh from the country at the beginning of March 1810, and within six weeks was writing to friends in England of 'this Northern Athens'. She was still calling it such thirteen years later. 'Of persons of rank there are many from different quarters,' she had written in 1810, 'attracted by the fame of this Northern Athens, as it has become fashionable to call it.' But 'Athenianism' came at a price: 'though the feast of

reason abounds, there is not so much of the flow of soul.' There was certainly—
among an elite 'too well bred, too well informed'—spirit, intelligence, verbal
wit, animated conversation (but maybe with excessive, self-consciously brilliant,
epigrammatic expression), acuteness, profundity; but heart, imagination and
playfulness were perhaps lacking in the Northern Athenian constitution.[4]

Writing to Robert Pearse Gillies, the eccentric and increasingly absurd
Earl of Buchan—who posed as sort of tutelary deity of Edinburgh's cultural
firmament—referred to 'the Caledonian Athens'. 'The season of Folly is over
and gone', Buchan once proclaimed, 'and the voice of the lyre is heard in our
land.' It was comments such as this that caused Gillies, who was making a
name for himself as a *littérateur* on the Edinburgh scene, to recall how
Buchan 'conceived that all the artists, literary men, and scientific men of the
modern Athens, were under his especial care and patronage ... [as their]
Magnus Apollo.'[5] Buchan did indeed like to imagine himself the Apollo of
later eighteenth- and early nineteenth-century Edinburgh in all possible ways.
Sometimes he even dressed the part, accompanied on at least one occasion by a
retinue of nine young women dressed appropriately as the Muses and by a boy
in no dress at all in the role of Cupid, all being attendants upon his 'divinity'.
Gillies delighted in describing this 'classical scene'.[6] In 1803, the caricaturist
John Jenkins drew the Earl as 'Apollo Prince of the Muses', bespectacled and
sitting on a very ordinary Scottish chair supping very ordinary Scottish brose
out of his helmet with a very ordinary Scottish ladle, while the nine Muses, with
their appropriate attributes, disport themselves on the staircase behind him.[7]
(Fig. 20) Buchan's music-room in his Edinburgh house contained paintings of
'the three Muses '—he presumably meant 'Graces'—which were joined by one
of 'The Education of Achilles', in which the old centaur Chiron was shown
'instructing [his pupil] to sing the Hymns of Orpheus ...'.[8]

Buchan laid himself open to ridicule on account of his fantasy of a classical
realm where he set much of his own quasi-autobiographical writing. A small
printed pamphlet, anonymous but certainly by Buchan and probably produced
on his own private press, gives a flavour of his notional early mornings before
he spooned that porridge from whatever receptacle he actually used. *The Four
Repasts of the Day: Repast First. Breakfast* begins thus:

> It was where the maiden fortress of Edina hides the ascending chariot of the
> Archer, that a hoary-headed son of Apollo went forth to take his morning
> walk ... In the eye of his mind he sees the sluggish stream of Lethe pressing on
> his view [presumably the Water of Leith, where Buchan did indeed walk near
> St Bernard's Well], and the rebounding cataracts of Acheron come upon his
> ear—He walks forth from the gay city: his sleep had been airy, light; from pure
> digestion bred, and temperate vapours bland:—O virgins of Edina, virgins of
> the Sun! Why do ye thus plunge into the caves of Erebus, and scatter your roses

in the regions of Pluto? [Why do young women stay up late, partying?]—Was
it for this that the Graces gave you that celestial rosy red, those blushes of love
and of innocence, those lips that were formed to enchant the sons of the earth,
and to send forth the accents of melody and of friendship?—Arise virgins, and
come away; come with me, and taste the pleasures of breakfast.—It was thus
that the hoary-headed man did preach to the morning air.[9]

In one of his essays, specifically one of his 'Letters in Imitation of the Ancients',
Lord Buchan assessed the Greeks in such a way that it is difficult not to read
into the passage a cryptic judgment on his own code of ethics, not to mention a
self-identification with the Greeks in many of their characteristics.

> I hold the men of Greece to have been the first of human beings, and to have
> exhibited in their character all that mortals can attain. *Their* genius was great
> and transcendent; *their* government free, and fitted to form heroic minds;
> *their* language was copious, philosophical, varied, and sublime, beyond all
> the languages on earth; and even when they became corrupted and sunk into
> depravity, still they were Greeks, for they transgressed with a high hand, and
> sinned (as I may say) in a superior style …[10]

Perhaps it was on account of such an amalgam of eccentricity and arrogance as
Lord Buchan customarily displayed that it was never without a certain frisson
of humour, verging on disapproval, that Gillies would refer to the 'Modern
Athens' (with or without quotation marks) or to his 'Athenian world'.[11]

When people called Edinburgh 'The Athens'—as some, indeed, did—they
seldom meant to be complimentary. Nor did they imply that, in the city thus
labelled, anything amounted credibly to emulation of the 'other' Athens, and
all that the concept of genuine 'Athenianism' suggested. Distaste was indicated
by the use of both the definite article and those quotation marks: 'The Athens'.

The writer of the remarkable essay published in *The New Edinburgh Review*
(much cited in the last chapter) was fulsome in his praise of Greek buildings
and a neo-Greek identity for Edinburgh. Even he, however, appears to have
jibbed at going so far as to adopt the actual name of *Athens* for the northern
'counterpart'. Buildings reflected social and cultural attitudes and aspirations,
and those were, in turn, reflected in the buildings of a city. The *New Edinburgh
Review* contributor felt it important not to be carried away by ideas of
parallelism: '… the Athenian Parthenon serves to indicate the far removed and
much changed character and pursuits that belong to a city which has been (*idly
we admit*) [my italics] invested with the title of "the modern Athens".'[12]

Looking back in old age to Edinburgh immediately after the conclusion of
the Napoleonic Wars in 1815, Henry Cockburn condemned the adoption of
the epithet 'The Modern Athens' as silly and ill-judged. This was, he wrote, a

'foolish phrase ... a sarcasm, or a piece of affected flattery, when used in a moral sense; but just enough if meant only as a comparison of the physical features of the two places.'[13] Much is summed up in Cockburn's shrewd analysis. The idea of the 'Athens of the North' carried baggage both useful and cumbersome. There was, he conceded, a topographical parallel: this was undeniable. Indeed, topography was key; and it was of much greater significance in seeking for a likeness to Athens than any perceived intellectual distinction that allowed a cerebral similarity to be boasted about. The more that citizens of Edinburgh saw on the Continent (Cockburn was unashamed to confess) the more they understood just how little, in the way of artistic and architectural progress had, up till then, been achieved in their city. Yet, equally, those who visited other places did come—through 'taste, or conceit, or mere chattering'—to appreciate the 'general picturesque grandeur and the unrivalled sites of their city'. Of this Cockburn noted, rather enigmatically: 'but it all did good'; and he surmised that 'money, travelling, and discussion will get us on.'[14] But not, perhaps, *too* much discussion, for he also noted that 'There were more schemes, and pamphlets, and discussions, and anxiety about improvement of our edifices and prospects within ten years after the war ceased, than throughout the whole of the preceding one hundred and fifty years.' However, he mused further that 'The opportunities of observing, and the practice of talking of foreign buildings in reference to our own, directed our attention to the works of internal taste, and roused our ambition.'[15]

The principal focus of that ambition would be the National Monument, conceived in the form of a new-built Parthenon on Calton Hill; and in that campaign Cockburn himself, along with Walter Scott, would bend to the Athenian yoke, or rise to the Athenian challenge—whichever way it can be seen. Cockburn and his generation, and his kind of citizen of taste and discernment, would see some, at least, of what he called 'the beauty of the bravery which the Queen of the North has since [the Napoleonic Wars] been putting on'.[16] But, equally, he would witness many other fine architectural or planning projects fail for want of adequate funding, sufficient civic pride, effective civic leadership, and simply in the absence of the right conjunction of moment, opportunity seized, and vision. 'But we have no Pericles', Cockburn ruefully accepted.[17] It is a lapidary phrase that might well stand as epitaph on the grave of Edinburgh's Athenian ambition.

*   *   *   *   *

It is certainly true that crowing over being 'Athenian' or 'Attic' long rebounded on the Modern Athenians. As early as 1774, Gilbert Stuart, son of the Professor of Humanity and Roman Antiquities, turned on Edinburgh and its men of letters:

I mortally detest and abhor this place and everybody in it. Never was there a city, where there was so much pretension to knowledge, and so little of it. The solemn fopping and the gross stupidity of the Scottish literati are perfectly insupportable.[18]

Greek was hardly taught, if at all, to the boys of Edinburgh before they entered the 'Town's College' (as the University was generally known). Yet Cockburn gave it as his opinion that 'there is no solid and graceful foundation for boys' minds like classical learning, grammatically acquired'. The 'early discipline of the mind' proved to be the real benefit. Andrew Dalzel, Professor of Greek, was a very distinguished scholar, but he was an ineffective teacher of the rudiments to a large and unruly class: even such absolute basics as the very alphabet was new to Cockburn and most of his fellows. Still, Cockburn remembered him as 'a general exciter of boys' minds', and as 'an absolute enthusiast about learning— particularly classical, and especially Greek ... he inspired us with a vague but sincere ambition of literature, and with delicious dreams of virtue and poetry.'[19]

As early as 1804, however, Dalzel expressed some dismay about the future of his beloved classical studies in Edinburgh. This was a serious confession by a man who must be seen a torch-bearer of the ideas of classical civilisation that underpinned the ethos of a Modern Athens in the making. He wrote to Richard Porson, Regius Professor of Greek at Cambridge:

All that I have been able to do, or shall be able to do, is to endeavour ... to inspire the youth in this northern part of the Island with a love and admiration of Greek literature, without some knowledge of which no nation can be considered as truly learned ... It is difficult to stem the torrent of taste which is at present, in this part of the country, moving with impetuosity towards chemistry and mineralogy and natural history and such like sciences, and there is some danger of our philosophers (I believe it is pretty much the case already), when they meet with a Greek quotation, saying, with the monks of yore,—'*Græcum est, non possum legere*' He who can in any degree prevent this sort of ignorance is surely doing good service to the cause of letters.[20]

Dalzel's lectures extended beyond language teaching to Greek history and antiquities, philosophy, literature and even art; his personal scholarship encompassed work on the topography of Troy. In this last field he translated and edited lectures given to the Royal Society of Edinburgh by the French traveller and archaeologist Jean-Baptiste Le Chevalier, later to befriend Walter Scott. These were published in Edinburgh in 1791 as *Description of the Plain of Troy: with a Map of that Region, Delineated from an Actual Survey*.[21]

Strange as it may seem, the world of Homer and of Greece of the archaic period was rather more to the taste of many Modern Athenians than the high point of fifth-century classicism. The notion of the radical democracy of Periclean Athens worried the Edinburgh establishment. This was particularly the case in the era of the French Revolution and its aftermath, and during the period of industrial and social unrest of the late 1810s and 1820s. The first two lines of John Gillies's dedication to King George III of his *History of Greece* of 1786 even anticipated these events. 'The History of Greece', Gillies loyally informed his sovereign (who would subsequently reward him with the office of Historiographer Royal for Scotland), 'exposes the dangerous turbulence of Democracy.'[22] Gillies was not alone in his suspicion and fear of demagoguery, populism and the rabble: William Robertson (not the University Principal and great historian, but the other of that name), Deputy Keeper of the Records at Register House, and also an historian of Greek antiquity, had expressed himself in similar terms in 1778.

It is, therefore, on the face of it, rather strange that Edinburgh became so mesmerised by 'Athenianism' on a cultural level, as demonstrated by the way it affected daily life in everything from women's dress, porcelain tea-cups, silver-ware and book-bindings, through fabrics and furniture inlays, to house exteriors and interiors, public buildings and monuments great or small. Attention has wisely been drawn to the surprise of, and paradox inherent in, Edinburgh's 'selectively embracing some of the less contentious facets of the city's [Athens's] experience under the incomparable Pericles—its cultural richness, its architecture … even its military effectiveness and imperial aggrandisement.' The result was that, by the later 1820s, 'the city's [that is Edinburgh's, this time] modern character was now assumed … to be wrapped up in that of classical Athens.'[23] A country whose scholars had once been fixated on discovering the tangible links with its *Roman* occupation now came to be more interested in identification with aspects of the classical past—with *Greek* culture and ideals—having no direct links to the history of Scotland itself.[24]

* * * * *

The young Walter Scott also sat under Dalzel, distinguishing himself for his wilful disregard of even the rudiments of the Greek language. Scott was, in consequence, known as 'the Greek Blockhead', an opprobrious title he did nothing to eschew.[25] Sheepish regret about lack of classical knowledge remained characteristic of Scott to the end of his life, albeit masked by a kind of insouciance that led him to make light, or the best, of his situation. That he was 'no Grecian' and 'almost totally ignorant of the language' were phrases frequently used in his correspondence. Nevertheless, Scott would come to appreciate the value of the mental discipline bestowed by a classical education.

And yet no one was more central to the 'Athenian' standing of Edinburgh in the early nineteenth century than this same 'Greek Blockhead', Walter Scott.

'Athenian' ideas had come relatively late to him. When writing to his bride-to-be Charlotte Carpenter, on 21 November 1797, he had alluded only to 'Auld Reekie which you must know is the Scotch nickname for Edinr.'[26] Even though he wrote from George Street in the New Town, it did not occur to him to stress any Northern Athenian claims for the city, or more specifically those of its fashionable new 'classical' quarter which was to be his fiancée's future home. In 1814 he could mock the pretension that was seemingly summed up in the 'Athenianizing' of the city. As we noted in the previous chapter, Archibald Alison and others would try to suggest that Scott—thinking of the Edinburgh of his own day when he wrote some lines in the dedicatory epistle to George Ellis prefacing the Fifth Canto of *Marmion* (1808)—meant really to praise the developments in town planning and street architecture of the late eighteenth and early nineteenth centuries. Reading Scott's lines

> Dun-Edin! O how altered now
> And liberal, unconfined and free
> Flinging thy white arms to the sea …

these keen Athenians liked to imagine that Scott was in some way prophesying a bright neoclassical future for what he also—and more famously—called, in the same poem, his 'own romantic town'.[27] In that famous passage, Scott's thoughts were in fact very much on the city that was Auld Reekie, the historic huddle of its Old Town, not on the classical terraces and squares of a new city on the way to becoming the Modern Athens.

Twice only in his correspondence did Scott refer to Edinburgh as Athenian: in these two letters he wrote unflatteringly of the place some seemed to want to become somewhere else. The first occasion was in 1812, and thus relatively early for such terminology.[28] There is some sarcasm in Scott's tone as he writes of learned circles in 'our northern Athens' being 'agitated' by scientific and educational dispute. The context of his comment two years later was the tardy delivery of new publications by the booksellers from whom they were ordered. Scott wrote: 'For a Northern Athens as Edinburgh has been called by some conceited persons we are unpardonably slow …', thus making clear his disapproval of such civic vanity and self-importance.[29] It is interesting to note that a correspondent of Scott's, writing five years later, should have suggested that he might ask for a certain book 'at a circulating library in your *Northern Athens*', a gently satirical hint that both the notion of Edinburgh's new status and the soubriquet itself were in relatively wide use throughout Great Britain.[30]

In the third number of his pamphlet satire *The Visionary* of 1819 (composed of three letters, signed 'Somnambulus', and originally published in *The Edinburgh Weekly Journal*) Scott ridicules those who wanted to promote 'the insane idea' of extension of the franchise, and even universal suffrage.

He imagines the radical Edinburgh populace casting their votes by means of inscribed oyster-shells deposited, for want of a more suitable receptacle or ballot-box, in a glass-kiln at Leith. Scott has a character in the saga declare that this voting process was 'in imitation of Athens'—the allusion being to the use, in classical antiquity, of inscribed potsherds (*ostraca*) in the process of 'ostracism'—and adds the aside that 'all the world knows how like Edinburgh is to Athens'. It has been suggested that, as well as attacking the movement for reform, Scott here mocks the pretension prevalent among the Edinburgh Whigs to be Northern Athenian.[31]

The so-called 'Trial of Queen Caroline' took place in 1820. It led to a welter of journalism and pamphleteering for and against both her and King George IV. It was also a time that saw political unrest in England and Scotland, with serious radical disturbances. At the end of the year, the Tory *Blackwood's Magazine* printed an article in which the Edinburgh Whigs (notably Francis Jeffrey and Henry Cockburn) came in for criticism on account of their desire for governmental and constitutional change. This embraced sarcastic mockery of just such 'Athenian' intellectual and moral pretension: ridicule of (as *Blackwood's* put it) 'the wits and wise men of the North—the "Arbitri Elegantiarum" of the world—the "deliciae generis humani"—the all-be-praised, all-admired geniuses of the modern *Athens*.'[32] Yet they were taken to task in Latin tags rather than in Greek phrases, presumably as likely to be better understood even in the vaunted city in question.

In the privacy of his journal, Scott described his celebrated 'Letters of Malachi Malagrowther' as epistles to 'the Athenians', thus again mocking Edinburgh's 'Athenian' identity and alluding, in passing, to St Paul's epistles to Greek cities.[33] However, as we shall see, Scott could himself be 'Athenian' at a critical moment when he lent his name in support of the 'Parthenon' National Monument campaign.

And yet, at another critical moment just months later, it was Edinburgh's identity as 'Auld Reekie' that came most readily to Scott's mind or welled up in his heart. As the royal visit of August 1822 drew nigh, he wrote two sets of verses entitled 'Carle, Now the King's Come!' In these, Edinburgh is made to address her people, and the 'high heid yins' due to be closely involved in the extravaganza. She speaks in the character of 'Auld Reekie, in her rokelay [a short cloak] grey'. Scott did not think to make his city cheer on the populace, or welcome the King, in the alien character of the Northern Athens wearing a 'chiton white'.

In his *Provincial Antiquities and Picturesque Scenery*, Scott would describe the social and cultural changes that had overtaken his city, and would do so almost in 'Athenian' terms, yet without contriving to resort to these actual words. His assessment of this Northern Athenian society includes a pen-portrait of that class of 'the most successful professional men' who were now 'both aspirants after, and dispensers of, literary fame; and there is spread through society at large a more general tinge of information and good conversation than is to be met with elsewhere.' This progress in manners manifested itself in the encouragement of the fine arts; in the purchase of books; even in the purchase of pictures by 'the opulent'. The rise of taste and a consciousness of aesthetics was inspired by 'noble scenery' and 'ruins of antiquity'. The mornings of such a man 'may be spent in study ... and his evenings with friendship or with beauty.'[34] Without saying as much, Scott managed almost to evoke a world of the ancient academy and the symposium.

In 1816 Scott had reviewed the Third Canto of Byron's *Childe Harold's Pilgrimage*. It is difficult not to see a glimmer of rising philhellenism in his article; the spell of the Greece of the past is manifest, and a nascent admiration of the Greece of the present may be sensed.

> Greece, the cradle of the poetry with which our earliest studies are familiar, was presented to us among her ruins and her sorrows. Her delightful scenery, once dedicated to those deities who, though dethroned from their own Olympus, still preserve a poetical empire, was spread before us in Lord Byron's poetry, varied by all the moral effect derived from what Greece is and what she has been, while it was doubled by comparisons, perpetually excited, between the philosophers and heroes who formerly inhabited that romantic country, and their descendants, who either stoop to their Scythian conquerors, or maintain, among the recesses of their classical mountains, an independence as wild and savage as it is precarious ...[35]

He continued with a passage adapted from sentiments first expressed by John Wilson Croker in a letter to the publisher John Murray, but changing Croker's original 'forests decay' to the more specifically and effectively Grecian 'temples decay', and Croker's long-winded 'he who has had the good fortune to stand on that sacred spot' of Marathon to the more antiquarian-sounding 'he who has trode it'.

> Pictures fade and statues moulder and temples decay, and cities perish: but the sod of Marathon is immortal—and he who has trode it has identified himself with Athenian story in a manner which neither painter, nor poet, nor sculptor could have accomplished for him.[36]

Reviewing the Fourth Canto of *Childe Harold* two years later, Scott was again open in his praise of Greece as 'the country whose sun, so long set, has yet left on the horizon of the world such a blaze of splendour'.[37] In 1819 Greece was once more the focus of Scott's tribute. In his essay on the Drama for the *Encyclopaedia Britannica* he wrote of '... that wonderful country, whose days of glory have left such a never-dying blaze of radiance behind them'.[38]

Scott was keen that his younger son Charles apply himself, as he himself had not done, to ancient languages. In 1820 Charles was sent to the Revd John Williams's school in Lampeter, Wales. The boy received a letter from his father encouraging application to his Greek and Latin grammar. 'A perfect knowledge of the classical languages', the elder Scott wrote,

> has been fixd upon and not without good reason as the mark of a well-educated young man and though many people may have scrambled into distinction without it, it is always with the greatest difficulty just like climbing over a wall instead of giving your ticket at the door ... [I]f you are not a well founded grammatical scholar in Greek and Latin you will in vain present other qualifications to distinction.[39]

John Williams came north in 1824 to be the first Rector of the new Edinburgh Academy, at the opening of which establishment Scott gave the address. Scott's speech was reported in the press. Scotland had not produced many eminent classical scholars, he had conceded. The teaching of Greek must begin earlier and had to be 'prosecuted to a greater extent' than hitherto. Making a direct comparison or identification with Greece—this was a new school in the 'Modern Athens', after all—

> [Scott] would have the youths taught to venerate the patriots and heroes of our own country, along with those of Greece and Rome; to know the histories of Wallace and Bruce, as well as those of Themistocles and Caesar; and that the recollection of the Fields of Flodden and Bannockburn should not be lost in those of Plataea and Marathon.

Greek was 'the language of the fathers of history, and of a people whose martial achievements and noble deeds were the ornament of their pages.'[40] A Greek motto was devised for the Edinburgh Academy by John Williams, and settled upon by the directors: Η ΠΑΙΔΕΙΑ ΚΑΙ ΤΗΣ ΣΟΦΙΑΣ ΚΑΙ ΤΗΣ ΑΡΕΤΗΣ ΜΗΤΗΡ ('Education is the mother of wisdom and virtue'). It was inscribed across the architrave of the austere Doric portico of William Burn's building on the northern edge of the New Town.[41] Paradoxically, the austerity is almost more suggestive of Sparta than of Athens and, significantly, the school's prefects later came to bear the ancient Spartan magisterial title of 'ephors'. With its unfluted, almost primitive columns, the Academy is more reminiscent of Segesta in Sicily than of anything in Athens. But Segesta was actually unfinished; in Edinburgh, unfluted columns were (presumably) cheaper than a fluted Doric order, and economy was an important matter when commissioning a new school building or anything else dependent on private funds rather than government or civic largesse. The contrast with the flamboyant architectural decoration of the

Royal Institution is notable, as it is with the much more imaginative massing, variety, elaboration and sheer splendour yet enormous subtlety of the buildings of the very slightly later (and publicly supported) High School.

※   ※   ※   ※   ※

Hugh William Williams's first exhibition of his Greek watercolours made some of the Modern Athenians feel more 'Athenian' than previously. Henry Cockburn reported to Sir Thomas Dick Lauder, at Relugas in Morayshire, that the show had afforded 'a most beautiful display of art and taste'. Over-optimistically, he thought it seemed to be succeeding well, and that it might make Williams some money.

> It is becoming a fashionable lounge and if he can only get some poor, blind, snuffy, old card playing harridan of a Dowager to take him up, Greece may do after all. By Minerva let me implore you to inspire taste and patriotism in the Shire of Moray.

Cockburn continued with an account of the convivial and classical private view. 'Oh! what a glorious—what a God-like bouze we had on the opening of Williams' exhibition in the rooms.' Twelve good men, true to the ideals of the ancient and the modern Athens—'the nine muses and three graces', as Cockburn whimsically jested of an all-male group of lawyers and scholars—had gathered at the Calton Convening Rooms. The group included the classicist, James Pillans. Sometime Rector of the High School, and subsequently Professor of Humanity in the University of Edinburgh, Pillans would later be recipient of the dedication of John Patterson's essay *On the Character of the Athenians*. They 'dined surrounded by Greek scenes ... and had we not a night of it ... with Jeff [Francis Jeffrey] piping as a little Pan, with a Pyrrhic dance!'[42]

Two decades on, Modern Athenians dining together would have had the ideal crockery for such a supper. From the later 1840s to around 1854 the Bo'ness Pottery, established on the shore of the Firth of Forth west of Edinburgh, produced a series of transfer-printed dinner-wares marketed as the 'Modern Athens' pattern. Though clearly inspired by the Shepherd and Britton book of 1829, the plates and dishes are decorated with views differing from the steel engravings in that publication. Two showing Calton Hill and its surroundings are of particular interest. One illustrates the High School, the Nelson Monument and the unfinished National Monument. The other shows Regent Terrace, the Burns Monument, the Nelson Monument and a *completed* National Monument in all its vast splendour. A Modern Athenian could finish his last Scotch collop or Finnan haddie and reveal on printed earthenware what had failed to materialise in reality.

'Athenianism' appeared in many guises. Long before this, the tickets for 'Mr Ritchie's Ball', held in the new Assembly Rooms in George Street in 1785, had borne the image of an elegant female attired in 'Grecian' dress supporting one side of an oval cartouche. The moulding of this is plain and unornamented. The other side is held by a putto in swirling drapery, sufficient to hide his modesty but no more. His portion of the 'frame', however, is transformed into something much more suggestive of classical antiquity, for an elegant spray of laurel authentically evokes the Mediterranean or Aegean. (Fig. 30) Notions of an 'Arcadian' dream-world persisted. Nearly sixty years later, in 1843, tickets for the Edinburgh Musical Festival Ball were adorned with the image of three terpsichorean 'Greek maidens' engaged in a musical and choral dance between elements of monumental or domestic interior furnishing that could come from the nineteenth century's ideas of Greek vase painting or Pompeiian wall-decoration.[43] (Fig. 38)

About the same time, those same Modern Athenians cavorting at an Assembly Room ball would have been able to enjoy a series of graphic caricatures of themselves in day dress rather than evening attire. In 1839 Hugh Paton published the first plates in what eventually grew into a substantial series of caricature portraits by Benjamin Crombie. Paton wrote thus in *Men of Modern Athens*, which presented the first six portraits to the public:

> Tourists have declared that, travel where they may, they have never seen a city that can stand comparison with Modern Athens. There are the *Buildings* of Modern Athens ... the beauty of its situation and the scenery immediately surrounding it, some of which has been rendered classical by the pen of its own Scott. There are the *Women* of Modern Athens; and in this, what some call the degenerate age ... the silver age ... there are—yes there are—the MEN OF MODERN ATHENS! ... a delineation of them is indeed a desideratum ... making the 'MODERN ATHENIANS' speak for themselves. Such appears the popularity and general approval of the present undertaking, that Candidates are already in the field for a place amongst the Men of Modern Athens, some of whom will be allowed a corner.[44]

A further set of twenty-one *Modern Athenians* (the title by which the prints became better known) followed in 1844, and a complete series of forty-eight appeared in 1851.

In 1882, in a spirit of affectionate antiquarian retrospection, William Scott Douglas and the Edinburgh publishers A. & C. Black re-issued Crombie's *Modern Athenians* prints of 1839-51. This re-publication was in keeping with the earlier spirit of veneration that had motivated Hugh Paton to produce the original sets; for it was Paton who had previously published, between 1837 and 1838, the extensive and invaluable collection of caricature etchings by John

Kay. These capture, as nothing else does, the characters of late eighteenth- and very early nineteenth-century Edinburgh. Paton described the further exercise of what might almost be called filial piety as 'acquitting his duty to Athens as it was'. His *Modern Athenians* venture—making available a very much less varied and rather less interesting and appealing series of portraits by Crombie—was aimed at capturing the likenesses of the kenspeckle characters of the Edinburgh of his own day.

*   *   *   *   *

A key figure in Edinburgh's assumption of an 'Athenian' identity was, of course, Archibald Alison. In the last chapter, we traced Alison's advocacy of an Edinburgh Parthenon as the single most spectacular building that might advance an 'Athenianism' in stone. In this chapter we investigate Alison as a Modern Athenian in a wider context. He had won a prize at Edinburgh University in 1808 for an essay on 'Causes of the Eminence of Athens in the Arts and Science'.[45] It seems that the notion of some sort of subliminal parallel between his own city and that of ancient Athens must have struck him then, and that the idea remained vivid in his mind to resurface with real force in 1819.

Alison's thesis was that Edinburgh could play the cultural and intellectual part of a Greek city-state. He first set this out in his influential initial article in *Blackwood's Magazine* that July, pursued it later in the same journal and took it up again, later still, in *The Edinburgh Review* in 1823. In the 'ardent spirit' of such small communities, 'the human mind arrives at its greatest perfection', and 'the freest scope is afforded both to the grandeur of moral, and the brilliancy of intellectual character.' The sub-text is that Edinburgh was then, or was poised to be, another Athens. It was able to aspire to this position due to its constellation of great minds and wealth of cultural achievement. Edinburgh must strive to preserve its distinctive cultural identity within the United Kingdom. A National Monument would serve to keep alive Scottish pride in artistic and cultural distinction.

Up to this point, Alison had not actually said that the proposed monument should be in the Greek style; but the implication was that if the city *felt* Greek it should *look* Greek and *build* Greek. Alison argued that Edinburgh was already 'Athens' in the mind. It could also yet be so in stone.

The Athenian 'substructure' supporting Alison's case was now revealed.

The statesmen of Athens, when they wished to rouse that fickle people to any great or heroic action, reminded them of the national glory of their ancestors, and pointed to the acropolis crowned with the monuments of their valour; and invoked the shades of those who died at Marathon and Plataea, to sanctify the cause in which they were to be engaged.[46]

Clearly these ancient struggles—Salamis, too, of course—had their modern parallels in the Nile and Trafalgar, in Salamanca and Waterloo.[47] The hoped-for national memorial would 'stand at once the monument of former greatness, and the pledge of future glory.' Alison suggested that Edinburgh was the real intellectual centre of Britain, a united multi-national state dominated by England: it was a situation akin to that conveyed by the old Horatian adage of captive Greece taking captive her wild Roman—for which read 'English'— conquerors.

> The taste of Athens continued to distinguish its people long after they had ceased to be remarkable for any other and more honourable quality ... To this day the lovers of art flock from the most distant parts of the world to the Acropolis, and dwell in rapture on its unrivalled beauties, and seek to inhale, amid the ruins that surround them, a portion of the spirit by which they were conceived.[48]

Alison returned to his theme in *Blackwood's Magazine* for November 1819, making the renewed observation that the monuments of Athens had continued to attract the admiration and interest of travellers long after the political decay of the city.[49] The older 'Athenian' greatness of Edinburgh, presumably that witnessed at the height of her Enlightenment distinction, was waning. Some 'great and permanent objects of attraction' must be established to hold people to the city as a cultural centre, and to draw them thither as by a magnet. If built on the Greek model previously outlined, the National Monument might achieve that grand object. As once in Athens, so now in Edinburgh might peace and prosperity usher in an era of unmatched fertility and achievement in culture and the arts. By 'transferring to our city the most perfect monument of ancient art', advantages such as Phidias and Pericles had conferred on ancient Athens would likewise be enjoyed by the people of Edinburgh, and inspiration be given to the 'rise of Scottish genius in the fine arts'.[50]

Alison also pointed to the views that Williams had made of Grecian scenery which would surely convince their countrymen of the similarities in landscape and layout between the two places.[51] Typically, Alison suggested that Phidias himself would have recognised in Calton Hill the ideal location for the great temple. But, equally typically, Alison allowed his enthusiasm, and his obsessional wish to create a new, 'Athenian' Edinburgh, to subvert historical fact. It is strange that Alison did not consider that Phidias and his ancient architectural colleagues—the men actually more likely to have been instrumental in determining the siting of the Parthenon—would not have thought first and foremost of Edinburgh's original and existing 'acropolis' as equating to the historical and religious importance of their own ancient citadel. The 'Castle Rock versus Calton Hill' conundrum continued.

Alison's tireless prose flowed on in praise of Scottish smeddum, Edinburgh enterprise and Northern Athenian ambition. He urged his fellow citizens to 'draw at once from the pure fountain of Grecian excellence than lower down, where the stream has been polluted by the intermixture of more turbid waters'.[52] This article would have been read by many of the professional and legal elite of Edinburgh, now returned to the city from their long vacations in the Highland or Borders air and beside the clear rivers of their country estates. The metaphor will not have been lost on them. Alison continued:

> And would it not be a proud thing for this country, that, while all nations, from the time of Pericles, have concurred in admiring the Parthenon, in Scotland alone were artists to be found of sufficient magnanimity to renovate that edifice, and a people to be met with capable of appreciating the benefits which would attend its restoration? ... It is ... in our power to raise an edifice which will attract the eye of taste even from the splendid façade of the Louvre, or the pillared scenery of Venice.[53]

*   *   *   *   *

The writer signing himself 'A Traveller', contributed an article, in epistolary form, largely supportive of Alison's arguments.[54] The contention was that Edinburgh people were not yet truly Athenian, but that they were progressing on that course. The building of the National Monument on Calton Hill might still at this point be deemed 'an undertaking so foreign to their ordinary thoughts'. This disarming admission was one Alison himself would hardly have made, and its candour is sobering. But though they were not yet Greeks, classical refinements were certainly less strange to Edinburgh citizens than once they had seemed. 'Works of pure taste' had come to the city; and if the writer of the piece here had in mind merely the County Hall, the Observatory and 'the new designs for the College', then these buildings were at least a start. To become Athenian was no longer an alien thought. Greek buildings on the Calton Hill and elsewhere in Edinburgh would be the physical manifestation of 'its eminent moral rank in the scale of cities, for the reception of a great Classical Temple'.[55]

An anonymous writer makes several important statements about what it was, or meant, to be a Modern Athenian. 'Athenian' feelings were clearly elitist sentiments. As that 'Athenianism' was expressed specifically in a wish to see a Parthenon on Calton Hill, the feeling was one that was (so the author argued) 'universal among men of taste and education'. But so pervasive, persuasive and powerful were these sentiments that even the lower orders were, or would soon be, touched: 'Athenian' feelings would become 'very general even among those of inferior aquirements'.[56] The original Parthenon having been *designed* 'by men of the greatest taste whom the world has ever seen', it was, presumably, then actually *built* by the craftsman and labourers of ancient Athens. The same would, equally presumably, apply in the Modern Athens, where the men of learning and taste (the equivalent of the *hippeis* and *zeugitai* ranks of Athenian society) would dictate policy and contribute or raise the funds, and the execution of the building would be in the hands of a skilled but always respectful workforce (the *thetes*). As in antiquity all had pulled together to create what had been 'the *National Monument of Athens*', so a similar phenomenon would occur in the Modern Athens in raising the National Monument of Scotland. The northern Parthenon would be built by, for and 'among a people capable of appreciating the benefits which it is fitted to confer upon the progress of the arts'.[57]

The identification between 'Athenianism' and elitism is also stressed by the writer of the long article in *The New Edinburgh Review*. Architecture and the arts of design should not be confined to 'the educated orders only'; 'profit and advantage will arise from diffusing it through the very lowest ranks of society.' Such a transfusion of taste was to be hoped for among 'all classes of artizans as well as through those leading members by whom their activity is put in motion and their industry directed'. The art of drawing was essential in many manufactures.

> The cabinet-maker and the upholsterer are, in a certain sense, architects; but even the saddler, the shoemaker, the common working gardener, nay the very turner of a mopstick ... are guided by some principles of taste, and may be better guided by better ones.

Much was to be gained from the diffusion of taste, 'even among the refuse of society, among idle children, and through the general multitude, ungraciously called *canaille* ...' Regrettably, this lack of taste could be perceived to extend 'to a considerable height in society ... too often to its very capital.' (One has the image of Edinburgh's 'stratified' appreciation of taste and culture being likened to a Greek column.) A diatribe about lack of knowledge and taste leading to public vandalism follows: the prevalence of such behaviour extended from base to abacus of that metaphorical column. The common people were wildly and widely destructive of everything they could set hands on. But,

> If they commit these injuries from wantonness and ignorance, the motives of their betters cannot be much different, when they carve their insignificant names on ancient monuments, or break off a volute or the finger of a statue, as a specimen of the building or the sculpture.[58]

Had he read this passage in his respectable mid-forties, Henry Brougham might have reflected on his wild escapades as a young man in Edinburgh, wrenching off door-handles and bell-pulls from New Town houses after a too-convivial evening at the Apollo Club. Jessy Harden, a Queen Street resident, had been shocked by such goings-on, and by such loutish behaviour. The judge Lord Meadowbank was greatly concerned that 'the rabble' might (as he put it) 'chip the Columns' of the Royal Institution if the supposedly temporary hoardings around its building-site were ever removed.[59] In an early 'Athenian' Edinburgh, there was clearly much room for improvement in manners.

Northern Athenian elitism manifested itself in all manner of ways. In 1824, George Cleghorn was outraged at the scheme to construct burial lairs, otherwise called 'catacombs' or, more quaintly, 'dormitories', within the stylobate of the National Monument. If built beneath a hall perhaps destined to receive the likenesses of some of the greatest men of the nation, these spaces might attract the wrong type of corpses. Death and burial, Cleghorn implied, ought to be subject to the same sort of class-distinction as anything else in Edinburgh. Modern Athenians clearly felt that they should rest for eternity with their own kind.

> Now, if these dormitories be put up to the highest bidder—to every grocer and tallow-chandler who has fifty pounds to spare … would it be consistent with the dignity or character of the edifice, that vulgar ashes should repose under a pavement destined for monumental sculpture?[60]

When Cleghorn set out once more on his crusade for the Parthenon, this time in the hope of injecting life into a moribund project, it was these same 'dormitories' that especially concerned him. Any suggestion of an ecclesiastical function for the Calton Hill Parthenon remained the principal stumbling block to further progress. With that idea of a church had come the notion of the burial lairs. Their inclusion in the massive platform supporting the colonnade risked not just the physical stability of the entire superstructure. The demand to have them also induced a kind of moral instability, and provoked the 'indecency and absurdity' of turning a national monument into a 'mercenary, jobbing, and joint stock operation' simply to benefit the over-inflated aspirations of little people that they and their kin might lie within a temple dedicated to the memory of great men and heroic deeds.[61]

The Parthenon project, 'so momentous, with a view to the future advancement of taste', could be accomplished 'only *at this time*, and *in this city*'.[62] Truly was the hand of destiny upon the Modern Athenians. Edinburgh was 'the only city in the empire, where a situation fitted for the restoration of so sublime a structure can be obtained'; where the materials were readily and economically to hand; 'and where moral feeling, most likely to realise its advantages, is to be found.'[63]

It was only in Edinburgh, and certainly not in London or anywhere else in England, that the objective of building a Parthenon could be achieved. The English, however, were ideally fitted to be Northern Parthenon proselytes:

the Scottish project might take with 'the public spirit and classical enthusiasm of that generous people'. England sent numerous Grand Tourists 'into all the classical regions of the South': they brought home Greek sculptures; increasing numbers 'of the most distinguished youth' made the 'pilgrimage' to the Acropolis, returning with 'the warmest admiration for its beauties'; engravings of the ruins of Greece sold widely and well. Nevertheless, English travellers to Greece, no matter how strong their interest and sincere the wish to 'realize in this country the delight and the advantages which they have experienced from [Greek] remains', had to accept that 'the restoration of the Parthenon, so earnestly desired by all men of taste in England, is hopeless in that country'.[64] There was no suitable situation in London, and freestone of appropriate quality was not readily available. Therefore, the English also looked to Edinburgh, to the Calton Hill, and to the quarries of Craigleith for realization of the 'Athenian' dream in Britain. The long-established 'classical habits of England' would, perforce, defer to those more recent ones in Scotland, if only the Parthenon could be definitely decided upon.[65]

*   *   *   *   *

Northern Athenians and their opponents drew breath for some eighteen months. Then, in December 1821 and January 1822, appeared the printed circular letters from the Sub-Committee of the General Committee of Subscribers to the National Monument. These letters advocated the choice of the Parthenon as model, and solicited subscriptions for the project. The language was persuasive, and the sentiments those of men fully convinced of the ability of Edinburgh to surpass the ancient city of their inspiration. That the signatories should have included 'Grecian' Williams and Archibald Alison was hardly unexpected, and that the Earl of Elgin should have appended his name by way of expiation for his sins of 'dilapidation' of the prototype is wholly understandable. The intervening period had, after all, seen Williams half-excuse the stripping of the Parthenon of its sculpture, for the sake of the likely long-term benefit to the development of 'correct' classical taste that the presence of the marbles in London would convey: they were now 'where the wisdom of Minerva is centred—in Britain.'[66] But to find Walter Scott and Henry Cockburn signing variants of the circulars comes as a surprise in the light of the former's comments on the conceit of thinking of Edinburgh as a Northern Athens, and the latter's memories of the foolishness of the adoption of the Grecian epithet.

When the artist Benjamin West, President of the Royal Academy, wrote to Lord Elgin after being permitted to draw from the Parthenon marbles at Elgin's house in Piccadilly, he declared that the Earl, 'by bringing these treasures of the first and best age of sculpture and architecture into London' had 'founded a new Athens for the emulation and example of the British student.'[67] Edinburgh might not have the Parthenon sculptures; but it did appear to be on the way to having a full-scale replica of the building itself. There was a genuine feeling in the city that, in erecting a 'facsimile', the citizens would be ensuring that the memory of the original might be preserved in the event of its destruction.

The critical years of Edinburgh's assumption of its 'Athenian' identity coincided with the outbreak of the Greek Revolution in 1821, and the events of the ensuing war of independence. The second circular letter of the Committee of Subscribers to the National Monument, issued on 24 January 1822, carried dire warnings. Its sense of foreboding about the likely fate of the Parthenon was palpable. It is 'a matter of very serious regret to the lovers of the arts in every part of the world', the Committee said,

> that this structure, the most perfect which human genius ever conceived, is not only already in a very dilapidated state, but is placed in a situation where its existence is liable to the utmost danger, in consequence of the political conflicts by which it is surrounded. Not only is it at the mercy of ignorant barbarians, totally incapable of appreciating its value, but its situation on the Citadel of Athens, and on a military station of such importance, renders it liable to the still greater danger of being destroyed in the course of the conflicts of which that country is already the theatre. From this cause it has already suffered many serious injuries, and there is every reason to fear that the first struggles of Grecian freedom may be followed by the entire destruction of the monuments of that [freedom] which is past.[68]

James Simpson, a lawyer of literary inclinations, a friend of Walter Scott and himself one of the signatories of this document just quoted, composed a series of letters to Scott 'on the Moral and Political Character and Effects' of the King's visit in August 1822; they were published that autumn. His musings included whimsical notions of how hopeless it would have been on that occasion to 'call out and embody the heathen gods ... to build an actual Parnassus, and stock it with the professors of the university with the Principal habited as Apollo on the summit.' But Simpson also imagined how the King himself would have caught his first glimpse of the real Calton Hill, which Simpson called 'the cliffs of the Acropolis, whose summit was already prepared for the Parthenon.' He continued:

> Nothing could be better timed. A new impulse has been given to that noble undertaking, superadding to all its former attractions of patriotism and taste, a powerful, and, it is trusted, most effectual association of affectionate loyalty. The day is the nearer that we shall see realized that ornament to our country, that record of her past, and incentive to her future greatness; and when even possessing such a model of taste, while a few years more will for ever obliterate its Greek prototype, we shall proudly say,—

> ... Oh mark on high
> Crowning yon hill with temples richly graced,
> That fane august in perfect symmetry
> The purest model of Athenian taste,
> Fair Parthenon! Thy Doric pillars rise
> In simple dignity ...[69]

Simpson was not alone in believing, quite genuinely, that an Edinburgh Parthenon—when it came—might well replace the original. John Stark inserted a whole passage on the National Monument in the text of his *Picture of Edinburgh* (1823), in which he pointed out that the building would not just 'perpetuate the remembrance' of the deeds of the late Napoleonic Wars, but would stand as symbol of 'the desire among men of taste of restoring to the arts the model of a building which *time and barbarism* [my italics] will soon annihilate.'[70] That Edinburgh, as the Modern Athens, might be able to uphold the glory of ancient Greece in the face of current oppression and 'barbarism' was a widely held conceit.

Scott himself was moved to acknowledge that same Greek cause: the report of his address at the inauguration of the Edinburgh Academy included the following passage:

> At no moment was the study of that beautiful language [Greek] so interesting as at present, when the people among whom it was still in use, were again, as he trusted, about to emancipate themselves from slavery and barbarism, and take their rank among free nations.[71]

Not long after this, George Sibbald threw in for good measure the almost obligatory, if insouciant, comment on the current state of Greece in the early stages of its revolution against the Ottoman Empire.

> And we may add, that every one who knows the value of liberty & independence, & can be proud of the grandeur & ornaments of his country, must deplore the fate of the fallen & wretched Greeks, enslaved by the oppression of cruel & lawless barbarians, &, in order to gratify an idle & useless curiosity, stript even by the learned & civilized, of those monuments of art, which have justly immortalized both the architects & architecture of their country.[72]

The Duke of Hamilton had made two significant and interrelated points in his speech at the laying of the foundation stone of the National Monument. 'Long has that Grecian edifice', he said, 'been the object of universal admiration, and, until now, has survived the vicissitudes of fortune, and arrested even the unhallowed hands of Barbarian conquerors.' Imitating the model of the Parthenon might lead to a more general emulation of Greek taste in the arts in Scotland.[73] A product of that new-found taste might preserve the memory of the ultimate symbol of Greek artistic perfection, itself very possibly at hazard from Turk and warring Greek alike. However, to balance the opinion of Modern Athenians, who thought they were saving the spirit of Ancient Athens from barbarians, Francis Cohen delivered a sober corrective view.

> If the Parthenon is at the mercy of barbarians, we are sorry for the fact; but the Turks have done their utmost to prevent further injury: Lord Strangford prevailed upon the Porte to issue an order especially commanding the Turkish troops, during the present warfare, to respect the monuments of Grecian antiquity. But if the Parthenon should unfortunately be destroyed, if the Greeks should finish the spoil which the Venetians began, still the copy of it will in no respect answer its proposed end ...[74]

An unexpected architectural dimension to philhellenism, or at least to a consciousness that what Edinburgh built might possibly reflect opinion on the struggle for Greek independence, is to be found buried in the text of one pamphleteer's response to another writer's argument on an entirely different point. In 1825, a war of words, almost as fierce as the war of gunpowder and sword in Greece, was being waged in pamphlet and counter-pamphlet on the development of The Mound and approaches to the centre of the city, by way of new streets and bridges, from the south and south-west. This is far too complex, not to say tedious, a matter to concern us here. Nevertheless, it included an item of relevance to ideas of Edinburgh architecture and town planning, and their relationship to wider notions of philhellenism and the Greek cause. The writer signing himself 'A Builder', and terming himself a 'Practical Man', had expressed perfectly reasonable doubts, on technical grounds, about an idea that a crescent of houses might be built on the upper, south-west slope above The Mound; this would have led up from its head, by Ramsay Garden and the Castle bank, towards the esplanade. The 'Builder' reasoned that the 'acclivity' would mean that any development in the form of a crescent would imply a 'discordant' stepping-up of the houses on the steep rise: 'nothing', said the writer, 'surely could be so barbarous in architecture'. This was just the sensible concern of an experienced, professional man, one used to the difficulty of building on the often-challenging slopes of Edinburgh.[75] He was rapidly answered, however, by the author calling himself 'A Plain Honest Man' who, interrupting his own discussion of new streets and approaches, took the opportunity to indulge in a little facetious banter about this suggested crescent. It was only one proposal within a slew of schemes for the head of The Mound. But,

The dislike of the Honest Builder ... towards Crescents, may arise from some
confused association in his mind of the struggles of the Greek Patriots and the
atrocities of the Musselmans, with the symbol by which the latter are typified.[76]

*   *   *   *   *

It is in the context of the Greek Revolution that we should also consider another
aspect of 'The Athens' from Within. Paradoxical as it may seem, some Modern
Athenians, otherwise so much fixated on proving the unique worthiness of their
city, actually looked outwards too. Between 1822 and 1825 they wanted to
extend an eleemosynary hand from the Modern Athens to what remained of its
southern sister. A northern city inspired by the ancient Athens wished to seize
the opportunity to try to repay a spiritual and educational debt by interesting
itself in the welfare of the modern Greeks.

Central to this wish was the dissenting clergyman and ecclesiastical historian,
Dr Thomas M'Crie. In his biography of his father, M'Crie's son (also Thomas)
would address the feelings of a man so thoroughly grounded in ancient Greek
learning as was this eminent churchman. In 1822, said M'Crie the younger, his
father had been moved by

> the spectacle of a whole nation, once so famous for literature, laws and
> civilization, rousing itself from the lethargy of ages, and by the strength of its
> unaided arm releasing itself from the yoke of a barbarous despotism ...

Many thought the modern Greeks 'unfit for and unworthy of the blessings of
freedom', and could not see beyond the 'contrast of [Greece's] ancient glory
with her modern degradation.'[77] M'Crie senior spoke powerfully against this
preconception at two large public meetings in Edinburgh. At both, he looked
beyond classical scholarship and sentimental attachment to the romantic
notions of the ideal represented by ancient Greece, especially Athens.

The first meeting was held at the Merchants' Hall on 7 August 1822, only a
short time before the King's visit. M'Crie's address is considered the first to have
been delivered in Great Britain on behalf of the Greek cause.[78] Its purpose was to
establish a relief fund for the 'sufferers' of the Chios (Scio) atrocity perpetrated
by the Ottomans earlier that same year. In promoting the subscription, M'Crie
sought to reward modern Greek resolution by means of Modern Athenian
philanthropy: '... what man that has a spark of patriotism in his breast, or that
has any taste for liberal knowledge, does not feel himself concerned in every
thing connected with the name and the fates of Greece?' Feelings might have
been 'blunted and become torpid'. But it would not require 'any vast powers,
any preternatural charm to awaken it', for 'pronouncing the name of Greece still
occasions ... a mixed emotion of veneration and delight ...'.[79]

The second meeting that M'Crie addressed was held at the Assembly Rooms in George Street on 9 April 1825. His speech was to the 'Scottish Ladies' Society for Promoting Education, Especially that of Females, in Greece' (the exact title of the organisation varies between sources). The underlying purpose was to repay, in some measure, Edinburgh's—and Britain's—debt to ancient Greece by returning the opportunity for educational advancement to its fountainhead. M'Crie had some telling remarks to make. 'There is in the very name of Greece', he ventured, 'a charm which is felt by those who cannot explain the cause of their emotions ...'. And he went on, later, to say much—in what might now be regarded as a rather a patronizing way—of how Northern Athenian womenfolk were not sufficiently classically educated to appreciate the beauties of Greek literature in the original, even if they might still enjoy its sentiments through the medium of translation in English verse by the likes of Alexander Pope.

What is most significant in M'Crie's address is a somewhat saccharine (not to say sexist) passage that links the Ancient with the Modern Athens.

> Edinburgh, which used to be contented with the name of the *Gude* [Good] *Town*, has of late years been saluted with the flattering title of the *Modern Athens*. Without stopping to inquire if there has been a general acquiescence in the imposing of this title, or if it is likely that our city shall be known to posterity by it, I hope ... that you will agree with me when I say, that she has never presented a fairer or more attractive claim to this appellation than she does this day, when her daughters are assembled in such numbers to express their sympathy with the Greek nation, to pour the only salutary balm into the still bleeding wounds of that long oppressed people, and to help them to the means by which they may gradually attain their former distinction in knowledge and refinement, and even surpass, in point of extent at least, anything which Greece had reached when her illumination was at its meridian: for ... however great my admiration of the august institutions and never-dying, though at present faded glories of that country, I must be allowed to say, that ancient Athens herself never presented a spectacle of the same interesting kind as this assembly, in which the flower of the female population of a great city [Edinburgh] is collected, in order that the expressed fragrance of its benevolent feeling may be wafted to a distant land ...[80]

The frontispiece portrait ornamenting M'Crie's biography is by J[ohn] Horsburgh after a sculptured bas-relief portrait by A[lexander Handyside] Ritchie.[81] The image is framed by a wreath close in style to those which Playfair added to the previously blank metopes of the frieze of the Royal Institution building when that structure was enlarged in 1831-36. (Fig. 84) The fillet binding the lotus fronds is simplified from Playfair's prototype, and the wreath is shown reversed. But the image is distinctly that of a Modern Athenian, and indeed the wreath and its orientation is derived from a detail in Stuart and Revett.[82] (Fig. 85)

In April 1828, the second report of the Directors of the National Monument was still mentioning the likelihood of destruction of the Parthenon in the Greek War of Independence. The potential consequences of that were laid on with a trowel. While the 'Grand Original' that was Temple of Minerva in Athens was 'at this moment perishing amidst the ravages of war', 'an exact fac-simile of that "jewel in architecture" was now rising at the gates of the Metropolis of Scotland'.[83]

Michael Linning, the lawyer who served as Secretary of what came to be known as the Royal Association of Contributors to the National Monument of Scotland, was consumed not just by his own self-importance but by the nobility (as he saw it) of the cause to which he devoted so much time and effort. Yet even he must have appreciated that the project had stalled, probably fatally. The various papers he brought together and published in 1834 under the title of *Memoranda Publica* preserve the record of his personal attempt to make Edinburgh the Modern Athens.

First, however, he had tried to make it a Modern Rome. He had proposed two giant commemorative columns for the New Town: one, to be based on the Column of Trajan, in tribute to Henry Dundas, first Viscount Melville; the other, after the Column of Marcus Aurelius, was intended as a memorial to William Pitt the Younger. The former only was erected, in St Andrew Square.[84] Though based (very loosely indeed) on what Linning termed 'an approved model of antiquity', their prime begetter saw nothing anomalous in the fact that both these were to be fluted monumental columns: they were to be built without the continuous spiral sculptural friezes that characterise the Roman *columna cochlis*, and which render the ancient originals such important works of art and invaluable historical documents. Yet Linning could describe the columns proposed for Edinburgh as being instances of 'restoring' an antique prototype.[85] There is a clear parallel with the equally fatuous idea of a 'Parthenon' National Monument *without* the Parthenon's sculpture. Both his columns and his beloved Parthenon were, in a sense, structures lacking the essential message their antique prototypes had been intended to convey. It is perhaps little wonder that, in due course, Linning would find nothing unsettling about Edinburgh's Parthenon being planned, from the outset, without the essential sculptural decoration of the original. In the self-serving memoir of his involvement with the Parthenon project, Linning summed up the ideal of what was dreamed of, if not quite the reality of what little had actually been achieved.

> The portion of this edifice that has been already built, is admitted by architects to be, in point of taste and execution, one of the finest and most chaste pieces of masonry in the world, worthy of its grand prototype, which, as it

commemorated the victories of Marathon and Salamis in ancient [Athens], so will its representative, commemorate, as it is destined to do, those of Trafalgar and Waterloo in Modern Athens ...[86]

There were repeated instances of referencing parallels between ancient Athens and modern Edinburgh (and Scotland as a whole) in matters of war as in taste. In his speech at the inauguration of the Edinburgh Academy, Walter Scott had paired Scottish valour of old with ancient Greek patriotism and martial intrepidity. Young Athenians of the new school would later learn not just to study, but to fight and perhaps die for their country in a quasi-ancient way as citizen-soldiers beneath the same inspiring legend of Η ΠΑΙΔΕΙΑ ΚΑΙ ΤΗΣ ΣΟΦΙΑΣ ΚΑΙ ΤΗΣ ΑΡΕΤΗΣ ΜΗΤΗΡ. When the school's Officers' Training Corps was established in 1908 this motto was emblazoned on the cap-badge, within a wreath of laurel, round a portrait bust of Homer.[87] (Fig. 105) In a similar Greek spirit, the High School war-memorial, placed in the oval assembly hall and dedicated in 1923, evoked ancient sacrifice and applied it to modern times. In the elegant form of a Doric aedicule with acroterion and antefixes, and built of marble not from Pentelicon but rather from Skye and Iona, its inscription is derived from a verse of Simonides: ΟΥΔΕ ·ΤΕΘΝΑΣΙ · ΘΑΝΟΝΤΕΣ—'Though dead, they live still'.[88]

*   *   *   *   *

Many writers used 'Athenian' terminology almost as second nature and without thought or explanation. A publication of occasional verse bears the actual imprint not of 'Edinburgh' but of 'At Modern Athens'.[89] But the best example is that of Charles Kirkpatrick Sharpe. Between 1817 and 1844, Sharpe's whimsical correspondence was peppered with allusions to Edinburgh's vaunted status. He wrote in one letter of the 'chorus of sighs and groans, much duller than that in Greek tragedies', which he might have introduced to his lament: but he confined himself to addressing his epistle to Lady Charlotte Campbell as from 'Athens, Siberia'.[90] On another occasion he wrote to her of the dullness of 'The Modern Athens ... much deserted.'[91] The chosen terms suggest, on the one hand, just how ridiculous Sharpe considered it to think of Edinburgh—or perhaps even to mention the city in the same breath as the Athens of antiquity—as a hotbed of world culture; and, on the other, how distant Edinburgh often seemed, for cultivated people, from other, more vibrant centres of civilisation where the arts were more truly esteemed. In 1818 Sharpe took to task the writer and publisher of a review of one of his own publications, which he considered poor and inaccurate: the cynicism of the response was somehow magnified by Sharpe's suggestion that this 'ignorant' and shoddy piece of Edinburgh journalism had emanated from 'that wonderful town, the Modern Athens'.[92] 'New Athens' was the specious address from which he communicated with two female correspondents in 1832 and with others in 1834, 1836, 1838 and 1844, Sharpe using also the more abbreviated 'of Athens', or 'to Athens'—terms in fact referring to the genuine Edinburgh—in his correspondence.[93] He bemoaned the fact that 'No pamphlet ever sells in the Modern Athens!'; but such publications might do better, if someone were to come and teach good breeding 'to our modern Athenians'.[94] A bad concert had not been well attended, proving the 'generality of the Athenians are wiser than your humble servant'. But, on the other hand, 'three Athenian fools … have been lately drowned at Duddingston: they were all drunk, as was the fellow who should have saved them', when the ice gave way as they skated or horsed-about on the frozen loch. Sharpe remembered that '… nobody was drowned at Duddingston when I was young. Can the ice be weaker, or the brain of those who venture upon it? I guess the last.'[95] The implication was that 'Modern Athenian' good sense had not permeated to the lower orders.

Sharpe's caricature self-portrait sheds its own light on the 'Athenian' age of the city. (Fig. 21) The kenspeckle figure of this great Edinburgh eccentric stands before the outline of some buildings. These are not noticeably 'classical', and the small human figures in the background appear to be approaching the houses with some caution. Above these buildings, in the sky and among the rising chimney-smoke of Auld Reekie, Sharpe has written the words 'Modern Athens'. There is a cryptic message here: Sharpe was a doughty defender of the historical and picturesque sights of old Edinburgh. In 1817, the very year that the County Hall was erected as a Greek interloper in the still predominantly late-medieval atmosphere of St Giles and the adjacent High Street, the Old Tolbooth was demolished. Sharpe expressed his outrage to Walter Scott: 'as to beautifying the old town of Edin., the idea is ridiculous. Every invasion of this nature destroys its character … I would not move one stone of it.'[96] Making a Modern Athens had the unfortunate effect of diminishing the essence of Auld Reekie. Some, like Sharpe, thought the price too great, and they continued to cherish the city of the past. Some, conversely, welcomed a new world into that of the old, and greeted the Modern Athens with pleasure or even relief, precisely because it spelled the end of the insalubrious Old Edinburgh they had known. The Old Town became ever more separate from the 'Athenian' New. In 1825 a writer mused sarcastically on how

> your superfine people, persons of cultivated taste, literary folks, and those whose clothes will spoil, dread the Grassmarket as the devil does holy water … Antiquaries, however, and English artists, coming in search of the picturesque, still continue to poke about the Stinking Close, and all the odd corners … as far as the Vennel.[97]

Alexander Trotter of Dreghorn devoted much time and enthusiasm to his proposals for the redesign of The Mound. Conceived in the late 1820s, these were revisited in 1836. At that time Trotter imagined what a visitor might have

seen and felt on looking northwards from the Old Town towards and over
the New: how (as he put it) 'the stranger, in emerging from an ancient city,
is astonished, on the sudden, with a bird's eye view of our Modern Athens.'[98]
Trotter had dearly hoped that the stranger would by then have been able to
look down, too, on the 'Gallery' into the design of which Trotter had put
so much thought. His ideas for this commercial development continued the
slightly earlier schemes we have already noted for a shopping arcade behind,
and southwards of, the Royal Institution. In Trotter's vision, this would have
been a nodal point of the *agora* at The Mound. In 1829 Trotter had described
the sort of 'Gallery' he had in view. It would serve many purposes for the
Modern Athenians, for it would be

> a shelter in that much-frequented passage from the violent gales and piercing
> winds so prevalent in the Good Town of Edinburgh ... To the infirm, it would
> afford the opportunity of taking exercise without exposure to the eastern
> blast;—the stranger would enjoy the variety and novelty of the scene,—the
> lounger would here find subject to pass the hour, and kill the time.—The
> Shops and a Bazaar Establishment would not fail to attract the Belles,
> and Beaux would follow in their train. Judges and Gentlemen of the Law,
> Professors and others connected with the University, all now chiefly residing
> in the New Town, would daily have occasion to pass and repass to and from
> the Courts of Law and the College; and all would contribute to the prosperity
> of the Shopkeeper.[99]

Young women such as those to whom Trotter alluded, or as the one Sharpe
included in the background of his caricature portrait (wearing an example of
the absurdly enormous hats of the period), were notable for the distinctive
contribution they made to the society of New Athens. Sharpe once wrote
of the musical daughters of an acquaintance in Abercromby Place as a 'nest
of owls':[100] a delightful Modern Athenian conceit, given the iconographic
importance of the owl in ancient Athens. But bluestockings were also mocked
for their classical attainments. Robert Mudie later turned his gimlet eye on the
ladies of 'The Athens'.

> Notwithstanding all the beauties, physical, mental, and erotic, of which the
> Scottish metropolis boasts, it does not please always. The Calton Hill, the
> Craggs on Arthur's Seat have their pleasures by sun-light and by moonlight.
> There romancers go in the morning, to witness the rising sun; there the belles
> of the Athens display to the noon-tide sun the flexures of their forms, the folds
> of their drapery, and between whiles also the furrows of their brows—the
> prints not of time, but of talent—the notched chronicle not of how many years,
> but how many systems of philosophy, and snatches of tales, are recorded upon

those perennial brasses of Athenian science and Athenian small-talk; and then the swain steals out at eve to visit the glimpses of the modest moon, and of his yet more modest daughter of that queen of madness and amatory decorum.

It is utterly impossible to be in Edinburgh without philosophizing,—aye, without having a theory to one's self or living a sceptic of all theories whatever ...[101]

The ideal visual accompaniment to Mudie's vision of amorous belles and beaux on the slopes of Arthur's Seat is provided by a detail in a drawing by George Meikle Kemp of about 1830. The view (lithographed by Nichol) is taken from near St Anthony's Chapel towards the Calton Hill. Against a background of the most notable of the existing Calton buildings—the High School, and also of a notionally completed Parthenon set on a stylobate that is more in the nature of an imposing terrace—a top-hatted and bonneted couple canoodle in a way that is highly unusual for *staffage* 'accessories' in the topographical views of the period. They seem a Northern Athenian Pericles and Aspasia. (Fig. 94) Interestingly, a print of a view that is very similar or indeed more or less identical—but one published (and possibly also engraved) by J. West in 1843—shows a happy Modern Athenian family on the same slopes. (Fig. 95) Father, mother, son and daughter play together: Pericles and Aspasia have settled down.[102]

Robert Pearse Gillies had witnessed the occasion when Walter Scott's house, and its contents, were sold on Scott's financial ruin in 1826. Gillies thought 29 Castle Street might have been preserved as a sort of monument to Edinburgh's 'Athenian' talent. 'Yet with cold, stolid, iron visages, Modern Athenians witnessed that profanation; with perfect *nonchalance* they took possession of his old-accustomed abode, which he was never more to enter.'[103]

Gillies was by no means alone in commenting on a certain coldness and hardness characteristic of the temperament of the Northern Athens. A certain smugness and self-satisfaction, too. Even Captain Basil Hall, a staunch supporter of the Parthenon project, who wrote so assiduously to many of the protagonists, seems to have been in two minds about the worthiness of the wider setting into which the building was to be introduced. The New Town of Edinburgh, Hall would later conclude, was 'a city with more pretensions, and less title to distinction, so far as picturesque effect of mere buildings is concerned, than any capital in Europe'. He knew many of them, and could judge fairly. By contrast, he saw across the Nor' Loch valley and the Earthen Mound the 'happy elegance of outline of the Old Town'.[104] There it was, in all its claustrophobic hotchpotch of towering tenements and its cries of 'Gardy Loo', that the Modern Athenians had lived before they knew that they were Athenian, and had to find fresh air in fresh fields to match their new-found graces.

In 1826, also, we have a further insight into the lonely domestic world of William Henry Playfair, the architect par excellence of the Modern Athens.

Playfair had informed Cockerell, his coadjutor in the National Monument project, that he had

> taken the freedom to hang up your beautiful restoration [of the Parthenon] in my drawing room to refresh myself when I am fagged and to exhibit to all those who are curious on the subject. My enthusiasm is much raised upon the matter and I entertain no doubt that the Building will be finished, although probably at a distant period.

Prophetically, Playfair added: 'If it stick fast, the disgrace will not attach to those who suggested the idea, but with those who have not energy or public spirit sufficient to carry it forward.'[105] 'Grecian' Williams wrote to Cockerell in 1828:

> With regards to the engraving of the Temple of Minerva it is admired here very much & your name, my dear friend, is blown from the Trumpet of Fame in a noble style. It will shew what we are to have on the Calton Hill with good effect & help if anything will to obtain subscribers ... I may tell you that many Gentlemen propose to undertake to get subscribers sufficient to build a Column each when the funds are getting low ... I need not again repeat how much I am obliged to you for your offer of *the Athens* ...[106]

Williams was referring to the 'restorations' of the Parthenon drawn by Cockerell and engraved by John Horsburgh that Williams included in the first volume of his *Select Views in Greece*. (Fig. 62) A note to the text accompanying an image of the west front of the Parthenon, also contributed by Cockerell and likewise included among Williams's engraved views in the second volume of this work, explains that John Henning had modelled a 'beautiful restoration' of the Parthenon frieze to a small scale, 'well deserving a place in the cabinets of persons of taste'. These miniature models by Henning did indeed find their way into such collectors' cabinets.[107] At a much larger scale, some of Henning's reproductions are also to be found in the entrance halls of Edinburgh New Town houses, where Modern Athenians might have looked at them before stepping out for a day's work in the institutions of New Athens, or on their return to enjoy one of the celebrated and cultivated 'Attic nights' of the period.

*   *   *   *   *

Archibald Alison was not a man to forsake a cause he had so early and so eagerly espoused. He was always ready to strike home for the Modern Athenians once again; and he did so in a further article in *Blackwood's Magazine* in 1836, by managing to introduce the unfinished Edinburgh Parthenon in a general essay entitled 'The British School of Architecture'. Possibly conscious of what Robert Mudie had said so waspishly on the subject of 'the vanity of the Athens' (we shall examine Mudie's extraordinary onslaught later), Alison asserted his unwillingness 'to encourage the vanity which provincials in general, and the citizens of Edinburgh in particular, are so apt to exhibit'. This assessment of Edinburgh's pretension was disarming in its frankness. But then, in complete contradiction of this professed aim, Alison went on to state his clear preference for the 'purer taste and more manly character of building in the Scottish metropolis' as opposed to that displayed in London.[108] This was partly the triumph of high-quality Craigleith or Cullalo freestone over stock brick and stucco. But greater achievement had been vitiated by lack of money. 'It is an easy matter', thundered Alison, 'for the citizens of London, revelling in their superior wealth and in the possession of the seat of government, to deride the fourteen columns, the fragment of a mighty undertaking, on the Calton Hill.' Alison's over-heated imagination had increased the number from the twelve columns that then actually existed (and still do). But he continued:

Those fourteen columns … are the same benefit to the arts and public taste which the poems of Virgil and Homer are to literature; they will exist, if not destroyed by external violence, for thousands of years, and be admired when the meretricious piles of London are reduced to heaps of their mother clay. Even now, they are the most imposing objects of the kind in Britain; they impress strangers more than any edifice in the island; and if the structure is completed … on the same scale of primeval magnificence, it will give to the Scottish metropolis a distinction beyond what any capital in Europe can boast.[109]

Now completely seduced by his subject, to the extent of drawing extravagant comparisons between the incomplete, cash-starved temple of the Northern Athens and great piles far and near, Alison went on to write:

Much of the sublimity of the unfinished structure, as of its far-famed original on the Acropolis of Athens, is to be ascribed to the great blocks of stone of which it is composed. Those who have seen the gate of Agamemnon at Mycenae, in Greece, or the Cyclopian [sic] walls of Volterra, in Italy, will be at no loss to appreciate the immense effect of such massive blocks in the production of architectural effect … Stonehenge, rising like the work of giants on the solitude of Salisbury Plain … the monolithe [sic] obelisks and gateways of Luxor exceed in sublimity the tenfold bulk of York cathedral …[110]

Alison appeared to suggest that in order to achieve their 'Athenian' apotheosis, Edinburgh folk—now chronically short of money, for the city had been declared bankrupt in 1833—did not actually have to *achieve* the great Greek building they wanted, but merely to have *conceived the desire* for it.[111] The token columns on the Calton Hill might, in Alison's architectural synecdoche, stand for the wished-for whole because the *spirit* behind the conceit was there. John Parker Lawson drew specific attention to what he praised as 'the admired columns of the National Monument', and even went so far as to tell his readers how much the shafts and capitals, and the platform they stood on, had cost when he was seeking something to say by way of description to accompany James Duffield Harding's lithograph of the Calton Hill, first published in *Scotland Delineated* (1847). This fine image manages to convey an almost 'Arcadian' feeling to the view of 'ruins in a landscape': one hardly senses that the scene is, in fact, not in rural Greece but at the centre of a teeming, northern city.[112] (Fig. 65)

A mere three years later, however, a similar compilation of equally fine images appeared, but this time with a commentary much less favourable both to the National Monument as it existed and to the ethos that had brought it into being. The reader is not to be fooled by the tone at the beginning of the essay accompanying an illustration by the late George Meikle Kemp (an excellent draughtsman, and designer of the Scott Monument). A shaft of light over the Observatory dome illuminates the huge portico of the National Monument on its stylobate, jagged-edged with its toothing-stones; Turneresque lightning flashes between the columns. (Fig. 66) 'The point on which the finest evidence, alike of the liberality of Edinburgh, in the encouragement of art and the capacity of accomplishment, evinced by her architects, is found on the Calton Hill …'. But the confidence apparently expressed here is immediately dissipated, for the commentary moves on to consider 'the flattering idea' that a building 'similar in appearance to the Parthenon of Athens' might complete the city's 'fancied resemblance' to Athens. Seeds of all manner of demeaning doubt are being sown, and much is to be read into the imprecision of words such as 'similarity' and 'ideas'. Then comes the denouement: the unfinished National Monument is 'the embodiment of a grand mistake in hewn stone! … a very striking "national monument" of pride and poverty.'[113]

*   *   *   *   *

All the major Greek buildings of the Athens of the North, the National Monument excepted, were connected in some way with the world of the mind. Institutions devoted to education, science and the arts were accommodated in temple-like structures, with one—the Royal Institution itself—providing rooms for a drawing school, an art gallery, and two learned societies with their libraries, museums, and meeting rooms. Monuments to philosophers, mathematicians and poets were designed like choragic monuments in Athens, or tombs in Magna Graecia. Medical colleges were built in magnificent Greek-inspired style. Schools or charitable educational institutions were given superb new buildings of a Doric grandeur hardly to be paralleled elsewhere.

'The taste which sprung up round the work of Phidias might then be transferred to our northern regions ...', Archibald Alison had proposed in 1819.[114] It was deeply shocking to him, therefore, and to many others, that in 1832 a sculptor of a somewhat different calibre should have been permitted to establish a workshop and exhibition in a series of sheds within the curtilage of the uncompleted National Monument (itself now surrounded by 'a coarse and clumsy palisade') and sheltering behind the columns of the western portico. Contemporary prints clearly show these shanties.[115] Robert Forrest was certainly not without talent.[116] But the fact that, almost as soon as the Edinburgh Parthenon project had ground to a halt, he was granted use of the site, and encouraged to display his work in such a prominent position, struck many as a sort of betrayal of the ideas of 'Athenian' Edinburgh. The long-lived judge Sir John Macdonald, Lord Kingsburgh, harrumphed in his reminiscences (published in 1915) that the enclosure known as 'Forrest's Statuary' was 'hideous and discreditable', its contents 'unworthy to be provided with accommodation on our classical hill'. But the Calton had declined in status since the days of the Modern Athenians of the 1820s. With regret did Macdonald recall its use for carpet-beating, linen-washing and as a drying-green. Prints of the mid-nineteenth century also show this mundane function of the erstwhile ethereal 'Acropolis' of Modern Athens. The columns of the National Monument, thought Macdonald, 'tell of Scotland's folly'.[117]

The greatest proportion of Forrest's output consisted of representations of characters from Scottish popular literature, or interpretations of episodes from Scottish history, though he also carved large likenesses of British military heroes. But one of Forrest's other works seemed to stand in a class of its own, and to enjoy a tenuous link to the Greek ideals of Calton Hill and of an Edinburgh with a concern both for the Greece of the present and Greece of the past. This was the sculptural group representing 'The Sisters of Scio', a subject from the aftermath of the massacre of Chios, itself infamous among atrocities of the Greek War of Independence.[118] Forrest's immediate inspiration had been the poem by Felicia Hemans, 'The Sisters of Scio', which first appeared in *The Literary Souvenir* in 1830. This includes the lines 'Thoughts of our own lost home/ our sunny isle', and the doleful 'Desolate, desolate our chambers lie!' It may not, perhaps, be entirely fanciful to make a connection here with the abandoned National Monument and its use as Forrest's showground.

The anonymous author of *Edinburgh Dissected* was in no doubt that 'the desecration of this noble fragment by the wretched sheds' should be stopped forthwith, 'no matter if these sheds were the studio of Praxiteles himself'.[119] And the writer wanted to see the completion, for some suitable purpose, of the Parthenon, soon to acquire the unfortunate nickname of 'Edinburgh's disgrace'. Others wished the same. Robert Batty, in 1832, had speculated that

The spirit and patriotism of the inhabitants of Edinburgh will probably in time crown the whole of the Calton Hill with beautiful and magnificent buildings, and render this fine northern capital worthy of its boasted title of 'The Modern Athens'.

Enough of the 'great National Monument' had been erected 'to give fair promise of its future grandeur'.[120] Successive editions of Black's *Picturesque Tourist* likewise pondered the future of a building that, despite the evident masterly workmanship, seemed destined to stand as but a 'modern ruin'. The National Monument had been conceived as something worthy of a patriotic cause and was to have risen as 'a literal restoration of the Parthenon'. But, unfortunately,

> the architectural taste of the projectors was far in advance of the pecuniary means at their disposal; and the monument, we fear, is doomed to commemorate the inadequacy of metropolitan means to give effect to the designs of metropolitan taste.[121]

The misplaced 'architectural ambition of the projectors' likewise figured in the second edition, coupled with the reflection that

> It cannot fail to be lamented, not only by all Scotsmen, but by every man of taste, that this attempt to restore one of the "glories of the antique world" upon a site worthy of its fame, should thus be defeated by the want of funds.

The guidebook added a melancholy observation illuminated by a slight ray of hope:

> How long the structure is destined to languish in its present condition it is impossible to calculate—possibly till some auspicious occasion, when Her Majesty may be pleased to visit her Scottish Metropolis, and to acknowledge a royal interest in the progress of the work.[122]

Queen Victoria indeed came to Edinburgh later that year, 1842. But the niece of George IV dispensed as little royal largesse towards the northern Parthenon as her uncle had done in 1822.

Henry Cockburn lamented the failure to complete the National Monument and the decline of its surroundings on Calton Hill—what he called the 'hurtful temptations' to ruin the place.[123] In 1835, he had been outraged when the city resolved to move the place of public executions to the vicinity:

> ... my whole time, thoughts and soul are engrossed amidst astonishment, horror, rage, disgust and indignation at a resolution of the Town Council to make the front of the Calton Jail the hanging place!!! There's a scheme

for you! The Parthenon of Edinr, the Westminster Abbey of Scotland, the National Acropolis, the scene hallowed by the ashes of Hume, Burns, Playfair, and Stewart ... And for what! To remove an established nuisance from the Old Town ... to the New Town! And if the said New Town be not degraded below the lowest dirt in spirit, it will rise into rebellion ...[124]

This Golgotha-like notion having been quashed, the hill was now a public washing- and drying-green, and Cockburn queried if this could possibly be right.[125] In his cynical and celebrated *Letter to the Lord Provost on the Best Ways of Spoiling the Beauty of Edinburgh* (1849) he wrote of the hill as 'the glory of Edinburgh', and then of 'that striking fragment of the Parthenon ... which I can never permit myself to doubt that some future generations will complete.'[126] He contrasted what might have been with the present actuality, expressing relief that the Calton Hill had still, as yet, not become the execution ground. In the privacy of private correspondence he went further, allowing himself not just italics but multiple exclamation marks, writing of the Calton Hill

getting itself converted into *a public washing green*!!!!! With iron poles, and ropes, and wells, and streaks of worn grass—i.e. mud—and yellow, ragged blankets, and tubs, and stones, and bitches [the washer-women]. All this on the Calton Hill! ... a voluntary magisterial act, cursed by a few, but applauded by many!! Do keep your eye on all such pieces of Hunnism.[127]

Cockburn's feelings for the National Monument are very significant, as his outbursts bring together a number of thoughts engendered by the 'classical hill'. From the outset of the Edinburgh Parthenon project, there were those who had stressed its function as a national 'Pantheon' or 'Valhalla', a potential 'Westminster Abbey' which might in due course hold memorials to the great of the Scottish nation; this enhancement of its role would further manifest the Calton's credentials as 'the National Acropolis'. The terms and notions may have become mixed up and used freely and variously, but the general concept was always there.

Lord Cockburn's elitist 'Athenian' view of 1849 was immediately challenged by James Begg, who pointed out a little peevishly (not to say pedantically) that the Hill was just a 'bleaching green' and that actual washing did not come into it; also, rather more significantly, that the Lord Provost was the guardian of the rights of the real people of Edinburgh and not just some sort of airy 'protector of the beauties of the "Modern Athens"'.[128] This was a city where, in the post-reform age, democracy was beginning to matter. No longer could the old Town Council, with its thirty or so self-perpetuating members, be compared to the rule of the Thirty Tyrants of ancient Athens after the end of the Peloponnesian War. In these circumstances it is strange to find that Professor John Stuart Blackie does not appear quite the democrat we might expect. In January 1869 he delivered a three-hour lecture 'On Democracy', which highlighted what he saw as its shortcomings, whether in antiquity or the present. Greater rights should be granted to those with more education or property, or to members of learned and elite bodies such as the Faculty of Advocates or the Royal Society of Edinburgh—to both of which Blackie himself happened to belong. Henry Longueville Mansel, an Oxford philosophy don of conservative views, wrote thus to Blackie: 'I marvel ... at your boldness in delivering it [the lecture] at Edinburgh—the Modern Athens like her ancient prototype, being far gone in the worship of Demos ...'[129]

In his posthumously published *Memorials of his Time*, Cockburn also reflected on a further inappropriate use of the Calton slopes and crags. 'It was a piece of undoubted bad taste to give so glorious an eminence to a prison.' Robert Adam's castle-style Bridewell of 1791 had been joined by Archibald Elliot's Calton Gaol of 1815-17, also in a castellated idiom. Together, these institutions saw that the felons of Edinburgh were housed in as magnificent a topographical setting as might be imagined. This Cockburn did not like. 'It was one of our noblest sites, and would have been given by Pericles to one of his finest edifices.'[130]

Another who hoped that construction of the National Monument might be resumed and taken to completion was James Ballantine, a stained-glass artist of distinction but also a versifier of somewhat less merit. His collection of couthie pieces published in 1843 with the title *The Gaberlunzie's Wallet* includes a long 'Address to Edinburgh'. The rhyme-scheme of the poem is eccentric. But the text contains some very interesting insights on Calton Hill, and what might have been, and what Ballantine hoped might still be, its crowning glory. Leaving apart his peculiarity of expression—and quaintness of sentiment about a Northern Athens once imagined, since lost, but perhaps still yet reclaimable—these lines may form an ending to this chapter.

> Behold that Hill which towers sublime,
> Gay, green as Youth, and dark as Time,
> Bank, slope, and ridge appear;
> While Temple, Tower, and Monument,
> In one bold rugged outline blent,
> Their lofty heads appear;
>
> One new-born Temple caps its top
> To Scotland's bosom dear,
> Yet, while her breast swells high with hope,
> She sheds a silent tear;
> Lest all her tried valour
> No other meed should gain.
> To story her glory,
> Than this unfinished fane.

Awake my country, why delay?
Ye slumber in the blaze of day,
All shameless in your shame;
To let this noble fragment stand
A wreck unfinished, and a brand,
Upon the Scottish name; ...

Come, start men, shew heart, men
Be soul and sinew strained,
Till ample, this temple,
Shall tell the conquest gained ...

Resume your noble work of love,
Stint not your country's fame,
Until her glory gleams above,
In characters of flame;
Then flourishing, and nourishing
Art, science, love, and peace,
Our north home shall forth come,
And rival Ancient Greece.[131]

NEW ATHENS FROM WITHOUT

'THE SOUL OF THE SCENE, THAT TO WHICH ALL BOW'

Edinburgh's undoubted intellectual eminence, coupled with its outstanding natural setting and increasingly elegant streets and buildings, could and did lead residents into exaggerated praise of their city—sometimes to a ridiculous extent.

This tendency was observed and mercilessly mocked by Thomas Jefferson Hogg when he travelled north to join his friend Percy Bysshe Shelley in Edinburgh in 1811. One consequential little man with whom Hogg shared the coach would not be silent on the matter of the 'Athenian' status of the place: 'You will find it a most remarkable city; by far the most remarkable under the heavens, without any exception.' Hogg was sarcastic indeed about his goal, certainly when he found his accommodation:

> If such be, in very deed, the beauteous city of Minerva, the chosen residence of
> Apollo and the Muses, the true abode of Beauty, of the Loves and Graces, I wish
> I were back again in my lodgings in York, or at one of the inns near the Lakes ...

The distaste of squalor and sense of disappointment remained even when Hogg had encountered 'glorious spectacle', 'magnificence' and the 'triumphs of art and nature'.[1]

To Sir Nathaniel Wraxall the common people of Edinburgh seemed very far removed from the Athenian ideal. His visit to the David Hume mausoleum was spoiled by the intrusion of contemporary life upon the contemplation both of modern genius and great architecture in the antique taste:

> ... in this *nasty* city—for such the inhabitants certainly are—however beautiful
> may be the Aspect of the Place, the near approach ... was impeded by many

abominable Nuisances; & I was driven from offering my Hommage at his Tomb, by a Worshipper of another Description, who could not be approached without Disgust.[2]

Yet, for every visitor who mocked Athenian pretensions and the actuality of life in an Auld Reekie that had given itself 'Athenian' airs, there were many more who actually were impressed by the city, and sympathetic to its claims of intellectual and topographical distinction. Dr Peter Morris may only have been a figment of J. G. Lockhart's imagination as the eponymous writer of the brilliant *Peter's Letters to his Kinsfolk* (1819); but Morris spoke for many genuine visitors to the Northern Athens from southern parts of the United Kingdom. At one point, Lockhart has Morris report on a visit to Playfair's observatory on Calton Hill. One must overlook the inexact understanding of authentic Greek architecture and concentrate on the opinions of a visitor affected by the classical atmosphere of this little cultural and scientific precinct:

> Its fine portico, with a single range of Doric pillars supporting a graceful pediment, shaped exactly like that of the Parthenon—and over that again, its dome lifting itself lightly and airily in the clear mountain sky—and the situation itself, on the brink of that magnificent eminence ... just where it looks towards the sea—altogether remind one of the best days of Grecian art and Grecian science, when the mariner knew Athens afar off from the Aegean, by the chaste splendour of pillars and temples that crowned the original rock of Theseus. If a few elms and plantains could be made to grow to their full dimensions around this rising structure, the effect would be the nearest thing in the world to that of the glorious scene, which Plato has painted so divinely at the opening of his Republic.[3]

The visual imagery Lockhart was calling for would, in some measure, be provided when Hugh William Williams produced his romanticised view of 'The Academic Grove' showing Plato and his pupils debating below a statue of the patron goddess Athena, the buildings of the Acropolis forming the background to the scene. (Fig. 33) It would not be long before another writer could comment on how 'the pure Grecian architecture' had somehow come to find a natural and happy habitat on a 'craggy hill' seeming to 'offer sites equal to the Athenian Acropolis itself', with the result that 'various structures of that kind have been erected upon it'. The Observatory stood out, giving 'the whole scenery a Grecian aspect, its form and situation being alike calculated to remind the spectator of the temple-crowned steeps of Achaia.'[4]

At the same time as the fictional Peter Morris was in Edinburgh, the real Nassau Senior arrived in the city. He was a newly called London barrister, and later a distinguished political economist. His enthusiasm for the Observatory matches Lockhart's—coincidentally, because by his own account, Senior specifically said that he had heard of *Peter's Letters* but not yet read them. 'Lockhart', wrote Senior, 'is a prominent person in the Edinburgh world, not only from his general literary accomplishments, but as the reputed author of Peter's letters, which give, I am told ... a very animated picture of the place.' On a fine day in 1819, Senior made his way up Leith Walk.

> The sun had just got behind the Calton Hill, & the slanting rays doubled the apparent height. The observatory at the top, which is of Grecian architecture, was magnified till it resembled my idea of the Parthenon & the magnificent architectural bridge which connects it with the town [the Regent Bridge, by Archibald Elliot, forming part of Waterloo Place] might have stood in Athens. My admiration increased as I went on. Imagine Oxford or Chester on one hill, Bath on another, & Windsor Castle between them. And the situation is worthy of it ...[5]

Frances, Lady Shelley, was also in Edinburgh in 1819. She was a woman susceptible to the Picturesque in both its Romantic and Classical manifestations—those contrasting yet complimentary characteristics that Edinburgh could demonstrate so well. Observing the city from the south, as Walter Scott's Lord Marmion had done, she 'gazed in rapture on this truly romantic city, where Art has proved a true sister to Nature, both having combined to adorn this unrivalled capital.' The sites she knew from her reading of Scott 'conjured up fairy visions of historic, classic, and poetic interest, all equally absorbing.' But now, in actuality, the Calton Hill presented a totally different view of Edinburgh. She had evidently come to terms early with its new 'Athenian' designation. 'From its summit, the straight streets, the Grecian buildings, the white freestone, and the crags of Arthur's Seat give an impression of elegance and taste nowhere to be seen but in this modern Athens.' Rapidly, however, Lady Shelley found a parallel in another great city of the ancient world and of modern Europe: 'In my opinion, the walk up the Calton ranks next in beauty to that of the Monte Pincio at Rome.'[6]

A third visitor of 1819, Robert Southey, differed from both Nassau Senior and Frances Shelley in seeing little or nothing of the emerging elegant 'Greekness' of Edinburgh, and everything of the grimy face of Auld Reekie. It was the smuts and odours of the town that he commented upon, summed up in his acerbic comment that one might 'smoke bacon by hanging it out of the window'. Southey would not have known that Playfair was, at the time, planning the layout of the city north-eastwards of Calton Hill towards Leith; but he did examine Playfair's work at the University, though he is unlikely to have been aware of the architect personally, or of how much Playfair's designs impressed those who had commissioned him. Rather, such 'Grecian' classicism as Southey observed, he dismissed for its pretentious extravagance. 'The people of Edinburgh have acquired a taste, or more properly a rage for splendid buildings. The expenditure upon the College is profuse, even to absurdity.' This was demonstrated by what Southey condemned as 'the preposterous ceiling of their intended Museum [that is, the upper Natural History Museum, now the Talbot Rice Gallery], a rich specimen of ill-directed expenditure.'[7] (Figs. 55-56)

Like Lady Shelley, Benjamin Robert Haydon was also a great admirer of Scott, whose writings had formed his expectations of Edinburgh's character and scenery. In 1820 Haydon professed himself astonished by what he described as a 'wild dream of great genius', and went on, in the abbreviated form of his diary entries, to describe Edinburgh as 'finest city in Europe—may be in time [in] the World'. Conscious of where the real parallelism lay, he added: 'The only city in the World where the Parthenon might be erected with something of its ancient splendour—.'[8]

A 'passing visitant' was how William Hazlitt would have classed himself when in Edinburgh in the spring of 1822.[9] Although he reviewed (as we have seen) the first exhibition of Hugh William Williams's watercolours, and did so enthusiastically, it was not such refined interests that had brought him to the city in the first place. Hazlitt was seeking a divorce so that he might marry a much younger woman, and was fulfilling the necessary residence requirement in order to obtain one under Scots law. He seems to have spent some, at least, of that time closely studying the young ladies of Edinburgh. The vision of them intruded on his appreciation of Williams's pictures, for in his piece for *The London Magazine* he waxed lyrical about

The slender, lovely, taper waist (made more taper, more lovely, more slender by the stay-maker), instead of being cut in two by the keen blasts that rage in Prince's [*sic*] street, is here supported by warm languid airs, and a thousand sighs, that breathe from the vale of Tempe. Do not those fair tresses look brighter as they are seen hanging over a hill in Arcadia, than when they come in contact with the hard grey rock of the castle? Do not those fair blue eyes look more translucent, as they glance over some classic stream? What can vie with that alabaster skin but marble temples, dedicated to the Queen of Love? What can match those golden freckles but glittering sun-sets behind Mount Olympus? Here, in one corner of the room, stands the Hill of the Muses, and there a group of Graces under it![10]

Its overt lasciviousness apart, this passage constitutes a remarkable assessment of what contact with the vision of Greece, as conveyed by a series of views painted from nature, or filtered through the eye of an artist who was convinced of the similarity of Scottish and Greek scenery, might do to the corporeal form as much as to the psyche of Modern Athenian womanhood! Looking at Greece made the women of Edinburgh look their best; they became the Graces.

The purported memoirs of an unusually literate non-commissioned officer of the Royal North British Dragoons (Scots Greys) record two separate tours of duty at Piershill Barracks, Edinburgh. Corporal (later Troop Sergeant Major) William Clarke was first posted to the city in 1807, and returned when his regiment formed one of the mounted escorts for King George IV in 1822. Whereas the precise status of the manuscript is in doubt, a comment of Clarke's should nevertheless be considered here, for he records his appreciation of 'the unequalled architecture of modern Athens'. Although the supposition must be that this comment was written some time subsequently, the terminology of later years being applied retrospectively to the first decade of the century, the very fact that urban architectural achievement and Northern Athenian notions should have entered the dragoon's head at all is of some interest.[11]

Thomas Bewick revisited the city in 1823 after a very long interval. He wrote of

> ... the new town, or city of palaces, as it is now sometimes called, [which] had been added since I had seen it [in August 1776]. But all these splendid buildings are of trivial import compared with the mass of intellect and science which had taken root and had been nurtured and grown up to such a height as to rival, and perhaps to outstrip, every other city in the world ... Edin., now the seat of learning, and rendered brilliant by gems both of art and science with which it is adorned.[12]

William Deane Ryland, an undergraduate of St John's College, Cambridge, visited that same year. Coincidentally, he illustrated his travel journal with some pleasing sketches which prove to be either copied from, or based upon, original drawings by Bewick. So carried away was Ryland by all he encountered—he even glimpsed Sir Walter Scott (to whose novels he was devoted) in the Advocates' Library—that he imagined he actually *saw* the Northern Athenian Parthenon. This is an interesting instance of someone who had become so seduced by the very idea of Edinburgh as another Athens that he envisioned a completed building even before it had been started. Presumably he had learnt that such a monument was to be built; but he must surely have discovered that only the foundation stone was in existence to give some hope and substance to the dream. Ryland's ascent of Calton Hill seemed to convince him, also, of an aspect of Edinburgh's contemporary 'Athenian' spirit, and of how it had percolated down from the people with whom he mixed more naturally during his Edinburgh days and nights. A working man he encountered

> gave a very favourable impression of the intelligence of the lower orders of the Scotch, for although he had been but a private soldier he seemed perfectly acquainted not only with the history of his own country, but with the present state of affairs on the Continent, with the sanguinary character of the French and the evil influence of the Roman catholic priesthood.[13]

Hugh Miller, whose career as geologist and evangelical Christian writer still lay in the future, first came to Edinburgh in May 1824 in pursuit of his trade as a stonemason. Miller's poetic description of the Modern Athens he saw is striking—except for the fact that he never referred to the city as the Modern Athens. In writing of how the city's 'monuments rising above the cloud' seemed to him akin to 'spears and banners on a field of battle', he continued with the reflection that the scene 'reminded me of those cities which Heaven visited in judgement when the sun had risen on that morning on which Lot took his departure from them.' Edinburgh, whether as Auld Reekie or Modern Athens, had not often been mistaken for Sodom or Gomorrah. Miller continued, remembering his sense of disappointment: 'I had read of its streets of palaces, but I had acquired my ideas of palaces from the descriptions of fairies and genii.' What is most interesting about Miller's memories of his first encounter with Edinburgh, and specifically with its buildings, is his disdain for the architecture of the city. He confessed that he had been less impressed by its grandeur in actuality than he had been in anticipation and in imagination. Stonemasons such as he were realists. 'The more conversant a person is with the tricks of a juggler the less will he admire his skill.' Miller was able to reduce all of the glories of the Modern Athens, as its majesty was expressed in individual buildings, to its essential structural and mechanical parts. Looked at that way, the city held little in the way of awe for him: 'Give me matter and motion, said I, and I will build an Edinburgh.'[14]

The Scottish Tourist (1827) was one of several guidebooks to Scottish sites and scenery published to cater to the ever-increasing market for visitors to both Edinburgh and Scotland as a whole. The publication supplied a useful corrective to the idea that the rash of neoclassical buildings, which contributed so much to the changed townscape of Edinburgh, made the city what it now was, and what it might become. Nature had done that job. 'Much as Edinburgh owes to the taste with which its recent buildings have been planned, its principal features derive their character from its situation.' This was a city part Classical, part Romantic, but one set in a tremendous landscape wholly that of the latter realm.[15]

In the journal of his Scottish tour of 1832, William Cobbett did not even feel he had to name the city to which he was setting out: his memoir simply records that he was bound for 'Modern Athens'. It is clear that he regarded this, above all, as a city of the mind, for he makes plodding jests about the 'antallect', 'feelosofers', and 'about feelosofical' matters: Edinburgh was inhabited by 'so many *really* learned and *really* clever men'.[16]

The American man of letters Nathaniel Parker Willis, who had travelled widely in Europe and who knew both Turkey and Greece, arrived from London by sea. On board the *Monarch* steamer he had struck up conversation that had led to his mentioning his time in Greece. Hearing this, a female passenger turned to him and asked if, when there, he had happened to meet 'Lady ——'.

Indeed, Willis had met her in Athens; his fellow-passenger was her sister. This en route to the *Modern* Athens. Willis was impressed by the setting of, and approach to, Edinburgh, the prospect of which, from the Forth, struck him as being second only to that of Constantinople. But then he moved on to the comparison with Athens:

> The singular resemblance, in one or two features, to the view of Athens, as you approach from the Piraeus, seems to have struck other eyes than mine; and an imitation Acropolis is commenced on the Calton-hill, and has already, in its half-finished state, much the effect of the Parthenon. Hymettus is rather loftier than the Pentland-hills, and Pentelicus farther off and grander than Arthur's seat; but the Old Castle of Edinburgh is a noble and peculiar feature of its own, and soars up against the sky, with its pinnacle-placed turrets, superbly magnificent.[17]

When Willis wrote of the 'other eyes' that had seen Edinburgh, and compared it with Athens, he perhaps meant Hugh William Williams. Certainly, their ways of seeing the two cities, and 'twinning' them, were similar.

In Edinburgh Willis met John Wilson, 'Christopher North' of *Blackwood's Magazine*, and they talked of the particular kind of satire and humour associated with that journal and its contributors. The most exotic visitor to Edinburgh at the height of its Northern Athenian conceit was a *Blackwood's* creation: the entirely fictitious Tahitian chief, Omai. In 1822, *Blackwood's* carried two long articles purporting to be Omai's memoirs of his visits to Edinburgh, the second of which coincided with that of King George IV. This entertaining spoof, apparently the work of the printer John Stark (author of successive editions of *The Picture of Edinburgh*), has been overlooked by all who have subsequently written about both the National Monument and the Royal Visit; it has also been neglected by writers on the celebrated real-life eighteenth-century figure of Omai (or Mai) himself, to whose story this *jeu d'ésprit* provides an amusing post-script. The fictional Omai who comes to Edinburgh is said to be the grandson of the genuine Omai.[18] On Day Thirteenth of his second visit, headed 'The Parthenon.—The Theatre', Omai joins the Freemasons of Scotland at the ceremony of the laying of the foundation stone of the National Monument. He calls this 'the Parthenon Church on the Hill of Calton'. Having seen a perspective view or other drawing of it, he proceeds with a word of explanation: 'And the Parthenon, if I, Omai, am asked what it is—it is a true church, with pillars, for I have seen its picture in the theatre-house; and it is the National Monument.'

Another contributor to *Blackwood's* that same year, regrettably anonymous, was probably as genuine as 'Omai' was imaginary: he wrote an article published under the name of 'a Londoner but no Cockney'. Offering what purports to be a view of 'the King's Visit to Edinburgh', the piece is in fact an excellent analysis of what was going on in the city—in architectural and other realms—and in the minds of its more 'Athenian' citizens.[19] The Londoner looked at the Calton Hill as a place that was both a precious natural asset while remaining largely unbuilt upon, but also as a *tabula rasa* ripe for tasteful development in the classical style. The reference within the following passage is to Charles Robert Cockerell, designer of the Edinburgh Parthenon.

> The hill is a favourite, and, like all favourites, runs a hazard of being spoiled. A celebrated London architect, availing himself of the popular propensity, has recommended that it should be stuck over with pillar and pyramid without delay. The advice is natural to an architect; no man can resist his calling; and this fine hill will be nothing better than an inordinate pin-cushion.—*Oremus pro paupertate Edinensi.*[20]

The final words of the quotation above are fateful and prophetic ones: the 'prayer' for the 'poverty of Edinburgh', thus prohibiting further exploitation of Calton Hill, would indeed be answered as money for the National Monument ran out.

Past architectural development in Edinburgh, the 'Londoner' observed, had been tentative and cautious. So should it continue, even now that the will to be Athenian was abroad.

> In this prudence, they have built a little Greek house on the Calton, as a preparative to the Parthenon. They have called it an Observatory; they might more wisely have called it an ice-house. They already had an Observatory, an old hard-featured thing, that stood wrapt up in grey rock, like an eternal watchman on the brow of the hill. But they must try their skill in pediment and pillar, and, as the result, have produced a little three-or-four cornered thing, like a Ramilies hat squeezed to the top of the hill. It was to have been among the lions of Edinburgh, and strangers were to have wondered and worshipped at it five miles off. But it was found to be the very temple of the winds; Eurus, Notus, and Agrestes made sport of it with impunity. The little Observatory was in hazard of being carried off into the Ocean. To obviate the deportation, they have buried it within walls, where it lies as snug and viewless as an oyster between its valves.[21]

In contemporary usage, 'the lions' meant the celebrated sights or sites to be seen by tourists. Like Lockhart in *Peter's Letters* before him, the 'Londoner' was none too precise about the specifics of Greek architecture, but he was right about the way that the Observatory, so exposed to the elements, was soon equated with a 'Temple of the Winds', by which name it was sometimes called by visitors of the period. (There was some confusion with the actual, so-called Tower of the Winds in Athens, which had never been a temple.) The resting lion suggested by the silhouette of Arthur's Seat, and the menagerie of other, human, 'lions' in the city, attracted 'lion-hunters' in large numbers to Edinburgh in its 'Athenian' years.[22]

*   *   *   *   *

Many in pursuit of these animate and inanimate 'lions' were European tourists. French visitors to Edinburgh in the early 1820s were generally impressed by most of what they encountered in a city they appear to have accepted readily as the Modern Athens. Their eagerness to tour Great Britain matched that of Britons' enthusiasm for rushing over to France immediately after the conclusion, at the Battle of Waterloo, of the long wars with the old enemy (as they had in the earlier brief intervals of transient peace in 1802 and 1814-15). As a former place of exile for the French royal family and its entourage, Edinburgh had its attractions. But one does sense that, in the years after 1820, many highly intelligent and observant French visitors were swallowing their national pride and a predisposition to place Paris at the apex of European civic achievements in terms of culture, beauty and amenity.

Charles Nodier came to Scotland in 1821. His account, published in Paris in 1822, has a title-page vignette of Holyroodhouse (where the French exiles had lived), and a frontispiece engraving of a rather androgynous 'Chef de Clan' looking like an epicene Greek *kouros* in too-short kilt, plaid, feather bonnet and his other accoutrements. It was issued the same year in English translation by Blackwood in Edinburgh and Thomas Cadell in London, but without either vignette or Highland chief—which was probably deemed just too silly for the British market.[23] Nodier's account of Edinburgh launched straight into Athenian comparisons. The city was unquestionably one of the most interesting in modern Europe. Independently of this fact, due to its political and literary institutions, and taking into account

> the edifices, or the recollections which give it a title of rivality [*sic*] with the most celebrated cities of ancient Europe, it seems that the name of the Athens of the North, *which nobody contests* [my italics], is a privilege of locality founded on very striking topographical resemblances.

As other visitors before Nodier had already asserted, Leith took the place of the Piraeus. The Castle Rock brought to mind the Acropolis, and the similarity set him musing: 'absorbed in I know not what sentiments, I dreamt of nothing but Athens, and was looking for the Parthenon.' Interestingly, Nodier was definitely thinking here of the formula 'Castle equals Acropolis', for he goes on to mention the Calton Hill without drawing any Athenian parallels at all in its case.[24] (Despite the chronological disparity, this comment may actually be what James Simpson was referring to when he told Walter Scott of a French writer—about twenty years before, Simpson confusingly said—who had similarly been looking for the temple of Athena on the Calton Hill.)[25] In the New Town, what must be Royal Circus (then being built) promised, so Nodier reckoned, an urban quarter 'worthy of Athens herself'. A group of Highland chiefs glimpsed in the streets in full fig—probably en route to an Edinburgh Celtic Society gathering—appeared to him to sport 'Grecian drapery' rather than to resemble the kilted Romans that so many before (and since) had seen as the obvious antique parallel.[26] Continuing the Greek theme of an Edinburgh turning increasingly to an 'Athenian' outlook, Nodier amused himself by speculating that 'There will never again be Romans but the Parthenon may one day rise from its ruins', adding the little barb '… if Lord Elgin has left any'.[27]

Amédée Pichot's visit coincided with that of King George IV. His account, which took the form of a series of perceptive letters to friends in France, was also translated into English in 1825. It is one of the best commentaries on Edinburgh ever written by a foreigner, and unquestionably one of the most penetrating on the subject of the city in its 'Athenian' persona. The view from Arthur's Seat was said by Pichot, without equivocation or preliminary justification, to be that of 'the northern Athens; that is to say, the most extraordinary panorama which any city in Europe can supply.' It was superior to that of Rouen, or even Marseille. For a Frenchman to admit this at the start was surely exceptional. Everything that the eye embraced was 'worthy of the Athens of the north'. The city even had its own Piraeus: 'I designate the port of Leith by that name.'[28]

> There is talk of raising a national temple on Calton Hill, and it is proposed, for that purpose, to make it a copy of the Parthenon; this will, perhaps, be the only edifice truly worthy of the designation of Athens; but, as I have before said, the *tout ensemble* of the city astonishes the stranger at first sight.[29]

A Parthenon would at least lend character to the treeless, 'sterile eminences on which the Modern Athens is erected'. It is true that Pichot was not blind to what he saw as the many deficiencies, even downright 'bad taste', exhibited in the design of the residential streets of the New Town. Nor were public and monumental buildings excepted from criticism of this aspect of the fabric of a city, 'the site of which alone ought to have inspired a true taste in architecture'. Even Robert Adam did not escape castigation.[30] But Pichot was especially acute in appreciating the essential nature of Edinburgh's 'Athenianism'. This did not depend upon topography and architecture alone, he suggested, but rather more truly upon its distinction as a city of the intellect. And here Pichot was even more perceptive when he made the suggestion that 'Edinburgh, in proudly proclaiming herself the Athens of Great Britain'—this recalls those remarks made in the 1760s—was perhaps applying the epithet more subjectively than objectively. Still, and undeniably, the Athenian parallel

> does not alone refer to the analogies of her site, to her Piraeus (Leith), her Acropolis, with its citadel (the castle), to her future Parthenon, (the projected temple on Calton Hill), &c. Edinburgh is still more proud of aspiring to the designation, on the score of her philosophers, orators, critics, and poets, or rather of her learned societies, which are not all, unfortunately, Academies. But every body here occupies himself more or less with literature and science ...

The 'Athenian' character of the city extended to the fair sex. 'Even the ladies', Pichot declared, in a passage mixing patronising bemusement with an element of French male chauvinism, 'aspire to the exertion of their little literary influence. Nous sommes tous d'Athènes sur ce point.'[31] These Modern Athenian females should have been displeased, as Pichot was, by the spectacle of the crudely sculptured statue of a lumpish Hygieia in the rotunda of St Bernard's Well, when the picturesque setting, and the wider literary context, would have suggested a more elegant 'Grecian Hebe, worthy of the Modern Athens'.[32]

Adolphe Blanqui visited in 1823. Much struck him as 'Athenian': like its prototype in classical antiquity, the Modern Athens, and most specifically the New Town of Edinburgh, was 'la fille de civilisation ... riche, elegant et somptueuse comme elle'. Once again, the location of Leith suggested the Piraeus, 'car Edimbourg a des ressemblances [sic] frappantes avec Athènes'. The projected Parthenon would add to the physical and topographical similarity. The fame of the city's institutions, and the eminence of her learned men, made her the Athens of the North. Of all these luminaries, none was a greater attraction than was Walter Scott. (Pichot had felt exactly the same.) Blanqui therefore called at Scott's house in Castle Street.

> Quand les étrangers visitaient Athènes, ils couraient voir d'abord Socrate et Platon: notre première visite était due à l'auteur des Puritains et de Waverley...

All in all, Blanqui was exceedingly impressed by a city without physical or intellectual rival in Europe, where 'rien ne lui manquera des beautés de Rome et d'Athènes'.[33]

François Alexandre Pernot, who published his collection of picturesque views accompanied by a commentary in 1826, saw principally a city of contrasts: 'les sombre édifices du viel Édimbourg et l'élégance de la Nouvelle-Athènes'; 'une ville sombre, enfumée, irrégulière ... une ville toute modern ... ou l'on a prodigué des péristyles grecs, et que surmonte une élégante colonne trajane!' Viewed from Calton Hill, Leith naturally assumed the identity of 'le pirée de l'Athènes du Nord'. Pernot, however, was in no doubt that as 'comme un autre souvenir d' Athènes, l'antique citadelle comparée à l'Acropolis'. But everything offered an easy association of ideas and souvenirs of all the ages.[34]

Given French visitors' interest in, and understanding of, contemporary Edinburgh's obsession about feeling and looking 'Athenian', it is something of a corrective to note that Gustave d'Eichthal—later to be so eminent as a promoter of everything Greek, and of the Greek language—makes no allusion whatsoever to the notion of Edinburgh as the Modern Athens. Edinburgh was, he freely admitted, 'certainly one of the most beautiful cities in the world, the most beautiful if you except Naples which is hard to better.' But he drew no comparisons, either topographically with Athens or, culturally, with the Athens of antiquity. In fact, he suggested that the citizens of Edinburgh 'have been careful to erect only buildings in the Gothic style to ensure that they harmonise with those that have been there a long time.' Perverse and factually wrong though this statement was, the very fact that d'Eichthal made it at all is significant. It is almost as if he had turned his back on the development of Greek—or even classical—Edinburgh. Paradoxically, he did discuss what he considered the less frequent use (than in France) of the Corinthian order in Edinburgh buildings, and singled out for mention as memorable 'the temple-like building that the Society of Arts [*sic*] has had constructed by North Loch'. He was referring to Playfair's Royal Institution, executed in the architect's interpretation of Greek Doric.[35]

Also referring to the Royal Institution, Léon de Buzonnière proceeded to comment on a building he thought 'imposant, mais un peu lourd'. This was even before Playfair enlarged it so considerably. He did, however, admit to the reader that he had made copious notes on Edinburgh—hence, perhaps, his subsequent confusion, and his mistake in saying its order was Ionic. Buzonnière seemed hopeful about the ultimate completion of the National Monument, not mentioning the fact that building was at a halt and writing that it was 'copie fidèle' of the Parthenon.[36]

George Elder Davie long ago drew attention to the important essay on Edinburgh by Charles de Rémusat of 1856, writing that

> Edinburgh for de Rémusat was in a quite genuine sense an Athens of the North, and, in his eyes, the elegant classical monuments to Stewart and Playfair on the Calton Hill bulked just as large in the Princes Street scene as the Gothic confection in honour of Sir Walter Scott.[37]

Though very slightly later in date, Jules Verne's novel describing the Scottish tour of two young men, Jacques and Jonathan, may be conveniently dealt with here. The manuscript was written in 1859, but it passed to a provincial French library and remained unpublished until 1989. It is a lightly fictionalised autobiographical account. The English translation of 1992 was published, appropriately, in Edinburgh.[38] Of Calton Hill, Verne wrote that the 'civic leaders ['l'édilité Édimbourgeoise'] have adorned it with various monuments, all imitations of ancient edifices, in keeping with local taste'. But of that taste a not very flattering opinion was given. 'Up there ... the unfinished portico looks successful, and overall the group of monuments is attractive in that setting, even if, taken individually, each one is poorly designed, nastily cluttered with detail and unstylish. Nonetheless, this architectural attempt to look like something is preferable to looking like nothing, as so many French monuments do.' The High School was described as Greco-Egyptian—this presumably on account of the form of some of the windows on its main façade.[39]

*   *   *   *   *

The Athens of the North also attracted its share of visitors from northern and eastern Europe. In fiction, these may be represented by the characters in Honoria Scott's novel *A Winter in Edinburgh; or, the Russian Brothers*. The tourists are conducted round the city by a guide who, combining 'national pride with architectural knowledge, asserted truly, that few cities could boast more magnificent public edifices than Edinburgh'.[40] The visitors came just too early to marvel at the St Petersburg-like grandeur of Playfair's Royal Terrace, one of the most splendid domestic manifestations of the Northern Athenian spirit in classical architecture. The huge terrace is not archaeologically accurate 'Greek' by any means in external detail, though there are good 'Grecian' interiors in many individual houses. It is in fact predominantly Roman in feeling and, as such, it embodies the stylistic imprecision of Edinburgh classicism.

A real visitor was the perceptive Pole, Krystyn Lach-Szyrma. He agreed with contemporaries who, on account of 'the exceptional beauty of its position', compared Edinburgh with Lisbon, Naples and Constantinople. But he went on to observe that, for Scots imbued with poetry, 'cold comparisons are not enough'.

They speak of their native town in parables and with great sentiment. The common people call it 'The City of Palaces'; sentimentalists, in accord with the ballads, 'The favoured seat of Edina'; the romantics, led by Sir Walter Scott, 'Our romantic town'. The classicists find that it is like Athens and, disregarding whether or not they will meet with general approval, they call it: 'The Athens of the North'. The likeness is indeed striking. Like Athens, Edinburgh is beautified by a bay, for the Firth of Forth is certainly worth the Aegean Sea: Leith is good enough to take the place of the Piraeus; the castle on the rock that of the Acropolis. The Parthenon alone seems to be missing but even this is to be erected ... It will be erected on the top of Calton Hill and, as there is not enough room for it, the monument of Nelson will have to go. This is certainly not a pity, as it is nothing but a satire on the lack of taste of the Athenians of the North ...[41]

Lach-Szyrma's most telling point is surely that the Athenian parallel did not find universal approval, and that it was the *fons et origo* of the sort of mixed emotions that were so much in evidence at the time of his visit.

Some years later, C. S. Graffman's *Skottska Vuer* (Stockholm 1831), with its lithographs by C. J. Billmark, gave a Swedish audience a picture of a city plainly called (and called so *in English*) 'The Modern Athens', in which much was made of the 'national-monument, likt Partenon i Athén … de flesta I Grekist stil…'.

Edinburgh and its Society in 1838 was published in Edinburgh by a pseudonymous author whose name appears on the title-page as 'Sebaldus Naseweis', thus suggesting some vaguely Central or Eastern European nationality. In German, 'naseweis' means precocious, cocky, know-all, or impudent—in other words, a smart-alec; and, as a given name, 'Sebaldus' is one suggesting bravery and inquisitiveness. The book displays a typographical detail not without relevance: 'Reflections on Modern Athens' appears as the running head throughout the book, which purports to be the memoirs of a European traveller to Scotland. We learn it had been decided that Naseweis should spend some years in 'a city vulgarly called Edinburgh; but which the learned, for reasons best known to themselves, have rechristened by the name of Modern Athens.' The captain of the ship bringing Naseweis into Leith points out landmarks of the city of Edinburgh beyond.

> Those pillars which you see at the other extremity of the town, on that eminence, is a monument of Scottish pride and poverty, intended to commemorate the warlike deeds of our countrymen. It has stood for years in that unfinished state; and it would be well, rather than leave it as it is, to plant some ivy round it, to hide the nakedness of our resources, and to name it the 'modern ruins of Modern Athens'.

The captain continues:

> Our city, sir, is crowded with monuments from one end to the other. But you will see them afterwards at more leisure, and be able to judge, from personal observation, how far they are creditable to the national taste, or affording evidence of unwarrantable expenditure or ignorant pretension.[42]

*   *   *   *   *

A perfectly genuine visitor to Edinburgh also published his account in 1838. This was the Revd Dr Thomas Frognall Dibdin, whom we have already encountered as a most enthusiastic, albeit gushing, commentator on the scene. His excitement at approaching 'this ATHENS OF THE NORTH' accounted for his breaking unto upper case by way of emphasis. But paradoxically, in calling Edinburgh a city of palaces, he also labelled it the 'GENOA OF THE NORTH', as if the New Town were in some way to be equated with the magnificence to be seen in the 'Strade Nuove' of 'La Superba'.[43]

Dibdin was a bibliomaniac, and the 'book-haunts of the Modern Athens' were his special delights, even if he was discomfited by the 'Cimmerian darkness' of some of the lower rooms of the Advocates' Library, where the gloomy way to literary treasures was lit by permanently burning, smelly gas-lights: 'It is inconceivable how long they have borne this state of things in the modern Athens.'[44] But his pleasure at entering the glorious room now known as the Upper Signet Library made amends for everything. 'It is like the "purple light" of Virgil's Elysian fields', Dibdin thought, his opinion compounded by sight of the painting by Thomas Stothard running round the interior of the shallow cupola.[45] This has been called a 'delightfully improbable conversazione of Scottish and Classical literati'.[46] It features Apollo and the muses, together with Homer, Herodotus and Demosthenes as representative ancient Greeks. But Roman, English and Scottish authors, including even such Enlightenment figures as David Hume, William Robertson and Adam Smith, were added to the strange assemblage, the iconography being a unique statement of what seemed suitable for a decorative library ceiling (only moderately pretentious in conception, however risible in ultimate effect) in the Athens of the North.

Dibdin examined the libraries of private men 'in this Northern Athens', and he commented on the general hunger for learning and the pursuit of taste that was universally evident. At no time, he thought, 'had there been a more general and anxious desire among these *Athenians* to explore the crumbling treasures of Antiquity [the word is set in bold black-letter]—whether in the shape of a *boke* [Dibdin's customary pseudo-archaism for 'book'], a *church* or a *castle*...'. The several historical book-clubs were (he felt it necessary to point out) most certainly not intended 'for the haunt of, or as the receptacles of debauchees'.[47]

On the progress of the arts of painting, sculpture and architecture 'in this renowned *Athens of the North*' Dibdin had some interesting observations to make. 'The strides towards perfection in each department, within this century, have been enormous.' Referring to painting in particular, he pointed to the contrast with the 'limited list, so sparingly commended' by his friend Sir John Stoddart at the beginning of the century: 'behold here, gentle reader, a more copious list or grouping, in colours more glowing and encomiastic ... There is a sort of heart's worship in the cause.'[48]

But, still, Edinburgh people had to look to their laurels, for the rival city in the west might match them at their game. Dibdin admired the buildings and monuments in Glasgow's George Square, where a Scott monument (a statue on an enormous classical column) had already been erected some years before Edinburgh's huge Gothic space-rocket appeared. 'The Spartans have here shot ahead of the Athenians', Dibdin commented wryly.[49] When Edinburgh classicists themselves wanted (perhaps unwisely) to demean the Merchant City of Glasgow, they searched for an ancient Greek allusion and tended to opt for 'Boeotian', the implication being one of dullness or stupidity.

Sated with all he had experienced in Edinburgh, Dibdin at length

> bade farewell to that city which by courtesy has been called the MODERN ATHENS. It has been so designated in the preceding pages: a title, of which the local and architectural character of the place, as well as the pursuits and talents of the citizens, should seem to justify the assumption. But, whether fitly or unfitly bestowed, is of secondary importance. The City of Edinburgh wants no fanciful, titular adjunct to bind the 'form and fashion' of it upon my memory by cords as numerous as they will be lasting. If I have turned my back upon its buildings for ever, the 'windows of the soul' (to borrow Primaudaye's expression) shall be always open, whence to survey its beauties, and to waft the warmest wishes for the prosperity of its Inhabitants ...[50]

The note of reservation discreetly expressed here is surely every bit as interesting as any element of uncritical acceptance of the Athenian comparison.

Watching from London, *The Times* missed few opportunities to mock Edinburgh's airs and graces, and even its emergence as a tourist centre. In the year that Dibdin's Northern Tour was published, the newspaper ridiculed the 'extravagant expenditure ... laid out in architectural embellishment and landscape-gardening—which contrived to make [the] city a place of attraction and profitable resort', but which had also driven it into bankruptcy.[51] So much for the physical setting of 'Athenian' pretension. As a city of the intellect, Edinburgh was (so *The Times* implied) vastly over-rated, and particularly so by itself. 'If Edinburgh be entitled to her self-arrogated description of "Modern Athens" it is surely not to her displays of public eloquence that she can justify her claim.' Quite to the contrary, in the orotund opinion of *The Times*,

> this Northern Capital seems to be fatal to all but the very heaviest heavings of humdrum intellect, which in its sympathetic fondness it enshrouds in congenial vapour. Were it worth the while, we might prove that talents of a high order—nay, genius itself, have been dimmed and darkened by the density of this political atmosphere.

Sir John Campbell, Member of Parliament for the city of Edinburgh and Attorney General in the government of Lord Melbourne, was in the firing line.[52]

*   *   *   *   *

A series of German visitors in the 1830s and 1840s were enthusiastic in their praise of Edinburgh, and for its 'Athenian' airs. This was despite the fact that construction of the National Monument was at a dead halt, the city bankrupt, and the high-tide of 'Athenianism' ebbing. Friedrich Ludwig Georg von Raumer is an excellent example. 'The Edinburgh architects', he wrote

> excel those of London, and the enthusiasm of the public authorities for the embellishment of their native city is deserving of great praise, though they have been blamed for it in many quarters. It is to be hoped that Calton Hill will be transformed more and more into an Athenian Acropolis; and as the glory of Pericles and Phidias has survived all censures, may Heaven grant their Scotch imitators resources and perseverance; they may be certain that glory will follow.
>
> Some of the lately-built portions of Berlin may be compared with Edinburgh; but we have not the beautiful prospects and striking points within the city and out of it …

Palermo came to Raumer's mind in the way that its surrounding rocky hillsides encroached on the city rather as they did in Edinburgh. The view from Calton Hill struck him as similar to that from Capodimonte in Naples. Naples, indeed, was uppermost in his consciousness when in Edinburgh—and Naples really won out. Raumer noted how some of the streets of Naples ran right to the bay, whereas in Edinburgh 'the less transparent Firth' (a tactful assessment of a frequently gurly Forth estuary) was some distance from the city. The coast of Sorrento and the islands of Capri, Ischia and Procida were more varied than the shore of Fife. Vesuvius was 'an accessory in the grandest style'. It had to be admitted that the southern light was rather superior to that of the north.[53] Perhaps it was as well that 'Grecian' Williams was no longer on the Edinburgh scene to argue the toss over what landmarks in or near the Modern Athens might lord it over those of Attica.

Queen Victoria and Prince Albert (of Saxe-Coburg and Gotha) first saw Edinburgh in September 1842. As in the case of George IV's visit twenty years earlier, public excitement ran high. *The Times* newspaper reported that the steamer *Modern Athens* (which normally served the Granton to Dundee route) had plied down the Firth of Forth to meet Her Majesty's ship. The vessel was 'beautifully decorated with evergreen', and had on board 'an excellent band of musicians'.[54] The royal couple were deeply impressed by the city. As they drove to Leith from Dalmeny Park, they saw the unfolding scene of Calton Hill with its rugged backdrop of Arthur's Seat and Salisbury Crags: 'Albert said he felt the Acropolis could not be finer; and I hear they sometimes call Edinburgh "the modern Athens."'[55] In his memoir of the royal visit, Sir Thomas Dick Lauder commented on the Calton Hill topped by the Observatory 'like a Grecian temple', and near it

> the half-finished façade of the great National Monument, designed as an accurate fac-simile in style, dimensions, and execution of the celebrated

Parthenon of Athens, but in its present embryo state so perfectly presenting the picturesque appearance of a ruined temple, as in defiance of the inferiority of climate, and all other attendant circumstances, to fill the mind with associations of Greece.[56]

'All other attendant circumstances' is a phrase that covers a multitude of sins. It might well serve as a sort of epitaph on the stalled 'Athenian' ambitions of Edinburgh, and to epitomise everything from the whole improbability of the notion itself, to the inappropriateness of building a temple in an alien Greek style on a wind-swept Scottish hill-top.

Johann Georg Kohl and Carl Gustav Carus both visited Edinburgh in 1844; their accounts were published in English translations in 1844 and 1846 respectively. The latter contains possibly the last positive statements by foreigners in support of the 'Athenian' identity of the city. Carus was in medical attendance on Frederick Augustus II, King of Saxony, during his visit to Great Britain, and therefore approached Edinburgh with the aesthetic assumptions of a citizen of Baroque and Classical Dresden. He early declared his admiration of the Modern Athens: 'I certainly consider Edinburgh the most beautiful and most interesting looking city I know; Rome and Naples not excepted.' The resemblance of the Calton Hill to the Acropolis was naturally commented upon, and repeatedly so. But, in his enthusiastic account of neoclassical Edinburgh, Carus became confused not only by what he had seen there, but by the Greek prototypes themselves. What he calls the Observatory, but which is in fact the High School, is described as 'a perfect imitation of the buildings about the gates of the Acropolis of Athens'; and neither of the 'choragic' monuments of Dugald Stewart and Robert Burns, though certainly Athenian in inspiration, were imitations of the ancient Tower of the Winds. Carus was, however, right in pointing out that the High School's Propylaea-like structure bore a somewhat similar relation to the National Monument then in (suspended) construction as did the Acropolis entrance buildings to the crowning Parthenon.

Of the Monument ('in this half finished state ... wonderfully like that of the ruins at present on the Athenian hill') Carus offered a most interesting observation, comparing it with contemporary German neoclassical structures, and terming it, with justification, 'a kind of Walhalla for Scotland'. This may well be the earliest instance—Carus's book had first appeared in Berlin in 1845—of such a parallel of architectural types (the Greek peripteral temple) and functions (those of a national memorial shrine to sacrifice or genius) being applied to a British building. It also places developments in 'Greek' Edinburgh nicely within the setting of European neoclassicism. As we shall see, in 1846 (the year of Carus's publication in English), and again in 1848, George Cleghorn would make extensive reference to the Walhalla at Regensburg in Bavaria in the context of his campaign for completion of the National Monument.[57] It is significant, however, that Carus seems rather to have preferred the Edinburgh

Parthenon as an *unfinished* structure, 'let alone for some years'—'for the last two or three lustra', he actually writes, thus mixing Roman five-year time periods with Greek Doric columns and epistyles: 'perhaps the building is more beautiful as it is', than it might be when finished, in a city where 'the taste for monumental art on a large scale appears to prevail very much'.[58]

Kohl, a native of Bremen and a citizen of Dresden, was vastly impressed by almost everything, lamenting only the absence of a fine river flowing through the city. Clearly the Water of Leith did not count. 'We may read about Edinburgh as much as we please', he wrote,

> and yet be ever pleased and delighted with the singularly beautiful situation and laying out of the city. I believe everybody would declare Edinburgh to be one of the finest cities in the world, if envious fate had not entirely denied her a great embellishment, namely, a fair mirrored stream, of which she has nothing. She is a pure inland—a pure hill and dale city, and possesses every charm a human habitation can enjoy in her hills, crags, dales, hollows, and ravines; but the living stream she is entirely deprived of.[59]

But Kohl was prepared to overlook this deficiency in favour of other topographical and intellectual advantages.

> On account of her beautiful situation, (partly, indeed, on account of the flourishing state of science here,) Edinburgh has been compared to Athens, and hence has been called the Athens of the North. In truth, the resemblance is wonderfully striking. Athens, too, is almost entirely a hill and dale city. Perhaps, however, her Ilissus was somewhat greater, and nearer to the city, than Leith water. Athens, like Edinburgh, lies inwards, and had her Piraeus, as Edinburgh has her Leith harbour. The hills in the neighbourhood of Edinburgh, too, are like those in the vicinity of Athens.

Kohl continued with what constitutes, perhaps, in all its concision, the clearest statement of praise in favour of the concept of the Athens of the North ever recorded.

> But I believe that Athens has earned decidedly far more honour from being compared to Edinburgh, than Edinburgh has from being placed side by side with Athens. For there can be no doubt, that, in the Northern Athens, whatever is comprised in situation, is more magnificent and beautiful than it ever was in the Southern Athens.[60]

The German visitor went on the compare the Castle Rock favourably with the Acropolis, improbably crediting its buildings with 'as high an antiquity as the

Acropolis of Athens'. He noted that a monument modelled on the Parthenon was designed to crown the Calton, already a hill of monuments, in a manner reminiscent of the Athenian Acropolis. So this city had effectively not one acropolis but two—as 'Grecian' Williams had found himself suggesting in the early 1820s, and forgetting himself in so doing. But perhaps this was only fitting for a place with a university which Kohl (who had himself attended great German universities) unashamedly and flatteringly classed as a seat of the Muses. Nevertheless, one can detect that the transformative, 'Athenian' power of Auld Reekie was checked, and its impetus spent. Kohl observes of the unfinished Parthenon that 'either the inspiration of the idea was not lasting enough, or better management was required for its full development ...'[61] As Henry Cockburn well understood, the Lord Provost and Magistrates of the City of Edinburgh were evidently no match for Pericles as patron and promoter of a golden age.

Dr Gustav Friedrich Waagen of Berlin, director of the Gemäldegalerie and the first professor of art history in any university, came to Edinburgh from Prussia in pursuit of the 'art treasures in Great Britain'. He was compiling the celebrated survey, published in 1854, that still constitutes an important work of reference. That he was impressed is abundantly clear. He had, he confessed, always wanted to see this 'wondrous city'. He was astonished by the variety and richness of the picturesque views that unfolded before him. 'I felt as if some gorgeous dream had been actually realized.' The Calton, with its 'peculiar forms', was a topographical highlight.[62] Waagen was conducted over it by David Octavius Hill, the artist and pioneer of photography, and admired the various classical monuments, the twelve columns of the unfinished Parthenon 'which have a very good effect', and the High School, 'on which the eye willingly dwelt'.[63] Sir John Steell's magnificent equestrian statue of the Duke of Wellington was examined in the studio (the great monument was unveiled in 1852, but Waagen was on his tours of inspection in 1850-51). Writing of this sculpture, Waagen praised 'the union of a genuine plastic style, as preserved in the Greek marbles, with the conditions of a modern costume.'[64]

The single structure of which Waagen wrote most was the Royal Institution. This was

> like a Doric temple of the richest form, with a portico of eight pillars, three pillars deep. Four small projections, supported by two pillars, on the long colonnaded sides, and an attic behind the portico, on which the statue of Queen Victoria enthroned, constitute the chief departures from the Doric form. The execution of the building is sharp and precise in a beautiful stone.[65]

It is significant that Waagen should have chosen to mention a watercolour painting 'of singular power and freedom' in the collection of the Royal

Institution.[66] The artist was Hugh William Williams, the subject was the Temple on Cape Sounion, and the effect it had on the Prussian visitor recalls the impression made on the citizens of Modern Athens some thirty years previously by Williams's vision of Greece. The spell was not yet broken.

*   *   *   *   *

Florence Nightingale knew and loved Athens. She kept an owl (rescued while in the Greek capital) as a pet, which she named Athena. In 1852, Nightingale wrote to her family of a recent visit to Edinburgh.

> The passage over the firth to Burnt Island [*sic*] was beautiful, though very cold, and the curious likeness, which everybody has remarked between Edinbro' and its castle and Athens and her Acropolis seen across that glorious firth, though seen by me only in a mist, made the comparison still more striking. But no one will ever grapple with the question, they will only say, oh! *you* are mad for Athens (as if it was a question of *you*) or oh you can't bear the north.[67]

And the question? Surely that was: why did the parallel loom so large in the consciousness of travellers? And the answer? Perhaps essentially that people derived some strange satisfaction from seeing a place as somewhere else, especially if northerners could dream of sunnier climes and more historic scenes, and even in their mind's eye translate a Scottish city to the south.

ATHENIAN EDINBURGH IN BRITISH SATIRE
'THAT FALSE AIR OF A MODERN ATHENS'

Sometimes it is difficult to know whether an observation by a visitor is either complimentary or derogatory. Onesiphorus Tyndall (later Tyndall-Bruce), wrote from Edinburgh to his friend, C. R. Cockerell, then the overall, but absentee, designer of the Parthenon on Calton Hill, to say that he had arrived at his hotel in 'this Athens'.[1] Did Tyndall use the term admiringly, because Cockerell was attempting to give the city its most distinctively 'Athenian' feature, and was thus supporting Cockerell's endeavour; or, sarcastically, because both men knew inwardly that the scheme was preposterous, and that the city was in fact no Athens, and could never really be such?

William Wordsworth captured well the paradox in a sonnet intended for his series *Yarrow Revisited, and Other Poems*, written probably in 1831, but not included in the published collection of 1835.

'Now that a Parthenon ascends, to crown
Our Calton Hill, sage Pallas! 'tis most fit
This thy dear City by the name be known
Of modern Athens.' But opinions split
Upon this point of taste; and Mother Wit
Cries out, 'AULD REEKIE, GUID AND HONEST TOWN
Of Ed'nbro', put the sad misnomer down,—
This alias of Conceit—away with it!'
Let none provoke, for questionable smiles
From an outlandish Goddess, the just scorn
Of thy staunch gothic Patron, grave St Giles;
—Far better than such heathen foppery

The homeliest Title thou hast every borne
Before or since the times of, *Wha wants me?*[2]

The 'point of taste' and the 'alias of Conceit' will be readily understandable to anyone who has pursued the story of 'the Athens of the North' before, or who has followed the discussion in the pages of this book.

The allusion to '*Wha wants me*' may, however, be obscure. The 'Wha [Who] Want's me? man' was a distinctive character on the Edinburgh urban scene of the eighteenth and early nineteenth centuries who supplied the services of a mobile 'public convenience' by providing a bucket and a voluminous cloak to conceal the user. He, and the circumstances, were the stuff of many a graphic satire since 'The Flowers of Edinburgh' caricature was published by J. Langham in 1781. Wordsworth appears to adapt the street cry to a different and more subtle purpose. Who needed or 'wanted' the un-called for soubriquet of Modern Athens when the time-honoured, more homely and in every way more apposite Auld Reekie was good enough for anyone's intellectual, topographical and visual 'ease'?

*   *   *   *   *

The claim of Edinburgh to be another Athens drew some adverse comment just as it drew praise. It may be helpful to penetrate beyond the casual remarks in the accounts of bemused visitors, or the occasional barbed comments by jaundiced residents irritated by vainglorious self-importance, and to consider some calculated satirical treatments of place, people and pretension.

Some of these *jeux d'esprit* we have encountered already, such as the clever spoof entitled 'The Second Voyage of Omai the Traveller' which appeared in *Blackwood's Edinburgh Magazine* in September 1822. Many visitors' accounts contain an element of satire, with fun poked at refined Edinburgh society, institutions, manners or the wished-for status of the Modern Athens. Examples of wit at the expense of the Athens of the North pervade the writing of the time, and can be found widely scattered through the whole body of evidence available to the student of the phenomenon. Even instances of more balanced journalism, ostensibly focusing on other matters, may still be rich in mockery and irony.

An early example of satire turned against the pretension of the Modern Athens—in this case, against the fashionable classical attainments of the literary ladies of the city—is to be found in Christian Isobel Johnstone's *The Saxon and the Gaël; or, The Northern Metropolis*. In a long novel, the witty author describes society's view of 'Mrs —— the scholar'. The gossips discuss her nature and attributes, and set these off against her undoubted learning, which seemed to have been maintained at the expense of her outward appearance. 'You see what a horrid mouth she has, which is no wonder, poor woman; for Miss Macdugald told

1. Hugh William Williams, *Athens towards the South-West*, seen from near the foot of Mount Lykabettos and looking to the Acropolis. The Temple of Olympian Zeus is to the left, and the Monument of Philopappos crowns the Hill of the Muses. Watercolour, pen and ink, *c.* 1820-22. *RISD Museum, Providence, Rhode Island, USA*

2. *Edinburgh from the summit of Arthur's Seat*, *c.* 1830. Calton Hill, with the incomplete National Monument and the High School, is in the middle distance at the extreme right. Aquatint by Richard Reeve after a drawing by William Purser. *The New Club, Edinburgh*

3. *Athens from the East*, engraved by James Stewart after a drawing by H. W. Williams from Williams, *Select Views in Greece* (1829). *National Library of Scotland*

4. Edinburgh seen across the Firth of Forth from Fife: a detail from *Edinburgh from Hillside*, by John Thomson of Duddingston, oil on canvas, 1824. Around the time this large and fine landscape was painted, many thought the view of Edinburgh from the water equal, or even superior to, that of Athens from the sea. *Author's collection*

5. Detail from *Edinburgh from Duke's Walk*, studio of Alexander Nasmyth, oil on canvas, about 1820. The most distinctive topographical features of central Edinburgh, the Castle Rock and Calton Hill, are prominent elements in the view. *Author's collection*

6. 'That ancient and martial acropolis of Caledonia.' *Edinburgh from the Glasgow Road*, engraved by George Hollis after an oil painting by Alexander Nasmyth. First published in 1821, in Part V of Walter Scott's *Provincial Antiquities and Picturesque Scenery of Scotland*, it was later reprinted in this fine coloured impression. *The New Club, Edinburgh*

Top: 7. *Edinburgh from the North West*, engraved by Robert Scott after a drawing by Andrew Wilson; folded plate tipped-in to George Robertson, *A General View of the Agriculture of the County of Mid-Lothian* (1795). The New Town spreads out northwards between the Castle and the Calton. *National Library of Scotland*

Middle: 8. *Edinburgh, from Craigleith*, engraved by William Tombleson after a drawing by Thomas Hosmer Shepherd; from *Modern Athens!* (1829). Edinburgh appeared a city boasting not one 'acropolis' but two. The Castle is at the right; Calton Hill, crowned by the unfinished National Monument, is at the left. *Private collection*

Bottom: 9. Detail from *View of Edinburgh from the Dean*, oil on canvas, attributed to James Giles. The presence of the completed Donaldson's Hospital, designed by W. H. Playfair in the Jacobethan style, dates the picture to the years shortly after 1851. The unfinished National Monument crowns Calton Hill to the left. *Author's collection*

Top: 10. The Acropolis of Athens, with the Tower of the Winds in the centre foreground, from Stuart and Revett, *The Antiquities of Athens*, vol. 1 (1762). *National Library of Scotland*

Middle: 11. *Edinburgh Castle and The Mound*, engraved by William Home Lizars after a drawing by John Wilson Ewbank. Allan Ramsay's 'guse-pie' house appears at the upper left centre, below the Castle's Half Moon Battery. *Private collection*

Bottom: 12. Detail from *Edinburgh from the Calton Hill*, engraved by William Tombleson after Thomas Hosmer Shepherd; from *Modern Athens!* The circular Panorama House on The Mound bears a similar relationship to the Castle as the Tower of the Winds does to the Acropolis in Stuart's plate. Allan Ramsay's 'guse-pie' house uphill nearby, which was octagonal in shape, reflects even more the profile of the Tower of the Winds. *Private collection*

13. The east front of Robert Adam's University building (today's Old College), begun in 1789. Its dramatic and massive vestibule is perhaps the most 'Roman' structure in Edinburgh. *Photo: Author*

14. Archibald Elliot's 'Pantheon' proposal for a 'national monument' cum church, engraved by W. and D. Lizars as a fold-out plate illustrating the report of a 'numerous and respectable meeting' held in 1819 to discuss the most suitable form of a monument to commemorate the Scottish dead of the French wars. *National Library of Scotland*

15. A triumphal arch commemorating the Battle of Waterloo, proposed by James Gillespie (later Gillespie Graham), 1816, to stand at the west end of Princes Street. *National Library of Scotland*

16. Richard Crichton's 1814 designs for the western end of what later became Waterloo Place. The feeling is almost that of the Roman Baroque; a Roman 'Pantheon' is visible at the far end of the new street. *City of Edinburgh Council—Edinburgh Libraries*

Above left: 17. *Archibald Alison,* by John Watson Gordon, oil on canvas, dated (bottom left on the chair) 1839. Alison was a key writer on the idea of an 'Athenian' Edinburgh. *East Lothian Council*

Above right: 18. *Hugh William Williams,* engraved by Charles Thomson after an oil painting by William John Thomson, 1827. In both painting and travelogue, Williams pointed up the similarity between Athens and Edinburgh. *National Library of Scotland*

Below: 19. Profile relief portrait of H. W. Williams on his monument in the Canongate Kirkyard, Edinburgh. *Photo: Author*

Above left: 20. *Apollo Prince of the Muses Suping Browse [supping brose] out of his Helmet*, engraving by John Jenkins, 1803. The eleventh Earl of Buchan was obsessed by Scottish history and iconography, and equally by his own self-importance as patron of arts and letters. *National Library of Scotland*

Above right: 21. *Charles Kirkpatrick Sharpe, Esqr.*, doughty defender of the fabric of Old Edinburgh and mocker of 'Athenian' pretension, captured in a self-caricature of 1831. 'Modern Athens' is written in the ascending smoke of Auld Reekie. *Author's collection*

Right: 22. *William Henry Playfair*, statue by Alexander Stoddart, 2016. The young Playfair, who became the architect of the Modern Athens par excellence, clutches a portfolio of drawings and leans against the fragments of classical buildings of the kind that, in actuality, he never saw. The statue stands in Chambers Street, near the University building which Playfair completed triumphantly. *Photo: Author*

23, 24 & 25. In 1822, the very year that the foundation stone of Edinburgh's 'Parthenon' was laid, James Hall and two other young Edinburgh advocates made an expedition to southern Italy and Sicily as part of a remarkable Grand Tour. In one of his illustrated travel journals, Hall drew Adam Paterson standing against a drum of an unfinished column in the Campobello quarries in Sicily and, again, sitting on a fragment of fluting from the top of a shattered column shaft at Agrigento. James Veitch was sketched lying full-length in a groove of a huge triglyph block of the Temple of Olympian Zeus at the same site. The pages of the sketchbook measure a mere 14.5 × 10 cm. *National Library of Scotland*

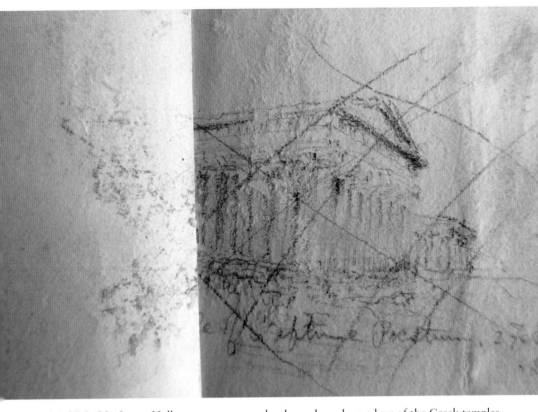

26, 27 & 28. James Hall was so overcome by the scale and grandeur of the Greek temples at Paestum, south of Naples, that he was really unable to record the scene adequately on paper measuring only 8.5 × 12 cm. We have the eloquent evidence of an abandoned sketch of the Temple of 'Neptune'. He fared better with the Temple of Athena, which he called 'of Ceres'. Later, in Sicily, Hall was able to capture two of the temples at Agrigento (those of 'Concord' and of 'Hera Lacinia') on a single page. But Paestum remained supreme in his memory. *National Library of Scotland*

Above left: 29. The bindings of some presentation copies of Stuart and Revett's *Antiquities of Athens* are ornamented by a gilded leather appliqué, itself set within a circlet of anthemion enclosing an olive wreath. The plaque shows a statue of Athena Parthenos with her attributes. This is a powerful symbol of devotion to the ideology of ancient Athens. *National Library of Scotland*

Above right: 30. Lady's ticket for Mr Ritchie's Ball at the New Assembly Rooms, George Street, Edinburgh (opened in 1787), engraved by Robert Scott, probably in the early 1790s. *City of Edinburgh Council—Edinburgh Libraries*

Below: 31. Medallion ornament, designed by Robert Adam and engraved by John Beugo, borne on the title-pages of the first volumes of the *Transactions of the Royal Society of Edinburgh* (Adam was an early Fellow of the Society). The Greek inscription is from Thucydides, whose words (given to Pericles in the famous funeral oration) about Athenian love of the arts and pursuit of philosophy are here applied to Edinburgh. *Royal Society of Edinburgh*

32. In 1788 David Allan of Edinburgh drew and engraved this emblematic frontispiece for R. E. Raspe's catalogue of the vast collection of gem casts by the Glasgow-born modeller James Tassie. The book was published in London in 1791. There were several important collections of coins and classical gems in Edinburgh by this date. Athena, seated on a Greek *klismos* chair, opens the door of a medal cabinet of splendid neoclassical design. *National Library of Scotland*

33. *The Academic Grove*, a romanticised vision of what Hugh William Williams imagined Plato's Academy in ancient Athens might have been like. This reconstruction, published in Williams's *Select Views in Greece* (1829), places the site far too near the Acropolis; but the Propylaea entrance building on the Acropolis of Athens had, by that date, been reflected in the design and siting of the High School of Edinburgh, built on the southern flank of Calton Hill. *National Library of Scotland*

Above left: 34. The warlike Athena was, with Apollo, the patron deity of the arts. Classically minded people in the age of the Modern Athens liked to have her image around them. This early nineteenth-century statuette, probably French, is characteristic of a wish to identify with the taste and learning encapsulated in the image of the goddess. *Author's collection*

Above right: 35. A modern print made from the handsome early nineteenth-century binding-stamp of the Advocates' Library, displaying the Medusa-head device associated with the shield of Athena, and thus emblematic of the Library's place as promoter or defender of learning. *Author's collection*

Below: 36. Detail from a panorama of Edinburgh drawn by Mary Stewart, Lady Elton, and lithographed by William Westall, 1822. Central in this image is the half-round colonnaded eastern end of the Calton Convening Rooms, venue that same year of Hugh William Williams's first exhibition of his Greek views. *The New Club, Edinburgh*

37. This attractive device was drawn and engraved by William Home Lizars for use as an ornamental heading on the policy documents of the Edinburgh Life Assurance Company, established in 1823. A vignette after Raphael's *Madonna della Sedia* is the central feature of this masthead. Around and below the tondo, luxuriant thistles surmount a Greek Doric portico, emblematic of the Athens of the North; Edinburgh Castle looms in the background, symbol of Auld Reekie. Here were the twin identities of early nineteenth-century Edinburgh. This particular policy is the one taken out on the life of Sir Walter Scott, 1824. *Aviva Archives, NU3853*

38. Ticket for the ball held in association with the Edinburgh Musical Festival in 1843 when the Music Hall, adjoining the Assembly Rooms, was opened. The lithographer had premises in Greenside Place, below the northern slopes of Calton Hill and the unfinished National Monument. Edinburgh might not have had its completed Parthenon; but the ticket suggests that the ladies of the city might still affect 'Grecian' drapery and 'attitudes' nonetheless. *City of Edinburgh Council— Edinburgh Libraries*

THE COUNTY HALL

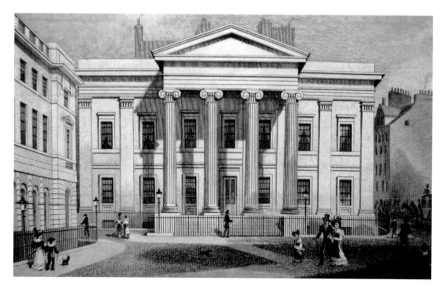

Above: 39. The County Hall had more contemporary detractors than admirers. To many, its massive Ionic portico seemed out of place in its surroundings, both in relation to the slightly earlier neoclassical frontages to its south, and the vulgar hustle and bustle of the High Street to its north. The engraving is by Lizars after Shepherd, published in *Modern Athens!* (1829). *Private collection*

Below left: 40. Patrick Gibson drew the County Hall in 1818 for his *Select Views in Edinburgh* in order to illustrate the imperfections (as they were widely perceived) of its north elevation on the High Street. This is a detail of his plate. Out of loyalty to the old Edinburgh that was then passing, Gibson also showed the historic Old Tolbooth—even though it has been demolished the same year that the County Hall was constructed. *National Library of Scotland*

Below right: 41. J. M. W. Turner also drew the north elevation of County Hall in 1818. It was engraved by John Le Keux, with figures by George Cooke, as a plate in Part III of Walter Scott's *Provincial Antiquities*, 1819. Here again is a detail of a larger view. *National Library of Scotland*

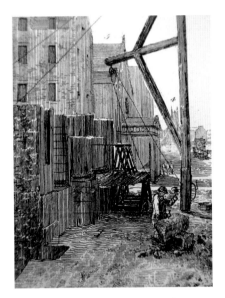 

Above left: 42. Detail from a plate in Patrick Gibson's *Select Views* (1818) showing the columns of the south side of the Regent Bridge in Waterloo Place under construction. In a foreshortened view, the north portico of the Theatre Royal in Shakespeare Square appears at the left. *National Library of Scotland*

Above right: 43. Gibson's plate also shows the other side of the Regent Bridge, the view similarly telescoped so that the bridge appears almost abutting Register House, which in actuality is some hundreds of feet away. *National Library of Scotland*

Below: 44. J. M. W. Turner included an interesting view of the Regent Bridge under construction in his general prospect of Edinburgh from Calton Hill, engraved by George Cooke for Part IV of Scott's *Provincial Antiquities* in 1820. In this detail, the masons' sheds and the impedimenta of construction can be seen. *National Library of Scotland*

Above left: 45. Waterloo Place was, and still remains, one of Edinburgh's finest and most interesting Greek thoroughfares. In this view by T. H. Shepherd, engraved by Thomas Barber for *Modern Athens!*, Archibald Elliot's elegant Erechtheion Ionic porticoes frame the view to Calton Hill, crowned by the National Monument shrouded in scaffolding. In 1829, when this plate was published, few realised that no more of Edinburgh's Parthenon would ever be built. Ironically, the Nelson Monument, so greatly disliked, had been completed. *Private collection*

Above right: 46. The south-east block of Waterloo Place adjoining the Old Calton Burying Ground, with the Post Office and the Regent Bridge. Shepherd's drawing for *Modern Athens!* was engraved anonymously. *Private collection*

Below: 47. Inscription tablet on the north arch of the Regent Bridge, naming the Lord Provost at the time of its foundation in the 'ever memorable year 1815' (Sir John Marjoribanks), and the architect (Archibald Elliot). *Photo: Author*

Above: 48 & 49. The architecture of Waterloo Place reflects the familiarity of its designer, Archibald Elliot, with the most authoritative archaeological sources. The columns and their capitals are derived and adapted from those of the Erechtheion, as published by Stuart and Revett in *The Antiquities of Athens*. The pilaster capitals are imaginative variants of a type noted on the Temple of Apollo at Didyma, near Miletus in ancient Caria, and published in the Society of Dilettanti's *Ionian Antiquities* in 1769. *Photos: Author*

Below: 50 & 51. Column capital from the north porch of the Erechtheion and a pilaster capital of so-called 'sofa' type from Didyma. *National Library of Scotland*

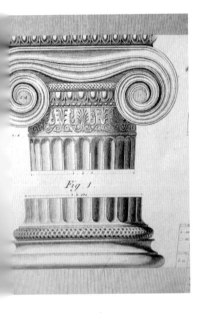

A Fantasy World on Calton Hill

Above: 52. Playfair's highly romanticised perspective view of an early design for his Observatory on Calton Hill is interesting in several respects. The building is given a distinctly Roman character with its Corinthian porticoes and its Pantheon saucer-dome (the structure as actually built is quite different and much simpler). Romantic ruins occupy the background here, as if the site had a long continuity of ancient civilisation. Two of the figure groups—those in the centre and left foreground—are derived from the *staffage* included by Stuart and Revett in their view of the Monument of Philopappos in Athens. © *Royal Incorporation of Architects in Scotland. Courtesy of Historic Environment Scotland*

Below: 53. The source for Playfair's exotic figure-groups in the drawing above is clear: they are lifted from Stuart and Revett, *Antiquities of Athens*, Vol. III (1794), Chapter V, Plate I. In this plate, the figures in swirling oriental drapery are actually Stuart and Revett themselves, dressed the part to appear inconspicuous in Ottoman Athens. The figures in Western costume are other visiting British antiquaries: Playfair omitted these in order to magnify the would-be exoticism of the scene. Coffee for all is being prepared by the Turkish man and boy in the foreground. *National Library of Scotland*

54. W. H. Playfair's Lower Natural
History Museum (now part of
the University's Law Library)
can be likened to a Greek Doric
temple turned inside-out. Though
unconventional, and displaying
solecisms to upset the purist, it is
nevertheless a very distinctive interior.
Photo: Author

55. An engraving by W. H. Lizars
of Playfair's Upper Museum, made
originally as a letter-head for Robert
Jameson, Professor of Natural
History. Two large dogs crouch under
the table-cases on each side, while the
professor's tame puma, which had
the run of the building, peers over
the central display case. Some thirty
years later, the plate appeared as an
illustration to a memoir of Jameson
published in *The Edinburgh New
Philosophical Journal*, 57 (1854).
National Library of Scotland

56. The rich decoration of the
Upper Museum was called by
many contemporaries 'Grecian'.
The mouldings are, in fact, more
generically 'classical' rather than
specifically and authentically Greek,
though the column capital in the
foreground displays elements derived
and adapted by Playfair from
archaeological source-books illustrating
the Erechtheion. The current bland
colour-scheme hardly does these fine
details justice. Thomas Frognall Dibdin
would not have thought it 'saucy'
enough. *Photo: Author*

TWO 'GRECIAN' LIBRARIES

Above: 57. The glorious room now known as the Upper Signet Library was designed by William Stark, and built and fitted out for the Faculty of Advocates. It is perhaps Edinburgh's most spectacular neoclassical interior space. Contemporaries called it 'Grecian'. In fact, it is Imperial Roman in its splendour, but with elements of Greek detail. The iconography of the allegorical and faintly absurd frieze, painted by Thomas Stothard around its shallow central dome and oculus, shows Apollo, the Muses and assorted poets, philosophers and historians, thus evoking a certain aspect of the city's would-be 'Athenianism'. This is a finely tinted copy of the engraving by William Watkins after Thomas Shepherd, made for *Modern Athens!* (1829). *Society of Writers to H. M. Signet*

Below: 58. Within the University, the great and richly decorated library room that now bears Playfair's name is also neither truly Greek nor yet truly Roman either. Here its huge Ionic columns can be seen rising beneath the coffers of its barrel-vaulted ceiling. It illustrates well the originality of the architect and many of his fellow practitioners in creating an idiosyncratic style for 'the Athens of the North'. *Photo: Author*

59. Playfair's original Royal Institution (1822-26) before its later enlargement and elaboration. The plate, by Samuel Lacy after T. H. Shepherd, was included in *Modern Athens!* Viewed down Hanover Street in the New Town, the Greek temple forms a contrast with the background of towering buildings on the ridge of the Old Town. The 'pyramidal' structure, visible over (but apparently on) the roof, is the Panorama House on The Mound. *Private collection*

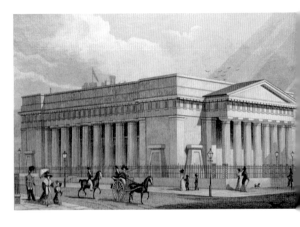

60. The boxy, Greek Doric temple of the Royal Institution is seen from its north-east angle. The Egyptian-style plinths designed to support sculpture at each corner are visible. So is the flag-tower of the Castle, which looms over the Institution's roof. Engraving by A. Cruse after T. H. Shepherd for *Modern Athens! Private collection*

61. Just how great was the transformation that Playfair wrought on his own original Royal Institution building between 1831 and 1836 is clearly shown in the fine lithograph by Samuel Dukinfield Swarbreck, made in October 1837 for his *Sketches in Scotland*. Princes Street appears as a stylish boulevard where commerce, though already present in many shops—some still with Greek-columned frontages—had not yet wholly overwhelmed the elegant residential life of the Modern Athenians. *National Library of Scotland*

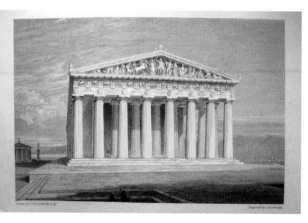

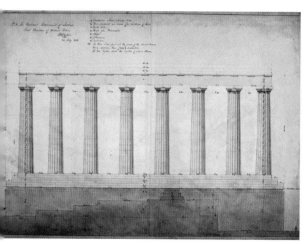

Top: 62. An intense stylistic and moral debate between 1819 and 1822 resulted in the decision to build a monument to the Scottish dead of the French wars, modelled on the Parthenon of Athens. Charles Robert Cockerell emerged as the overall architect, with Playfair as his local collaborator. This is a reconstruction by Cockerell (in some measure fanciful) of the original ancient building that inspired the 'facsimile'—never to be completed—on Calton Hill. The engraving was included in Hugh William Williams's *Select Views in Greece*, of 1829, the same year that construction of the Edinburgh Parthenon ceased. *National Library of Scotland*

Middle: 63. Playfair prepared a series of drawings for the National Monument, including this one for its western portico. These eight columns, with their architrave, together with two further columns on each flank, on a massive stylobate, were all that the funds would pay for. What had been intended as a northern Parthenon became 'Scotland's Folly' or 'Edinburgh's Disgrace'. *Edinburgh University Library*

Bottom: 64. The western portico today: many think that the National Monument looks better as a pre-fabricated 'ruin' than it would ever have done if completed as a replica Parthenon. *Photo: Author*

65. John Duffield Harding's drawing (which he lithographed himself) of the incomplete National Monument, with Professor John Playfair's monument brought into the same view, was included in topographical publications from the 1840s onwards. By the time Harding drew the scene, the sheds of Robert Forrest's statuary workshop and exhibition, and their surrounding palings, impinged on the scene. But, these apart, what Harding captured might almost be a vision of rural Greece. *Author's collection*

66. The 'Turneresque' effects of weather and light in this drawing by George Meikle Kemp, engraved by Thomas Dick, add greatly to an attractive view of the Calton Hill ensemble. The jagged toothing-stones of the stylobate of the National Monument seem to call for building work to continue. *Author's collection*

THE HIGH SCHOOL

Above left: 67. By common consent, Thomas Hamilton's High School is not just the finest building of 'Modern Athens', but also one of the great monuments of international neoclassicism. Its perfection of style and execution is matched by the Romantic splendour of its setting. But this architectural achievement has been greatly compromised by civic neglect in modern times. As Lord Cockburn said even in his day: 'Alas, we have no Pericles.' The High School was completed in the year that J. Henshall's engraving after Shepherd's drawing for *Modern Athens!* was published. *Private collection*

Above right: 68. Greek Revival perfection in the High School. Hamilton studied the published archaeological source-books assiduously, drawing upon and adapting them very successfully. *Photo: Author*

Below: 69. George Meikle Kemp's drawing of the buildings and monuments on and around the Calton Hill, with Thomas Hamilton's eclectic Burns Monument of 1830 and his much purer Greek High School in the foreground. This was engraved at small scale by James Johnstone for the fourth volume of the Glasgow-published *The Republic of Letters* (1833). *National Library of Scotland*

THE THRASYLLOS THEME

Above left: 70. The Choragic Monument of Thrasyllos in Athens, as recorded and interpreted by Stuart and Revett, provided a recurring theme for Edinburgh architects to borrow from (notably in its wreaths, or its continuous band of guttae below them), or even to reinterpret as a whole. The monument of the builder-architect George Winton in St Cuthbert's Kirkyard is an excellent example of copying and adapting the ancient original. Ironically, not long after this was erected in Edinburgh, the Thrasyllos monument itself was destroyed in the Greek War of Independence. *Photo: Author*

Above right: 71. A somewhat freer translation of the Thrasyllos original is found in the monument of William Trotter, sometime Lord Provost and also the great furniture designer of 'Athenian' Edinburgh, which stands in Greyfriars Kirkyard. *Photo: Author*

Below: 72. A handsome conjoint pair of door-pieces in Broughton Street echoes elements of the ancient Athenian prototype. *Photo: Author*

The Dugald Stewart Monument and Its Sources

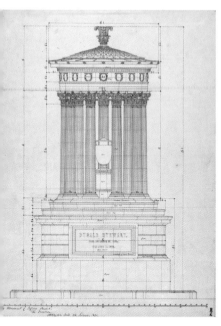

Left: 73. Playfair's monument (1831) to the philosopher is derived from the Choragic Monument of Lysikrates in Athens, as recorded by Stuart and Revett. Playfair further re-interpreted that record, for example by replacing the frieze of tripods—alluding to the prize won by the patron or 'impresario' Lysikrates in an ancient dramatic festival—with a frieze of wreaths, emblematic of the fame and glory won by Dugald Stewart in the fields of literature and philosophy. This is one of Playfair's drawings associated with the commission to design the monument. *Edinburgh University Library*

Below: 74. Samuel Dukinfield Swarbreck drew the Stewart Monument in its dramatic setting on the south-western escarpment of Calton Hill for his *Sketches in Scotland* (1837). *National Library of Scotland*

Above left: 75. A capital and column shaft of the Monument of Lysikrates, as published by Stuart and Revett in *The Antiquities of Athens*. Playfair replicated the sophisticated fluting with the turned-over leaf-effect at the top, but omitted the lowest tier of vegetable ornament in the capitals. *National Library of Scotland*

Above right: 76. Fastidious attention to detail was Playfair's hallmark. Note the 'turned-over' tops of the flutes—an expensive feature for the masons to execute—and the adapted but still exquisite capitals. The form of wreath in the frieze was Playfair's favourite type: adapting it from a small-scale decorative tailpiece detail in the third volume of *The Antiquities of Athens*, he used it lavishly in the Royal Institution when he began the redesign of that building the same year, 1831. *Photo: Author*

Below: 77. The Lysikrates order, with its distinctive fluting and with its full capital with all three tiers of vegetable ornament, elegant helices and palmettes on the faces of the abacus, is to be found on this mid-Victorian porch in St Andrew Square. Changed ownership to hotel use in very recent times, and the insensitive introduction of out-of-place and unnecessary spotlights, has damaged the effect. *Photo: Author*

Above: 78. A corner of the central 'temple' element of Thomas Hamilton's High School. The wreaths in the metopes are derived from the Choragic Monument of Thrasyllos. *Photo: Author*

Below: 79. The angle of one of the corner porticoes of the Royal Institution, in its enlarged and elaborated incarnation, shows Playfair's favoured but less elegant form of wreath, and the opulence of much of his other detailing. Remodelling of his earlier construction gave Playfair the chance to create a sort-of alternative 'Parthenon', distinctly in his own eclectic idiom, at just the moment when it was clear there was little possibility of completing the much purer and more authentic 'reconstruction' of the original 'Parthenon' on Calton Hill. *Photo: Author*

80 & 81. The elegant Thrasyllos-type wreath, adopted by Thomas Hamilton at the High School. His source was a plate in Stuart and Revett's *The Antiquities of Athens*. *National Library of Scotland* and *Photo: Author*

82 & 83. Playfair's somewhat less elegant but preferred form of wreath decoration was also derived ultimately, if less obviously, from a detail in Stuart and Revett. Examples are to be found in profusion on the Royal Institution, and on both the frieze of the Dugald Stewart Monument and on the series of stele-like posts that surround the tholos itself. *Photos: Author*

84 & 85. The frontispiece portrait in the biography of Thomas M'Crie, philhellene and advocate of women's education in Greece, is framed by a wreath derived from a tailpiece decoration in the third volume of Stuart and Revett's *Antiquities of Athens*. Playfair favoured this style of wreath, which he derived from the same source, using it—inverted—to decorate both his Dugald Stewart Monument and the metopes of his enlarged and elaborated Royal Institution. *National Library of Scotland*

86. After designing the Royal Institution not once but twice—that is, in its original, and in its greatly enlarged forms—Playfair subsequently found himself in competition to design a new National Gallery of Scotland, on a site at The Mound immediately south of the Institution. In this lovely perspective view, with tonality and setting that render it almost a glimpse of Greece in Edinburgh, Playfair offered an early proposal. The new Gallery is the building on the left: an austere Doric stoa, to match the existing, though much more elaborate, Royal Institution, on the right. In the end, the National Gallery would be in Ionic dress; and something of the magic of the Greek vision captured here was undeniably lost. *Edinburgh University Library*

87. Playfair's competitor for the National Gallery commission was Thomas Hamilton. Playfair's ingenious, revised (and implemented) scheme provided accommodation for both the National Gallery and the Royal Scottish Academy in the same building. Hamilton proposed two separate but matching structures in the Doric order: buildings of such elaboration that they would have complemented, in a backhanded sort of way, his great rival's existing Royal Institution rather well. Hamilton's twin stoas—the Mound roadway itself was to run between them—would have constituted perhaps the single greatest set-piece of design and urban planning in the Athens of the North. But it was not to be. Playfair, better connected with men of influence, got the job. *Royal Scottish Academy*

88 & 89. These two illustrations are from a pamphlet of Hamilton's, his *Letter to Lord John Russell ... On the Present Crisis Relative to the Fine Arts in Scotland* (1850). They provide more information about his proposed Mound Galleries. A folding lithograph shows the Doric porticoes of the north front of the easternmost range, with a profusion of sculptural ornament. The other illustration, which takes the form of a woodcut set in the text, shows how a viewer of Modern Athenian sensibility would perceive the relationship of the 'Tower of the Winds' octagon roof-light, or cupola, of the east range to the Castle rock rising behind. *National Library of Scotland*

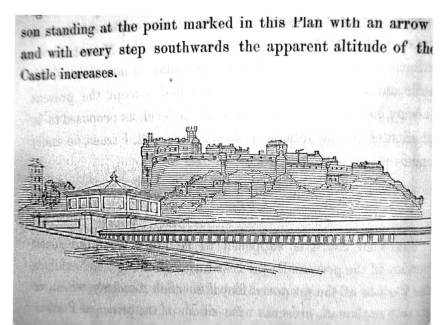

son standing at the point marked in this Plan with an arrow and with every step southwards the apparent altitude of the Castle increases.

PLAYFAIR'S 'STYLOPHILY'

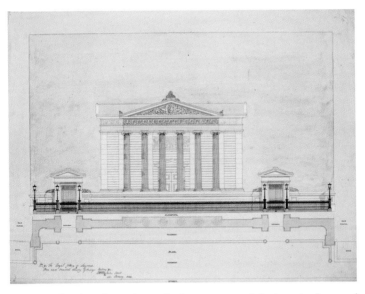

Above: 90. Playfair loved a colonnade. In an unusual design, the hexastyle Ionic portico of his Royal College of Surgeons (the whole building is generally known as Surgeons' Hall) stands on a screen wall. The vegetable forms of the honeysuckle ornament of the tympanum of the pediment, and the anthemion and lotus of the frieze, are particularly luxuriant and well-executed. This elevation is preserved in the great collection of Playfair's architectural drawings in Edinburgh University Library. *Edinburgh University Library*

Below: 91. The blank return wall terminating a row of houses of equally unusual design in Blenheim Place is ornamented with a parade of six engaged Doric columns. Built on a vertiginous site, these properties appear single-floored with sunk basements at the front, but are actually of four storeys to the rear. A tetrastyle Ionic portico looms over the low houses as a grand gable termination to the tenement block behind, at the end of the terrace. The higher flats here enjoy a view up to the slopes of Calton Hill, crowned by their classical structures. *Photo: Author*

92. Despite Edinburgh Academy having been founded as a private establishment for the sons of the upper middle-class professional families of the New Town, the design of the school, by William Burn, is austere in comparison with the new buildings constructed only a short time later for the city-funded High School. The Doric columns are unfluted, giving the building the (probably unintentional) character of an unfinished Greek temple such as Segesta in Sicily; there is no concession to superfluous ornament. The serious, classical ethos of the establishment is conveyed in the two inscriptions on the entablature, one in Greek, one in Latin. *Photo: Author*

93. Economy is also shown in the less visible parts of the High School. The wreaths in the metopes of the Doric frieze stop at a point where their absence would be noticeable only to those ascending the Calton slopes behind the building, to the north. Their omission is invisible from the south front and almost wholly so from the sides. *Photo: Author*

94. Several artists and architects imagined how the National Monument might look if ever completed. George Meikle Kemp, later to gain fame as the designer of the Walter Scott Monument in the Gothic style, amused himself in a more classical realm by drawing this prospect of the Calton Hill with the Parthenon rising above the High School. Both the Burns and Stewart Monuments are shown, so the image must date from after 1831. The costume of the canoodling couple in the foreground corroborates this date. *The New Club, Edinburgh*

95. A variant of Kemp's view was also engraved by J. West in 1843. A happy family group (their costume fits the later date) has replaced the lovers, but they are equally oblivious to the Greek Revival splendours of Calton Hill. *Edinburgh University Library*

96. John Dick Peddie's idealised view of Edinburgh in 1866 includes several proposed schemes for city-centre development, notably at the east end of Princes Street and around Waverley railway station. He has also completed the Parthenon. A photograph of his scheme, published some forty years later, is entitled 'The Calton Hill and its Capabilities'. From William Mitchell, *The National Monument to be Competed ... on the Model of the Parthenon at Athens* (1907). *Private collection*

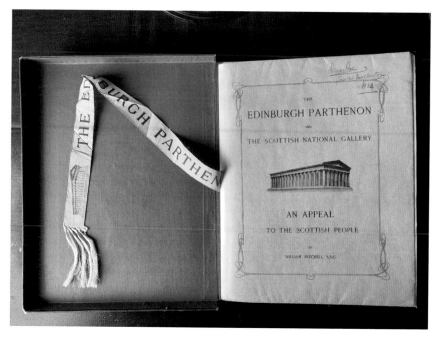

97. William Mitchell's book was published in various states of luxury presentation, one being as a soft-covered volume within an enclosing box. An image of the inspiration for the National Monument, in the form of the now-lost model of the Parthenon by the Edinburgh sculptor Peter Slater, appears in several places and forms: printed on the cover of the book itself and likewise in the text, blocked on the exterior of the box, and yet again woven in the silk ribbon that is neither bookmark nor mechanism for easing the printed volume from its container. *Private collection*

98. Michell's treatise includes this rather crude vision, by George Shaw Aitken, of the completed National Monument 'as it may be'. There is no pedimental sculpture, though the metopes do appear to bear some form of indistinct decoration. *Private collection*

Bravura in Bavaria; Triumph in Tennessee; Embarrassment in Edinburgh

Above left: 99. Ludwig I of Bavaria's great architect Leo von Klenze designed the 'Walhalla' overlooking the River Danube near Regensburg. That this enterprise succeeded, and in a comparatively short time (1830-42), should have given the proponents of the Edinburgh Parthenon pause for thought. In fact, few in Edinburgh other than George Cleghorn gave it a moment's notice. Illustration from Samuel Green, *Pictures from the German Fatherland* (1892). *National Library of Scotland*

Above right: 100. The Parthenon in Nashville, Tennessee (a city known as 'the Athens of the South'), was first constructed at the end of the nineteenth century of impermanent materials, then subsequently rebuilt of high-quality concrete. It is remarkable for recreating the sculpture of the original, and for the astonishing opulence of its interior, which attempts to show what the cella of the Parthenon of Athens may have looked like. No-one in Edinburgh even mentioned its existence. Photograph by the studio of Marvin Willard Wiles, 1925. *The Parthenon, Nashville, TN*

Below: 101. Edinburgh's ill-fated and ill-conceived attempt to build a 'facsimile' of the Parthenon. Twelve columns only, with their architrave, were ever built. *Photo: Author*

102, 103 & 104. In July 1918, George Washington Browne published his designs for the conversion of the unfinished National Monument as a memorial to the Great War, then still in progress. These illustrations show the 'interior' and 'exterior' of the unfinished western portico, which was to be adapted for what might have been a very successful memorial. On what could be called a stele of pseudo-antique kind, Washington Browne paid tribute to his predecessors in Edinburgh Parthenon-building, C. R. Cockerell and W. H. Playfair, adding his own name at the foot. These photographs from *The Builder*, and from a privately printed pamphlet by Washington Browne, show evidence of wartime economy in paper and production. *National Library of Scotland*

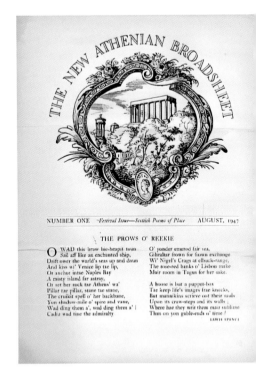

Above left: 105. When the Edinburgh Academy established its Officers' Training Corps (OTC) in 1908, the cap-badge harked back to the 'Athenian' age of Edinburgh when the school was founded. Around the head of Homer (long used in school symbolism, and on prize medals), and within a laurel wreath, was the same motto as that inscribed on the portico of William Burn's building: Η ΠΑΙΔΕΙΑ ΚΑΙ ΤΗΣ ΣΟΦΙΑΣ ΚΑΙ ΤΗΣ ΑΡΕΤΗΣ ΜΗΤΗΡ—'Education is the mother of wisdom and virtue'. *Author's collection*

Above right: 106. The first number of *The New Athenian Broadsheet*, August 1947. Publication coincided with the inauguration of the Edinburgh International Festival of Music and Drama. A refreshed sense of hope for, and expectation of, post-war 'Athenianism' is evident in the use of the imagery of the Calton Hill monuments. *Private collection*

Above left: 107. Adam House, in Chambers Street, was designed by William Kininmonth, 1954-55. The prominent Greek inscription on the elegant and unusual façade repeats a much earlier one, erected in the nearby old University premises in 1616. The text explains that learned men enjoy double insight. Unfortunately, this does not apply to those who erect street lights, as a thoughtlessly placed and obstructive lamp standard now prevents the taking of such a photograph today. *Photograph: Ian McHaffie (1997)*

Above right: 108. The back endpaper of Eric Linklater's *Edinburgh* (1960) bears Don Pottinger's plan of the New Town, ornamented by the figure of an imaginary ancient Greek architect or town-planner—a northern Hippodamos of Miletos, perhaps—evidently considering the possibilities of some new building or street layout in 'the Modern Athens'. *Author's collection*

A.B.MEARNS LTI

MASONRY SPECIALIST
Restoration Conservation

55 Bangor Road, Edinburgh EH6 5JX
Tel: **0131 554 7753** Fax: **0131 553 2460** Email: **abmearns-stone@btconnect.**

109. In an allusion to the notion of 'the Modern Athens', the specialist stonemasonry contractor A.B. Mearns has capitalised on the image of the Parthenon of Athens in its current state of ruin. The unstated implication is that even such an iconic building might be restored by the skills of Edinburgh masons. This attitude would have found favour with Archibald Alison, who suggested that Edinburgh was the best city in which to build a replica Parthenon, on account of the skills of its masons and the local supply of excellent building stone. *Author's collection*

Above: 110. Style and wit combine in the restoration, by the leading conservation architectural practice Simpson & Brown, of a bland 1960s George Street shop front as smart premises for an optician. The Ionic ('Eyeonic'?) capitals have volutes formed as *pince-nez* spectacles. *Photo: Author*

Right: 111. In Haddington Place, part of the long parade of Leith Walk and once a row of stately Georgian shop fronts articulated by Ionic columns, there stands a sorely mistreated door-piece. Here the columns bear the character of traditional barbers' poles. There is nothing 'Victorian' about this building of about 1825. *Photo: Author*

Above left: 112. The Hillside Crescent 'unconformity'. A street of grand houses, begun to the design of Playfair, was completed much later only in parts, and some of those sections were themselves subsequently demolished in the twentieth century. One gap site was filled by a building of 'cynical irrelevance' (to quote *B o S Edinburgh*). That itself has since been reworked and improved; but all too jarring is its juxtaposition with the elegance of the 'Athenian' age of Edinburgh, or the architecture of its afterglow. However, to the right of the original house is another gap-site fill-in, dating from 1990, which attempts more respectfully to echo, to some degree at least, the style of its neighbour. *Photo: Author*

Above right: 113. William Burn designed this once-fine mausoleum in St Cuthbert's Kirkyard for his MacVicar relations. It is a variant of the Monument of Thrasyllos theme, though it adheres less faithfully to the prototype than others of its kind. Its current state suggests more classical ruin than monument to a well-doing Modern Athenian family. *Photo: Author*

Below: 114. Another house-tomb in decay is the Suttie of Balgonie mausoleum in the Canongate Kirkyard, with its Greek detail. The wreaths are of 'Playfair' type. *Photo: Author*

Above left: 115. The superb, but long vacant and neglected High School was passed over as the location for the new Scottish Parliament. From the near vicinity of the 'Holyrood' parliamentary complex, one can look up towards Calton Hill and see those symbols of democracy and the 'democratic intellect': the unfinished Parthenon on the hill-top and, lower down, the Greek temple portico and colonnaded stoa forms of the old High School itself. *Photo: Author*

Above right: 116. Willowherb grows wild on the superbly cut masonry of the substructures of the High School. *Photo: Author*

117 & 118. Greek detail on the western pavilion of the High School, overtaken by ivy, not of romance but of neglect. The Modern Athens of the North resembles the ancient Athens of the South as a place where buildings in ruin can be inspected, and lamented, in their decay. *Sic transit…* (sometimes, only a Latin expression will do). *Photos: Author*

119. Hope remains. Alexander Stoddart's statue of William Henry Playfair (2016) bears upon its pedestal a deeply symbolic bronze relief, 'Edina Reflecting the Glory of Athena'. The personification of Edinburgh, 'the Modern Athens', wearing a mural crown and bearing a mirror of classical form, is showing to Athena—patron goddess and personification of ancient Athens—an image of herself. For a brief period, the Scottish city had thought itself a reincarnation of the Greek original. The memory of that time, and of the ideas symbolised by the notion of parallel, remains vivid. *Photo: Author*

me, but pray keep it secret now   she speaks Greek, only think! and snuffs …'.
Lady Mary Murray opines that 'Latin and Greek certainly do spoil the mouth'.
Lord Macallan gives the male opinion on such female paragons of learning.

> I own it is pleasant enough when the Ladies can cleverly make us play bo-peep
> with the blue-stocking; but when like Mrs ——, they display it to the very
> garter, I think they ought to put on breeches at once, and then we would know
> what to take them for—like a gardener's ticket you know, 'man traps and
> spring-guns here'.[3]

A wave of satire swept over Edinburgh in 1820, and the tide remained high
for the next fifteen or so years. This inundation, which carried along with it
several three-decker novels, certainly enlivens the debate. These works, in
which the 'Athenian' ways of the city are derided, are mostly mediocre. They
are not without interest, however, and as a series they have not been examined
before from this point of view.

The anonymous author of *Edinburgh: a Satirical Novel* (perhaps the
pseudonymous 'Thomas Brown, the Elder', author of comparable works on
Bath and Brighton) found plenty to mock in a city he had 'been led to think
was the centre of science, of industry, and of literature'. As things turned out,
there was much amusement to be had at the expense of the poorer, less à la
mode inhabitants, largely untouched by Modern Athenian ways of living and
thinking. They had their existence in Old Town garrets or *attics*, where at the
end of the working day they spent their *noctes atticae*. There they displayed
their 'attic salt'—that is, the elegant wit that characterised their betters, but a
less erudite or polished measure of which was possibly also theirs—which had
to be distinguished, of course, from the other kind of salt that they used on their
porridge.[4] A snide comment of another kind is here ill-concealed, as the people in
question presumably had little time left over from the pursuit of a hard and basic
existence to enjoy drawing-room repartee or Speculative Society bons mots.

*Glenfell; or, Macdonalds and Campbells. An Edinburgh Tale of the
Nineteenth Century*, is a little-known work in the John Galt canon, and copies
of the novel in its first edition are exceedingly rare. The work was published
anonymously. It is interesting for its side-lights on New Town customs, and the
novel offers its own contribution to the Athenian debate. At its very outset, the
novel makes reference to Edinburgh as a seat of 'talent and genius' rendering
the place the '"intellectual city"'; and we immediately learn of the arrival of
an English tourist in '"the Athens of the North"'. Both the last two terms are
printed within quotation marks: we can infer that they were in common usage
and were to be widely understood—and thus open to mockery. But printing
them this way also suggests Galt's slight sneer of contempt at the affectation
implied. Even the arrangements for, and the social distinctions between, the use

of bells and door-knockers in New Town houses—phenomena entertainingly observed—are labelled instances of 'the ingenious refinement of the modern Athenians'.[5]

David Hume had relished mocking the ignorance of Londoners. 'The Barbarians who inhabit the Banks of the Thames', was how he characterised them in a splenetic moment.[6] In *Glenfell*, Galt refreshes Hume's jibe in damning London as 'the flat Boeotian region of the dull and muddy Thames', while not exactly endorsing the claim of Edinburgh to assert an 'Athenian' superiority. Indeed, Galt made a sustained satirical thrust of his own at the Northern Athenians; but he was, of course, a West of Scotland man, and he was not going to yield the palm readily.

The Edinburgh hostess and would-be *salonnière* Mrs Campbell is to give a dinner party. Her guests will include some of the *literati*,

persons who, in the opinion of their fellow-citizens, equalled in the different modifications of talent and acquirement, the most illustrious of any age or country. It is, however, necessary, to explain in what manner it happens that individuals so extraordinary are so little known out of the circles of the intellectual city, while they are so strenuously celebrated within its romantic bounds.

In the first place, there is the invidia of contemporary rivals, and national as well as local prejudices ... The poets, the orators, and the lawyers, of [London] ... being under the influence of the envious spirit of conscious inferiority, make a point of rarely noticing the pre-eminent endowments of the northern Athenians; and when they do quote their verses or opinions, thay [sic] always select such as are only remarkable for their conceit or mediocrity, disguising the malice of this insidious detraction by exorbitant epithets of admiration. But their cruel applause is as nothing compared with the effect of national or local prejudice. The whole English people, the Irish, and all Europe, are chagrined at the superiority of the wise and learned of Edinburgh; yea, every other town that participates in the intellectualising keenness of the Scottish air, turns the sharpness of its wits against the pretensions of the provincial capital ... within the circles of the romantic town. These narrow circles of the different orders of society, may be compared to those maps which illustrate the plurality of worlds, wherein we see different systems linked together by the long elliptical orbits of unappropriated wandering stars of singular and transient splendour.—What these stars are in the universe, the Edinburgh men of genius are in the spheres of Edinburgh; they are found glittering and decorating, not only where with heavenly harmony the feast of reason and the flow of soul is dispensed, but even where Mrs Campbell and her daughter —— [,] the earth and moon of the system, hold their diurnal course ... [T]he plain fact is, that the highest public characters of Edinburgh are possessed of an agreeable affability, which induces them to accept of invitations to the show dinners of all their various degrees of acquaintance, by which they respectively acquire a numerous host of partizans to buy their books and speak their praise, contributing to a species of literary federalism that exists no where else.[7]

Connected with *Glenfell* is another offering by Galt, said by a twentieth-century authority to predate that novel in terms of composition if not publication. *Auld Reekie; or, a Mistake in Edinburgh* is a drama preserved on account of its inclusion in an omnibus edition of some of the writer's minor works.[8] A retired English general officer, accompanied by his wily and forward ex-army servant, Saunders, arrives in Edinburgh. This, the General proceeds to explain pedantically, is a place of great civilization, unlike the wilds of North America where the two had soldiered together. Here the coarse stories they had been wont to tell in camp would not (as the precocious servant points out) 'take with the *beau monde*' of the city. Agreeing, the General goes one better, asserting: 'Why, man, this is the Athens of the North.' He is then teased by his servant, who (in the way that servants sometimes do in English theatre) seeks to tie him in intellectual knots. 'You began, sir, by saying that Edinburgh was Athens. Now, with such a beginning, what would have been the end of the tale?'[9]

John Galt was familiar with both Athens and Edinburgh. This fact gives added piquancy to what he said *en passant* of an 'Athenian' Edinburgh in *The Last of the Lairds* (1826). In this novel we encounter 'Athenian philosophers', 'Athenian gentry' and even a 'Mr Threeper of Athens' (that is, Edinburgh), a lawyer who possesses an 'exquisite feeling of propriety in art'—very much as did the real lawyers of Edinburgh, such as the advocate Archibald Alison or the solicitor Aeneas MacBean.[10]

Published in the same year as Galt's *Glenfell*, and bearing a rather similar title, was *Glenfergus*. The anonymous author was Robert Mudie, whom we shall discuss in more detail later. The locus of the story in *Glenfergus* is the fictional Fergustown, on the West Highland coast. Edinburgh features merely as a place where some of the characters go to, or have gone to, for education, or to further would-be literary careers. Thus, the parish minister's son, George Cymbal, sets country female hearts a-flutter with his sophisticated Edinburgh dress. He was 'a handsome young man, fresh from Prince's [*sic*] Street, and in the height of Scoto-Athenian foppery'. Even his footwear is deemed classically perfect: '"How divinely picturesque the young gentleman looks", said Clarinda. "Those boots of his are quite the Grecian buskin, of which my dear uncle used to speak."' Another character seeks literary fame in 'the Scottish metropolis, the very seat and temple, as he observed, of literature and science.' An older *littérateur* adds a corrective note about Edinburgh as this mart of polish and learning ... This city, like Athens of old, is wholly given to idolatry, and perhaps the whole world does not exhibit such another instance of affected freedom of thought, and real servility both in judging and acting.[11]

*   *   *   *   *

Another fictitious visitor to Edinburgh who made his appearance in 1821 was the Revd Dr Paul Prosody. This splendid creation of William Combe sets out for Scotland with the intention of out-doing, in the sphere of antiquarian and picturesque tourism, his celebrated 'Southron' contemporary, Dr Syntax.[12] On arrival, the clergyman is immediately drawn into a circle of like-minded Scottish antiquaries led by Dr Factobend, of the Antediluvian Club, with whom Dr Prosody explores the historic buildings, picturesque landscapes and collections of Edinburgh. But first Prosody dines with Factobend, as if at some memorable supper of the days of the great classicist and judge James Burnett, Lord Monboddo, of whom Lord Cockburn said that his entertainments had been 'the most Attic' of the day.[13] Dinner is served 'in the manner of the Ancients', the table set with 'ancient urns and bronzèd vases'. Disaster strikes. Prosody's servant Archy had been intending to dress as a Roman, but in the end (in a revolution in antiquarian taste) appears accoutred as a knight in armour. He is discomfited when his vizor snaps shut just as he attempts to serve the wine, contained in a magnificent Greek *krater*, said to resemble one of Sir William Hamilton's vases. Archy trips, falls against the table, and smashes to smithereens Factobend's prize specimen of Greek antiquity.[14] An amusing aquatint plate allows us to be spectators of the tragic scene.

Factobend's ire, Prosody's shame, and the sherds of the Greek pot forgotten, the English visitor is invited to inspect what he has come north to see.

> And when the dawn of morning gray,
> Tips our stern crags with orient ray,
> I move that we do sally forth.
> To view this Athens of the North.

In fact, Dr Prosody has already called the city as much when he greets his welcoming hosts with the remark that he had never expected to visit Edinburgh, or to be so received:

> That it should ever be his fate,
> To enter thus in gorgeous state
> The Athens of the North, or be
> The object of such courtesy.[15]

A witty interchange takes place between Prosody and a university student upon North Bridge, metaphor for the link between the two contrasting worlds of the Romantic and Picturesque Old Town, so much admired by Prosody for its 'hoar antiquity', and the rational, enlightened order of the classicism of the New Town. The student's talk is all of the improvements evidenced by the modern (that is, neoclassical) architecture and town-planning of the Athens of the North.[16] Prosody symbolises the tensions underlying the idea of Edinburgh as the Modern Athens. He admires the intellectual ethos of the contemporary city, alluding as he does to Smollett's famous designation of the place at an earlier time; yet, as an antiquary, he also admires the idiosyncratic romance and the historic appeal of the buildings of Auld Reekie. In the end, however, he achieves a satisfactory antisyzygy, apostrophising the Athenian qualities of the city thus: 'Adieu, a long adieu', he cries,

> Illustrious seat of arts and letters;
> Antiquities and all such matters;
> Hot-bed of genius, seat of science,
> Long may'st thou hold at proud defiance,
> Each rival who thy fair renown,
> Would try to blast with Envy's frown ...[17]

*   *   *   *   *

The September 1822 number of *Blackwood's Magazine* was devoted to the royal visit of August that year. Several contributions are relevant here. The piece entitled 'Hogg's Royal Jubilee', which is attributed to John Wilson ('Christopher North'), takes its title from James Hogg ('the Ettrick Shepherd'), also of the Blackwood circle. It includes an imagined poetic interchange between (the late) Robert Fergusson and (the late) Robert Burns on the subject of the King's jaunt. In this, Edinburgh is referred to many times as 'Auld Reekie'. But, at the outset, Fergusson is given the following lines, the second of which alludes to the topographical similarity between Athens and Edinburgh, then very much in the mind of the literary public, and also the eye of an artistic coterie which had just seen the paintings of 'Grecian' Williams:

> What Kintra's [country's] this, what City's that,
> Which sits as auncient Athens sat?...[18]

Burns himself (the real Burns, that is) might have sympathised with these sentiments, for he was, after all, the poet of the 'Address to Edinburgh', with its praise of the elegance and splendour of architecture, the wealth of trade, the realm of learning and the rule of science. Burns's poem was composed in December 1786, and it therefore stands at a point in time almost exactly equidistant between the drawing up of James Craig's plan for the classical New Town (1766) and the period when Edinburgh really began to assume 'Athenian' airs. In 1830, Burns himself, by then perceived as one of the greatest geniuses of the Golden Age of Scotland, would be commemorated by a version of the Choragic Monument of Lysikrates on the flank of Calton Hill.

Also published in the September 1822 number of *Blackwood's* was the sixth instalment of the 'Noctes Ambrosianae'. This famous series features imaginary conversations that took place over suppers at Ambrose's tavern. This particular instalment has a complex scene involving in the action and the discussion many of the regular characters of this whimsical cycle—some of them real, some fictitious, and most with identities mixed between fact and fiction.

The political affairs of contemporary Greece in the throes of revolution are introduced. Specific mention is made of the horrific massacre on the Greek island of Chios (Scio) by the Ottomans in April that year, and the abduction and abuse of its women. This is in order to allow 'Mr Bunting' to allude to 'the inhabitants of modern Athens', as well as to events in Greece. Bunting also mentions having attended a recent meeting in Edinburgh 'at which the affairs of Greece were admirably discussed': this must be that at which Thomas M'Crie had spoken. A breathless and somewhat confused interchange among some five characters takes place. The subject is the architecture of Edinburgh, and the proposed Parthenon in particular. The Nelson Monument is defended, condemned and defended again by succeeding speakers. Interestingly, an Englishman favours its demolition to make way for the Parthenon: it disfigures 'the modern Athens'. Christopher North asks whether 'monuments to the illustrious dead [are] to lie at the mercy of Dilletanti [*sic*]?' Another participant weighs in: 'I admire the Parthenon ... I am glad the foundation-stone has been laid.' North speaks again: 'So am I. Let Scotland shew now that she has liberality as well as taste, and not suffer the walls to be dilapidated by time before they have been raised to their perfect height.'

This speech is significant, both in its echo of concerns for the current state of the original Parthenon, and its prophetic musing on the possible fate of the 'facsimile'. The Irishman, 'O'Doherty', declares that the Edinburgh Parthenon will be an elegant 'testimonial'; but, as a national testimonial, should not it be paid for by Scots themselves, rather than by hand-outs from a government in London? 'Timothy Tickler' (the real Robert Sym, a prominent Edinburgh lawyer) rises to this challenge. 'We admire the Parthenon. We resolve to build it. We call ourselves Athenians, and then implore Parliament to pay the piper. Poor devils! We ought to be ashamed of ourselves.' The Englishman, 'Buller' (presumably a generic 'John Bull' figure), joins in the reproach:

A rich nation does well to be magnificent. Up with towers, temples, baths, porticos, and what not; but for one nation to build splendid structures, and then call on another for their praises and their purses, is, in my opinion, not exactly after the fashion of the Athenians.[19]

This was not the first time that the friends who convened at Ambrose's had turned to the question of an 'Athenian' Edinburgh. In the second number of the 'Noctes' series, published in April 1822, the debate is warmly contested. 'Buller' opens proceedings: 'You will pardon me, my beloved and honoured friends, but do you not think that the "Modern Athens", as applied to Edinburgh, is pure humbug?' 'North' and 'Tickler'—one in real life an Edinburgh advocate, the other an Edinburgh solicitor—agree. The latter fulminates, and many of his thunderbolts strike home:

> Such an impertinence would not have been tolerated in Auld Reekie. In the days, of [Adam] Smith, and [David] Hume, and [William] Robertson, we were satisfied with our national name, and so were we during a later dynasty of genius, of which old [Henry] Mackenzie still survives; but now-a-days, when with the exception of [Walter] Scott, yourself North, and myself, and a few others, there is not a single man of power or genius in Edinburgh, the prigs call themselves *Athenians*! Why, you may just as appropriately call the first Parallelogram, that shall be erected on Mr [Robert] Owen's plan, the Modern Athens, as the New Town of Edinburgh ... Where are our sculptors, painters, musicians, orators, poets, and philosophers? ... The ninnies have not even the sense to know that our Calton Hill is no more like the Acropolis than Lord Buchan is like Pericles, or [Francis] Jeffrey like Demosthenes. It is the Castle Rock that is like the Acropolis ... if the Parthenon is to be built at all, it *must* be built on the Castle Rock. This is the first egregious blunder of our Modern Athenians ... We are Scotsmen, not Greeks ... There are not ten persons in Edinburgh—not one Whig I am sure—who could read three lines of Homer "*ad aperturam libri*". There are pretty Athenians for you! Think of shoals of Scotch artisans, with long lank greasy hair, and corduroy breeches, walking in the Parthenon![20]

Not so long after they had digested this very telling outburst, with its reference to what properly constituted the 'acropolis' of Edinburgh—Castle or Calton?—and its deflation of so much 'Modern Athenian' flummery, Edinburgh readers would have been able to enjoy the image of Tickler's real-life original, Robert Sym, WS. Sym was caricatured by John Kay in all the supercilious elegance of demeanour for which he had been celebrated, with his tall, spare, upright figure setting him apart from the crowd. Yet Hugh Paton, in his commentary on Kay's portrait, described Sym—so long-lived (1752-1845) that he witnessed almost the entire 'Athenian' phenomenon—as 'one of the handsomest men of Modern Athens'.[21] Clearly many were reluctant to let go of the notion despite any amount of mockery of it.

In 1830, the men of the Ambrosian Nights were still discoursing on the 'Athenian' question. Thomas De Quincey, a more recent recruit to the company, launches forth:

> No wonder Edinburgh is such a city. There is something sublime, Mr North, to my imagination, in its mid-summer solitude. Still almost as a city of the dead, yet serene as a city of the living ... I envy the stranger within your gates. The dullest wight ... must become a poet beneath your Castle Rock—sublimer, sir—believe me—than the Acropolis: though pardon me for hinting, that I am scarcely sensible of the propriety of the term—when self-applied to the ingenious and learned inhabitants—Modern Athenians.

'The Ettrick Shepherd' joins in, his intervention ranging from mundane concern about his dessert to some homespun moralising on the absence of any literary talent in the Modern Athens resembling the ancient tragedians: 'Nor me either—my aipple's dune—and its hanged nonsense. Whare's Pericles? No the Provost—perfek gentleman though in a' things he be ... Whare's Eskluss, Yourippidays, and Suffoclaes?'[22]

*   *   *   *   *

The Hermit in Edinburgh: or, Sketches of Manners and Real Characters and Scenes in the Drama of Life is an interesting analysis of, among other matters, 'the taste of the modern Athens'. The author was Captain Felix McDonough, who noted that 'The resemblance which has been discovered betwixt Athens and the Metropolis of fair Scotia, has been too often asserted and too floridly described to need any comment on that head ...'. But McDonough maintains that Edinburgh actually has 'a very small proportion of *Greek* inhabitants or visitors within its limits', adding the somewhat opaque comment that 'the hand of Donald and Sandy do not open so readily to these tolerated depredators as the warmer palms of the more southern cities'. This seems not very comprehensible until we realise that 'Greek', as employed here, probably carries a derogatory connotation. In contemporary usage, a 'Greek' could mean a cunning, wily person: a 'sharper'. It could also mean an Irish immigrant. McDonough, Irish himself, returns to the similarity between the Greek and Scottish cities:

> ... the concentration, however, of talent and of science, on the northern soil gives a colouring for the parallel alluded to, and where localities are imperfect genius and invention may bear out the comparison. The progress which the graces and the muses have made on Scottish ground, aided by the operations of the arts and sciences ... and the sharp edge of reviewer's criticism, could not

fail to bring Scotland and her capital into notice and fashion, into admiration and imitation ...[23]

Thomas Love Peacock subtly and wittily satirised Edinburgh's 'Athenian' pretensions in *Crotchet Castle* (1831). Richard Monckton Milnes, Lord Houghton, concluded that Peacock had exhibited

> an indiscriminate repugnance to Scotland and everything Scotch ... Thus the assumption of the name of the 'Modern Athens' by Edinburgh, seemed to him absolutely profane: the only possible application could be its occasional festivities; but even a good supper could not make an Athenian without Attic salt ...[24]

Underlying the humour of *Crotchet Castle* is the fact that the eponymous Mr Crotchet had been born 'MacCrotchet'. He had left Scotland for London, like the real John MacMurray, from Edinburgh, who had similarly reinvented himself as the plain, less overtly Scottish Mr *Murray*, the London publisher. Both had turned their backs upon the Northern Athens in favour of the Mecca-like magnet of the southern metropolis. Amusingly, Crotchet states as fact that 'very few intellectual noses point due north'. Hearing this, Mr MacQuedy [=QED], the Edinburgh economist, responds, seeing a chance to score a victory for Edinburgh's intellectual, 'Athenian' leadership: 'Only those that point to the Modern Athens.' The Revd Dr Folliott joins in: 'Where all native noses point southward.' Equivocating, MacQuedy balances the argument: 'Eh sir, northward for wisdom, southward for profit.'[25]

Athenian satire is heavy during the debate over breakfast at Crotchet Castle, which occurs in Chapter II of the novel, entitled 'The March of Mind'. Dr Folliott, the English clergyman, and Mr Skionar, the transcendental poet, are pitted against MacQuedy. Folliott is a gourmand—but a thinking one. He likes fish for breakfast, and praises the Scots for this taste. 'We have much to learn from you in that line at any rate.' MacQuedy responds:

> And in many others, sir, I believe. Morals and metaphysics, politics and political economy, the way to make the most of all modifications of smoke; steam, gas, and paper currency; you have all these to learn from us; in short, all the arts and sciences. We are the modern Athenians.

Warming to his theme, MacQuedy disputes Folliott's assertion that the Modern Athenians 'sup upon sandwiches'. 'Nay, sir; the modern Athenians know better than that. A literary supper in sweet Edinbroo' would cure you of the prejudice you seem to cherish against us.' But Folliott renews the attack:

... much more is wanted to make up an Athenian. Athenians, indeed! where is your theatre? who among you has written a comedy? where is your attic salt ... The great business is, sir, that you call yourselves Athenians, while you know nothing that the Athenians thought worth knowing, and dare not show your noses before the civilised world in the practice of any one art in which they were excellent. Modern Athens, sir! The assumption is a personal affront to every man who has a Sophocles in his library. I will thank you for an anchovy ...

After a testy interchange about comedy—MacQuedy had advocated *The Gentle Shepherd*, by 'the divine Allan Ramsay', only to be countered by Dr Folliott with 'The Gentle Shepherd! It is just a comedy as the book of Job'—MacQuedy reposts again:

Metaphysics, sir; metaphysics. Logic and moral philosophy. There we are at home. The Athenians only sought the way, and we have found it; and to all this we have added political economy, the science of sciences.[26]

Lady Clarinda, the voice of feminine common sense, subsequently assesses MacQuedy as 'the Modern Athenian, who lays down the law about every thing, and therefore may be taken to understand every thing'.[27]

*   *   *   *   *

This short survey of Modern Athens in satire began with a glance at Christian Isobel Johnstone's *The Saxon and the Gaël* of 1814. It draws towards its close with the same author's 'Mrs Mark Luke; or the West Country Exclusives', which is a long story included in the three-volume collection given the overarching title of *The Edinburgh Tales, Conducted by Mrs Johnstone*, published some thirty years later.[28] Although this is billed as an 'Edinburgh Tale', it is in fact a West of Scotland one, and it deals with the pretensions of a Glasgow grocer's wife. Its significance for our enquiry lies in the occasional references to Edinburgh made by Clyde-side folk, rising or risen in society. The humour lies in the way one side of the country views the other, and in the different kinds of middle-class attitudes and aspirations. At the outset, Christian Johnstone explains that her story relies on the very human instinct to keep others 'without a certain pale and boasting of being within it ourselves.'[29]

Mark Luke, a Glasgow grocer, marries Barbara Peaston. They have an only daughter, Marjory Robina, known as Mysie. A well-doing pillar of what the writer calls the 'shopocracy', Mr Luke prospers mightily. With prosperity comes pretension. The circles in which they move become grander; Mysie attends the 'Belle Retiro Establishment'; the focus of life gradually moves down the Clyde to smarter locations than the city itself. The Lukes keep company with the rather more polished Stronachs of Port Glasgow, whose daughter Flora has been 'finished' in Boulogne. The Stronachs

> seemed to despise the whole province as commercial, and vulgar, manufacturing, and impracticable to the refinements and graces of life. They had little more reverence for the poor provincial gentry, than for the purse-proud *mercantiles*. Edinburgh itself, the very Modern Athens, was despised, with all its architectural, literary and aristocratic pride and splendour. Mrs Mark Luke was overcome with amazement.

Metaphorically, Miss Stronach then puts the closely buttoned boot (enclosing her, presumably, elegant foot) into the capital of her country, despite all the interest that the young ladies have shown and will show in winning the hearts of smart and 'weel-conneckit' young Edinburgh advocates on the Western Circuit.

> What is Edinburgh, after all, but a provincial town, where the Scottish law courts sit ... with all the formality, and more than the conceit of such kind of places? Even *your* city of Glasgow, ma'am, is, in some respects, superior to that town of poor cousins, with its stiff professional air and ridiculous pretensions.

Mrs Mark Luke, who 'usually affected to yield the palm to the City of Palaces'—as Edinburgh was sometimes known at this time, or earlier in the century—'as proof of her own refinement', bridled at this double onslaught, but appeared 'as became her, at heart sound and unfaltering in her allegiance' to her native Glasgow.[30]

*   *   *   *   *

In 1824, the pseudonymous author 'Lawrence Longshank, Gent.' published the orotund and vaguely titled work *Things in General* (its full and enormously long title includes the phrase 'Autobiographic Sketch in Limine [*sic*] and a Notice Touching Edinburgh'). These were the rambling memoirs of Robert Mudie. He was an embittered Dundonian school-teacher who had migrated to London and turned to journalism, in which capacity he had covered the King's visit to Edinburgh three years previously, publishing a comprehensive and valuable account. What he wrote of Edinburgh in *Things in General* was merely an appetiser for what was to follow the next year.

> Yea, of a surety it may be said of this city, which, *soi-disant*, and of her own proper assumption, claimeth and moutheth the epithetion of the modern Athena, that

like as the Athena of old, she is wholly given to idolatry; but ... her worship and her oblation are votive to nothing saving that which [either] springeth of herself, or is begotten of the lucre of place or the abundance of Mammon.

For Mudie, Edinburgh had once been 'the city of Anticipation': 'that paradise of youngling scribes, studyless students, and all the *exuviae* and efflorescence of the provinces'. But the bitterness of disappointment and rejection by society had set in, consuming the writer and prompting attacks on lawyers, ladies, literary men:

Yea, when this pseudo-Athena waxeth proud,—when she boasteth of her literary fame,—when she telleth of her Maecenases—of farthings and counterfeit half-pence ... I will speed me from her as from the city of the plague—lifting up my voice to others that they may follow mine ensample ...[31]

The ground was thus marked in acid. In 1825 a further book appeared that must have infuriated all supporters of the Parthenon scheme, or indeed all Modern Athenians. In the 'Noctes Ambrosianae', not unnaturally, this work came in for some discussion—but, strangely, not nearly as much as one might have expected, given the sensation the book had caused. 'The Ettrick Shepherd' wondered why 'Christopher North' had not boxed the author's ears. But 'North' himself was surprisingly tolerant of an author he did not consider 'absolutely a blackguard'.[32]

Under the title of *The Modern Athens*, and under the pseudonym of 'A Modern Greek' (therefore a 'cunning rogue', perhaps?), Robert Mudie published his full-scale satirical and acerbic analysis of what he saw as the essence of contemporary Edinburgh. It is an example of astonishingly bitter and jaundiced reportage in which Mudie took satire of 'Athenian' Edinburgh to both new depths and vitriolic heights. Mudie's chosen pen-name has nothing whatsoever to do with real Greeks in the era of the Greek struggle for independence, and Mudie actually makes no pretence whatsoever to view the city and its inhabitants as a Greek might possibly have done, or from a 'Greek' perspective of any kind.

To *The Modern Athens*, Mudie gave the subtitle of a 'Dissection and Demonstration of Men and Things in the Scotch Capital', a place and a people he evidently loathed and despised. At the outset, he declared cynically that his intention was 'to enwrap the whole in one pure and perennial blaze of glory'.[33] His mockery of what he saw as the pretensions of the city and its unself-critical inhabitants, described throughout as 'the Athens' and 'the Athenians', was merciless and excoriating. The book, though in some ways distasteful and often cruelly cutting, is actually extremely well-written. Early on, Mudie states—with a retrospective glance at the King's visit three years previously—that

... the Modern Athens holds herself up to the world as a sort of concentrated tincture or spirit of all that is fine or feeling in the country,—as being the throne of learning—the chosen seat of sentiment and song; furthermore, when there was upon this occasion gathered in and about the Athens, all the lights which are acknowledged as shining, and all the fires which are recognised as burning, in taste and talent throughout Scotland ...[34]

Perhaps having digested the polemical articles of Archibald Alison and his fellows, Mudie—ever the outsider—drew the conclusion that the leading characteristic of 'the Athenians' was to

esteem their own idols in preference to the idols of every other people on the face of the earth. Their own situation is the finest that can possibly be found; and their own mode of improving it is superior to any that could be suggested. Their men ... excel all others in wisdom ... which, shining from the Athens, [has] dazzled and illuminated mankind.[34]

The planned Parthenon was seen as but the vanity of vanities distinguishing (or making farcical) a city desperately trying to become what it could never be. All the arguments of the supporters of the project were rehearsed and then damned to scathing ridicule. Mudie's principal target was 'the vanity of the Athens', and what he termed its characteristic 'self-adoration'.[36] His central contention was that this had assumed ridiculous and damaging proportions. In this it was as if he were picking up the comments made in a similar vein, if very much less cruelly, by Scott and Cockburn before they had forgotten themselves and had become 'Athenian', along with their peers, in supporting the Parthenon project.

Ancient Greek historical events, personalities and cultural achievements had found their modern equivalents, and indeed superiors, in Edinburgh's varied contributions to modern British historical development. Ancient parallels came

gradually a little nearer home ... Edinburgh was very much like Athens,—it was, in fact, the Modern Athens, or the Athens Restored; the Calton Hill was a far finer thing than the Acropolis; the freestone of Craigleith excelled in beauty and durability the marble of Pentelicus; the Firth of Forth outstretched and outshone the Egean or the Hellespont; the kingdom of Fife beat beyond all comparison Ionia and the Troad; Ida and Athos were mere mole-hills compared with North Berwick Law and the Lomonds; Plataea and Marathon had nothing in them at all comparable with Pinkie and Preston Pans; Sir George Mackenzie ... excelled both Aeschylus and Aristophanes; Macvey Napier was an Aristotle; Lord Hermand a Diogenes; Macqueen of Braxfield had been a Draco; the Lord President was a Solon; a Demosthenes could be found anywhere; and Lord Maconochie [Mudie means the judge Alexander Maconochie, Lord Meadowbank] was even more than a Plato. Then to make the parallel perfect, and indeed to make the Modern Athens every way outstrip the Athens of old, only one thing was wanting ... that there should be erected upon the top of the Calton Hill, a copy of the Temple of Minerva Parthenon, to be called the national monument of Scotland ... and that the independence of the modern city and the modern land should survive the building of the monument as long as that of the old had done. The proposal took amazingly; for, in an instant, every quill was up to the feather in ink, every tongue was eloquent, and every lady and gentleman took an Athenian *nom de guerre*— Alcibiades there, Aspasia here, till they had Athenized the whole city ...[37]

With specific reference to the unbuilt *omphalos* of this new Athens, Mudie took ill-concealed pleasure in pointing-up current and future difficulties of this 'slow-going Parthenon'.

Still, however, fine as the situation was, and fond as they were of it, a Parthenon in speech was a cheaper thing than a Parthenon in stone; and so, though Edinburgh had, beyond all doubt or dispute, become the Modern Athens, it still wanted the temple of Minerva upon the Calton Hill as the national monument of Scotland. It was still wished and resolved, however, that this finishing touch should be given to the likeness and the glory of the Modern Athens ...[38]

For Mudie, there was precious little glory in 'Athenian' Edinburgh. Something of the paradox, and the larger question of the validity of the Athenian identification, was all too tellingly observed when he summed up at the end of his evisceration of 'the Modern Athens'. He had, he wrote, tried to analyse

those features and traits which stamp upon the Modern Athens, the isolation and individuality of her character, as she stands away from other cities, and appears in herself ... The Athens boasts of herself as a model of elegance and of taste: I found her a compound of squalor and of vulgarity.

Mudie heaped sarcasm upon vituperation, and cynicism upon misanthropy. Every aspect of the city's life and culture was attacked; all its faults were laid bare. He concluded his character-assassination in a way that demonstrates that he was alluding to the (alleged) exclamation by the Turkish *Disdar* of Athens, when witnessing the dropping and destruction of a Parthenon metope due to the carelessness of Lord Elgin's labourers when removing the sculptured panel. Edward Daniel Clarke asserted that the Ottoman official had muttered sorrowfully, in Greek, 'Telos', meaning 'the end', or 'never again'; the comment had become celebrated through Byron's having incorporated it in a note to the Second Canto of *Childe Harold's Pilgrimage*.[39] The peroration to Mudie's long diatribe incorporates these ideas.[40] It runs thus:

> When she [Edinburgh] redeems herself from them, and becomes in reality even something like what she would call herself in name [Athens], let her then make comparisons with the Gem of ancient Greece. Let her give some proof that Minerva Parthenon is her tutelar goddess; when she has done so, let her build the temple to that divinity; and, as she finishes the sculpture of the last metope, with deeds of her own worthy of being recorded, I (as the Turk did when her countryman completed the spoliation of the ancient Athena,) shall to the completion of the merit which she claims, subscribe
>
> ΤΕΛΟΣ.

THE ANTI-GREEKS OF MODERN ATHENS

'UNBLUSHING SERVILITY AND BITS OF BORROWED LUSTRE'

Not everyone in Edinburgh wanted to feel Greek, or to express commitment to 'Northern Athenianism' by building Greek. As we have seen, a whole genre of literary mockery of Edinburgh's pretensions developed. This chapter looks specifically at intellectualised hostility to the Greek style in architecture and townscape as an alien and inappropriate import.

In the October 1819 number of *Blackwood's Magazine*, a pseudonymous writer calling himself 'A Journeyman Mason' contributed an essay with the somewhat demeaning title 'Decorations of Edinburgh'.[1] This choice of title seems to reduce the grandest dreams of Greek Doric architecture to the level of ephemeral bunting for a street party. The author, however, had a much more earnest purpose: to counter the arguments of Archibald Alison and the other contributor to *Blackwood's* known only as 'R'. In an article that was refreshingly short by the standards of other writers on the subject, the 'Journeyman Mason' suggested that it would be unwise, indeed shameful, to think and build in the Greek style, thus denying—betraying, even—the home-grown national heritage in architectural design. Classical Greece should inspire, certainly; but it should not dictate and dominate.

I have read with some sorrow, and more shame, your correspondent's proposal to adorn Edinburgh with a Greek temple. Is he serious? Or does he write it as a satire upon Scottish invention? and is it true, that no living man is capable of conceiving a suitable structure to commemorate the glories of Scotland? That your correspondent shews good taste in admiring the Parthenon, who would deny—but he is unwise in recommending its restoration by his countrymen. The use to be made of ancient works, of the majestic remains of

Grecian greatness, is not to transfer them in the gross into marble or stone, to carry them off, pillar and rafter, like the fabled church of Loretto,—but to contemplate and admire them, to elevate the mind and kindle a fire which may excite an emulation of their glories.

Had the 'sun of Scottish invention' sunk so low, or had it never risen? Was Edinburgh, he was effectively suggesting, supposed always to eschew the autochthonous, and never to create anything new? It appeared that the aim of civic taste was to 'restore the old ... works which exercise the memory in recollections of Athens and Rome, rather than [to] aspire after an hazardous reputation for originality ... and earn the immortality which awaits imitation and forsakes invention.' Edinburgh citizens should 'look at the Parthenon, contemplate its simple beauty, then conceive something in the same lofty spirit ...'. The 'Journeyman' continued to lament the idea that 'where you cannot lead you should limp after ... There are too many buildings in Edinburgh already which remind one of other people's productions ...'. Having mentioned 'the insulted genius of his country', he condemned a taste that would

> show the Scotch to be miserable copyists of fine marble in coarse stone. Let us not look at Scotland and her heroes and sages through Greek spectacles—let us make something that Phidias might have done had he been a Scotchman.[2]

After this admirably clear statement of sound principle, the writer turned against both the proposed Parthenon model and the Calton Hill as its location. In doing so, he apparently ignored the fact that the Athenian Acropolis was a substantial and prominent high point, even though other Greek temples had indeed been built on lower ground. Thus, he further confessed that he felt

> afraid the Calton Hill, (if it is the Calton *now* that it *once* was, for I cannot look out at any window and see the tricks which *improvement* has been playing with this admired rock), would be too large a base for this building, the mountain would devour the monument—you must have a building of colossal magnitude to associate with this mighty pedestal. I am surprised that your correspondent did not feel some classical scruples about recommending a hill, even of solid rock, for the scite [*sic*] of his Parthenon ... he might have advised you to build your monument in the North Loch.[3]

In a second article, entitled 'Public Buildings of Edinburgh', the same 'Journeyman Mason' returned to his self-appointed task by delivering himself of a further forthright condemnation of what he saw as the unwarranted and undesirable 'Athenianizing' of the city.[4]

... we cannot create architects like soldiers—by conscription—nor rear splendid edifices by a spell—nor rob Athens to decorate Edinburgh, as Constantine did Rome to ornament Byzantium. We must maintain the same air of originality in our buildings which reigns in our literature, and make the one worthy of the other ... Homer and Virgil are pointed out as the well-springs of poetical genius ... we are not permitted to *adapt* their verse to our achievements ... How this privilege is denied to poets and conceded to architects I cannot comprehend ... the tables and shelves of architects are loaded and encumbered with drawings of all the buildings Greece or Italy possess.—They accumulate there, till native taste is terrified at the contemplation ... till original talent is frightened into servile imitation ...

Classical buildings and monuments might be unwisely and inappropriately copied or adapted 'as beacons to light the way for public taste—an expensive mode of instruction, sacrificing ready money, and originality together—for the sake of erecting *something* that means *nothing* ...'. Greece itself, after all, 'was no importer of the architecture of other nations'. In a nimble riposte to Alison and others, the 'Journeyman' wrote of 'stolen morsels' to be put into hungry mouths, 'till something better can be made ready'. Edinburgh was now threatened with a 'resurrection of the Parthenon', 'taken "cut and dry" from the architect's portfolio', because

a traveller, it seems [this was probably a hit against Hugh William Williams], has discovered some resemblance between the Acropolis and the Calton Hill—they are both rocky elevations—overlook two ancient cities—'they are both rivers, look you,' says Fluellen, 'and there be salmons in both.'

The allusion is to a sophistic truism uttered by the character Fluellen in Shakespeare's *Henry V*, Act IV, Scene vii, adapted and quoted with no great accuracy. The 'Journeyman Mason' might well have added to equal effect Fluellen's further observation of similarity between places and natural features: '...'tis all one, 'tis alike as my fingers is to my fingers ...'. But the 'Journeyman' went on to counter the argument that Craigleith freestone and the local masons' skill might make all possible:

... because Waterloo-place possesses capitals delicately carved, exactly resembling some Athenian antiques, we must have an imitation on a grander scale; we have been but puny thieves of porticos and capitals hitherto—despise these petty larcenies—make a bold grasp, and become the greatest and most unlimited architectural thieves of the age. But then, this will enable Edinburgh to have a school of architecture—to become the centre of taste, and the mistress of chaste design—and you cannot imagine what wonderful things Scottish genius may accomplish, by placing a Parthenon before it. It may teach us to be honest, but we begin basely—it may instruct architects in the honourable feeling of the genius of the one land to another—to abandon their predatory inroads on broken down nations—but it sets a bad example; and ... there will be no end to the importation of ancient temples, while folly has a pound in her pocket, or Scotland an acre of rock for a foundation.

The 'Journeyman' accused Alison (though not by name, for Alison had written anonymously) and others of his persuasion of rushing precipitately to 'occupy this classical rock—this Caledonian Acropolis, before native and original genius can come modestly forward with her proposal of a rival edifice.' Such an action would be disloyal to Scottish taste and talent: 'your Caledonian Parthenon would only be a Greek Parthenon, degraded in a baser material.' Warming even more ardently to his theme, he mocked what he saw as a shameful attempt to make Scottish architects speak Greek, as it were, against their nature or their better judgment, 'to instruct and elevate the grovelling intellects of the Caledonian architects', and inveighed against 'the unblushing servility of the whole race of architects, and which nothing can equal but the imprudent fortitude with which the restoration of the Parthenon has been proposed and pressed.' Too much building in Edinburgh was, even then, little more than 'bits of borrowed lustre'. The person who advocated a wholesale surrender to classicism forgot

the fame of Scotland whenever he thinks of the Greeks—he loves a Doric portico better than he loves his country, and the dust of Athens or the cinders of Herculaneum have more of his reverence than the dust of all the Douglasses [*sic*]. He considers that the keystone in the arch of Scottish renown is not in its place till a successful inroad has been made on the Doric—he contemplates former thefts with a rapture he seeks not to suppress—still his joy is not perfect—nobody has stolen an entire Doric temple—how blind we have been to our own greatness! To select with taste, to single out an object worthy of being stolen, is the greatest proof, in his eyes, of good taste and genius ...

Not the least of Alison's sins, in the Journeyman's view, was to contemplate a Parthenon restored and translated to Edinburgh as a complete temple, but without its sculpture:

Perhaps he prefers it plundered of its brightest jewels, and robbed by time and the hand of man of its chief attractions, to what it was in its proudest hour, when its pediments and friezes spoke audibly in sculpture as with a tongue ...

Without its marbles, a facsimile Parthenon would be merely 'a crown deprived of its gems, or a nocturnal firmament without stars', and thus 'present this empty Doric cup to the thirsty lips of his countrymen'. Without appropriate sculpture, the Calton Hill monument would be 'inferior to its prototype, and will no more have the effect of the Parthenon than a prentice's cap will look like a bonnet of gold sparkling with precious stones.'

*   *   *   *   *

When the 'Journeyman Mason' was writing so forcefully, Edinburgh people had at least enjoyed some opportunity to become acquainted with the Parthenon sculptures. In 1811, as we have noted, Benjamin West thought the arrival of the Elgin Marbles would make London into 'a new Athens'; Edinburgh therefore needed to look to its classical laurels if it sought to compete for the title.

Drawings, and some casts, of the Parthenon marbles were acquired for the Trustees' Academy in 1816, for the sum of £120, on the recommendation of Hugh William Williams and with the support of Gilbert Innes of Stow, merchant banker and maecenas of sculptors and sculpture. (Innes was a 'mover and shaker' in Edinburgh's commercial and cultural worlds. A bachelor involved with innumerable societies, clubs and institutions, he owned one of the city's finest houses in St Andrew Square; and with his 67 illegitimate children he went some way by himself to populate the Modern Athens.) Made in London by the Italian *formatore* Matteo Mazzoni, these Parthenon casts were housed, somewhat incongruously, in the attic flat of a tenement at 5 Picardy Place, where the Trustees' Academy was then accommodated. This property was at the west end of the street—on its now-demolished south side—and so its windows would have looked directly across to and down Broughton Street, to those elegant and interesting door-pieces derived from the Athenian Monument of Thrasyllos, which we noted at the end of Chapter 4.

Many more high-quality casts, also struck from primary moulds of the original sculptures, would follow once the Academy had been transferred to Playfair's Royal Institution in 1826. Indeed, it would appear that the necessity of accommodating an expanding collection of Parthenon casts was one of the motivating factors in the campaign to build the multi-purpose Royal Institution in the first place, and certainly a major reason why it was subsequently enlarged between 1831 and 1836.[5] There the casts were displayed at a height roughly corresponding to that of the original Parthenon frieze, so replicating more faithfully the authentic arrangement of the sculptures when *in situ* on the ancient temple than was the case with the display of the actual originals at the British Museum, where the Elgin Marbles were shown almost at eye level. Playfair designed the cast gallery of the Trustees' Academy to accommodate the frieze around its walls, in a substantially complete form as casts from primary moulds taken from Lord Elgin's sculptures. In providing permanent exhibition space for the Elgin casts to be displayed in this way, Playfair effectively created another sort of 'inside-out temple'—the frieze being mounted facing *inwards*—following that which he had earlier conceived in the lower hall of the Natural History Museum of the University. This enlarged cast collection formed the best such assemblage in Great Britain at the time. It might even be argued, that in being readily accessible to the public, this represented in some small way the (admittedly not very strongly marked) egalitarian credentials of late-Georgian Edinburgh as some sort of latter-day 'Periclean democracy'.

In the course of a dispute on the question of legitimate ownership of certain drawings, Lord Elgin had previously asserted that he had exhibited some Athenian drawings, incontrovertibly his own, in Edinburgh for an extended period before 1815. Then, in 1827, he presented the Trustees' Academy with some casts from the sculptures of the Theseion, and of the Temple of Athena Nike on the Acropolis, which he had previously housed at Broomhall. Despite the opprobrium he may have acquired in other quarters, Elgin remained to a great extent a hero in an Edinburgh which saw itself as the Modern Athens. Admittedly, Walter Scott entertained an ambiguous view of the Earl's most famous 'achievement', writing in 1818 that 'though I am glad that the marbles are brought here [that is, to Britain] yet I would have cut my own hand off rather than have displaced one of them.' However, to balance this ambivalence, there were other equally strongly held and more clearly positive opinions. In the catalogue of the Trustees' Academy casts, Charles Heath Wilson paid due tribute to the Earl for having 'saved from entire destruction these memorials of the arts and civilization of the Greeks', when 'Time and barbarism seemed intent on the destruction of these magnificent remains.'[6]

Between 1835 and 1838 another, full set of very high-quality casts (also from primary moulds) of the Parthenon marbles was obtained for the Trustees' Academy: these casts included the sculptures of the west frieze, which Elgin had left in place on the ruined temple. The combined run of casts was then displayed as an archaeologically correct whole or 'integral structure', as distinct from being isolated in a series of tasteful, individual 'museum exhibits'; and other casts of some metopes were also skilfully arranged in a scholarly way, being set between made-up timber and plaster triglyphs.

That Edinburgh acquired this invaluable collection was due to the enterprise and foresight of two men. Both played a thoroughly 'Modern Athenian' part. James Skene of Rubislaw, Secretary to the Board of Trustees for Manufactures—which administered the Trustees' Academy—argued for the purchase of the casts and found the money to pay for them. George Thomson, Chief Clerk to the Board, went to London to negotiate the deal, and to buy additional handsome casts of individual Parthenon pedimental sculptures.[7]

Interestingly, James Skene, who had done this considerable service for classicism in the Athens of the North, actually lived in the Athens of the South for some years in the later 1830s and early 1840s, during which time he made many drawings of Greek sites and Greek landscapes. Skene was, from early manhood, a celebrated European traveller and he was drawn to Greece at this later time by reason of his son's marriage to a Greek. Skene's own translation from Edinburgh to Athens as a resident was an uncommon tribute by a pillar of society in the one city to the other—a destination that had so much inspired that same Scottish society through the power of its ancient ethos and the magic of its immortal name.

Edinburgh was not, however, entirely marble-mad. In November 1820 Benjamin Robert Haydon brought to the city his celebrated painting of *Christ's Entry into Jerusalem* for what proved to be a highly successful public exhibition. But Haydon brought other work to Edinburgh as well. What has been largely overlooked is that he showed some of his drawings of the Elgin Marbles at the same time, and in the same venue. The rooms of the auctioneer William Bruce at the Regent Bridge, Waterloo Place, were not far from the site favoured for the Parthenon facsimile.[8] Haydon had worshipped the Parthenon sculptures and had drawn them repeatedly ever since his first encounter with them in 1808, when he was taken to see them by the Scottish painter David Wilkie.[9] *Blackwood's Magazine* was lavish in its praise of the *Jerusalem* picture. But below the review of Haydon's exhibition was a separate, mere one-and-a-half-line paragraph, mentioning the drawings without any comment whatsoever; these records of the Parthenon sculptures were thus accorded a very subsidiary billing.[10] Haydon himself once referred to the Elgin Marbles as the 'Ruins of Athens', just as Thomas Campbell, the Edinburgh-born sculptor, had initially been disappointed, indeed going so far as to think them (as he put it) 'Rubbish!'.[11] It seems odd that the Modern Athens did not pay the drawings greater attention.

Haydon had earlier lambasted the same David Wilkie, not only for his tardy appreciation of the merits of the marbles themselves, but also for meanness both in spirit and in pocket in trying to obtain for himself a plaster-cast, cheap or even gratis, from Haydon or his Italian 'plaisterman'. The pretext was that this specimen, if and when presented to John Graham of the Trustees' Academy, might persuade Graham to subscribe for a complete set of casts of the Parthenon frieze and metopes for the use of the Edinburgh drawing school. It was in this context that Haydon poured out his injured feelings to his diary: 'And so, to save 5 shillings, he [Wilkie] will be nervous & falter & hesitate & have all the feelings of meanness. Think of a man bargaining to save five shillings on an *Elgin Marble*!'[12] Here, at roughly the same time that Scott and Cockburn had belittled and thrown doubt upon Edinburgh's claiming to be the Athens of the North, is the thinly veiled suggestion that even Wilkie could think himself Athenian only if the price were right.

*   *   *   *   *

The single most devastating criticism of the drive towards a Greek Edinburgh in stone is to be found in the verses of James Aikman's *The Cenotaph, a Poem* and in its substantial prose introduction, published in the city in 1821.[13] Aikman's work is a remarkably assertive statement of Scottish nationalism. This being so, then what (as Aikman phrased it) 'in the estimation of Scotsmen … is all Greek and Roman fame?' Aikman wanted a National Monument that would speak Scots, not Greek; one that would reflect the native traditions of design; and one that would express Scottish national sentiment. Indeed, the words 'nationality' and 'native', and the notions they nurtured, fall thick and fast on Aikman's pages. It meant, in fact, that he wanted something Gothic, a style carrying Scottish national associations that are 'not *classical*, it is true, but they are dearer'.[14] Warming to his task, he let rip against the Greek and for the Gothic, expressing himself almost as if he were taking the oath in a court of law:

> My predilections are for a monument SCOTTISH;—wholly SCOTTISH; and *nothing* but SCOTTISH; I would rather have a building of inferior grade, if truly Scottish, than one 'of 'unapproachable glory', if it were merely the transplant of an exotic to be set down and nourished in the forced earth of the Calton Hill.[15]

In condemning 'the Grecian style' in general, Aikman made an interesting distinction between two modes of neo-Greek architecture. One, 'of a light airy gracefulness … connected with the idea of gaiety, pleasure, and amusement', might best be adopted chiefly 'in buildings where these sensations were intended to be produced in the embellishment of our theatres, squares, terraces, and crescents.' This was, perhaps, suitable enough for the New Town: for domestic buildings, elegant shop-fronts, and so on. The other kind of Greek building was to be found in those 'more massy specimens': namely, public buildings. The example he singled out was Archibald Elliot's County Hall, with its Erechtheion Ionic order, a structure very often commented on (as we have seen) both favourably and unfavourably, but the setting of which—at the junction of Parliament Square and the High Street—was frequently held against it. Aikman had his own decided views on this building:

> The universal impression which has been produced, is exactly the reverse of admiration, and confirms the previous prejudice which in Scotland had been attached to the shape and form of Heathenism; it is inanimate, heavy, dull, and uninteresting,—the rites of the Heathen were literally deeds of darkness,

their temples were constructed to exclude light, except by the door, and as a *whole*, total darkness is connected with the idea of the interior, and is an association which attaches to the very name.[16]

Turning to the proposed National Monument, a structure intended to be on a very much larger scale, and in a different order from that of the County Hall, Aikman felt that the inappropriateness would merely be writ larger.

It is NOT *Classical* recollections and associations that such a structure is intended to foster,—it is *Scottish* feelings which it is intended to preserve,—it is Scottish associations which it is intended to produce,—it is all the feelings and associations essentially connected with the glory of our *own* country, our beloved Caledonia, which ought to be identified in a *Scottish* National Monument, and not the recollections, however pleasant to the scholar, of the glory of Athens and the age of Pericles.[17]

Aikman's verse continues the attack on the classical, and carries forward the torch for the national style of Scotland, whatever that was: his was an onslaught against the derivative and uncritical copying of the Greek, and in favour of the originality of native design.

> ... And shall it not? Shall we despairing seek
> No Adams now, a model from the Greek?
> A Temple—not a Church—a borrowed plume,
> For second Athens, like the second Rome!! ...

An endnote reads: '... by the second Athens, is meant "The Intellectual City", a name that might afford the ground-work of a Tome.' But his verse continues:

> I ask no modern Parthenon to deck
> Our Calton's rugged summit—*a la Grec* ...
> What freezing language ever yet expressed
> More chilling praise—*a copy at the best*! ...

to finish with this flourish:

> Perish the Grecian column, ruin seize
> The polished architrave—and sculptured frieze.
> No! Scotia be each recollection thine
> And every sculptured wreath thy artists twine,
> Be Scottish all—both execution and design![18]

Although the pro-Greek vision was now focused firmly on a Parthenon 'facsimile', John Galt added a necessary corrective to an excessively Hellenic view of the future architectural development of an 'Athenian' Edinburgh. Under cover of a nominal review—of *An Inquiry into the Principles of Beauty in Grecian Architecture* by George, fourth Earl of Aberdeen—Galt, writing under the pseudonym 'Viator' [traveller], and as one of the few commentators who had actually been to Greece, set out his own opinion as to the 'appropriateness' of the application of Greek forms.[19] Aberdeen had been lambasted by Byron in *English Bards and Scotch Reviewers* as 'The Travelled Thane, Athenian Aberdeen'. Thus, one experienced traveller in Greece was giving his opinion on another; and Galt had already expressed in no uncertain terms, in his *Atheniad*, just what he thought of those like Aberdeen, every bit as much as Elgin, who wished to despoil the monuments of Athens.[20] Galt, in fact, held that, of all the ancient Greek building-types, only the temple was successfully adaptable to modern monumental buildings. Lord Aberdeen had declared that

> We can scarcely deny that the pleasure which is derived from surveying the ancient models of Grecian architecture, is incalculably heightened by ideas connected with learning, with science, and with art, accompanied, as they ever must be, by all the nameless charms which imagination combines with the history of the Greeks, and which it throws over all their productions ...

The temples of the Greeks provoked in the thinker or viewer 'sentiments of admiration, and feelings of delight.'[21] Lord Aberdeen had prefaced the passage cited by Galt (and quoted immediately above, from Galt's review) with the following thought:

> If then, admiration of Grecian architecture result from intellectual association, it will be found to exist only among men of knowledge; and its just proportion will be determined by those whose taste is the most cultivated, and whose science is the most extensive.[22]

The case for Edinburgh's regarding itself as another Athens, or *the* Modern Athens, seems yet further strengthened. Galt, however, cautioned his readers not to go too far in pursuit of what they thought might be desirably Greek only to achieve something that was unhistorical, archaeologically inaccurate, and intellectually and artistically indefensible. In any application other than the temple form, Greek architecture was 'among the clumsiest styles extant'.[23] In his sights was the County Hall. Yet again was this building viewed with contempt, not just as an inferior example of architectural design, but also on account of its unfortunate siting.

In every other situation, the columns and ornaments of the Grecian architecture appear heavy and inordinate; and perhaps no better proof can be given of this truth, than by referring to that monstrous *two*-storied [*sic*] combination of sandstone and masonry, which stands with its pillars up to the ankles in the dirt and mud of the High Street, and which, with a degree of ignorance quite intolerable, we so often hear spoken of as a copy—a copy! of the Erectheum [*sic*].[24]

Galt wrote just too early to have turned his sarcasm on James Milne's St Bernard's Crescent, well described by twentieth-century commentators as displaying an 'alarmingly Grecian façade' and as 'the most uncompromising of all essays in house-building for Modern Athenians', being 'fronted with a hectoring array of two-storey Doric columns crammed between giant antae'.[25] 'One of the most daring uses of Greek Doric in domestic architecture' is the most recent scholarly view.[26] Indeed, the central portion of the west side of St Bernard's Crescent, its houses appearing almost to be a single public building rather than a series of private dwellings, might well exemplify the coldness and severity for which 'Athenian' Edinburgh has been (respectfully) criticised.[27]

*   *   *   *   *

An increasing consciousness of Edinburgh's campaign to be Athenian informs the London-published *Quarterly Review*'s venture into the debate on the most suitable style for the National Monument. As has already been demonstrated, what begins as a 'review' of a book on one topic soon turns, unashamedly, into a critique of the 'Athenian' pretensions of Edinburgh, becoming a vehicle for attacking the proposal for the 'restoration' of the Parthenon.[28] Having taken issue with the January 1822 circular letter from the National Monument committee, Francis Cohen (the author of the *Quarterly*'s essay) went on to controvert each argument in favour of the Parthenon scheme, expressing outright the earnest hope that it would prove abortive.

> Possibly we are mistaken; but it seems that it is, at least, desirable that a *National Monument* should bear some assignable relation to the people by whom it is erected ... Posterity will surely require that the National Monument should be an enduring specimen of the genius and talents of the age when it was planned and executed. Such certainly was the Parthenon of Athens, which we so justly admire. The Parthenon on the Acropolis ... was truly Grecian ... But the Parthenon on the *Calton Hill*, the Parthenon of *Edinburgh*, if it perfectly represents its prototype, will therefore necessarily be a Grecian national monument, and not a monument of Scotland in the reign of George IV.[29]

A 'prefect restoration' had to be more than mere walls and columns: there was the *spirit* of the place, too, and this Edinburgh could not really hope to emulate—still less achieve. 'The purple peplum must be extended; Athene must be called to inhabit her abode. The naked empty copy would be as mournful as a ruin.'[30]

In a paragraph seeking a literary parallel for a Greek-style monument constructed by and for Scots, in Scottish stone on a wind-swept Scottish hill-top, and in a passage moreover taking its cue from the great printing and publishing traditions of Scotland in the age of the Enlightenment, Cohen muses that

> If a sumptuous edition of the Persae were to be published at Edinburgh or at Glasgow, we could hardly give the title of a 'national tragedy' to the drama of Eschylus [*sic*], although the type might have been cast by Foulis, or the presses worked in Mr Ballantyne's printing office. A simile, we confess, is always a bad argument; yet, we really do not understand by what poetical right or legal fiction, the new edition of the temple of Ictinus [with Kallikrates, one of the architects of the Parthenon] can become the property of the Scottish nation, although the freestone ... may have been quarried in the Lothians, and though the masons of Edinburgh may have executed the mouldings with all possible delicacy and fidelity.[31]

The argument that the Calton Hill made a finer setting for the reconstructed temple failed on a very vital point. For that case depended on an impossibility: '... provided the Calton Hill stood in Attica, where the Acropolis stands—but it does not—and we have some suspicion that it makes a great deal of difference.' A Doric temple in Edinburgh would be completely out of place: 'Whilst the abbey and the castle continue to hold their state'—the allusion was to a famous (but paraphrased) line in Walter Scott's *Marmion*—'the Parthenon will be a perpetual and painful solecism'. The name and fame of Scott was further evoked; and the fact that he himself had signed the circular letter soliciting subscriptions to the National Monument in Parthenon form was an aberration best forgotten:

> Justly may the people of Scotland be proud of their *own romantic town*, and of *him* whose transcendent genius has conferred upon all its historic monuments a more than classic immortality. Therefore they should seek to decorate it worthily and nobly, obeying the yearnings of *his* mighty spirit, and so as to recall the memory of the ancient days of energy and independence, not by creating a perpetual dissonance in the landscape, jarring to all moral perception, and hostile to all national feeling.[32]

Cohen saw no value in a 'restoration' of the Parthenon in Edinburgh, either as a teaching aid or as source of inspiration towards improvement of Scottish national taste. The student of architecture would in no way benefit from a reproduction of the building: 'there is no lesson … which he cannot now learn upon paper', from all the accurate drawings in existence. If the purpose of having an Edinburgh Parthenon was to give

> instruction in Grecian architecture, it will be simply a useless and expensive work … if it is to form the taste of the student and rouse his emulation, then we are not without apprehensions that it will be worse than useless.[33]

The article suggested, in sum, that the National Monument—*any* 'national monument'—should remain an enduring specimen of the genius and talents of the age when, and the society by whom, it was built. So, indeed, its passionate advocates believed, it would be—if only Edinburgh considered herself rightly, properly and in all earnestness as the Modern Athens, and was generally accepted to have deserved and achieved that accolade. But the *Quarterly* thought the case was not proven, and that the title was undeserved.

Cohen's article had evidently rankled with George Cleghorn, and the offence remained. One of the essays Cleghorn included in his collection of *Remarks on Ancient and Modern Art* in 1837 was an 'Analysis of Publications on Architecture'. Quite apart from demonstrating the writer's broad knowledge of the topic, this piece indicates just how much *The Quarterly Review*'s attack had actually wounded some at least of the Modern Athenians—despite Williams's assurance to Cockerell that the article had made 'but a small impression' in Edinburgh, and had not checked the enthusiasm of the proponents of the Parthenon.[34] Cleghorn's remarks of fifteen years later show that the reverse was true. The *Quarterly* reviewers (Cleghorn wrote of them in the plural) had lauded 'the perfection of the Greeks' in architecture. But, at the same time, they (that is, 'the reviewers') 'declare open hostility to restoration, or even imitation, not only because they think it would be unsuitable to modern times, but degrading to the genius and dignity of modern art.' The reviewers also lauded the Gothic and the Italian, but Cleghorn pointed out that 'Their chief object, however, in this article, was to put down and ridicule the restoration of the Parthenon as the National Monument of Scotland, then in its highest popularity.'

> Every argument and allusion that sophistry, wit, ridicule and even flattery, could suggest, was brought to bear in this devoted undertaking,—and unfortunately, as it turned out, with too much success, in spite of an able vindication in the Edinburgh Review and some spirited articles in Blackwood's Magazine.[35]

Cleghorn's reference was to the journalism of Archibald Alison, both proactive and reactive, in the cause of a huge Greek temple looming over the would-be Northern Athens.

On the vexed question of the educational value of a vast 'reconstruction' of a ruined ancient building, as opposed to the study of measured drawings, a significant report on art education in Scotland of 1837 appears to have come down in favour of drawings. This was in the very same year that George Cleghorn argued so vigorously for physical 'restorations of a few of the most celebrated temples of antiquity' as 'the most powerful means of fixing and improving the national taste ...'.[36] Informed in part by evidence submitted to their enquiry by the eminent authority Dr G. F. Waagen of Berlin—who stated that students of manufactures in Prussia received instruction in architecture by means of *models* of the Parthenon—William Dyce and Charles Heath Wilson recommended the teaching of classical architecture to students of design by means of scale drawings of plans, elevations, details and mouldings. The actual stone-and-lime Calton Hill Parthenon, either in itself or as potential vehicle of instruction, was not even mentioned.[37]

*   *   *   *   *

Modern Athenian though he was, and doughty fighter as he proved to be through his extended campaign for the adoption of the Parthenon as model for the National Monument, George Cleghorn nevertheless added a useful corrective to the somewhat blinkered classical view of the Northern Athens. He contested the questionable suggestion that the prospect of, and from, the Calton Hill was almost wholly 'Grecian'.[38] Anyone who asserted this seemed

> to have overlooked Bridewell, the New Jail, Jailor's House, and Nelson's Monument; which, being all of a castellated Gothic, and situated on the hill itself, form decidedly the most conspicuous objects in the view. The only building on the hill, of a Grecian character, is the small Temple of the Observatory ... masked by high walls, as if it were deemed sacrilege to be permitted to approach too near, or even catch a glimpse of it, except at a respectable distance. It does not indeed necessarily follow, that a Grecian Temple is inadmissible, because Gothic structures happen to be in the vicinity, or within the range of its visible horizon, though it must be confessed, the National Monument would appear to greater advantage had these structures been less of a Gothic character, and still greater had they never been built at all. With respect to Nelson's Monument, in particular, there can be but one opinion—it ought to be pulled down as disgraceful to the taste of the age, and incompatible with the favourable effect of the Parthenon on its proposed site.[39]

And, in a discrete section of one of his essays on art and architecture, Cleghorn wrote tellingly of the specifically Scottish medieval tradition of excellence in building, both ecclesiastical and secular.[40] Here was a man who, despite his almost obsessional commitment to the cause of the Edinburgh Parthenon, and concomitant involvement in the promotion of the idea of an 'Athenian' Edinburgh, still recognised the Gothic cathedral and the baronial castle as national achievements of which to be proud.

In light of the divergent opinions of Alison and Cleghorn about how 'Greek' Edinburgh actually was, it may be useful to consider the contents of Shepherd and Britton's *Modern Athens!... or, Edinburgh in the Nineteenth Century*—and to do so in the full knowledge of the part that the book played, and continues to play, in helping to enshrine the idea of 'the Athens of the North'. The title of this book suggests that epithet and time can be completely identified, one with the other. And yet, remarkably, the text never once actually mentions Athens, or Greece—or, for that matter, Edinburgh as Athens. The phrase 'Modern Athens' is confined to the two title-pages. This makes the presence of the rather strange exclamation mark in the book's title on the second, or principal, title-page all the more intriguing. The first title-page, more typographically elaborate, carries a view of the Castle with old houses and hostelries in the Grassmarket below. The *staffage* in the plate consists not of elegant Modern Athenians promenading, such as one finds in many other plates in the collection, but of carters, porters and other tradesfolk. In a sense, this is the enduring image of Edinburgh: the 'Auld Reekie' side of a Janus-faced city. Does the exclamation mark on the second title-page hint at the contemporary pomposity of the 'Athenian' epithet? Is the English author of the letterpress, and equally the London publisher, James & Company (with an address at the 'Temple of the Muses', Finsbury Square), smirking just a little at North British 'provincial' pretension?

The reader of *Modern Athens!* naturally expects that the album of some 100 plates will set out to illustrate that 'modern' Edinburgh has an 'Athenian' architectural air. However, the subjects of these plates give a rather different picture of the city and its townscape. The balance is not quite what one might imagine: the city and its environs seem not so comprehensively 'Athenian' after all. Forty-six engravings certainly show 'classical' buildings, or views in which the neoclassical face of the city predominates. But fifty-six have as their principal subjects what can loosely be called 'Gothic' or older structures, or modern buildings in the 'Gothic', or castellated styles, or which feature townscape views that stress the Romanic elements in nature or the built environment. Of these, six are scenes furth of the city itself, and include Sir Walter Scott's Abbotsford, a house—but the house of the book's dedicatee—stylistically as far from the dwelling of a 'Modern Athenian' as could be imagined.

Captain Basil Hall, who played a prominent part in pushing for the Parthenon—corresponding with the architect, and generally busying himself in promoting the Greek architecture that would enhance Edinburgh's 'Athenian' credentials—nevertheless becomes increasingly lukewarm about the 'Modern Athens'. As we have already seen, he appears not to have liked the New Town and, conversely, to have preferred what he described as 'the happy elegance of outline of the Old Town'. The 'New Edinburgh' was, in Hall's view, undistinguished despite its social and architectural pretensions.[41] This view accords with the opinion of several visitors and residents alike, who considered that the general mass of the Georgian planned quarter—what Robert Louis Stevenson would call its 'draughty parallelograms'—lacked drama and variety.[42] A bland sameness was matched by a strange soullessness. Tourists remarked on how empty the streets were, particularly when many residents were out of town in the summer. George Cleghorn made no secret of his opinion that the older portion of the New Town had 'little to boast of in point of architectural taste', and condemned its 'meagre sameness, and naked insipidity'.[43] Things were much improved, he admitted, as individual public buildings and whole streets had become more diversified in terms of height and variety of frontages; but, even so, he was able to find fault with (for instance) the superfluity of awkward angles in the plan of Moray Place, or with streets and structures where 'Grecian orders' had been adopted almost by rote as 'columnar ordinances'. He reserved contempt for the prevalence in the would-be Modern Athens of what he defined as 'a sort of Tuscan with an attic [*sic*] base', which constituted merely 'a bastard order'.[44]

Cleghorn's disdain for nominal adherence to classicism was trenchantly expressed, as was his mockery of illiterate attempts to employ the language of classical architecture as it filtered through the gradations of the building trades. 'The Grecian' was a fashion. But few had the real knowledge or skill to understand its subtleties or to achieve any real success in terms of source, derivation, emulation or replication.

> Every master mason, every plasterer, every carpenter who knows how to work a Grecian Doric column and entablature, piques himself on his knowledge of Grecian architecture, and looks with ineffable contempt on the Roman and Italian styles, and the ignorance of his predecessors. Every dwelling house and shop front must have its tiny, fluted, baseless, Pestum columns. Every public building ... has its Grecian Doric, or Ionic portico. Whatever may be the style or character of the building in other respects, it becomes henceforth a genuine Grecian structure. Graceful and appropriate as porticos are when properly applied, their constant recurrence on a paltry scale becomes sickening and nauseous—more especially the Doric, which is degraded to the most common and plebeian purposes, to petty porches, door-cases, and chimney-pieces; nor is it at all unlikely that it will descend at last to the classic decoration of our candlesticks, bed-posts, and other implements of domestic furniture.[45]

Cleghorn made a great deal of what he called the 'pomposity' of saying that this or that building was *after* such-and-such a structure at Athens, and of how one heard much of *restoration* or *imitation, after the manner or model of another*.[46] But at least Scotland escaped some of the worst excesses—or rather, perhaps, the more egregious diminutions or dilutions—of the classical tradition. It could 'boast the commencement of the Parthenon': the reconstruction (as it was hoped it would be) of an entire ancient Greek building in every detail, both externally and internally. This was a structure that, in its 'composition, decorations, dimensions, materials, and massive construction', had—with two other contemporary European buildings, one in Paris (Cleghorn means the Madeleine) and one in Bavaria (the Walhalla at Regensburg)—'a legitimate claim to the appellation of Grecian temples'. By contrast, English architects 'confine their practice to the working of the mere orders, to porticos, porches, and shop fronts, most of which are executed in stucco.'[47] Cleghorn's swipe was neither fair nor accurate, of course; but it was in keeping with his general disposition to mock the 'Anglo-Grecian' or the 'Cockney-Egyptian', and (echoing an article he quoted from the *Foreign Quarterly Review* of 1831) his colourfully expressed view that it was difficult to identify in the London street any building that offered the chance of 'obtaining the flavour of a single slice of pine-apple from a cart-load of turnips'.[48]

Walter Scott instinctively felt that Edinburgh was a Gothic city. The Calton Hill had previously been merely a 'solitary eminence', with a walk giving views of objects conducive to excite 'numerous moral associations'. But now 'Greekness' was fast taking over. Scott extolled those structures which evoked the castellated past, in preference to those which spoke for a neo-Greek present. The Gothic suited the site. In a location where Cockburn imagined that Pericles might have erected one of his best buildings, Scott actively praised the Bridewell, the Calton prison and its castellated Governor's House, as 'diversified by great variety of outline'. He wrote in the printed commentary on the engraving after J. M. W. Turner's view from the Calton Hill:

> There was indeed so little reason to reproach the persons concerned with debasing, by mean or heavy buildings, the romantic site where they were erected, that we have heard the architecture of those structures censured as too fantastic, and abounding too much in the caprices of the Gothic style. We cannot concur in this objection ... And surely, if the massive, yet irregular, style of a Gothic castle can be anywhere adopted with propriety, the Jail of a metropolis, built on the very verge of a precipice, and overhanging the buildings beneath, like an ancient citadel, is the most appropriate subject for the purpose.

And yet, Scott did not fail to praise also the 'daring spirit of modern improvement' of the Regent Road approach to the city, debouching into Princes Street by way of Waterloo Place, Edinburgh's most accomplished neo-Greek processional street.[49]

* * * * *

At the beginning of the nineteenth century, John Stoddart had been alarmed at what he regarded as the sacrifice of the fabric of old buildings for the purposes of new 'picturesque effect' or, worse, merely to supply the needs of the uncaring owner or tenant 'who, perhaps, undermines a tower, to build a pigsty, and destroys these ancient monuments, with as little feeling, as the stupid Turk does the splendid architecture of ancient Greece.'[50] In 1824, the so-called Great Fire of Edinburgh devastated the heart of the Old Town. A writer considered the impetus that this calamity might give to urban development on a scale, and in a taste, that would accord with the classical ambition of the city.

> This is an age of speculation ... and no sooner is room made by any accident for a new house or a new street—than all the architects in Edinburgh are scratching their heads for plans and elevations—and the public are inundated with sections and levels, and stuff about Athenian grandeur and Roman magnificence ... and whether or not calculated for convenience or for the climate, Grecian fronts and pillars, and pilasters and pediments, become the order of the day.[51]

Only a few months earlier, Charles Kirkpatrick Sharpe, concerned about Edinburgh (and Leith) becoming architecturally classicised at the expense of the picturesque buildings and street pattern of the past, had expressed his reservations wittily to his great friend Walter Scott. Now, even more, did the local heritage appear to be threatened with new 'Grecian' show-fronts. Thus Sharpe:

> The magistrates of Edin: whose good taste has long been the admiration of the world, not contented with making the old town of Edin: a new Athens, have extended their magic wand ... to Leith; and the front of the old jail ... a most beautiful morsel, is on the point of sinking down before it ... The foundation stone is laid of the new barbarity, designed by Mr Gillespie [James Gillespie Graham], and the destruction of the old building commences next week ... I need scarcely add that if you should resolve to stretch forth your saving hand, there is no time to be lost, and that the stately chief magistrate of New Athens [the Lord Provost, Alexander Henderson] hath his proud mansion-house in St John's Street.[52]

Sharpe enjoyed an extensive correspondence with several aristocratic ladies. Elizabeth, Marchioness of Stafford (Countess of Sutherland in her own right, and later Duchess-Countess of Sutherland on her husband's elevation to the dukedom), for example, had written earlier in 1824:

I lament, as you do, the innovations and repairs, if they are carried further than to prop up and support the memorials of former times. When lost, nothing can replace them; and it is an active stupidity to think that by making a Glasgow of Edinburgh the latter will gain ...[53]

Progress towards the status of the Modern Athens was being bought at the expense of the soul of Auld Reekie. Various Improvement Acts affected Old Edinburgh in the early to mid-nineteenth century. Two years later, Sharpe loosed off his most devastating salvo in the form of a letter to the editor of the *Edinburgh Observer*. This was headed 'Delenda est Carthago', and thus calculated to appeal to a classically minded readership. Sharpe's particular target was the damage to be incurred in the name of 'improvement' by the creation of what would become Johnston Terrace on the south side of the Castle Rock: 'little short of downright vandalism' by encroachment on 'the antique beauty of our metropolis'.[54]

Though I have lived to see, in the course of forty years, the old town lose much of its primitive features, from unavoidable decay, from the rage for *improvement* ... the Calton Hill utterly destroyed [Sharpe presumably implies the classical terraces of the Calton development scheme, round the southern and eastern flanks of the hill] ... yet never did I expect to witness such a bold attack as this upon the rock and Castle of Edinburgh.[55]

He pictured a sort of moral (or indeed mortal) struggle between 'rugged and picturesque localities' and what he demonised as the 'havoc displayed on the Calton'. The proposed lowering of the High Street was connected with the 'awkward position of the County Rooms'. Yet again this building, in itself and in its setting, was the target of reproach. Sharpe's solution was simple: why not just demolish the County Hall?

It is not very probable that the warmest admirers of modern architecture will much regret the destruction of a fabric which the Commissioners [of Midlothian] seem to have thrust down into a sort of *potato-hole* purposely for the sake of concealment ... so odd a figure does it cut there ...[56]

The editor of Sharpe's collected correspondence printed (after this letter to the *Observer*) a piece of what he called 'caustic irony' from Sharpe's often-waspish pen. Sharpe gave this pretend piece of Parliamentary drafting the title of 'Eiks for a new Act for Improving and Embellishing the Town of Edinburgh'. (In Scots legal terminology, an eik is an addition or supplement to a document.) One of its clauses ran as follows:

That, as it is a great point to direct the admiration of strangers to our modern improvements, the said strangers being too apt to inquire after objects of curiosity in the Old Town, and thus totally neglect the extraordinary beauties of the new, the following places are to be destroyed, and Grecian houses erected on their sites: The oldest part of Holyrood House, ... the Regent Murray's house in the Canongate, John Knox's House at the Netherbow, the Mint and the French Ambassador's House in the Cowgate, Queensberrie House, Tweeddale House, &c, &c.; these to be demolished and rebuilt according to prevalent taste ...[57]

Sharpe turned his antiquarian eye on 'improvements' being made to the Palace of Holyroodhouse. He told Sir Patrick Walker of Dalry he had noticed that

the persons entrusted with the reparation of the Palace are swerving from the old plan of the building, as well as from the express desires of his Majesty, and doing as much as possible to furnish the unfortunate inhabitants of this city—I say unfortunate, from a new infliction of a new taste which bears heavy on their prejudices and their purses ... Woe be to the hour when the Greeks first invaded Edinburgh, or rather the Goths in a strange disguise—the wolves in sheep's clothing! Along the top of the wall, on the back part of the Palace, these G.'s (take which word you please) have erected a sort of cornice (they probably may have some sort of sonorous Greek term for this, but cornice will make me and my ignorance understood) which projects beyond and over the slates of the roof ... [to] deprive the building of its resemblance to the old French palaces, ...; of its resemblance to itself ... Then why alter this? It may make it purer Greek ... perhaps (tho' I do not think so) a handsomer thing to look at; but then it is a *darn*, a botch, an alteration.[58]

Sharpe marshalled the opposition, and (as he was then able to tell Sarah Clementina Drummond, Lady Gwydyr) the much-despised and inappropriate classical cornice 'melted like snow off a dike'.[59]

Sharpe was also greatly exercised by the damage done to Salisbury Crags by unauthorised quarrying activity in order to produce road metal for the Modern Athens. This vandalism of a natural feature rather than an architectural one became a cause célèbre. Reports in *The Scotsman* were reprinted by the London *Times*, which delighted in the apparent slight to Edinburgh's self-aggrandisement as the seat of all civilisation, highlighting the

madness of the Edinburghers, who, piquing themselves on the grandeur of their city ... are quietly, and with their eyes open, suffering to be destroyed the chief ornament which it has received from nature ... And shall the inhabitants of Modern Athens—the learned advocates, physicians, ministers, the literati and dilettanti of Edinburgh, suffer to be completed, in a few days, a work of destruction which will be regretted for centuries, and is which is not more scandalous than irreparable?[60]

At Sharpe's behest, members of the Royal Household had moved to stop the vandalism, including Lady Gwydyr, daughter of the eleventh Earl of Perth and wife of Lord Gwydyr, Deputy Lord Great Chamberlain. Sharpe commended her intervention 'to save these rough rocks', saying that, by so doing, Lady Gwydyr had erected to her own vigilance 'a much richer and nobler monument than could have even been fashioned by Phidias out of the purest Parian marble.'[61] Sometimes, between educated people, only a Greek metaphor would do.

David Roberts, widely considered the most distinguished landscape and architectural painter of Edinburgh birth then living, had his doubts about an 'Athenian' city in terms of artistic taste. Wherever he was in his wide travels, Edinburgh remained for him (as his correspondence demonstrates) 'Auld Reekie'. 'The Modern Athens' was an epithet always used with a certain tongue-in-cheek smile. In 1842, he wrote to his friend, the decorator David Ramsay Hay, about the possibility of sending a painting of an Egyptian subject to the Royal Scottish Academy exhibition, 'if only to try the pulse of the Modern Athens on Antiquity'. He was not convinced that it would take with the 'Modern Athenians', and would have welcomed a better understanding of 'the artistic gossip of Modern Athens'.[62]

*   *   *   *   *

John Ruskin's celebrated lectures on architecture and painting, delivered in Edinburgh in November 1853, had three chief purposes in relation to architecture: the 'beatification' of the Gothic in construction and architectural decoration; the promotion of the idea that the style, with the craftsmanship that underpinned it, might be reverted to as a way of enriching the lives of his contemporaries; and a corresponding condemnation of the Greek Revival in all its manifestations. Indeed, the stentorian final words of the Addenda to his published lectures are these:

> ... the whole system of Greek architecture, as practised in the present day, must be annihilated; but it *will* be annihilated, and that speedily. For truth and judgment are its declared opposites, and against these nothing ever finally prevailed, or shall prevail.[63]

These were strong sentiments to lay before the citizens of the Athens of the North. And the Edinburgh Greeks were never spared throughout the two lectures. Those who had previously read Ruskin's *The Stones of Venice* could not have been unprepared for what he might say. In that work, Ruskin had damned classical architecture, whether in antiquity or the modern era. In order to revive and promote what he called 'a healthy school of architecture', it would first be necessary to 'cast out utterly whatever is connected with the Greek, Roman, or Renaissance'. Everything 'founded on Greek and Roman models ... is lifeless, unprofitable and unchristian [*sic*], in that same degree our own ancient Gothic is animated, serviceable, and faithful.' The classical was

> utterly devoid of all life, virtue, honourableness, or power of doing good. It is base, unnatural, unfruitful, unenjoyable, and impious. Pagan in its origin, proud and unholy in its revival, paralyzed in its old age, yet making prey in its dotage of all the good and living things that were springing around it in their youth ...; an architecture invented, as it seems, to make plagiarists of its architects, slaves of its workmen, and Sybarites of its inhabitants; an architecture in which intellect is idle, invention impossible, but in which all luxury is gratified and all insolence fortified;—the first thing we have to do is cast it out, and shake the dust of it from our feet for ever. Whatever has any connexion with ... any one of the orders,—whatever is Doric, or Ionic ... or in any wise Grecized ... that we are to endure no more.[64]

Now, in Edinburgh, Ruskin gave scant credit to the classical architects and builders of the city, or to their patrons and all who had sought to promote a would-be Greek city. He must have startled his audience very early on by telling them that he had counted 678 near-identical windows in the length of Queen Street, York Place and Picardy Place, not including any with mouldings. And that was not all: 'How many Corinthian and Doric columns do you think there are in your banks, and post-offices, institutions, and I know not what else, one exactly like another?—and yet you expect to be interested!'

The point still not sufficiently made, he turned to criticise the New Town houses in which so many of his listeners must have lived. They would already have known from Shepherd and Britton's *Modern Athens!* that, in the judgment of some outsiders, their houses were notable for 'tameness and monotonous appearance'.[65] But they also had to reckon with the view of a great insider, too: for even Walter Scott had earlier criticised the New Town plan for its 'tameness', 'uniformity' and 'monotonous simplicity'.[66] The entrances of these houses lining dull streets, Ruskin now said, were totally inappropriate for the climate. He imagined how difficult it was to deal with the closing of an umbrella in a high wind and lashing rain:

> ... you know how little these inconveniences are abated by the common Greek portico at the top of the steps ... You know how the east winds blow

through those unlucky couples of pillars, which are all that your architects find consistent with due observance of the Doric order.[67]

Lord Cockburn died the year after Ruskin delivered his devastating attack on the architecture of the New Town of Edinburgh. But Cockburn, in the manuscript of what would become his celebrated, posthumously published *Memorials*, had already made his own views clear. He had written that Scottish townscape as a whole displayed 'the dullest and baldest uniformity'.[68] He went on to comment, with specific regard to the New Town, on lost opportunity and poor taste:

> ... our escape from the old town gave us an unfortunate propensity to avoid whatever had distinguished the place we had fled from. Hence we were led into the blunder of long straight lines of street, divided to an inch, and all to the same number of inches, by rectangular intersections, every house being an exact duplicate of its neighbour, with a dexterous avoidance, as if from horror, of every ornament or excrescence by which the slightest break might vary the surface. What a site did nature give us for our New Town! Yet what insignificance in its plan! what poverty in all its details! ... Our jealousy of variety, and our association with magnificence with sameness was really curious.[69]

Thus, Ruskin must have known that some of his words would not fall on deaf ears. But Cockburn had, at least, expressed some satisfaction at the appearance of 'pillars' and 'porticoes' to 'lessen the baseness of the first ideas'.[70] And, looking back, Scott had already suggested that 'men's minds were not at that time ripe for the splendid ideas which have been since entertained.'[71] So even they were not entirely immune to classical flourishes, and Scott and Cockburn had (as we have seen) both lent their names to the Parthenon appeal in 1821.

The classical civic taste of the preceding generations was effectively mocked in the first of Ruskin's addresses. Edinburgh folk, he supposed, wanted a new building, so

> ... you send for the great Mr Blank, and the Great Blank sends you a plan of a great long marble box with half-a-dozen pillars at one end of it, and the same at the other; and you look at the Great Blank's great plan in a grave manner, and you daresay it will be very handsome; and you ask the Great Blank what sort of a blank cheque must be filled up before the great plan can be realised; and you subscribe in a generous 'burst of confidence' whatever is wanted; and when it is all done, and the great white marble box is set up in your streets, you contemplate it, not knowing what to make of it exactly, but hoping it is all right ...

Behind this, surely, lies the thinly veiled story of the Parthenon on Calton Hill, except that it never was 'all done'. A classical building was perceived to confer civic dignity and it cost a lot, this fact reflecting 'the greatest credit on the intelligent inhabitants of the city … and you remain in a placid state of impoverished satisfaction'. But where, Ruskin was asking in so many words, was the *passion* in a Greek building?

> Where do you go to eat strawberries and cream? To Roslin Chapel, I believe; not to the portico of the last-built institution. What do you see your children doing, obeying their own natural and true instincts? What are your daughters drawing upon their card-board screens as soon as they can use a pencil? Not Parthenon fronts, I think, but the ruins of Melrose Abbey, or Linlithgow Palace, or Lochleven [sic] Castle, their own pure Scotch hearts leading them straight to the right things, in spite of all that they are told to the contrary. You perhaps call this romantic, and youthful, and foolish …[72]

In his second lecture, Ruskin clearly hoped to strike a chord with the economical Scots in his audience. Sculpture and decoration high up on classical buildings was a waste of money, placed as it was almost invisibly.

> I know that this was a Greek way of doing things. I can't help it: that does not make it a wise one. Greeks might be willing to pay for what they couldn't see, but Scotchmen and Englishmen should'nt [sic].[73]

The people of Modern Athens were invited to look at what they had done; and they were encouraged to think again. Never had the New Town been criticised like this:

> Walk round your Edinburgh buildings, and look at the height of your eye, what you will get from them. Nothing but square-cut stone—square-cut stone—a wilderness of square-cut stone for ever and ever; so that your houses look like prisons, and truly are so; for the worst feature of Greek architecture is, indeed, not its costliness but its tyranny. These square stones are not prisons of the body, but graves of the soul.

Ruskin turned to what he called the 'despised workmen' of Edinburgh—to those very craftsmen whom Archibald Alison and others had praised for their consummate skill in working Craigleith sandstone and cutting it precisely for refined and elaborate Greek mouldings. He felt these men could do so much better if let loose on the ornamental parts of Gothic building, to carve vegetable and floral motifs. But, said Ruskin to his audience, 'it is you who have bound them down, and buried them beneath your Greek stones.'[74]

How much, Ruskin, asked, was there of 'nature' in the buildings of Modern Athens? The building he chose to examine in some detail was Playfair's Royal Institution—'the institution on the mound [sic]'. Paradoxically, this was in fact a 'Greek' building on which much of the enrichment was expressed in rather un-classical vegetable and floral forms. Ruskin chose to ignore this anomaly. In focusing on the Institution, Ruskin was (to be fair) at pains to make clear that he did not criticise Playfair's skill, merely the cultural and social climate in which he had been operating, and the taste that directed his commissions. 'It is not [the architect's] fault that we force him to build in the Greek manner.' Ruskin did his counting-exercise again, and perfectly correctly: there were, indeed, 66 identical lions' heads round the cornice, serving as ornamental antefixes, 'I suppose, executed on some noble Greek type, too noble to allow any modest Modern to think of improving upon it.' They must be good, and especially admirable, Ruskin added cynically, to be on 'the principal example of the Athenian style in modern Athens'. This was the single occasion in the long course of his lectures when he permitted himself the use of that tainted designation of the city in which he was speaking. But he showed a drawing, done for him by John Everett Millais, of a real lion's head; and, thereafter, another drawing of a lion head on the Royal Institution—'the Grecian sublimity of the ideal beast, from the cornice of your schools of design'—leaving the Modern Athenians in his audience to see for themselves what had been done to a building containing the Trustees' Academy, the Royal Scottish Academy and the rooms of two learned societies. The result? Ruskin lambasted it as 'barren and insipid absurdity ... false and futile'.[75]

In conclusion, Ruskin encouraged his hearers to be 'steadily determined that, even if you cannot get the best Gothic, at least you will have no Greek'. Revived Greek architecture ('Modern Greek') was an architecture of 'copyism'. And to have attempted 'to copy the form of the Parthenon without its friezes and frontal statuary, is like copying the figure of a human being without its eyes and mouth ...'.[76] Had he heard this, Archibald Alison—the man who, thirty years before, had thought the Greek was here to stay, and the Gothic at an end—would have swallowed hard. He might even have stormed out of the hall.

*   *   *   *   *

The very fine Trinity College Church, a late-Gothic gem which lay in the valley between the 'north back' of the High Street and the southern crags of the Calton Hill, had been demolished in 1848 to make way for the North British Railway Company's line.[77] Having been taken down, its stones were carefully numbered and deposited on the hill, a location which (as we have seen) Charles Kirkpatrick Sharpe thought had been 'utterly destroyed'. But nothing was done immediately about re-erection. This, too, became a cause célèbre, leading to much word-play about the changing nature of Edinburgh and its cultural standing. There were those who thought the church ought to be re-erected either on the upper or lower slopes of the Calton Hill—and if, in the latter case, on slightly elevated ground near the eastern end of Waterloo Place. Lord Cockburn, always influential, favoured an alternative, low-lying location at the south-east corner of East Princes Street Gardens, a site dismissed by others as merely 'a hole' or, worse, 'a filthy hole'. One of the numerous correspondents, who repeatedly joined an almost endless debate, invoked the name of that 'distinguished citizen ... the late Greek [*sic*] Williams', suggesting that Williams would have been the man of the moment to protest about the 'desecration of Modern Athens'. Regardless of whether the alleged 'desecration' was *potentially* that of the almost-sacred Greek enclave of the Calton Hill, or *actually* that of a superb medieval structure in the Old Town, the phrase 'Modern Athens'—as one suggestive of civic consequence and highest cultural dignity—evidently still had the power to move. Assuming the identity of 'An Old Traveller' who had 'examined both Greek and Gothic edifices', the writer just quoted maintained that the Calton might suit 'Grecian architecture', but was too elevated for a Gothic structure which required low ground to be appreciated.[78]

One participant in the vigorous discussion was William Mure of Caldwell, a politician but also the classical scholar who had travelled widely in Greece and whom we encountered in Chapter 2. Mure expressed the view that Edinburgh had deservedly acquired its Modern Athenian title, but that, if such disrespect to old buildings such as Trinity College Church continued, 'it would be the common opinion that the city contained in addition to its modern Athenians, a large and flourishing colony of ancient Vandals.' Another contrasted the 'proceedings of the municipality of Modern Athens' in the matter of the Trinity College Church with

the liberal and enlightened zeal with which the merchants of Glasgow,—a city styled by some of them [that is, by the Modern Athenians] the modern Boeotia,—were contributing for the decoration of their magnificent and venerable cathedral.[79]

*   *   *   *   *

The anonymous author of *Edinburgh Dissected: Including Strictures on its Institutions ...* (1857) effectively brings nearly to a close the era of Edinburgh's assumption of its Athenian dual personality. The writer took for granted that the allusions would be understood, so used those references without explanation. Thus, Calton Hill *is* the Acropolis, where *one day* 'the Modern Athenians' will erect a building 'more stately' than the Observatory. But hand in hand with the assumption of a long-standing tradition of such usage went a gentle mockery of how little had actually been achieved on the Edinburgh acropolis. The monuments to John Playfair and Dugald Stewart are written off as 'garden summer-houses, pretty though they be ...'.[80] One thinks of James Elmes, who in proposing the most suitable classical architectural types for adaptation as memorials to the Napoleonic Wars, wanted to see in London 'no pimping pepper-box'—nothing small, trifling or insignificant—but a

Monument of Lysikrates at full-size or, preferably, larger.[81] In fact, Edinburgh's versions of the choragic monument are possibly rather finer and certainly much more dramatically sited than the Athenian original.

The German novelist Theodor Fontane, who visited Edinburgh in 1858, also looked at these small monuments in the Greek taste. Rather significantly, Fontane did not rush to Calton Hill. Indeed, he put off his visit for some time. And when he did go, it was not (surprisingly) for the view. It was for the sake of

> certain things which are worth seeing and are connected quite directly with this particular hill. These things consist of half a dozen monuments ... What imparts to them a certain significance is the circumstance that the idea is implicit in them of a hall of fame for the Scottish people.

But, in fact, the monuments and memorials on the Calton could be dismissed in a way that Archibald Alison and his friends would have found incomprehensible nearly forty years earlier: they were pronounced mere 'imitations of classical models', and not, even then, of 'outstanding quality'. They could not 'claim the merit of original creation'; Fontane did not consider it worthwhile to describe or to criticise the structures.[82]

To Fontane, the 'classical' in Edinburgh seemed 'wholly alien'. He instanced the early exercise in Greek Revival that was the façade of County Hall, isolated in the overwhelmingly Romantic setting of the old High Street and so often before, as we have seen, singled out for disparagement. It was the *natural* landscape of Edinburgh that he thought notable, and that left an indelible impression. Who, after all, were [Dugald] Stewart and [John] Playfair, so commemorated by these classical monuments?

> What had they done to be thus monumentally glorified by their country? ... I had vainly believed that history or poetry had at least made me familiar with the name of every Scot who had any claim to have a monument erected to him ... The fact is that we foreigners know only the romantic side of Scotland ... Our sympathies have got themselves stuck in Scotland's past, while the Scots themselves regard it as their supreme task to break with that past and to honour men whose claims to fame were of an altogether different character.[83]

But the tale of the past, and the affecting poetry and songs of Robert Burns— whose right to a monument on Calton Hill (constructed in a classical style though it was) Fontane did not question—had 'visibly glorified the whole and lent to it a lustre which the more respectable side of the national character could never have achieved.'[84] Yet, for Fontane as for many others, the romantic element seemed at odds with the frigid, serious, humourless intensity of the Modern Athenians. Auld Reekie never really quite made it, heart and soul, to Modern Athens.

EPILOGUE

'Some Greek airs, and classic temples on her crags'

In his essay *On the National Character of the Athenians* of 1828, John Brown Patterson had included a passage that may perhaps (and without undue distortion) be thought applicable to the brief period when Edinburgh considered itself the Modern Athens:

> No town was ever so subject to mania as Athens, and nowhere was it more overpowering in its force, or more transient in its duration ... Besides, whatever attracted the notice of the Athenians whether for good or for evil, being generally seen by them associated in one way or another with the idea of *the city*, was placed by their patriotic feeling in an inconceivably striking light.

'Whether for good or evil' will take us back to the rhetorical question posed towards the end of the Prologue of this present book. Patterson continued:

> The nationality on which their [the ancient Athenians'] character rested was not a stable pillar, erected with the view of keeping the superstructure steady; it was a spire that supported a weathercock on a pivot polished by perpetual friction.[1]

Edinburgh, a Romantic city, set in a dramatic Scottish landscape, was a place that, for a comparatively short time, had been thought of as a Grecian city in a physical setting which evoked that of Greece. This may well appear to be a sort of mania. However powerful were 'Athenian' ideas, they proved transient, and they left a mixed legacy.

* * * * *

The author of *Edinburgh Dissected* (1857) had written of 'the Acropolis' and of 'Modern Athenians' without hesitation or further explanation. If some gentle mockery followed, it was in keeping with an established tradition.[2] But the writer admitted that he could never look on the National Monument 'without a sigh. A magnificent idea rendered abortive for lack of means—a ruin, yet fresh as the morning, when the first capital crowned its first column—a ruin, upon which no ivy seeks to entwine itself …'[3] He argued for its completion so that it might serve as a comprehensive national museum of material 'scientific, artistic, mechanical, archaeological': exhibits then scattered through the University, the College of Surgeons, the Society of Antiquaries, the Agricultural Association, even the Advocates' Library.[4]

But this was not the first proposal for use of the Edinburgh Parthenon should ever it be restarted and completed. The anonymous author just quoted was not alone in wanting to see the project brought to a conclusion worthy of a dream in fact now long overtaken by other civic priorities, by other tastes in architecture, and by changing perceptions of what Edinburgh was, or could be. In 1850, Adam White of the Zoology Department of the British Museum, born in Edinburgh in 1817, published his reasons for wanting to see a national museum established in his home city as a 'national monument' of another more general kind. 'Your site is the Calton Hill,—the ornament of your building the magnificent columns forming the NATIONAL MONUMENT …' But White added, as a footnote, the reluctant admission: 'It is feared that the place is almost out of the question on account of the expense.'[5] Writing as he customarily did as 'Ian', the Scottish nationalist John Grant argued in correspondence with the *Caledonian Mercury* in the early 1850s:

> The thirteen [sic] naked columns which rise on the Calton Hill must no longer continue an object of national ridicule. Let us now demand from the Government a share of what we are so rightly entitled to. Let the national monument be finished and occupied as a museum of geology, natural history, antiquities, and sculpture.[6]

This symbol of early nineteenth-century 'Athenian' ambition was now judged most fit to hold material evidence of all kinds relating to the past of Scotland. Thus, a twenty-first-century authority has been able to assess Edinburgh after its 'Modern Athenian' phase as 'a great *polis* of museums', representing a culture and a place that 'speaks of pastness'. By this judgment, too, the Edinburgh of the Victorian age became a cultural centre 'of curious and noble antiquity … rendered politically redundant by a modern … London'. It was 'Athenian' 'in the sense that it had been surpassed by a more modern imperial metropolis': a London that was a new Rome.[7]

*   *   *   *   *

In his *Scott-land: The Man Who Invented a Nation*, Stuart Kelly describes a climb to the top of the Gothic-style Scott Monument and the view from there to the classical National Monument on Calton Hill, reminding us that the National Monument is called 'Edinburgh's Folly'.

> It seems appropriate that while the National Monument was left unfinished, the Scott Monument was completed. 'Folly' is a delightful double-word—ill-advised foolishness on one hand and a whimsical, purposeless, architectural jeu d'esprit on the other.[8]

It is, perhaps, interesting to imagine what a visitor to Calton Hill between 1840 and 1846, when the Scott Monument was being constructed, might have thought when looking westward from beneath the colonnade of the unfinished Parthenon. Edinburgh had found itself unable to complete the one project, but had started another, even more extraordinary stone confection. From the classical to the gothic: all fourteen entries for the Scott Monument design competition in a neoclassical idiom (out of a total of a total fifty-four submitted in various styles) had been rejected. They had ranged from Greek temples to an enormous obelisk—the proposal of W. H. Playfair. The contention of Playfair and his supporters was that a classical design would be more in keeping with 'the great masses of building to which the eye is accustomed in Edinburgh'.[9] But George Meikle Kemp won the prize with his Gothic fantasy.

Playfair had one more throw of the classical dice at the nearby Mound, with his National Gallery of 1850-54, in Ionic style. This was itself a revision of his first, Doric, proposal. But the civic mood was swinging away from the austerely classical. Scott, as the embodiment of Scotland, had to be commemorated with something that suggested 'baronial Caledonia' and not ancient Greece. Playfair died in 1857. The Minutes of a meeting of the Board of Trustees for Manufactures held eleven days after his death recorded the view that his buildings at The Mound would 'transmit his name as the first of the Classic school of Scottish Architects'.[10] *The Scotsman*'s obituary, however, expressed the perverse sentiment of regret that he had not lived in a later age, when he might have been less engaged with the Greek style.[11] It was as if 'Athenian' Edinburgh should be regarded, in some quarters at least, as a kind of aberration. And yet, paradoxically, the epithet 'the Athens of the North' survived even into this post-Greek Revival architectural world.

*　　*　　*　　*　　*

Looking back around 1862 to his efforts some forty years before, Sir Archibald Alison congratulated himself and his fellow Modern Athenians on what they had achieved in their part-built Parthenon. 'The edifice was completed with success so far as contracted for, and now forms a most striking, because unique and faultless, ornament to Edinburgh.' It was if he could not come to terms with failure.

> Not more than a quarter indeed of the Temple has been erected ... but that quarter is the finest restoration of Grecian architecture which the British Islands can exhibit, and has contributed to introduce that pure and simple taste by which the edifices in Edinburgh have since been distinguished.[12]

A quarter! If he was thinking just of the number of columns of the external colonnade, Alison was strictly correct: twelve had been constructed, with their architrave, but another thirty-four columns would have been necessary to give him the peristyle of his Parthenon. And what of the other columns of the pronaos and opisthodomos? The frieze and cornice to add to the architrave of the existing western octastyle portico in order to make the full entablature? The entire entablature of the other end, and of both long sides? The external frieze with its triglyphs and ninety-two metopes—which might well have borne simple wreaths as substitutes for figurative sculptural decoration? All the necessary small elements and mouldings that characterise the refinement of the Doric order? The west and east pediments, for which some enrichment of the tympana would surely have been called for? The cella walls, and whatever form of frieze (not necessarily figurative) might or might not have been determined upon for the upper part of those exterior walls—as in the Parthenon itself, or (for that matter) Playfair's Royal Institution? Then whatever columns might have been intended for the interior of the cella: Cockerell's sectional drawings show forty-two of these, of various sizes and of the more expensive Ionic and Corinthian orders as well as Doric. The roof, of whatever form, probably partially glazed? Whatever complex system by which the interior would have been lit from above or from light-wells in the roof? And so on ...

Alison's insouciant statement is tantamount to disingenuous self-justification. It is notable that, after the passage cited above, no further reference to the National Monument was made in his vast autobiography.

Very far from content, however, had been George Cleghorn. In the Preface to his *Remarks on Ancient and Modern Art ... By An Amateur* (1837) he had anticipated one of the essays to be found in the body of his book. This, on the National Monument, was—as he disarmingly admitted—a topic

> far from being a popular one; but it is that very reason which has induced [the author] to resume the discussion, in the hope of rescuing the undertaking from the unmerited indifference and obloquy under which it has fallen, and awakening his countrymen to a sense of its importance, not only as affecting

national character and consistency, but as intimately connected with the advancement of Scottish art.[13]

In 1846, frustrated by the period of what he later called the 'torpor and inactivity' witnessed since 1829—a period when 'enthusiasm had subsided, and given place to disapprobation and indifference'—Cleghorn took up the torch again with renewed determination.

> These columns have long been, and still are a jest and a by-word—an object for the finger of ignorance and scorn to point at. Yet, desolate and imperfect—despised and neglected as they now stand—viewed as an example of the present Grecian Doric on its full scale of magnificence, and executed in massive blocks of superior masonry—they are unparalleled in modern Europe. If a part be so beautiful, *ex pede Herculem*, how much more the entire structure. Beautiful and interesting as this modern ruin must be in the eyes of every person of cultivated taste, it is deeply to be deplored that the commencement should not have been made at an earlier period—immediately after the foundation was laid, and when enthusiasm was at its height.[14]

Cleghorn continued to chide those who had failed to drive on the project for their 'boastings' that had merely seemed like 'pretensions', and for the cumulative failure that had provided Edinburgh with an unwelcome 'emblem of her pride, presumption, and inconstancy', a sentiment shortly to be expressed with even greater bitterness as 'the most signal and lamentable example of ... fickleness ... and failure'.[15] In 1837 he had upbraided the English architect, engineer and architectural writer William Hosking for omitting mention of Scottish architecture entirely and, more especially, for neglecting to highlight the National Monument, in the articles Hosking wrote for the seventh edition (1830-42) of the *Encyclopaedia Britannica*. This omission smarted particularly with Cleghorn on the grounds that the encyclopaedia was what he called 'a national work'. His grievance was probably centred on the fact that it was published in Edinburgh and edited by Macvey Napier of the Signet Library and the *Edinburgh Review*: a Northern Athenian had been, as it were, asleep on the job. Hosking's articles were subsequently revised and published as a monograph. But still there was

> not the slightest allusion to the commencement of the Parthenon, and its twelve matchless Doric columns ... unquestionably, the first and only attempt that has been made in Great Britain to restore a Greek temple of the first class in its true proportions, and on its full scale. Though the undertaking has failed for want of funds, it is not abandoned; and at all events, Scotland is entitled to some credit for having made the attempt and shown the way.[16]

Cleghorn also pointed out, again with ill-concealed disapproval, that in his *Lives of the Most Eminent British Painters, Sculptors and Architects*, the Scottish-born, but long London-based, writer Allan Cunningham also 'avoids all allusion to the National Monument of Scotland'.[17] The undertaking was either disapproved of for one reason or another, or was felt to be a Northern Athenian embarrassment best, and most charitably, forgotten.

However, it was with some evident relief that Cleghorn was able to confirm that the directors of the Royal Association of Contributors to the National Monument had at last decided that any ecclesiastical function for the structure should be forsaken: this on-off, Laodicean issue had bedevilled progress, and had confused matters, from the outset. Determined the Parthenon facsimile be completed, Cleghorn went much further. He stated that the pediments and metopes were to be enriched with 'national sculpture'; that the interior was to be decorated with representations of Scottish historical achievements in fresco, encaustic or oil painting; and that a 'Pantheon or Gallery of Honour' would be included.[18]

It appears that Cleghorn's ideas for the completion of the National Monument had become rather grander than they had been twenty or even ten years previously. Had something occurred to influence his vision? The answer to this question lies, first, in certain passages in his 1837 collection of miscellaneous essays; and, second, in a footnote to Cleghorn's line 'unparalleled in modern Europe' quoted above from his 1846 monograph. The note runs thus: 'The Walhalla of Ratisbon is now perhaps an exception, but it must be recollected that the Scottish structure was projected and commenced ten years before the other was ever contemplated.'[19]

Close reading of Cleghorn's 1846 text reveals that he had actually visited the Walhalla near Regensburg (Ratisbon) in Bavaria in 1839. He had been, on the whole, very impressed, and certainly greatly influenced by what he had seen of that astonishing construction. (Fig. 99) He stated (correctly) that it had been begun in 1830 and inaugurated in 1842. Edinburgh's Parthenon project had therefore (he maintained) preceded the Walhalla by nearly ten years. In his earlier text he had displayed a fair show of presumably second-hand knowledge of the Walhalla: that it had been founded in 1830 and designed to be an octastyle Doric temple with seventeen columns on the flanks—just like the ancient Parthenon. The information he then possessed (before personal inspection) had allowed him to draw the conclusion that 'When completed, it will be a noble specimen of pure Greek architecture, of the highest class, decorated with sculpture.'[20] Edinburgh's priority, though technically correct on chronological grounds, was defended with a certain querulousness in the face of the actual achievement at Regensburg—which, despite his over-confident bluster, Cleghorn must have found an uncomfortable truth.

Whether the King of Bavaria ever heard of the Scottish Restoration [of the Parthenon] is doubtful,—but whether he did or not is of little consequence,—Scotland … is entitled to the credit of having anticipated the plans of a prince universally acknowledged to be a man of the most refined taste, in all that regards art, in Europe.[21]

In the second edition of his collected essays on ancient and modern art, Cleghorn still railed at William Hosking's omissions, though by this date (1848) the passage on the Edinburgh Parthenon was modified so that it was now trumpeted as '… the first, and until the subsequent completion of the Walhalla at Ratisbon, the only attempt to restore a Grecian Doric temple of the highest class…'. The *Encyclopaedia Britannica*'s omission of the National Monument remained 'inexcusable'.[22]

Cleghorn enthused about the marble used internally at Regensburg, noting that it was stained to resemble ivory, and the lavish gilt decoration. He actually dreamed of chryselephantine 'Greek' statues finding a place in the interior decoration of the National Monument. The effect, he wrote, would be 'truly brilliant and classical'. He was undeniably more critical, however, of the siting of the Walhalla on a colossal terrace above the Danube, and of the general effect of a 'prodigious white mass—or as it were cascade of marble and limestone'.[23]

It would seem that George Cleghorn was almost alone among his contemporaries in paying heed to the King of Bavaria's Walhalla. Everyone else in Edinburgh ignored the fact of its existence. But surely intelligent, well-read people must have been perfectly aware that in Central Europe a reproduction Parthenon had actually been built in a comparatively short time, while the Edinburgh Athenians blustered and dithered. And that it was built of, or at least faced in, actual marble. And that it bore pedimental sculpture (even if not facsimilies of the originals). Its construction had, in fact, been undertaken only after lengthy debate on the most appropriate style for a Walhalla. William Beattie, who four years previously had praised 'the architectural magnificence of the Calton-hill' and who referred to the National Monument as a splendid record of a nation's prosperity, mentioned the Regensburg Walhalla in the most glowing terms in a topographical work on the Danube of 1842. It is significant that, in doing so, he made not a mention, retrospectively or comparatively, of the Edinburgh temple. That was now entirely forgotten. 'It is impossible to imagine a finer situation', Beattie suggested, 'than the hill selected for this magnificent edifice—that of the Parthenon [of Athens] excepted.' The Bavarian building was 'the wonder of modern times … entitled to universal admiration.'[24]

There had been those who thought a German national and patriotic monument should be Gothic not Greek, thus echoing some of the discussion about the Edinburgh National Monument, most notably the contribution of James Aikman. Leo von Klenze had been commissioned to design the temple in 1816, with a final plan being agreed in 1821; this was despite von Klenze's reservations about the suitability of the style.[25] It may have been a sobering thought for the Modern Athenians of Edinburgh, that not only did the Bavarians get their replica Parthenon, but they got (so to speak) Greece itself as well—in that the young Prince Otto of Bavaria, son of the begetter of the Walhalla, was nominated to the throne of the new Greek kingdom in 1832.

The matter of sculpture assumed great importance in Cleghorn's thinking.

> Even the Parthenon itself, how beautiful soever as a Doric temple, could have no pretension to be an Athenian National Monument, had it been destitute of its statuary and pictorial decorations, which, indeed, constituted its characteristic feature and chief glory.

Edinburgh must bear this in mind, and strive to emulate the original in some way. For it was Cleghorn's opinion that, deprived of the sculpture and painting of the prototype, any replica might be 'a handsome Doric temple', certainly; but it could have 'no pretension to be a restoration of the Athenian Parthenon ... A body without a soul, it would be a mere model or frame-work, devoid of meaning, expression, and nationality.'[26]

The indefatigable Cleghorn brought his 1846 essay towards it close with a mixture of rebuke to the past and resolution for the future. And although he accepted that it might, on balance, be preferable to leave the National Monument incomplete as 'a modern ruin' than to get it wrong through bad taste, poor judgment and penny-pinching, he yet hoped that success would prevail.

> Let not our country be longer exposed to the sneers and taunts, and fingers of scorn pointed at the twelve columns on the Calton Hill—a lasting and conspicuous monument we have raised—not, alas, to national glory, but to broken pledges and national dishonour. It is the duty of every Scotsman to remove this stigma from his country ... Edinburgh has been called the Northern Athens; were the restoration completed, she would have a better title to the comparison. Rome boasts of St Peter's—Paris of the New Louvre and Madeleine—London of St Paul's—but were the Caledonian capital to possess the Parthenon Restored, decorated with appropriate sculpture and painting, well might she hold up her head among those proud capitals, and in one respect at least, even surpass the glories of the Eternal City.[27]

*   *   *   *   *

Alexander Smith, then Secretary of the University, included a most evocative, indeed magical, portrait of Edinburgh in the first chapter of his *A Summer in Skye* of 1865. Here Smith looked back to a time 'when the city was really the Modern

Athens, and a seat of criticism giving laws to the empire'.[28] In Smith's book, the essential picturesque 'character' is the Old Town, even in its degradation of fabric and the wretchedness of its inhabitants. The Old Town, resembling 'a huge lizard, the Castle its head, church-spires spikes upon its scaly back, creeping up from its lair beneath the Crags to look out on the morning world …'; the Old Town, 'grey as a rocky coast washed and worn by the foam of centuries; peaked and jagged by gable and roof; windowed from basement to cope …'[29] The New Town, with the great public buildings of the city in their sharply cut Greek grandeur, and the long lines of unsmiling classical house-fronts, is passed over with much less mention, almost as if it were a mirage—like the age of the Northern Athens itself. But some fleeting shadows of that time remained.

> London is the stomach of the Empire—Edinburgh the quick, subtle, far-darting brain. Some pretension of this the visitor hears on all sides of him. It is quite wonderful how Edinburgh purrs over her own literary achievements … Edinburgh, looking some fifty years back on herself, is perpetually expressing astonishment and delight. Mouldering Highland families, when they are unable to retain a sufficient following of servants, fill up the gaps with *ghosts*. Edinburgh maintains her dignity after a similar fashion and for a similar reason … recalling the names … that of yore made the welkin bright. On every side we hear of the brilliant society of forty years ago … What blazes a sun at Edinburgh, would, if transported to London, not infrequently become a farthing candle.[30]

In an echo of what Theodor Fontane had felt just a few years before, Smith mused that the visitor from London finds Edinburgh

> possesses a Valhalla filled with gods—chiefly legal ones—of whose names and deeds he was previously in ignorance. The ground breaks into flowerage beneath his feet. He may conceive to-day to be a little cloudy—may even suspect east wind to be abroad—but the discomfort is balanced by the reports he hears on every side of the beauty, warmth, and splendour of yesterday. He puts out his hands, and warms them, if he can, at that fire of the past. 'Ah! that society of forty years ago! … What a city this Edinburgh once was!' [31]

Contemporary with Smith's book was an essay in *Macmillan's Magazine* by David Masson, who in that year became Professor of Rhetoric and English Literature at Edinburgh. Like Smith, Masson wrote lyrically of the city in its varied moods: of 'the bold, romantic outline of the whole—the high, rock-rounding Castle on one side, the monumental Acropolis of the Calton Hill on the other …'.[32] It may be remembered that, exactly forty years before, it was the *Castle* that had been the Acropolis, whereas the Calton was simply just a hill.[33] Interestingly, in describing 'that matchless Edinburgh of the nineteenth century ... which tourists have called the Modern Athens', Masson appears to shift responsibility for the epithet from the citizens themselves to outsiders looking in on the city.[34]

Daniel Wilson wrote of a yet older Edinburgh, contrasting the city and the age he described as that of 'the Modern Athens' with the genuine 'Old Edinburgh' that preceded it, still constantly asserting itself over such unnatural chronological and stylistic intrusions. Wilson described, in 1848, the visitor's approach from Granton harbour, up the long incline of Pitt and Dundas Streets towards the climax of the New Town: an ascent, as to an almost mythical city, 'our Modern Athens', which 'strikes a stranger with awe, not unmingled with fear ...'. Wilson recalled 'the Olden Time', contrasting it with this new time and new place, which he saw as a symbol of human vanity. The demolition of James Craig's Physicians' Hall, after a life of less than sixty-five years, was

> an amusing example of the vanity of the best laid schemes for future honour and fame. Already the *chaste Grecian architecture* of this Temple of Esculapius has been swept away with the same remorseless zeal with which its designer contemplated the supplanting and final extermination of the ancient Scottish capital.

Craig was the architect who proposed the successful New Town plan of 1766-67, which Wilson felt retrospectively had been designed to sound the death-knell of Old Edinburgh. The age of Modern Athens had been possessed by a 'mania for improving', that had 'raged like a contagious distemper'.[35] Then, casting his mind back in 1878, Wilson (born in 1816) wrote wistfully of that far-off 'Athenian' city, which 'had not even begun her still unfinished Parthenon, much less bethought herself of classic temples wherein to enshrine the memories of her philosophers, when the Calton Hill was my juvenile playground; though she was fast superseding Auld Reekie.'[36]

An Edinburgh Saturday 'newspaper' entitled *The Modern Athenian* ran to 119 numbers between 1875 and 1878. Its ethos was fully expounded in the first issue. The editor explained, with a candour and in words so striking that it is difficult to imagine them having been used even in 1820, that the title was chosen 'in deference to the city [Athens] which has given us birth'. The reader was offered some thoughts to ponder 'Before you can take a step with the Editor in his museum or his grove.' We sense a spiritual connection to ancient Athens with mention of such famous spots in its literary and cultural history— the 'grove' suggesting the Academy of Plato and the 'museum' the shrine of the Muses established in the same location or, alternatively, the Athenian hill of the Muses. The editorial continues:

> Not that a 'Modern Athenian' will grow insensible to the intellectual wants of his race or age, or that the mantle of wisdom would not become his shoulders,

but that, roaming abroad [in knowledge and wit] 'to see and hear things new',
in accord with the character of his ancient prototype, he shall so diversify
the feast that it will at all times be a pleasure to sit with him at the table his
ingenuity and resources enable him to spread out.

In its twelve pages the paper was to carry a lot on drama, 'now a real power in
the city whose classic name reminds one of that older Athens in which the Drama
originated.' The Modern Athenian reader was not necessarily or essentially
supposed to be a wit or a satirist; 'But at the same time, we fancy that a modern
Athenian, as was his prototype, may be very remarkable in both characters.' The
fine arts were also to feature prominently. The masthead of the editorial page shows
Athena enthroned, with Tragedy and Comedy at either hand, in an olive-strewn
portico with two outer Doric and two inner Corinthian columns supporting a
shallow pediment. There was also a section entitled 'The Athenian' which (as is
made clear in the second number) was a sort of 'club' like the Spectator or the
Pickwick, the characters of which were to bear a strange assortment of names
suggestive of senses, virtues and one—but only one—Greek letter.[37]

Samuel Henry Butcher succeeded John Stuart Blackie in the chair of
Greek at Edinburgh in 1882. It was said by the London press at the time of
Butcher's death in 1910 that there had been some initial resentment—'a
particular feeling', was the phrase—about a 'southron' being appointed to 'the
Athens of the North', though this seems to ignore the fact that Butcher was
in fact an Anglo-Irishman, Dublin born, and married to the daughter of the
Primate of Ireland.[38] It would appear that no such resentment of Edinburgh
applied the other way in academic circles, however. When, a generation later,
the Headmasters' Conference convened in the city in 1935, the Master of
Wellington College asserted that Edinburgh was considered by Englishmen as
a 'veritable Athens of the North', but that 'more than that they thought of it as
the city in the whole of the Empire where education had been the most valued
and most liberally endowed.'[39]

Robert Louis Stevenson's superbly evocative *Edinburgh. Picturesque Notes*
(1879) did not spare the 'Athenian' pretensions of the place, concluding that

> Her attraction is romantic in the narrowest meaning of the term ... She is
> pre-eminently Gothic, and all the more so since she has set herself off with
> some Greek airs, and erected classic temples on her crags ... above all, she is
> a curiosity.

His words 'all the more so since ...' are surely significant. It is as if the short-
lived, inappropriate and incompetently executed attempt to be 'Greek' merely
served to show up all the more just what Edinburgh had essentially been
all along. High on Calton Hill, Stevenson described 'the Modern Ruin'. His

assessment was not so much post-Athenian as Laconic: a structure that, in its present state, 'is a very suitable monument to certain national characteristics'. He meant, perhaps, the parsimony, faction and self-congratulation that were all manifest in the story of Greek Edinburgh. The columns gave Edinburgh 'even from the sea, that false air of a Modern Athens which has earned for her so many slighting speeches.'[40] For Stevenson, the city of his birth—ever fondly remembered despite 'the vilest climate under heaven' and for all its stifling social conventions—remained vivid in affectionate memory even in the days of his South Sea exile. It was 'Auld Reekie', never 'the Modern Athens'; and as such it was both subject and title of one of his last poems, published posthumously some six weeks after his death. The concluding lines echo through the years:

> Oh still, ayont the muckle sea,
> Still are ye dear, and dear to me,
> Auld Reekie, still and on.[41]

*   *   *   *   *

After his resounding plea for completion of the National Monument in 1846, George Cleghorn must have been stung by a comment made by James Elmes the following year. This, in fact, referred to the 'overgrown speculations' of the Adam brothers at the Adelphi in London. Elmes, however, then turned this to Edinburgh, home city of the Adams, where opportunistic building 'left the modern Athens for many years almost as much a heap of architectural ruins as was its ancient namesake'.[42]

The idea of the National Monument as a picturesque 'ruin' indeed gained ground in the later nineteenth century, thus making 'the best of a bad job'. People had forgotten what Lord Kames had said in his *Elements of Criticism* in 1762, at precisely the time when some of his contemporaries were beginning to think of Edinburgh as another Athens. 'Whether should a ruin be in the Gothic or Grecian form?', Kames had asked rhetorically, albeit he was musing in the context of an ornamental ruin designed for a park or landscape garden. He had answered his own question thus:

> In the former, I say, because it exhibits the triumph of time over strength, a
> melancholy but not unpleasant thought. A Grecian ruin suggests the triumph
> of barbarity over taste, a gloomy and discouraging thought.[43]

Edinburgh had its classical ruin—effectively an ornamental one filling the elevated, park-like landscape of the Calton Hill—to which the passing of time and a changing taste lent a romantic veil that concealed not any triumph of barbarism, but rather a failure of will and a damaging inconstancy of purpose.

As Allan Massie has suggested, dating the change of taste and the wider phenomenon to a period following the royal visit of 1822:

> no longer the city of the Enlightenment which could give lessons to all Europe, the Athens of the North was well on the way to becoming what the Athens of the South already was: a city given over to the picturesque. Its future was as a centre of Romantic tourism.[44]

The guides and handbooks of A. & C. Black and John Murray demonstrate this outlook well. These publications made a virtue of the fact that the Parthenon on Calton Hill looked like a ruin, and thus attractive in itself, quite irrespective of its original and unachieved purpose. What had been built in Edinburgh resembled more the Parthenon as it actually existed in ruin, than as it had stood in classical antiquity.[45] James Grant seemed content to allude to the enthusiasm and favourable auspices which surrounded the birth of the National Monument; to acknowledge it as symbolic of 'Scotland's pride and poverty' (thus consciously or unconsciously quoting Playfair himself, or at any rate the author of the text of *Scotland Illustrated*, of 1850); and to concede that 'As a ruin it gives a classic aspect to the whole city.' All these apparent contradictions were aired and given equal weight at the same time.[46]

Writing in 1898, Arthur Giles, head of the Princes Street booksellers Robert Grant & Son, recalled 'Edinburgh as Modern Athens' in the 1850s and 1860s: a city where 'wisdom' was still 'fashionable'; where the 'philosophers of Modern Athens' invited all the literary luminaries of the day—such as Ruskin—to address its 'Athenian' people; a city that had boasted 128 booksellers in 1867. Now, at the very end of the century, what Grant described as 'Usher Hall eyes' searched covetously for building-sites that would have insulted 'Scottish Athenian taste' by inappropriate development.[47] The brewer Andrew Usher had recently given a huge sum of money for a new concert hall, but a site had yet to be identified. The north side of Robert Adam's Charlotte Square—a supreme example of classical, if not actually 'Greek', Edinburgh urban design—was seriously considered for this new use. However, the City Council's preferred location was Atholl Crescent, an elegant Grecian terrace of 1825, immaculately planned and ornamented with a most effective parade of massed Ionic pilasters in the centre and at each end. This would have been wrecked by the imposition of a massive public building upon an essentially domestic piece of townscape.[48] Another, earlier, enterprise had found a site well enough: the National Monument, on Calton Hill. But the building had never been finished. Thus, in connection with the National Monument's appearance in a drawing by W. Banks (engraved by W. H. Lizars, published by Robert Grant's, and dating to about 1840), Giles recalled that 'It was to have given the new Athens the Parthenon of the past one', but reasoned that the greater age that has come upon it since has done more for the realisation of the city's ideal through its pillared pose than could have been done had the nation added to its number of pillars, and made that which was not as if it were. To perfect would have been ruin.[49]

Late nineteenth-century opinion on the National Monument as a ruin still generally held good into the mid- to late twentieth century, with Nikolaus Pevsner commentating that 'left unfinished', it had acquired 'a power to move which in its complete state it could not have had'.[50] In 1960, Eric Linklater observed that what existed had been built 'by pride, piety and patriotism', and so that was 'manifestly laudable'; nevertheless, Linklater was relieved that it had never been completed. Edinburgh's Parthenon had been 'left unfinished by the poverty that has saved so much of Scotland from vulgarity'. Completed, it would simply have been too much for the height of its hill. Thus, the Monument remained 'a celebration ... of that most likable spirit of humanity which recurrently compels it to set out on some gallant adventure without counting the cost ...'. The fragment, as actually built, stood 'delightful and slightly absurd ... and by the grace and favour of national limitations the impossibility of realising it has given Edinburgh one of its most engaging of its monuments.'[51] In the opinion of A. J. Youngson, it was fortunate that all schemes for completion came to nothing, 'for it is complete already ... a fragment is much better [than a full-scale copy of the Parthenon], mockingly, mysteriously, idiosyncratically "incomplete"; a ruin, or at any rate a seeming ruin ...'.[52] William St Clair concluded that:

> If the monument had been completed it is difficult to imagine how it could have escaped the bathos of pastiche. As events turned out, its twelve stark columns ... were more true both to the civic art of Athens, to the notion of enlightenment, and to the emerging romanticism than any completed version would have achieved.[53]

And for Robert Crawford, more recently—who sees, as so many do, Edinburgh's split personalities: the city of the Enlightenment on the one hand, and the city of Romance on the other, but sees them not 'distinct' but 'fused'— the unfinished Monument appears more 'doomed Romantic fragment than a neoclassical triumph'.[54]

*   *   *   *   *

In 1852, George Cleghorn added to his specifically National Monument-focused publications of 1824 and 1846 a third one, this taking the form of a long essay in an architectural journal. It is largely derivative of the earlier works, but it adds a measure of continued optimism.

The chaste, majestic, and faultless beauty of the Grecian Doric temple [on Calton Hill] will eclipse the most costly and magnificent works of modern times. Provided the restoration be correctly executed, and accompanied with appropriate sculpture and pictorial decorations, a certain and glorious success must be achieved, the influence of which on the future efforts of national taste and genius in the three sister arts, it is impossible fully to appreciate.[55]

But what is especially interesting is the note of nationalism—albeit 'unionist' nationalism—that has crept in. The completed monument, Cleghorn suggested, would

resuscitate and keep alive that patriotic independence and martial spirit for which our countrymen were so distinguished, when Scotland was an independent kingdom, but which is apt to die away when united to a larger and richer kingdom like England.[56]

In 1866, the architect John Dick Peddie created a striking view of Edinburgh, looking east from the Castle towards North Berwick Law, with the Parthenon complete and shimmering in sunlight on the Calton Hill. (Fig. 96) This truly Athenian image predates a rash of proposals by several architects for completion of the National Monument, or of turning it, once completed, partly completed, or otherwise adapted, to some noble purpose.[57] Their bright, watercolour visions, illustrating schemes of varying ambition, stand as memorials of what might have been.

More realistic was the attitude of Archibald Philip, fifth Earl of Rosebery, one of the most active advocates of cultural, intellectual and scholarly causes in the Scotland of his day. In making a public appeal in 1886 for the establishment of what was to become the Scottish History Society, he suggested that such a body

would preserve the perishable; it would form a collection valuable to the whole world, but profoundly attractive to Scotsmen; and it would raise a national monument, even more consistent and durable than those spectral and embarrassed columns which perplex the tourist on the Calton Hill.[58]

But already there had been a suggestion, made in 1884 by G. J. Forsyth Grant in a letter to *The Scotsman*, that the new Scottish National Portrait Gallery (which had been founded two years previously, but without permanent premises of its own) be accommodated in a completed 'Parthenon'.[59] This was a development of, or variant on, the old idea that a National Monument should have also the function of a 'Valhalla' or 'Pantheon' for the likenesses of great men. The notion of Parthenon as 'Pantheon' was to prove long-lasting.

In 1910 a plea, taking the form of a one-sheet printed poem, was made for completion of the National Monument as a tribute to 'Queen Victoria and the heroes of Scotland'.[60] Banal the verse may be; but the sentiments of the unknown poetaster were doubtless genuinely felt, and they continued the hope that some honour might be retrieved, and some dignified purpose found for 'Scotland's Disgrace'. The monarch who had done so much to make Scotland fashionable through the cult of 'Balmorality' was to be identified with many figures of the national past.

> Five British sovereigns their course have run
> Since this majestic edifice was planned, ...

> The Parthenon let 'Modern Athens' show
> Impressive in its symmetry sublime,
> For of its classic beauty much we know
> And wish more than a fragment spared by time.

> No grander site can any land supply
> Than that long waiting on the Calton Hill ...

> Now in this twentieth century we seek
> A vast Valhalla for the good and great ...

In the later 1840s George Cleghorn had at least acknowledged the existence of the Regensburg Walhalla. But no one concerned with the possible completion or development of the Edinburgh Parthenon around the turn of the nineteenth-twentieth centuries appears to have displayed any knowledge of what had just been built in Nashville, Tennessee or, if they did know of it, to have shown any interest or, still less, any shame. Nor did anyone reflect that Edinburgh, as the Athens of the North, had a rival city in the United States, which proudly bore the epithet 'Athens of the South'. Around 1824, the Princeton classicist Philip Lindsley had first christened Nashville, his adoptive home, 'Athens of the West' on account of its numerous colleges and educational institutions. Others followed his lead, taking their inspiration from the city's perceived dedication to education and the arts.[61] Like Edinburgh shortly before this time, Nashville was prompted to assume its other identity on cerebral grounds. There can have been no perceived topographical similarity whatsoever to Athens. As 'manifest destiny' ensured that the American frontier moved ever further from the Cumberland and the Mississippi Rivers, 'South' came to supersede 'West' in the soubriquet.

For the Tennessee Centennial Exposition of 1897, an exact replica of the Parthenon of Athens, complete with its sculpture, was constructed in less than two years, though of impermanent materials. That is half as long a period as the unfortunate hiatus between the founding of the National Monument and any construction work actually beginning on the western portico of the Edinburgh temple. Between 1920 and 1925 (but with some additional work lasting till 1931), the Nashville Parthenon was rebuilt in high-quality concrete, its sculpture likewise reproduced, and both this and the building itself coloured as we know the original to have been: an astonishing feat of civic pride and determination. (Fig. 100) The distinguished historian of Greek architecture, William Bell Dinsmoor, even acted as consultant.[62] The city's commitment to this extraordinary enterprise continued with the addition of a full-size replica of Phidias's cult statue of Athena Parthenos, as in the original Parthenon, complete with elaborate iconographic shield and the small (by comparison) statue of Nike in her outstretched hand; made between 1982 and 1990, this was finished with real gold leaf in 2002.[63] Edinburgh was thus beaten hands-down. Except that Edinburgh still had the better site by far for a Parthenon replica. It is ironic that the begetters of the Nashville temple, having paid all possible attention to every detail both external and internal, allowed topographical authenticity to end immediately outside the portico. As David Lowenthal notes:

> Nashville's Parthenon builders dispensed with the steep rise up to the actual Acropolis because 'it was feared that the effort needed to climb the hill might discourage visitors'; a mere ten-foot mound is meant to give it 'a commanding place'.[64]

Early in the twentieth century, William Mitchell, an Edinburgh solicitor, revived the dream of completing the Parthenon, observing as he did so that the Erechtheion-inspired façade of the County Hall had recently been removed to make way for 'a less classic building'.[65] Some citizens, Mitchell asserted,

> are beginning to think that the time has come for completing the National Monument, so long the national disgrace, the Parthenon of Athens being at last reproduced as a National Gallery for Scotland. Not only Scotland but the whole British Empire should embrace gladly the present opportunity for an object so worthy. Provided with improved access, the Calton Hill, now so shamefully neglected, is capable of being made not less attractive than the Acropolis of Athens.[66]

Here, surely, was a plea to revert to an 'Athenian' Edinburgh, where archaeologically inspired Greek-revival architecture was to be commended. In the 'Postscriptum' to his quaint travel memoir, Mitchell returned to the theme. Having now seen for himself Damascus, Jerusalem and Athens, Mitchell confessed his thankful pride that '"Edina, Scotia's darling seat"' need not fear comparison with any city in the world. A recent threat to the High School had been thwarted, saving 'that incomparable specimen of Grecian architecture' for posterity.[67]

Mitchell subsequently published a formal and very elaborate appeal for the National Monument to be completed as a National Gallery for Scotland. (Fig. 97) In doing so, he stated repeatedly that Edinburgh, so similar to Athens in setting and layout, was actually superior in every aspect, this transcendence extending from its existing Greek Revival buildings to its picturesque prospects, both inward and outward.[68] It could almost be Archibald Alison again. Mitchell was motivated principally by a sense of grievance that science and art in Scotland had been, in his opinion, shabbily treated—'starved and neglected', was his chosen phrase—by the United Kingdom government. His Majesty's Treasury should make amends by assigning funds to enable the completion of the National Monument as a new National Gallery which would be a tourist draw. The fact that, in antiquity, a wing of the Propylaea or entrance building to the Athenian Acropolis had been a picture gallery, offered the pleasing notion of a circle being completed. That Mitchell did not seek to complete the Monument as a 'monument' is significant. His reasons were interesting: in the era of the Edwardian *Entente Cordiale* he considered it insensitive, indeed embarrassing, to think any further about a triumphal monument which had commemorated the wars with, and victory over, France.[69] Tellingly, since at least 1833, there had been those who considered the Monument's 'war-memorial' function out-dated and irrelevant. It was, wrote one such, 'an unhappy object', evoking remembrance of a war already almost forgotten.[70] Though this view was, in fact, surely inaccurate and anachronistic, other wars would later bring the Monument to public consciousness once more.

Mitchell had proposed that access to the top of Calton Hill be facilitated by a funicular railway. He also drew a parallel with a rather unlikely place, namely the Casino at Monte Carlo. If that could be made easily accessible to its patrons, it was surely not too much to imagine that a national gallery on Calton Hill might be reached by an arrangement of lifts, 'gradation of broad, easy steps and promenades' by which to reach herbaceous gardens, statues, and fountains', where Edinburgh might provide 'a world's point of attraction', coincidentally designed to 'redound to the credit of the national character.'[71] The ignominy of 'Scotland's disgrace' might thus be expunged, but not much of the time-honoured parallelism with Athens seemed to survive this new, admiring comparison with the Principality of Monaco with its gambling tables. But the following year Sir Herbert Maxwell stated that Edinburgh's alias of 'Auld Reekie' might be a deterrent to visitors, and that the epithet 'Modern Athens' was likely to be found 'more alluring'; this seems like a return to the spirit of about 1820.[72]

*   *   *   *   *

The sociologist and highly influential pioneer of town planning, Patrick Geddes, who had established his 'Civic Observatory' in the Outlook Tower on Castlehill, looked coolly at Edinburgh in his celebrated *Civic Survey* of 1911. He reduced any past parallels with Athens to simple matters of geography and environment, just as he contended that 'Architecture and town planning ... are not mere products of the quiet drawing-office' but rather 'expressions of the local history, the civic and national changes of mood and contrasts of mind.'[73] Both Athens and Edinburgh were examples of what he called the 'port-fort', or 'Piraeus-Acropolis' form of civic development, a type actually not infrequent in Europe.[74] Geddes made an analytical 'comparison, side by side' of the two cities,

> each plainly a hill-fort associated at once with a sea-port, and with an agricultural plain. This combination of an Acropolis with its Piraeus and its Attica, is common throughout Mediterranean Europe, though less frequent in the north; and such a threefold cooperation is conducive alike to agricultural efficiency, to maritime enterprise and commerce, and to regional as well as civic culture. Thus we see the traditional comparison of Edinburgh with Athens has really little to do with our eighteenth and nineteenth-century imitations of Greek temples or Greek sophistries, but lies far deeper, in geographical and historical origins.[75]

In this single telling passage, Geddes wrote off much of the over-blown attempts of a century earlier to find a cerebral comparison between the one place and the other, or to identify specific sites with supposedly matching physical features. And when he did look at the Calton Hill monuments as a whole, he saw in the site 'a vast museum of the battle of the styles', where the classical—expressed at its best in the High School—contended with the romantic and the castellated. The National Monument itself was 'too colossal', whereas (and by contrast) the Greek art-galleries at The Mound were 'more temperate'.[76]

Geddes may have shown scant regard for the reasons why the Modern Athenians had wanted their city to assume the airs and graces of another Athens, but he did reserve a great deal of praise for the Roman classicism and town-planning vision of Robert Adam. Geddes would later write of 'the spacious dignity, the impeccable decorum of New Edinburgh.'[77] The New Town plan and its stately buildings were remarkable in the world. It was just that Edinburgh's Greek phase seemed an aberration.

Publications aimed at the tourist market still peddled the notion of Edinburgh— 'this citadel of beauty'—as 'the Modern Athens', even incorporating the epithet in their titles printed on tartan-bound covers and thus really muddling the homespun notion of Scotland's 'Auld Reekie' with the high-flown ideal of an intellectual and classical city. But for much of the twentieth century, Greek Edinburgh did not enjoy a good press among architectural historians. Arthur Bolton, for example, torchbearer for Robert Adam in a magisterial work of 1922, believed that 'the idea of "Modern Athens" has been responsible for a vast amount of architectural dullness ... the general air of monotony ... [flowing] in a pedantic Greek channel ...'.[78] Looking east across the Atlantic, and comparing the Scottish love-affair with the Greek Revival and the characteristics of the American application of the style, Roger Kennedy observed that 'Though Edinburgh delighted in calling itself "the Athens of the North" ... the Acropolis of Edinburgh, and that city's streets of Grecian town houses, though impressive, seem to an American to be somewhat heartless, dour, and cold.'[79] But even an anglicised American scholar, Robert Oresko, had earlier stated that 'the Athens of the North reflects more the dour, solid outlook' of men such as (perhaps predictably) Robert Reid and (remarkably) Playfair, both of whom Oresko dismissed, rather demeaningly, as 'craftsmen' lacking the 'classical vision' of the peerless Robert Adam.[80] Greek Edinburgh, with its hard, precise, architecture, and its unsmiling seriousness of mind, was indeed best denominated as 'dour'. In his history of architecture, David Watkin was happy to state that the Greek Revival 'was adopted ... with such panache that the city of Edinburgh, helped by the drama of its natural setting, became justly known as the Athens of the North.'[81] But the same writer, influenced increasingly by the achievement and the thoughts of Alexander 'Greek' Thomson, broadened his view to reflect the opinion that the Athenian epithet belonged more properly to Scotland as a whole rather than just to its capital city. A section of a major essay was entitled accordingly 'Scotland as the "Athens of the North": Edinburgh and Glasgow', and a catalogue of some of the latter city's greatest Greek buildings proffered to prove the point yet further.[82]

Almost exactly a century after Modern Athenian ideas had reached their zenith, W. G. Blaikie Murdoch (in 1924), and James Bone (in 1926) looked back at the attitudes of that era. Murdoch concluded with some high-flown reflections on Edinburgh classicism.

> ... Edinburgh, physically, was the ideal place for pseudo-antique architecture. With her stern, mountainous character she seemed verily born for the reception of the classic, whether in the form of streets or independent structures. She was able to offer sites of the loveliest to such, and do not some of her memories of Greece and Rome look as though they had risen at a wizard's incantation? It may be to the discredit of Scotland, that one of the most successful of her adventures in the quest for beauty should be no more than an imitation. Only, be it borne in mind, imitation is homage. And it is good to reflect that Scotland is in the forefront of the countries, having ... offered tribute to the genius of Hellas.[83]

Bone reinforced the old identification with Athens, but commented on the 'costly bauble' that was the National Monument 'stopped in the making' in the context of civic bankruptcy, while he lauded the High School as 'that marvel of harmony in site and design' (though in error it was to Hamilton, architect of the High School, that Bone attributed the Parthenon).[84] In one chapter, 'The Modern Athenian', Bone attempted a verbal portrait of the Edinburgh character, looking back to an age, a century earlier,

> whose very mistakes were heroic. Even those who know nothing of the mighty spirit that was stirring in the city at that time are moved by the great ruin on Calton Hill … to wonder what manner of men these Edinburgh people were. Desiring an impressive ruin (it would seem), they did not wait for Time's help, but promptly built one for themselves …[85]

He expressed satisfaction in the classicism of Edinburgh by relating the whimsical (and apocryphal) story of the self-improving shopkeeper of the New Town.

> No tradesman seems to be permitted to open a shop in the New Town unless he is soundly classic in his shop-front. There is a beautiful Corinthian grocer near one of the great squares … his romance of a business was something like this. He began in Stockbridge in quite a small way with one Doric pilaster. By and by, as things prospered, he thought he would make the venture and go up the hill, and so one fine morning behold the new shop half-way to Princes Street, and—yes!—Ionic columns a quarter engaged! … the last step is taken, and we see him today at the top of the hill with fluted Corinthian columns and a full entablature. May one not say that every grocer's boy in Edinburgh carries a Corinthian order in his message-basket?[86]

* * * * *

William Mitchell had several schemes up his sleeve. These varied from completion of the Parthenon in tolerably accurate Greek form (minus pedimental sculpture, and presumably without friezes or sculptured metopes) to an infinitely cheaper and much more economically manageable, more park-like layout, in which the uncompleted portico would stand as it was, but with the rest of the putative temple's footprint outlined by careful tree-planting. (Fig. 98)

More remarkable was the proposal of Frank Mears and Ramsay Traquair in 1912. This would have turned the skeletal outline of the temple of the 1820s into an elaborate precinct, heavy with statuary and articulated by a series of pavilions interspersed with semi-circular niches or *nymphaea* on either side of a rectangular pool. This would have created something reminiscent of Hadrian's Villa at Tivoli, or one of the Imperial baths complexes of Rome. Athens, ancient or 'Modern', appears to have been forgotten. Rome ruled once more.

The most poignant, and certainly the most effective proposal, was (Sir) George Washington Browne's of July 1918: the unfinished Parthenon was to be 'completed' or, rather, adapted, as a truncated temple portico to serve as a national memorial to the dead of the world war then still in progress.[87] (Figs 101-04) A memorial originally to one major conflict would thus be turned into a commemoration of a yet greater struggle. 'The design ... frankly accepts the twelve columns as a sufficient basis for an entire scheme.'[88] The original columns of the 1820s would have a completed entablature, a frieze and cornice being added to the bare epistyle, and the metopes ornamented with laurel wreaths in the manner of Hamilton at the High School or Playfair at the Royal Institution; this frieze would run round both the outside and the inside of the spectral portico. Enveloped within would be a sculptural group of Nike driving a quadriga (emblematic of four allied nations) and bearing before her the victor's wreath, with recumbent lions on either side atop the truncated stylobate. In front of the portico would be sculptures representing 'Heroism in the Field' and 'Endurance at Home'. The outer face of the stylobate was to bear bronze plaques listing the names of the fallen. A commemoration of a war *against* France would now become one memorialising a war fought *with* France as ally rather than enemy.

Another war later, when the descendants of the those who had smiled at Crombie's caricature portraits of the 1840s needed to be cheered in testing times, the artist Tom Curr produced (in 1944 and 1946) a series of cartoons of wartime Edinburgh personalities under the revived title of *Modern Athenians*. This was very much a 'city' effort, for there was textual assistance from the Lord Provost, Sir William Young Darling, and the Revd Ronald Selby Wright, Minister of the Canongate Kirk. Both were the kind of men who might have been prominent in the world of Henry Cockburn and Archibald Alison.

Victory achieved, and in an era of peace like that in which both the Parthenons of Athens and Edinburgh were conceived, a proposal was made by the architect Alan Reiach to transform the unfinished temple into the focus of a cultural complex for the 1951 Festival of Britain. The 'cella' of the Parthenon was to function as a sculpture court.

*   *   *   *   *

In every case outlined above, and also those imagined by other architects, planners and cultural impresarios, nothing came of all the good intentions. Yet notions of residual 'Athenianism' still clung to the city. The founding of the Edinburgh International Festival in 1947 had been accompanied by the establishment of a short-lived literary magazine entitled *The New Athenian Broadsheet*. (Fig. 106) The cover-page bears an elegant design by William McLaren, illustrator and decorative painter. Within a sub-rococo cartouche, with an oval cameo portrait of Athena at its base, appears a view of the bosky slopes of Calton Hill with the distinctive unfinished Parthenon and the 'choragic monument' of Dugald Stewart. Printed directly below is a poem by Lewis Spence entitled 'The Prows O' Reekie'. This captures well the pride of a patriotic writer. No city in Europe could compete with Edinburgh, whose physical grandeur matched by its literary achievement could outdo them all, Athens included.

> O wad this braw hie-heepit toun
> Sail aff like an enchanted ship,
> Drift ower the warld's seas up and doun
> And kiss wi' Venice lip tae lip,
> Or anchor intae Naples Bay
> A misty island far astray,
> Or set her rock tae Athens' wa'
> Pillar tae pillar, stane tae stane,
> The cruikit spell o' her backbane,
> Yon shadow-mile o' spire and vane,
> Wad ding them a', wad ding them a'! ...

At the start of the Edinburgh Festival's third season, on 21 August 1949, there was a revival of the old idea of the Modern Athens. In the forecourt of the Palace of Holyroodhouse the Duke of Hamilton, premier peer of Scotland and Hereditary Keeper of the Palace, received the mayors of a dozen cities. They included Edinburgh's namesake, Dunedin in New Zealand; and on a rather difference scale, Paris, Amsterdam, Hamburg and Lisbon. Athens was also represented. The mayor of that city brought with him his daughter, attired for the occasion as 'the Maid of Athens'. She presented to the Lord Provost of Edinburgh a 'Grecian urn'—the symbolism encompassed Keats and well as Byron—containing earth from the Acropolis as a further symbolic gift from the Athens of the south to that of the north.[89]

That 1949 Festival season included a revival of Allan Ramsay's pastoral comic drama *The Gentle Shepherd*, produced by Tyrone Guthrie. No matter that he described the whole extravaganza as 'Regency', the critic of *The Times* felt that this, in its setting of the candle-lit assembly hall of the High School on Calton Hill, offered a return of an Edinburgh which had once ('before the Industrial Revolution turned it from a metropolis into a railway terminus') been another Athens.[90]

The London press maintained a slightly patronising tone when it came to a revived 'Athenianism' induced by the Edinburgh Festival. The *Times* music critic wrote whimsically of the Muses taking their Scottish summer holidays. With Mozart on the programme, the Athens of the North turned itself into the Salzburg of the North, 'though Mozart was not a Scot and there was no Scottish Mozart'. The '*genius loci* [of Edinburgh] had done something for philosophy and literature and medicine but not for music'. Athenian ideas might be over-reached, and there were 'perils of success in complacency, too much money, and possible vulgarity'.[91] In 1960, when Athens had its own festival, commentators contrasted the more restrained civic mood there with the 'hurly burly' of the festival in 'the Athens of the North' (Edinburgh not being otherwise identified), where the visitor was subjected to 'bullying' by means of advertisements, banners and other street decorations.[92]

In 1949, however, an extraordinary claim had been made for Edinburgh. The eccentric writer Comyns Beaumont, proponent of many weird and fanciful theories, suggested not that Edinburgh looked rather like Athens and that it possessed 'Athenian' qualities, but that Edinburgh was, in fact—Jerusalem! There was a passing similarity with the opinions of Hugh William Williams, Archibald Alison and their friends in that Beaumont thought as follows:

> Old Edinburgh in its topography, its setting, the lay-out of its principal ancient streets, its wynds, its Castle rock, its former lakes or lochs, its Arthur's Seat, and its place names offers a most complete comparison with ancient Jerusalem.

But then the bizarre theorizing took over. His book *Britain—the Key to World History* includes a typeset table, and plans on the endpapers, that offer a full matching of Jerusalem landmarks with those of Edinburgh. '... *Edinburgh Castle is in all features absolutely identical with the City of David',* Beaumont wrote in italic for emphasis. George IV Bridge was the Tyropoeon Valley; the earthen Mound was really the ruins of the Antonia Fortress; Arthur's Seat was the Mount of Olives. And so on, to absurdity. Never once is Edinburgh compared with Athens; but, in Beaumont's distorted world-view, Edinburgh really was the City of David. And Athens ...? That was Bath.[93]

*   *   *   *   *

The Greek theme was revived in the medium of architecture when, in 1954, Sir William Kininmonth contributed his austerely elegant, neoclassical Adam House to the varied streetscape of Chambers Street, as a university examination hall-cum-theatre. The building commemorates both the name and location of Adam Square, which once occupied roughly the same site, and was the Adam architectural dynasty's city-centre property. Its most notable feature is a giant central *serliana*. However, some carved foliage over the central pedimented window might well have come from Playfair's Royal Institution. The University's shield of arms affects a rather medieval form. The date of construction is commemorated in attractive circular foliate cartouches suspended on a millinery shop's-worth of stone ribbon. Over the whole assemblage of decoration is the very same Greek inscription designed for the Town's College in 1616 which we noted in Chapter 3:

ΔΙΠΛΟΥΝ ΟΡΩΣΙΝ ΟΙ ΜΑΘΟΝΤΕΣ ΓΡΑΜΜΑΤΑ

It really does seem like a case of double vision to have a recension of the original which lauded the benefits of learned double insight. (Fig. 107) But maybe it is an example of a wish to maintain the 'Athenian' dream.

The endpapers of Eric Linklater's *Edinburgh* (1960) are ornamented by maps of the Old and New Towns by the artist and illustrator John Inglis Drever ('Don') Pottinger, whose work was renowned for its wit and lightly worn learning. The New Town plan bears as decoration, and as a sort-of presiding genius, the figure of an imaginary ancient Greek architect or town-planner—a northern Hippodamos of Miletos, perhaps—leaning on a pile of meander-ornaments, and sucking his teeth as he appears to assess the possibilities of some new building or street layout in 'the Modern Athens'. (Fig. 108)

An authentic Modern Athenian flourish was given to a previously unremarkable, and previously unsympathetically modernised, George Street shop front transformed by the conservation architects Simpson & Brown in 1985. The premises of Trotters opticians was upgraded (and returned to an early nineteenth-century appearance) by the application of style and humour in the creation of what could be called an 'Eyeonic' order—with the emphasis on the 'eye'. The new, slender-columned doorcase was given capitals with pince-nez spectacles for volutes. (Fig. 110) Archibald Alison might not have been amused; but surely Walter Scott and Henry Cockburn would have chortled at a delightfully whimsical take on how a Greek Edinburgh, which once saw itself through rose-tinted spectacles, might come to see itself through the lens of twentieth-century re-assessment.

Scholarship and wit of this kind was in complete contrast to the unfathomable decision taken by the City Council when it decided upon construction of a new 'temple' in the open square (the 'piazza' as it seemed now to be called) at The Mound. This monstrosity of limited life, which came and went with little or no record, appeared out of nowhere, and to no purpose, around the millennium. Its setting, east of the Royal Scottish Academy (the Royal Institution of yore) and north of the National Gallery, was all too close and visually intrusive to both buildings, and appeared a wilful mockery of both great temples of the arts. A travesty of taste, this shoddy shadow of the classical tradition of the Modern Athens had square 'columns' or, more accurately, piloti, and no entablature: the pedimented roof rested directly on the crudest of supports. It had no obvious function, there was no point in its existence, and it was unloved. Its disappearance was entirely unlamented. It had not expressed itself well in the classical language of architecture. In its relatively brief existence, it spoke only of two things, and it was not learned enough to express either in Greek. The first notion is that someone may have wished to pay homage, or at least to reflect, the neighbouring work of William Henry Playfair, but the result was merely to insult it. The second is that an ignorant, and unfortunately successful desire to emulate these monuments of Edinburgh's Athenian age simply demonstrated just how far the civic taste of Edinburgh had sunk by the end of the twentieth century. Had the city needed another 'folly' or 'disgrace', this surely would have claimed the palm.

*   *   *   *   *

Around 1970, fashionable young people about the New Town could still drink in Howe Street at 'The Athenian' bar. (There was also the 'Doric Tavern' in Market Street, on the northern fringe of the Old Town.) If they needed to have masonry repairs done to the exteriors of their elegant flats or houses (from 1977 within a City of Edinburgh Council Conservation Area, and from 1995 a UNESCO World Heritage Site) these New Town dwellers might call upon the services of the specialist restoration contractor A. B. Mearns. Established in 1975, the firm's acknowledgement of its credentials as a builder in the 'Modern Athens' is strikingly conveyed in its letterhead. (Fig. 109) This uses an image of the ruined Parthenon (the Athenian one), and the tacit implication is that some stone repair is necessary even to such an icon of world architectural history, and that the craftsmanship and local materials so much lauded by Archibald Alison are still to be found in the Athens of the North.

Hugh Trevor-Roper's witty 'Letters of Mercurius' first appeared in *The Spectator* in the late 1960s, and were published in book form in 1970. The collection of spoof correspondence, purporting to be that between academics in leading universities discussing matters of contemporary controversy, owes its particular eccentricity to the fact that the language is that of the early seventeenth century. One letter from 'Mercurius Edinensis' to 'Mercurius Londiniensis' is of interest here because it alludes to the epithets of Edinburgh. However, the writer and his correspondent appear to have bandied about the 'Athenian' epithet far too early for the historic period of the language, and the age of the Modern Athens appears to have been over long before, in reality, it had even begun.

> I hae received your letter of the 31ˢᵗ *ultimi*, in whilk you speir for news from this our Northern Athens, as it pleases you to call it; but I must send you a damping reply, for in truth we hae lang ceased to claim any sic exotick title, being weel satisfied with ourselves under our proper designation of Auld Reekie ...[94]

Wind was taken out of Northern Athenian sails, however, in Tom Stoppard's stage play *Jumpers* (1972). One character, Archie, says of another, Professor

McFee, who has shot himself: 'It was a trivial matter. He took offence at my description of Edinburgh as the Reykjavik of the South.' The jibe was taken up subsequently, and with relish, by Bernard Levin in a moment of vituperative journalistic sarcasm about the city's cultural pretensions. Others capitalised on what was increasingly regarded as the absurdity of a concept and a saying that were, perhaps, ridiculous even when first coined. The humourist Miles Kington wrote in his 'Moreover' column in *The Times* in 1983:

> I have never, truth to tell, quite understood the old description of Edinburgh as the 'Athens of the North'. A lot of talking went on in both places, no doubt ... But the only real links I can see between Edinburgh and Athens is that they are both full of unfinished monuments and retired Colonels. And Greece, of course, has stuffed vine leaves, which are only a kind of open-cast haggis.[95]

Norman MacCaig's 'Inward Bound' (1973), evoking visions of Greece in trans-estuarial views to Fife, might have appealed to Hugh William Williams or George Sibbald:

> On Calton Hill
> The twelve pillars
> Of this failed Parthenon
> Made more Greek by the Cargo boat
> Sailing between them
> On the cobwebby waters of the Firth
> Should marry nicely with the Observatory
> In the way compliments do
> Each observing the heavens
> In its different way.[96]

John Byrom, in 1983, compounded the idea in his delightful summary of the essential features of Calton Hill, including the Observatory, 'a miniature, bobbing chaste and demure enclosing its real telescopes beneath its handsome buns', and the National Monument 'a gaunt fierce fragment to full-size, beckoning Athena Nike'. He mused on the anomaly that, in this particular location, no replica of the Tower of the Winds was ever suggested, 'surely of all classical Greek buildings the most appropriate to the Calton Hill'. And he reflected, further, on the oddity 'that the Greeks themselves should need to travel to a windy Scottish hilltop to see such a close-entered catalogue of their own best buildings'.[97]

But only ten years later Allan Massie could say that 'The old name, the Athens of the North, is now meaningless, despite the Grecian temples on Calton Hill. The resemblance is rather to old Rome, which offers the same delight to the eye and the historical imagination.'[98] His views are compounded by the judgment of Robert Crawford, who suggests that a J. M. W. Turner view of the city from the Calton Hill makes it look 'a little like a North British Rome, if not quite a Modern Athens'.[99] Had Robert Adam been right all along, in trying to give Edinburgh a Roman grandeur? Was that more natural to it, really, with its seven hills, than any Athenian airs? Except, of course, that there are also seven hills in Athens ...

The most evocative twenty-first century statement of the idea of Edinburgh as the Athens of the North is to be found in the emblematic bronze relief panel on the pedestal of Alexander Stoddart's statue of William Henry Playfair, erected in Chambers Street in 2016. The iconography is as explicit as anything written in the entire literary debate on the meaning and nature of the Modern Athens. (Figs 22, 119) The plaque shows Edinburgh, 'Edina', wearing a mural crown as befits the personification of a city. She confronts Athena, patron goddess of the actual Athens, helmeted, adorned with the aegis and armed with shield and spear. Edina bears a polished bronze mirror of classical form. The symbolism suggests the Modern Athens reflecting back the glorious image of Athena—and thus of ancient Athens—to herself.[100]

*   *   *   *   *

A suggestion, perhaps more sentimental than serious, had been made in 1906 to complete the unfinished Parthenon as a monument to the forthcoming bicentenary of the Treaty of Union—considered by its proposer as 'surely one of the most blissful compacts that was ever vouchsafed by God to man'.[101] In a rather contrarian mood, it was then suggested in 1908 that, in an upsurge of sentiment provoked by aspirations to Home Rule, a Scottish parliament might be established on the site.[102]

Ninety years later, when a new Parliament—or rather a revived Parliament— was indeed decreed for Scotland, politicians and planners turned their backs upon the classical Calton acropolis, and its finest monument of all, the Greek Revival High School. This vacant building had already been fitted out for the Assembly expected to result from the Scottish devolution referendum of 1979; but, in the event, the electorate turned down the proposal for the creation of a Scottish Assembly. (Figs 68, 116-18) In 1997, however, a second referendum resulted in a majority for devolution, and this time for the establishment of a Scottish Parliament with a much more significant status and far wider powers.

The High School was Scotland's 'existing chamber-in-waiting'.[103] (Today, still-extant signs at the entrance to its precinct label it 'New Parliament House'). Most people expected it to become the seat of the newly decreed Parliament, for Calton Hill had long been seen, one way or another, as 'the embodiment of the Scottish soul ... What better place for a parliament, after all, than Scotland's national Valhalla, an acropolis resonating with the symbolic democratic virtues of Periclean Athens?'[104] But in 1997 the High School building was no longer considered suitable to house that Parliament. Nor was it recalled as a structure reflecting the aspirations of what had once been, for a short while, the Modern Athens. 'To the semi-educated and blinkered', wrote 'Piloti' in *Private Eye*, 'a Doric column may seem authoritarian, but ... it can represent democracy. The Greek Doric of the High School in fact symbolises everything that is, or was, noble and great about Scotland: the Enlightenment, education, civilisation.'[105] Gavin Stamp—the principal writer of *Private Eye*'s 'Nooks and Corners' page—had already observed, in 1991, that in Scotland the 'pure austerity' of the Greek Revival style had been made a symbol of nationhood. He went as far as to describe Edinburgh as 'the nearest thing to perfection achieved by man in the building of cities'. Significantly, he gave the accolade to the Athens of the North, and not to its erstwhile ancient inspiration in the Aegean.[106]

But a building that was both old and built in a classical style was not what the New Labour government of Tony Blair wanted for the people of Scotland. He himself had been educated at Edinburgh's Fettes College, an extravaganza mixing Scottish baronial and French gothic, thus redolent of the historic Auld Alliance rather than of any Northern Athens: a style very different from that of many other Edinburgh schools. Now, New Labour's 'Cool Britannia' ideology, with its 'manipulation of image and iconography' was fixated on a 'dreamscape of signature buildings and cutting-edge modernism'.[107] The people might actually have determined otherwise; they might, indeed, not have looked askance at a magnificent, superbly sited, time-honoured and universally praised building of far-reaching renown. But alas, the High School, and the Calton Hill in general, had become what Donald Dewar, Secretary of State for Scotland from 1997, called a 'Nationalist shibboleth'; supporters of Scottish independence had promoted a campaign that had adopted Calton Hill for its focus. The old High School had become a symbol of a devolved administration that might presage full independence. Even non-nationalists in Scotland, who paid no heed to political shibboleths, might well have been pleased to see the new parliament established in the High School, an incomparable location and an historic and beautiful building of the highest style and quality.

The decision, however, was made for them. Did some of the coterie that reached it lack historical knowledge or cultural nuance, or both? Or an understanding of what the concept of 'the Athens of the North' had once meant and might mean still? A site at Holyrood was fixed upon, ironically within sight of the Calton Hill with its unfinished Parthenon and magnificent High School, and the Scottish Parliament building was constructed between 1999 and 2004 to the designs of the Catalan architect Enric Miralles. (Fig. 115) The story of the entire Holyrood Parliament project has been well described as 'a metaphor for chaos, mismanagement, ineptitude, disappointment and recrimination'.[108] If this sounds familiar, it is because the unedifying Holyrood saga reflects in a strangely repetitive way something of the story of the National Monument. The Holyrood imbroglio also involved an episode of architectural infighting somewhat recalling the wider scene witnessed in Edinburgh during its 'Athenian' age. Proposals too grandiose, a seriously slipping timetable, incompetent project control and massive cost-overruns made many remember 'Edinburgh's disgrace' of the early nineteenth century. Through further 'folly' in visual terms, or in aim and purpose—albeit this perception depends on one's point of view—Edinburgh acquired a building that made it a little less the Athens, and more the Barcelona, of the North.

*   *   *   *   *

At the opening of this book, we noted that a mid-twentieth century authority wrote of how, some 125 years earlier, Edinburgh had come to see itself as 'a northern reflection of ancient Athens', and that the 'illusion' was taken seriously.[109] For a brief period, a metamorphosed Auld Reekie had thought of itself as something wholly different. It was as if some magic or sleight of hand had been at work.

Just before thoughts of a replica Parthenon on Calton Hill came to be enshrined in the city's aspiration, a nationally celebrated magician was indeed in Edinburgh. For four months he lived in Calton Street. This modest, steeply-sloping, low-lying thoroughfare was spanned by the Regent Bridge in Waterloo Place, soaring high above. (Fig. 44) The magnificent enterprise of the elevated, imperial roadway, product of the highest engineering and architectural skills, might well have seemed to some the result of a sort of magic in the town-planner's art. From his lodgings in lowly Calton Street, Mr [Thomas] Ingleby, 'Emperor of all Conjurors', sent forth a puff for his show. *The Caledonian Mercury* of 5 November 1818 carried word that he would perform at the Assembly Room in Musselburgh, just east of Edinburgh, for two nights. This celebrated master of illusion and legerdemain put it about that he would appear as from 'the modern Athens, the enlightened city of Edinburgh'. This single, ephemeral newspaper advertisement encapsulates much of the essential oddity of Edinburgh's contemporary aspiration to be another place in another time. 'Smoke and mirrors' may well seem a significant element in Auld Reekie's attempt to transform itself into the Athens of the North. Many in the conjuror's audiences will have been captivated by what they saw then, even as the inhabitants of Edinburgh as a whole will have been seduced by the literary and visual blandishments of Archibald Alison, Hugh William Williams, George Cleghorn and their Modern Athenian friends in the years to come, and by a most intriguing, persuasive, pervasive and enduring idea in the cultural history of Scotland.

NOTES AND REFERENCES

Chapter 1: Prologue

1 NLS, Acc. 12668. On Sibbald and his manuscript, and for some of the ideas and
   material dealt with in this Prologue, see 'Edinburgh as Athens', *passim*; see also
   Edina/Athena, p. 16.
2 Anon., '*Travels in Egypt and The Holy Land*. By William Rae Wilson', pp. 406
   and 411.
3 Thomson, 'Art and Architecture: A Course of Four Lectures', no. III, pt I, p. 51.
   For an edition of these lectures see [Thomson], *The Light of Truth and Beauty*,
   and for the quotation here see p. 147.
4 Thomson, 'Obstacles and Aids to Architectural Progress', lecture to the Glasgow
   Architectural Society, 15 March 1869: text printed in full for the first time in
   The Light of Truth and Beauty, pp. 89-99 at p. 95.
5 Thomson, 'Art and Architecture: A Course of Four Lectures', no. III, pt I, p. 51.
6 See two recent good, popular works: Herman, *How the Scots Invented the
   Modern World*; and Buchan, *Capital of the Mind. How Edinburgh Changed the
   World*. On these titles see the review article by Brown, 'One City in its Time:
   Views of Edinburgh in the Age of Enlightenment'. On the topic of Edinburgh as
   the Athens of the North, see several excellent short treatments in more general
   works, most notably Joyce, *Edinburgh. The Golden Age*; McKean, *Edinburgh*;
   and Cosh, *Edinburgh. The Golden Age*. Sheila Szatkowski's *Enlightenment
   Edinburgh* provides a useful and companionable guide to place and people.
   From an architectural perspective, Rowan, 'The Athens of the North Explored.
   Georgian Edinburgh—II' is full of perceptive insights; McKean and Macdonald
   provide useful summaries, also with a specifically architectural focus, in their
   respective articles, both entitled 'The Athens of the North', in *The Story of
   Scotland* and *Rassegna*.
7 'OROP', p. 306.
8 Necker de Saussure, *Travels in Scotland*, p. viii. It may be that from Necker's
   accolade is derived, consciously or unconsciously—it is certainly unreferenced—
   the title of Buchan's *Capital of the Mind*.

9 *Metropolitan Improvements*, pp. 2, 4.

10 Ian Duncan has written of how Edinburgh was 'promoting and redefining itself as a new kind of national capital … a cultural and aesthetic one' at a time when there was being developed a 'new ideology of imperial cultural nationalism': see *Scott's Shadow*, pp. 9, 16, cf. p. 18. See also the assessment of Edinburgh's 'Athenian' cultural standing in contradistinction to London's imperial Roman role in Robert Crawford, *On Glasgow and Edinburgh*, pp. 27-28.

11 On this fascinating topic, and specifically its architectural manifestation in a swing from a Roman to a Greek taste, see especially the impressive article by John Lowrey, 'From Caesarea to Athens'. Also valuable is Naik and Stewart, 'The Hellenization of Edinburgh', esp. pp. 368-71.

12 Elmes, 'On the best Situation and most proper Mode of commemorating the great Victories of the late Wars, by Sea and Land …', p. 33. For the reference to Thomas Howard, Earl of Arundel, and his collection of Greek sculpture—now in Oxford—see Henry Peacham, *The Compleat Gentleman*, p. 107. Adolf Michaelis, *Ancient Marbles in Great Britain*, Part I, charts the development of the Arundel collection; the history of other early collections up to and beyond Lord Elgin can be found in Parts II and III. See also the short study by D. E. L. Haynes, *The Arundel Marbles*.

13 *Metropolitan Improvements*, p. 4.

14 Cf. Rood, 'From Marathon to Waterloo', pp. 274-75. The Greek cause in 1821 was destined to appeal strongly and 'to touch the hearts and minds of European elites' precisely because these classes had been taught that Greek freedom won in antiquiy was, in essence, also the foundation of their own ideas of liberty. See Roderick Beaton, *The Greek Revolution of 1821*, p. 30. See also Ian Jenkins, *Archaeologists & Aesthetes in the Sculpture Galleries of the British Museum*, pp. 18-19, on Regency England's admiration for, and emulation of, a freedom-loving ancient Athens. One of the ways it did this was by offering what was quaintly described, in 1816, as 'an honourable asylum' to the Parthenon sculptures.

15 Alison, 1819 A, pp. 379 and 384-5. John Gifford appeared unaware of Alison's authorship of this article: see Gifford, pp. 48, 80.

16 Alison, 1819 A, p. 386. The phrase has been borrowed for the title of the essay by Brown, 'Gilded by the Rays of an Athenian Sun', p. 13.

17 See Michie, *An Enlightenment Tory in Victorian Scotland*, pp. 11, 157, 190-97.

18 On the concept of 'Romantic-Classicism' see Hitchcock, *Architecture: Nineteenth and Twentieth Centuries*, p. 13; and Crook, *The Greek Revival. Neo-Classical Attitudes*, esp. pp. xi and 63-69. However, for a slight corrective on the utility of the term 'Romantic-Classicism', see the comments by John Wilton-Ely in *The Age of Neo-Classicism*, p. 490. There is an excellent and sophisticated treatment of the topic in Chapter 5, '1800-1840. Romantic Classicism and the Emergence of a "National Style"', of Glendinning, MacInnes and MacKechnie, *History of Scottish Architecture*.

19 It is often said that George IV laid the stone himself. In fact, on the day in question—and evidently feeling himself not in a suitably 'Athenian' mood for such a task—the King remained at Dalkeith Palace enjoying the hospitality of the sixteen-year-old Walter, fifth Duke of Buccleuch, under whose roof he had preferred to stay for the duration of his Scottish visit rather than at the royal palace of his own Stuart forebears in the Old Town of Edinburgh: Holyroodhouse. From Dalkeith, the King went in the afternoon to nearby Melville Castle to partake of the further hospitality of Robert Dundas, second Viscount Melville. See Prebble, *The King's Jaunt*, pp. 330-32. In his admirable

discussion of 'Nationalism and Stylistic Debate', the American scholar Barry Bergdoll even insists that 'to launch this Doric enterprise George IV donned a tartan kilt!' See *European Architecture 1750-1890*, Chapter 5, pp. 152-54. Beaton (*The Greek Revolution of 1821*, p. 54) actually anticipates the laying of the foundation stone by a year, to make it 1821: a pardonable lapsus when so much talk of building an Edinburgh Parthenon was abroad, especially as he goes on to observe that, unlike the Greek revolution, the project was soon abandoned.

20 See the circular letter from the Sub-Committee of the General Committee of Subscribers to the National Monument, 25 December 1821, for instance in the example in NLS, MS.10958, f. 304. The text of this document opens by making reference back to the meeting on 18 June that same year.

21 McKean, *Edinburgh. An Illustrated Architectural Guide*, p. 85. See also McKee, *Calton Hill*, also at p. 85 with notes 47-49, albeit the description of the arch is not accurate. The drawings by Gillespie—said by McKee to be lost—are in an album in NLS forming part of Acc.14300 (Robert Naismith Collection).

22 See Anon., *Report of the Proceedings of a Numerous and a Respectable Meeting ... with a View to the Erection of National Monument ...*; Brown, *Rax Me That Buik*, p. 85; and Gifford, pp. 46-47.

23 See Glendinning, MacInnes and MacKechnie, *History of Scottish Architecture*, p. 189: '... images of Greek antiquity ... made an enormous impression, displacing Rome as the main inspiration for a national classical grandeur.' Glendinning elsewhere sums up the issue succinctly: 'The classical expression of the "national" changed from Rome to Greece ... many Scots saw Edinburgh as a pure, intellectual Athens to London's powerful but decadent Rome.': see *Architecture of Scottish Government*, p. 196, cf. p. 96.

24 Cleghorn 1, p. 4.

25 Emily Robertson, *Letters and Papers of Andrew Robertson*, p. 280.

26 Robertson, *The Parthenon, Adapted...*, p. 32.

27 *Letters and Papers of Andrew Robertson*, p. 282, quoting a letter of 24 July 1816.

28 Robertson, *The Parthenon, Adapted...*, pp. 26-27.

29 Cleghorn 2, 'Equestrian Statue of George IV in Front of the Parthenon', pp. 324-26.

30 Beattie, *Scotland Illustrated*, I, p. 117.

31 The terms occur in, for instance, the circular letter of the Sub-Committee of the General Committee of Subscribers to the National Monument, 24 January 1822, of which an example is NLS, MS. 15973, ff. 12-13. See 'Edinburgh as Athens', p. 3.

32 Lowenthal, *The Past is a Foreign Country*, p. 264.

33 Alison 1819 A, p. 384.

34 Alison 1819 B, p. 139.

35 Examples of these circular letters from the Sub-Committee of the General Committee of Subscribers to the National Monument are to be found in their different states in NLS, MSS. 638, ff. 9-10; 10958, ff. 304-5; and 15973, ff. 12-13. Sibbald may very well also have read the 'Address to the Citizens of Edinburgh' by Sir John Sinclair of Ulbster, Bt, statistician and agriculturist, published in *The Morning Post* of 20 November 1821. The context was 'His Majesty's expected visit to Scotland', which did indeed take place the next summer. In seeking, as it were, to summon up the blood of the citizens in anticipation of this potentially great event, Sinclair took it upon himself to remind them just what their city stood for, and what it might be. Mentioning

the proposed erection of 'The Parthenon' on Calton Hill—'so long anxiously wished for' as a 'favourite national object'—he reminded them that their city 'has been called the modern Athens. Its situation is, in some respects, similar to the ancient metropolis of Attica; and, in its devotion to literature, it bears a great resemblance to that celebrated city.' I am indebted to Dr Joe Rock for this reference.

36 Haynes, *An Historical Guide to the Sculptures of the Parthenon*, p. 5.

37 Whether this unknown writer could actually have ascended the Acropolis—if indeed this is what he was saying—in the prevailing military and political situation in Greece in 1831 must be open to some doubt. See 'An Assistant Surgeon in the Royal Navy', 'Letters from the Mediterranean', Letter IV (25 September 1831), p. 213.

38 Ewbank and Browne, *Picturesque Views of Edinburgh*, p. 210.

39 Williams, *Travels*, II, p. 274.

40 Many of these points were made eloquently in Alison 1819 A, and by 'R' in 'RPNM'.

41 Interestingly, Sibbald casts no aspersions on the architecture, or suitability for its site, of the Nelson Monument. As a naval man, he seems to be been well satisfied with it. In this, his view (or, rather, lack of any contrary opinion) is in marked contrast with that expressed almost universally by other contemporary commentators.

42 Sibbald greatly simplifies the extremely complex nature of the Erechtheion and the deities and heroes to whom the building was actually dedicated. Poseidon was honoured there, certainly, but it is entirely wrong to suggest that the temple was his alone.

43 Sibbald is evidently thinking of the area occupied by the Calton Hill Gardens, and Royal, Carlton and Regent Terraces round the eastern and south-eastern flanks of the hill. The Hill of the Pnyx was the meeting-place of the Ekklesia, or assembly, in ancient Athens.

44 The Theseion, as it was known (and is still popularly known), which stands above the Agora, is now recognised as the temple of Hephaistos.

45 The Olympieion, a vast temple which took many centuries to complete: the Roman Emperor Hadrian eventually achieved the task.

46 Mount Anchesmos, as a descriptive geographical name of antiquity, is generally reckoned to equate with the 'Lykabettos' of today's Athenian townscape. See Leake, *The Topography of Athens*, pp. 68-69 for a statement of the difficulty of being completely sure which names in ancient usage actually applied to features observable in the early nineteenth century. See also 'Edinburgh as Athens' note 44. To say, as Sibbald does, that Lykabettos is remarkably similar to the Castle Rock of Edinburgh, betrays his wish to identify the Calton Hill with the Acropolis. To do so, he had to find another feature for comparison, thus ignoring the much more obvious similarity between Acropolis and Castle.

47 In antiquity, the Ilissos (canalised early, and now largely culverted and invisible) flowed south of the Acropolis. It was a tributary of the River Kephisos.

48 This feature lies north of the Acropolis, outside the city wall.

49 Sibbald must in fact mean south-east; but one can forgive his error in this welter of distorted topography and in view of the general eccentricity of his notions.

50 This passage echoes the observations of Edward Dodwell, *A Classical and Picturesque Tour through Greece*, I, p. 344, and of Williams, *Travels*, II, pp. 301-2.

51 Dodwell, *Tour*, I, p. 291.

52 *Ibid.*, I, pp. 322-24.
53 Williams, *Travels*, II, pp. 321-23.
54 Williams, *Travels*, II, p. 382.
55 'OROP', p. 306.
56 *NER*, p. 601.
57 See Crook, *The Greek Revival*, RIBA Drawings Series, pp. 44, 23; and Crook, *The Greek Revival: Neo-Classical Attitudes*, p. 104. Crook also writes (*The Age of Neo-Classicism*, p. 612) of W. H. Playfair that he was 'brought up in "the Athens of the North"', where later he would be responsible for the design of the monuments adorning 'Edinburgh's Acropolis, Calton Hill'—*sic*, and without further explanation of how the one Scottish locality was turned into another, Greek one.

Chapter 2: The Northern Athens in the Eye

1 John Brown Patterson, *On the National Character of the Athenians*, pp. 56-57.
2 Matthews, *Diary of An Invalid*, p. 350.
3 Galt, *The Last of the Lairds*, p. 64.
4 [Anon.], *Memoirs of the House of Brandenburg*, p. 243.
5 See Schinkel, *The English Journey*, pp. 148-56 for Schinkel's account of Edinburgh.
6 Shepherd and Britton, *Modern Athens!*, p. 8.
7 NLS, MS. 3108, f. 37v.
8 'Londoner', p. 268.
9 Byron, *Complete Poetical Works*, I, p. 431 ('Hints from Horace').
10 NLS, Acc. 12676.
11 Beattie, *Scotland Illustrated*, I, p. 88 and note.
12 Gilpin had indeed drawn North Bridge very much as if it were a structure from classical antiquity. It hardly appears as if it were in Edinburgh, and seems more at home in the Roman Campagna. See Gilpin, *Observations, Relative Chiefly to Picturesque Beauty*, I, p. 63 and the aquatint view of the bridge opposite. Alexander Campbell, *A Journey from Edinburgh*, I, p. 3 also suggested that North Bridge was strikingly like a Roman aqueduct.
13 Stoddart, *Remarks on Local Scenery and Manners*, I, pp. 48, 54. Henry Tresham RA is not in fact known to have been in Greece, though he did spend years in Italy and also travelled in Sicily.
14 Carr, *Caledonian Sketches*, p. 47.
15 Scott, *Provincial Antiquities and Picturesque Scenery*, I, p. [67].
16 *Ibid.*, II, pp. [114]-15.
17 Batty, *Select Views of Some of the Principal Cities*, notes on plates 1, 3 and 4.
18 Stoddart, *Remarks on Local Scenery and Manners*, I, pp. 39, 78-79.
19 Lettice, *Letters on a Tour through various parts of Scotland*, p. 510.
20 *Ibid.*, pp. 511, 514, 525, 523.
21 Grant, *Old and New Edinburgh*, I, p. 2; II, p. 114.
22 See, for example, McWilliam, *Scottish Townscape*, p. 118; Daiches, *Edinburgh*, p. 195; *B o S Edinburgh*, p. 433; and Royle, *Mainstream Companion to Scottish Literature*, p. 13. Duncan still suggests this in *Scott's Shadow*, p. 14.
23 Stuart was responsible for the text and also for the general picturesque and topographical views; Revett for the measured drawings. *The Antiquities of Athens*, vol I, has a title-page dated 1762 but publication in London was in fact in January 1763. The second volume, containing the major temples of Athens,

and with a title-page dated 1787, actually appeared in January 1790. For publication details see Harris, *British Architectural Books and Writers*, pp. 443, 446 and 448.

24 *Ordnance Gazetteer of Scotland*, II, pp. 467-68.

25 *Black's Picturesque Tourist of Scotland*, p. 16, note.

26 Chambers, *Walks in Edinburgh*, p. 272.

27 *Life and Remains of Edward Daniel Clarke*, p. 232.

28 *Autobiography of John Galt*, I, p. 145.

29 *Life and Remains of Edward Daniel Clarke*, pp. 501-2.

30 Clarke, *Travels in Various Countries*, VI, p. 378.

31 Alison 1819 A, p. 385. See also 'Traveller', p.100. Gifford still adhered to the erroneous belief that Clarke had been responsible for a remark he did not in fact make: see Gifford, p. 48.

32 Clarke, *Travels*, VII, p. 77.

33 *Journal of Sir Walter Scott*, p. 101.

34 *SAHA*, no. 204.

35 Alison, *Autobiography*, I, pp. 154-56. Alison died in 1867. The text of his memoirs was compiled between 1851 and 1862, but mostly early in this period.

36 Alison 1819 B, p. 141.

37 *Peter's Letters to His Kinsfolk*, II, Letter L, pp. 281-82, 283-85.

38 Crook, *The Greek Revival. Neo-Classical Attitudes*, p. 104. Rowan, 'The Athens of the North Explored', p. 1052 is incorrect in saying that Williams first used the phrase in his *Select Views in Greece*: nowhere in that publication is the term used.

39 For this and the following statement see St Clair, *Lord Elgin and the Marbles*, p. 211.

40 *Ibid.*, p. 273. St Clair may have taken too literally the statement made by Williams in the Preface to the first volume of his *Travels*, p. xi. Williams here stated that his intention in his travel letters was 'to select' from all he had observed abroad 'what might be ornamental or useful at home', and so lend itself to 'any practical advantage, —particularly in the embellishment of our northern capital.'

41 Williams, *Travels*, II, p. 288.

42 *Ibid.*, II, p. 289n.

43 Galt, *Letters from the Levant*, p. 113.

44 Williams, *Travels*, II, p. 289n.

45 *Ibid.*, II, p. 384.

46 *Ibid.*, II, p. 382.

47 Galt, *Letters from the Levant*, pp. 113-14.

48 *Ibid.*, pp. 119, 121.

49 'C.', 'The Calton Hill', p. 145.

50 Gibson, *Select Views in Edinburgh*, Plate IV and letterpress p. 12.

51 See 'Additional Particulars Touching the Communication to be Formed from Princes Street to the Calton Hill', p. 405, with plate (following p. 408) entitled 'Elevation of the Approach from Princes Street by Wellington Bridge to the Calton Hill'. A coloured aquatint of the view is in Capital Collections, no. 9194. Remarkably, Butchart considered the building in the distance to be 'a view of the High School with its Grecian pillars'—which is an impossibility on several grounds. See Butchart, *Prints & Drawings of Edinburgh*, p. 35.

52 Gibson, *Select Views in Edinburgh*, Plates I and II with letterpress pp. 5 and 7.

53 Williams, *Travels*, II, p. 419.

54 *Ibid.*, II, pp. 419.

55 'Traveller', p.100.
56 Williams, *Travels*, II, p. 420.
57 Williams in Robert Chambers, *Walks in Edinburgh*, pp. 273-75.
58 *Ibid.*, p. 274.
59 *Ibid.*, p. 274.
60 *Ibid.*, pp. 274-75. These apparent topographical parallels and similarities evidently embedded themselves in the subconsciousness of writers on Edinburgh. In 1926 James Bone (a Glaswegian) paraphrased them unacknowledged, while managing to introduce an error or two: see Bone, *Perambulator in Edinburgh*, p. 20.
61 Williams in Chambers, *Walks*, pp. 274-75.
62 Mure, *Journal of a Tour in Greece*, pp. 56, 92n.
63 *Letters of John Stuart Blackie to his Wife*, pp. 132-33; cf. Stoddart, *John Stuart Blackie*, I, p. 289.
64 Stoddart, *John Stuart Blackie*, I, p. 290; *Letters of John Stuart Blackie*, pp. 133, 136-37.
65 *Handbook for Travellers in Scotland*, third revised edition (London 1873), pp. 44, 42.
66 Mitchell, pp. 9-10.
67 Williams, *Travels*, II, p. 419; Chambers, *Walks*, p. 275.
68 'Edinburgh as Athens', p. 8.
69 *Antiquities of Athens*, Vol. I, Chapter III, plate I.
70 *Walks*, p. 273.
71 On the visual connection between Athens and Edinburgh, and the shared geographical character of the two places, see Naik and Stewart, 'The Hellenization of Edinburgh', p. 368. See also the images reproduced in Edina-Athena, pp. 17-18.
72 See Edina-Athena, pp. 19-20.
73 *Select Views in Greece*. On Williams, see Joe Rock, 'Hugh William Williams, and especially Rock's excellent website http://sites.google.com/site/hughwilliamwilliams.
74 See Cosh, *Edinburgh. The Golden Age*, pp. 553-54 for this perfectly understandable, though incorrect, assumption.
75 *Catalogue of Views in Greece ... by Hugh William Williams*. Catalogues cost sixpence.
76 Anon, 'On Mr Williams's Exhibition of Water-colour Drawings', p. 239. The writer noted, however, that one 'brown sketch' of a Doric temple in particular—though reminiscent in tone of the 'Liber Veritatis' of Claude, or the 'Liber Studiorum' of Turner—was nevertheless 'emblematic of the wane of Grecian history', and so conveyed a melancholy thought (p. 241).
77 *Collected Works of William Hazlitt*, 9 (1903), 'On Williams's Views in Greece', pp. 324-26. The review appeared in *The London Magazine* in May 1822.
78 *Walks*, p. 272.
79 Williams, *Catalogue of Views...* (1822), p. 5, no. 7.
80 *Ibid.*, p. 12, no. 39.
81 Most unusually, on this occasion Sir Howard Colvin misread the evidence: see Colvin, p. 814. The mistake has been perpetuated by subsequent writers taking their information from this source.
82 Nisbet, *Catalogue of the Valuable Cabinet of Pictures ... of the late W. H. Playfair, etc.* Colvin actually cites the sale catalogue of Playfair's library (NLS, K.R. 16. f. 5(1)) rather than the sale catalogue of his pictures—which is K.R. 16. f. 5(2). In contemporary documentation, MacBean is also sometimes spelled 'Macbean'.

Chapter 3: The Modern Athens in the Mind

1 Daiches, *Paradox of Scottish Culture*, p. 73, cf. pp. 74 and 77.
2 Finlayson and Simpson, 'History of the Library 1580-1710', in *Edinburgh University Library 1580-1980*, ed. Guild and Law, p. 45.
3 Horn, *Short History of the University of Edinburgh*, p. [13].
4 See McHaffie, *Greek Secrets Revealed*, pp. 32-36.
5 Finlayson and Simpson, 'History of the Library...', p. 45.
6 See Brown, *Building for Books: The Architectural Evolution of the Advocates' Library*, pp. 1, 16. The Strangford Shield (now in the British Museum), a Roman marble reproduction of the shield held by Athena in Phidias's great statue in the Parthenon, had come to Britain from Athens in the 1820s.
7 See *Account of the Fair Intellectual-Club*, p. [2], 11, 32.
8 *Edinburgh Miscellany: Consisting of Original Poems ...* pp. 120, 122.
9 Gordon, *Itinerarium Septentrionale*, Preface. See also the letter of Gordon to Sir John Clerk of Penicuik, 12 February 1726, NRS, GD18/ 5023/ 3/ 17 where he contrasts attitudes to learning and scholarship in London with those in Scotland, much to the discredit of the latter. See also Brown, 'Precarious Preferment in Apollo's Favourite Residence', pp. 50 and 60.
10 *Poems of Allan Ramsay*, I, pp. 19, 21, 'The City of Edinburgh's Address to the Country'; *Works of Allan Ramsay*, IV, p. 262, 'On the Royal Company of Scottish Archers'; Brown, *Poet & Painter: Allan Ramsay, Father and Son*, p. 24.
11 Ramsay, *Poems*, Preface, p. vii.
12 See, for example, Galloway, *The Loyal Albany Museum*, pp. 31-32, 'Allan Ramsay's Study'. Galloway's is the line on 'Parnassus'; he also compares *The Gentle Shepherd* rather too favourably with 'the din o' Homer's strains'.
13 See Brydall, *Art in Scotland*, pp. 110-11, and, more generally, Irwin, *Scottish Painters at Home and Abroad*, pp. 83-84; also Smart, *Allan Ramsay*, pp. 15-16.
14 Campbell, *A Journey from Edinburgh*, II, p. 327.
15 *Ibid.*, pp. 332-33.
16 *Ibid.*, pp. 337, 340-41.
17 Brown, 'Robert Adam's Drawings: Edinburgh's Loss, London's Gain', p. 29.
18 [Gilbert Elliot], *Proposals for carrying on certain Public Works*, p. 5.
19 *Ibid.*, pp. 7-8, 10.
20 *Ibid.*, p. 32.
21 Stillman, *English Neo-classical Architecture*, I, p. 177, places the *Proposals* in the wider context of British urban development.
22 *Letters of David Hume*, I, p. 255.
23 *Ibid.*, I, p. 151.
24 See Stewart, *Dissertation, Part Second*, p. 452.
25 Quoted in Kerr, *Memoirs of William Smellie*, II, p. 252.
26 NLS, MS. 11015, f. 106v, 29 July 1761. See Sher, *Church and University in the Scottish Enlightenment*, p. 3. The Irishman Thomas Sheridan had famously come to Edinburgh to give elocution lessons to the Scottish literati, anxious to speak the King's English correctly.
27 Sher, *Enlightenment & the Book*, p. 67.
28 Quoted in McElroy, *Scotland's Age of Improvement*, p. 57.
29 On the Select Society see, most recently, Brown, '"A National Concern"', pp. 79-90.
30 NRS, GD331/5/22, Allan Ramsay to Sir Alexander Dick of Prestonfield, 31 January 1762; Brown, *Poet & Painter*, p. 36. It was first printed in Forbes, *Curiosities of a Scots Charta Chest*, pp. 198-99.

31 See Crawford, *On Glasgow and Edinburgh*, p. 27 for an example of just such confusion.

32 Brown, *Poet & Painter*, 40-41; Brown, 'Pamphlets of Allan Ramsay the Younger', pp. 67-71; Smart, *Allan Ramsay*, pp. 121-22, 139-48, 181.

33 Stuart & Revett, *Antiquities of Athens*, I, Preface, p. iii.

34 For thoughts along similar lines see Daiches, *Paradox of Scottish Culture*, p. 69 and, more recently, Allan, 'The Age of Pericles in the Modern Athens', p. 397. Allan's excellent article provides a view of the period, and the meaning of fifth-century Athens in later eighteenth- and early nineteenth-century Edinburgh, that is penetrating and rewarding on many levels. On Craig's plans see Fraser, 'A Reassessment of Craig's New Town Plans'.

35 *Isocrates*, edited and translated by Norlin, I (1928), pp. 148-49; 142-43: *Panegyricus*, 50; 40.

36 Gillies, *History of Ancient Greece*, I, p. 409.

37 *Ibid.*, pp. 410-11, 413.

38 John Knox, *A View of the British Empire, More Especially Scotland*, II, pp. 583, 578, 580-81.

39 St John, *Mary, Queen of Scots*, p. 6.

40 Heron, *Observations Made in a Journey*, II, p. 503.

41 *Ibid.*, pp. 504-5.

42 Brown, '"Spectator of the Busy Scene"', p. 162. The line, 'The Feast of Reason and the Flow of Soul', is in fact of Roman rather than Greek inspiration. It comes from Alexander Pope's *Imitations of Horace*, specifically from his 'First Satire of the Second Book Horace' (1733), line 130. As we shall see, both Mrs Grant of Laggan and John Galt also employed parts of the line to catch the spirit of an 'Athenian' Edinburgh.

43 Faujas de Saint-Fond, *Travels in England, Scotland and the Hebrides*, II, p. 225.

44 Mawman, *An Excursion to the Highlands of Scotland*, pp. 97-98; 100-1.

45 [MacNeill], *Town Fashions, or Modern Manners Delineated*, pp. ii, v, 3 and 78.

46 [Louis Simond], *Journal of Tour and Residence in Great Britain*, II, p. 50. On Simond, see *The Journal of Sir Walter Scott*, p. 500.

47 Simond, *Journal of a Tour*, I, pp. 375-76.

48 Andrew Lang, *Life and Letters of John Gibson Lockhart*, I, pp. 95-96, Lockhart to Jonathan Christie, 29 November 1815.

49 Necker de Saussure, *Travels in Scotland*, pp. viii, 24.

50 *Ibid.*, pp. 29, 100.

51 SNG, D 4250.

52 See Brown, *Rax Me That Buik*, p. 70.

53 Galloway, *Loyal Albany Museum*, pp. 11, 13.

54 Anon. ['Scotus'], *Letter to the Lord Provost, on the Mischievous Tendency of a Scheme for Abolishing the High School*, pp. 2, 22-23: copy in Edinburgh University Library, Research Collections, press-mark T.a.23/7.

55 See the article, 'High School: New Academy of Edinburgh', extracted from an unnamed magazine and with page numbers double-printed: copy is in NLS, shelf-mark Ry.IV.e.4(19), p. 527* [*sic*].

56 Edinburgh Town Council, *Address ... on the subject of the New Buildings for the High School*: copy in NLS, Ry. IV. e.4(18).

57 *Letter to the Lord Provost, on the Mischievous Tendency...*, p. 6.

58 On the High School and Academy buildings see Watters, 'Καλοι κ᾽αγαθοι (The Beautiful and the Good)'.

59 Stoddart, *John Stuart Blackie*, I. p. 143.

60 *Ibid.*, pp. 304-5.

61 Sir James Crichton-Browne, *Victorian Jottings*, p. 183.
62 *Scotland Illustrated*, p. 101.
63 *Ibid.*, p. 102.
64 On this see Davie, *The Democratic Intellect*. For Edinburgh's position about 1840 as a declining 'Modern Athens' see Davie, pp. 261, 255.
65 Beattie, *Scotland Illustrated*, p. 89.
66 *Ibid.*, p. 119.
67 Alison 1819 A, p. 384.
68 Anon., *Letter to the Directors and Members of the Institution for the Encouragement of the Fine Arts*, p. 10.
69 *Memoir and Correspondence of Mrs Grant of Laggan*, II, pp. 214-15, Letter ccix, 11 November 1818.
70 Williams, *Travels*, II, p. 256; see *SAHA*, no. 204.

Chapter 4: The Athens of the North in Stone

1 See Rowan, 'The Athens of the North Explored', p. 1052.
2 Campbell, *A Journey from Edinburgh*, II, p. 337.
3 NLS, MS. 963, ff. 51v-52.
4 *Ibid.*, f. 53v; see *SAHA*, no. 201.
5 Rowan, 'The Athens of the North Explored', p. 1052; Lowrey, 'From Caesarea to Athens', p. 136.
6 McMillan, 'The City of Edinburgh: Landscape and Building Stone', p. 129.
7 Alison 1819 B, p. 144.
8 'Cursory Remarks on Grecian & Gothic Architecture', p. 198.
9 Cleghorn 2, p. 79.
10 Gilpin, *Observations, Relative Chiefly to Picturesque Beauty*, I, p. 63.
11 Skrine, *Three Successive Tours*, p. 65.
12 Arnot, *History of Edinburgh*, p. 328; Campbell, *A Journey from Edinburgh*, II, pp. 157; Carlyle, *Topographical Dictionary of Scotland*, II, s.v. Leith, South; Storer, *Views in Edinburgh and its Vicinity*, I, [f. 23]. For the sources, see Brown, 'David Hume's Tomb: A Roman mausoleum by Robert Adam'.
13 Campbell, *Journey from Edinburgh*, II, p. 191; Heron, *Observations made in a Journey*, I, p. 15. Cririe, *Scottish Scenery*, p. 4. See also Andrew, 'St Bernard's Well and the Water of Leith'.
14 Sinclair, *Statistical Account of Scotland*, 1 (Linlithgowshire), pp. 235-36; quoted, with some changes, by Walter Scott, *Provincial Antiquities*, II, p. [199].
15 *Stranger's Guide to Edinburgh*, sixth edition, p. 203.
16 *Scottish Tourist, and Itinerary*, pp. 10-11.
17 Necker de Saussure, *Travels in Scotland*, p. 29.
18 *Walks*, p. 213.
19 *Antiquities of Athens*, vol. I, Chapter II, Plate III.
20 *Modern Athens!*, pp. 61-62.
21 Carr, *Caledonian Sketches*, p. 90.
22 *Ibid.*, p. 189.
23 On Duddingston and its sources in Stuart and Revett, *Antiquities of Athens*, see Macaulay, *Classical Country House in Scotland*, p. 174, from which the quotation comes.
24 Carr, *Caledonian Sketches*, pp. 222-23.
25 See Colvin, p. 823.
26 On the various schemes see Crook, 'Broomhall, Fife', p. 70.

27 See Smith, 'Lord Elgin and his Collection', p. 316. Cf William St Clair, *Lord Elgin and the Marbles*, p. 273, who states that Elgin 'lent his drawings of the Theseum to the architect of the new Royal Observatory which was to be built in Edinburgh.' But St Clair does not say when this was, nor offer any opinion as to who the architect in question is supposed to have been. Naik and Stewart ('Hellenization of Edinburgh', p. 371 and note 27) assume—possibly incorrectly—that the drawings in question had been *made* by Benjamin West, rather than that West (as is perhaps more likely, in the context) was merely the intermediary in sending north a parcel of existing drawings by hands other than his. But Naik and Stewart further rightly question the utility of dispatching to Edinburgh architectural drawings of the Theseion when measured drawings of the temple were already published and available. (This would have been in the third volume of *The Antiquities of Athens*). Their doubts lead them to suggest, plausibly, that the drawings West was to convey were of the *sculpture* of the Theseion, suggesting that such drawings were by West himself, an eminent figure draughtsman. Whether or not this is in fact correct, there would not seem to have been much point in sending drawings of sculpture either; for surely it is most unlikely that—purely on grounds of cost alone—any observatory building designed for Edinburgh would have borne sculptural decoration.
28 For an unexplained suggestion that Stark prepared a pre-Playfair design see *B o S Edinburgh*, p. 435, note.
29 NLS, MS. 3108, f. 9.
30 For an image and description of the porticoes of Rosneath, see Gow, *Scotland's Lost Houses*, pp. 116-17 and 119.
31 NLS, MS. 3108, f. 9.
32 *Ibid.*, ff. 54v, 59v.
33 *Ibid.*, f. 41.
34 Mawman, *Excursion to the Highlands of Scotland*, p. 103.
35 Stoddart, *Remarks on Local Scenery and Manners*, I, p. 72.
36 NLS, MS. 3108, f. 41.
37 Stark, *Picture of Edinburgh*, pp. 436-37.
38 *Ibid.*, p. 437.
39 'Additional Particulars touching the Communication to be formed from Princes Street to the Calton Hill', p. 405.
40 *Peter's Letters to his Kinsfolk*, I. p. 183, Letter XV, 'Mr Playfair'.
41 Playfair's drawing has several times been reproduced, with comment on the Romantic ruins but without tracing the source or these or, more particularly, of the figures. McKee describes the figures (*Calton Hill*, p. 112 and Plate 5.14) as 'classically swathed ... an oriental male smoking a hookah', although she fails to spot the borrowing from Stuart and Revett. The *staffage* is taken from *Antiquities of Athens*, Vol. III (London 1794), Chapter V, Plate I. For the biggest and best reproduction, but again without recognition of source, see McCall Smith, *A Work of Beauty*, p. 215.
42 *NER*, p. 577.
43 *Ibid.*, p. 577.
44 *Ibid.*, p. 585.
45 *Stranger's Guide*, sixth edition, p. 212.
46 'Londoner', p. 272.
47 Elmes, 'History of Architecture in Great Britain', p. 338.
48 *Ibid.*, pp. 338-39.
49 Stark, *Picture of Edinburgh*, p. 137.
50 Anon., *Letter to the Right Honourable the Lord Provost ... In Answer to a*

Letter … by 'A Builder'. By a Plain Honest Man, p. 30 note. A copy in NLS, Ry.1.1. 8(6), has the name 'David Bridges' inscribed on the title page beneath the printed pseudonym. Bridges, a clothier in Bank Street, had interests in the arts.

51 Gibson, *Select Views in Edinburgh…*, Plate IV and letterpress description p. 12.

52 *New Picture of Edinburgh for 1818*, p. 79.

53 *Letter to the Right Honourable the Lord Provost … By A Builder*, p. 20.

54 *A Letter to the Right Honourable the Lord Provost … By a Plain Honest Man*, p. 30, note.

55 Thomson, 'Art and Architecture…'. III, pt I, p. 51.

56 Cleghorn 2, p. 99.

57 Cleghorn 4, I, p. 178.

58 *Observations by Alexander Trotter … in Illustration of his Modified Plan of a Communication*, pp. 6 and 10.

59 *Scotland Illustrated*, I, p. 103.

60 *Topographical, Statistical, and Historical Gazetteer of Scotland*, I, p. 442.

61 *Picturesque Tourist of Scotland*, first edition, p. 41; second edition, pp. 45-46.

62 *Handbook for Travellers in Scotland*, third edition (1873), p. 48.

63 *Old and New Edinburgh*, I, p. 123.

64 For the scornful description see *B o S Edinburgh*, p. 183.

65 [Charles Kelsall], *A Letter from Athens, Addressed to a Friend in England* (London 1812), Notes, p. 40. On Kelsall, see David Watkin in *ODNB*.

66 *Letter from Athens*, p. 41. For Kelsall, the finest examples of a revived Greek style were to be seen in Paris, though London and Cambridge displayed some admirable specimens.

67 *Ionian Antiquities*, Vol. I, Chapter III, Plate VII.

68 Vol. I, Chapter IV, Plate VI).

69 Cf. *B o S Edinburgh*, p. 443.

70 *B o S Edinburgh*, pp. 118, 121.

71 *Ibid.*, p. 462.

72 *Modern Athens!*, pp. 48-49.

73 *Ibid.*, p. 43.

74 Joe Rock, *Thomas Hamilton Architect* is a valuable and well-illustrated survey of Hamilton's achievement. Ian Fisher's relatively brief essay in *Scottish Pioneers of the Greek Revival*, pp. 37-42, is slighter but judicious.

75 'C.', 'The Calton Hill', p. 147.

76 Colvin, p. 474.

77 On Burn, see the long and detailed essay by David Walker in *Scottish Pioneers of the Greek Revival*, pp. 3-35.

78 Rowan, 'The Athens of the North Explored', p. 1054.

79 See Colvin, pp. 185-86 for a very balanced assessment.

80 Rowan, 'Bicentenary of a Classical City. Georgian Edinburgh - I', p. 956.

81 Gow, 'Playfair: A Northern Athenian', pp. 37-38.

82 Robert Fleming Gourlay, *The Mound Improvement …*, p. 14.

83 My opinion as to a more likely possible source of the Monument is at variance with those of others: see *B o S Edinburgh*, p. 436 for the dubious suggestion of the Lion Tomb of Knidos as inspiration. The Lion Tomb does not seem to have been known at the time Playfair designed his uncle's monument.

84 *SAHA*, no. 188, quoting NLS, MS. 9704, f. 18.

85 NLS, MS. 638, f. 134, 30 June 1829; *SAHA*, no. 190, quoting NLS, MS. 9704, f. 146v.

86 Gow, 'William Henry Playfair', *Scottish Pioneers of the Greek Revival*, p. 46. Gow's essay is an admirable assessment of Playfair in all his aspects.

87 *Noctes Ambrosianae by the Late John Wilson*, IV, pp. 88-89. On Hamilton's work for the Blackwood family at 43-45 George Street, see Rock, *Thomas Hamilton Architect*), pp. 48-9.

88 NLS, MS. 638, ff. 131-32; and *SAHA*, no. 204.

89 NLS, MS. 638, ff. 132. The reference is to Hamilton Square, Birkenhead, by Graham, of 1825.

90 NLS, MS. 638, f. 116, Williams to Cockerell, 6 February 1828.

91 NLS, MS. 9704, f. 92; and *SAHA*, no. 189.

92 NLS, MS. 9704, f. 28; and *SAHA*, no. 261.

93 *SAHA*, nos 184 and 207. See also Colvin, p. 977; and Gomme and Walker, *Architecture of Glasgow*, p. 70.

94 *Memorials*, p. 279.

95 Schinkel, *English Journey*, pp. 150, 154.

96 The fullest treatment is John Gifford's posthumously published 'The National Monument of Scotland'. Detailed though this is, several citations and references are incorrect, and some sources are untapped. Other significant articles include J. E. Cookson, 'Scotland's National Monument', which is a largely political view of evolving architectural taste. There are three articles by Marc Fehlmann: '"A Striking Proof of Scotland's Pride"'; 'A Building from which Derived "All that is Good"'; and 'As Greek as it Gets: British Attempts to Recreate the Parthenon'. These last two are particularly interesting, although there is a great deal of duplication and overlap in all three publications. See also the excellent recent article by Matteo Zaccarini, 'The Athens of the North? Scotland and the National Struggle for the Parthenon'.

97 McKee, *Calton Hill*. This beautifully illustrated book is, regrettably, greatly let down by the large number of errors in both text and notes.

98 Alison 1819 A, pp. 383-84. The word 'not' in the second of Alison's sentences cited here seems misplaced, but the quotation is given exactly as in his printed text.

99 *Ibid.*, pp. 384-85, 382.

100 *Ibid.*, p. 385.

101 *Ibid.*, pp. 386-87.

102 Alison, *Autobiography*, I, p. 175.

103 *Ibid.*, p. 219.

104 On Greek temple-building effort see Dinsmoor, *Architecture of Ancient Greece*, p. 171.

105 Alison, *Autobiography*, I, pp. 218-20.

106 NLS, MS. 639, p. 10.

107 *Modern Athens!*, pp. 36-37, with plate showing the line of sight from the quarry to the New Town and Calton Hill. See also McMillan, Gillanders and Fairhurst, *Building Stones of Edinburgh*, pp. 118-23 and Plate 1.

108 Boardman, *Parthenon and its Sculptures*, pp. 28. See also Carpenter, *The Architects of the Parthenon*, p. 91.

109 Galt, *Letters from the Levant*, pp. 105-6.

110 Boardman, *Parthenon and its Sculptures*, p. 26.

111 See Cook, *The Elgin Marbles*, p. 18.

112 Gourlay, *The Mound Improvement*, p. 16.

113 Robertson, *National Monument*, pp. iii-iv.

114 Fehlmann, 'A Building from which Derived "All that is Good"'; see also Fehlmann, 'As Greek as it Gets: British Attempts to Recreate the Parthenon', especially pp. 355, 366-67.

115 Alison 1819 A, p. 384.

116 McKean, p. 152; cf. McKean, *Edinburgh. An Illustrated Architectural Guide*, p. 103.
117 Allan Massie, *Edinburgh*, p. 131.
118 See, for instance, the reports of the National Monument Committee of 1828 in which mention is made of the 'exact facsimile' to be constructed, but starting with the west front: NLS, MS. 352.
119 NLS, MS. 638, f. 105, 23 October 1826.
120 Alison, *Autobiography*, I, p. 219.
121 NLS, MS.638, f. 133.
122 'RPNM', pp. 509-12.
123 *Ibid.*, p. 510.
124 *Ibid.*, pp. 510-11.
125 Alison 1819 B, p. 146.
126 'On the Proposed Monument for Lord Melville. See also Godard Desmarest, 'The Melville Monument' which, however, fails either to note or draw on Alison's article.
127 'Monument for Lord Melville', pp. 563-64.
128 'Traveller', p. 100.
129 *Ibid.*, p. 105.
130 'OROP', p. 305.
131 *Ibid.*, p. 307.
132 *Ibid.*, p. 308.
133 *Ibid.*, p. 308-9.
134 Cohen, *passim*.
135 NLS, MS. 638, f. 22, Williams to Cockerell, 29 December 1822.
136 NLS, MS. 638, f. 35, Brewster to Cockerell, 18 March 1823.
137 Alison 1823.
138 See Michie, *An Enlightenment Tory*, pp. 134-35.
139 Alison 1823, p. 133.
140 *Ibid.*, p. 133.
141 *Ibid.*, p. 135.
142 *Ibid.*, pp. 140-41.
143 Fehlmann, '"A Striking Proof of Scotland's Pride"', p. 42.
144 *Ibid.*, p. 42. My quotations appended to Fehlmann's statement are from Alison 1823, pp. 137 and 138.
145 John Fleming, *Robert Adam and his Circle in Edinburgh and Rome*, p. 258, citing (but mistaking the context of) NRS, GD18/ 4852, Robert Adam to James Adam, 5 September 1758.
146 *NER*, pp. 563, 567.
147 *Ibid.*, pp. 561-62.
148 *Ibid.*, p. 563. The Tron Church is an interesting, elegant but hobbled mongrel of the seventeenth and eighteenth centuries, part 'Gothic survival', part vernacular Dutch-ish classical. Gillespie's Hospital, since demolished, was designed by Robert Burn in castellated style, 1800-01.
149 *Ibid.*, p. 564.
150 *Ibid.*, p. 566.
151 *Ibid.*, pp. 568-69.
152 *Ibid.*, p. 571.
153 *Ibid.*, p. 574.
154 *Ibid.*, pp. 576-77.
155 *Ibid.*, pp. 593-94.
156 NLS, MS. 638, f. 35, Brewster to Cockerell, 18 March 1823.

157 *NER*, p. 595.

158 *Ibid.*, pp. 598-99.

159 *Ibid.*, p. 599.

160 Luke, 14, 28-30 in the Authorized (King James) Version.

161 *Edinburgh Dissected*, p. 26. In our own day, Ian McHaffie, *Greek Secrets Revealed*, p. 1, similarly suggests that the quotation (which he gives in the New International Version) is applicable to the circumstances.

162 *NER*, pp. 582-83.

163 *Ibid.*, p. 603.

164 *Ibid.*, p. 600.

165 Cf. Dinsmoor, *Architecture of Ancient Greece*, p. 70; A. W. Lawrence, revised R. A. Tomlinson, *Greek Architecture*, p. 99; Tony Spawforth, *The Complete Greek Temples*, p. 58.

166 *NER*, pp. 601-2.

167 Cleghorn 1.

168 Cleghorn 3, pp. 2-4.

169 Cleghorn 1, pp. 44-45.

170 NLS, MS. 639, p. 15.

171 *Ibid.*, p. 71.

172 Cleghorn 2, p. 11.

173 Cleghorn 4, I, p. 328.

174 Mudie, *Historical Account of His Majesty's Visit to Scotland*, p. 265.

175 Stark, *Picture of Edinburgh*, pp. 78-79. This is probably the little-known William Reid, on whom see Colvin, p. 849. Another model of the Parthenon, the work of the sculptor Peter Slater (or Sclater) and presumably made at the time of the selection of the Greek design for the National Monument, and perhaps in close connection with the project, was presented to the Edinburgh Museum of Science and Art by Slater on 5 November 1870. It is said to have been six feet six inches in length and crafted of wood, and to have shown the ancient building restored but without its sculpture—which would accord with the aims of the National Monument projectors. No mention of this model is made in Roscoe, Hardy and Sullivan, *Biographical Dictionary of Sculptors in Britain* in the entry for Slater, pp. 1134-36, but see Mitchell, p. 11. My research indicates that this model was de-accessioned and transferred from the (then) Royal Scottish Museum to the Edinburgh Education Authority Museum in October 1949. It cannot now be traced. See the Museum of Science and Art Accessions Register for 1864-73, p. 303, preserved in the library of the National Museums of Scotland. However, what may be the model in question can be glimpsed in the bottom right foreground of a photograph of the Great Hall of the Museum of Science and Art, dated to *c.* 1880: see the record in the CANMORE (National Record of the Historic Environment) database of Historic Environment Scotland, SC834082. Its image also appears woven into the ribbon attached to William Mitchell's book of 1907 in one of its de luxe forms.

176 NLS, MS. 638, ff. 11-11v, Cohen to Cockerell, 30 July 1822.

177 NLS, MS. 638, ff. 92-3v, Basil Hall to Cockerell, 15 April 1825.

178 Brown, 'Intimacy and Immediacy: James Hall's Journals in Italy and Germany 1821-22', pp. 28-29 with Figs 1-3. See also Brown, '"Tre Volte Terra Classica": La Spedizione Siciliana di James Hall', pp. 1-15 and Plates VI-VII, and 20-27.

179 NLS, MS. 27628, ff. 25v, 22v-23, 26v.

180 NLS, MS. 27630, ff. 14v, 26v.

181 *Ibid.*, ff. 5, 28, 36v-37.

182 Brown, *Frolics in the Face of Europe*, p. 160.

183 NLS, MS. 638, ff. 68-69, Hugh Williams to Cockerell, 16 July 1824.

184 NLS, MS. 638, f. 47, Liston to Cockerell, 10 February 1824.

185 NLS, MS. 639. See Xenophon, *Memorabilia*, III, viii. 10, p. 93.

186 NLS, MS. 638, f. 75v, Archibald Alison the elder to Cockerell, 1 Nov. 1824.

187 NLS, MS. 638, ff. 73-74, Hall to 'R. C.' [*sic*] Cockerell, 1 Nov. 1824; *SAHA*, no. 205, pp. 61-62.

188 NLS, MS. 638, ff. 77-78, Playfair to Cockerell, 11 Nov 1824.

189 NLS, MS. 638, ff. 93-93v, Hall to Cockerell, 15 April 1825.

190 Dibdin, *Bibliographical Antiquarian and Picturesque Tour*, II, p. 485.

191 *Ibid.*, pp. 584-85.

192 *Ibid.*, p. 485, cf. pp. 480-81.

193 Fergusson, *History of the Modern Styles of Architecture*, pp. 307-8.

194 For helpful surveys of what characterised an acropolis and an agora, see Wycherley, *How the Greeks Built Cities*; also Hill, *Ancient City of Athens* and Camp, *Archaeology of Athens*.

195 *Letter to the Lord Provost on the Mischievous Tendency of a Scheme for Abolishing the High School*, pp. 2, 22-23.

196 McKee asserts that Archibald Elliot's 'Pantheon' national monument proposal was for a building at the *foot* rather than at the *top* of The Mound: see *Calton Hill*, p. 87 and no. 62. This view contradicts the unequivocal evidence of *Report of … a Numerous and Respectable Meeting … with a View to the Erection of a National Monument …* p. 25, and also the clear statements about the location made by Brown in *Rax Me That Buik*, p. 85, and in Gifford, p. 46.

197 *Letter … on the Mischievous Tendency …* pp. 24-25.

198 *Ibid.*, p. 26.

199 *Lord Cockburn: Selected Letters*, edited by Alan Bell, pp. 236-37.

200 For a first-rate study of the evolution of the National Gallery building see Gow, 'The Northern Athenian Temple of the Arts', *passim* but esp. pp. 21-28.

201 Thomas Hamilton, *Letter to the Right Hon. Lord John Russell …*

202 *Antiquities of Athens*, Vol. I, Chapter III, Plate I.

203 Gow, 'Northern Athenian Temple of the Arts', p. 17.

204 Hamilton, *Letter to Lord John Russell*, p. 27.

205 Rowan, 'The Athens of the North Explored', p. 1055; Crook, *The Greek Revival. Neo-Classical Attitudes*, p. 106.

206 Sir Albert Richardson's short but judicious survey of 'The Greek School in Scotland' is still worth reading for its assessments of what constituted 'all the attributes of the monumental', and of how the genius architects of Edinburgh managed to make ancient Greek forms 'pliant and docile'. See *Monumental Classic Architecture in Great Britain …*, pp. 69-73.

207 NLS, MS. 638, f. 65v, Burn to Cockerell, 10 July 1824.

208 NLS, MS. 638, f. 87, Cockerell to Alison, 29 March 1825.

209 Cleghorn 5, pp. 115-16.

210 Cleghorn 2, pp. 103-6; Cleghorn 4, I, pp. 123-26. Crook (*Age of Neo-Classicism*, pp. 550 and 612) calls Hamilton and Playfair, respectively, the 'Klenze' and the 'Schinkel' of Edinburgh.

211 Cleghorn 2, pp. 138, 140.

212 *Ibid.*, p. 73.

213 *Ibid.*, pp. 73-74.

214 *Ibid.*, pp. 108-9.

215 Cleghorn 4, pp. 128-29.

216 Cleghorn 2, pp. 138, 140-41.

217 *Ibid.*, p. 141.

218 *Ibid.*, p. 99.

219 On the proposed 'shopping mall' see Lowrey, 'Commerce and Conservation', p. 155 with Fig. 8.4. For the design and pretensions of one Edinburgh shop, see Brown, 'Daniel Macintosh and the Repository of Arts', which is based on study of the proprietor's elegant trade-card. Shops of a similar kind, often with classical door-pieces, can be observed at the right-hand side of Swarbreck's plate of the Royal Institution (Fig. 61).

220 *Letter to the Right Honourable the Lord Provost ... By a Plain Honest Man*, p. 11.

221 Cleghorn 2, pp. 99–100.

222 *Ibid.*, pp. 100, 140.

223 *Ibid.*, p. 99.

224 Dibdin, *Bibliographical Antiquarian and Picturesque Tour*, II, p. 588.

225 Cleghorn 2, p. 101.

226 Gow, 'Playfair: A Northern Athenian', p. 42; and *B o S Edinburgh*, pp. 244, 189.

227 For the quotation see Fraser, *Building of Old College*, p. 172.

228 *Ibid.*,, Figs 7.6 and 9.24.

229 *B o S Edinburgh*, p. 190.

230 Harris, 'C. R. Cockerell's "Ichnographica Domestica"', p. 15 quoting Cockerell's diary. See also Haynes and Fenton, *Building Knowledge*, p. 71 and Fig. 72, p. 69.

231 Fraser, *Building of Old College*, p. 172.

232 These columns are visible in Fraser's Figs 7.8 and 7.15, but without comment on the source.

233 Dibdin, *Bibliographical Antiquarian and Picturesque Tour*, II, p. 586.

234 *Antiquities of Athens*, I, Chapter III, Plate VII. Fraser reproduces Playfair's drawing for the capital as his Fig. 7.5 but again without comment.

235 *Antiquities of Athens*, III (1794), Chapter VI, p. 43, tailpiece.

236 *Antiquities of Athens*, I, Chapter, IV, Plate VI.

237 'C.', 'The Calton Hill', p. 148.

238 The New Club design is to be found in a volume of engraved plans, elevations and perspective views in NLS, R.251.d 2(2), catalogued as by Archibald Elliot and entitled 'The Edinburgh Hotel, Tavern and Coffee House, Waterloo Place'. For Cockerell's comments, see Harris, 'C. R. Cockerell's "Ichnographica Domestica"', p. 15.

239 The Source is *Antiquities of Athens*, Vol. II (London 1790), Chapter IV, Plate III. Alexander Thomson praised the Monument of Thrasyllos for the originality and inventiveness concealed by its apparent simplicity. See 'Art and Architecture...', III, pt ii, p. 82.

240 This and the preceding paragraph were written before the appearance of the second edition of McHaffie, *Greek Secrets Revealed*. See the comprehensive discussion there (pp. 177–79) of the Monument of Thrasyllos and its Edinburgh derivative, the Winton Monument (but only the Winton Monument), and the Broughton Street door-piece.

241 Aviva plc is the present-day successor company (via a series of mergers and acquisitions) to Edinburgh Life. Sir Walter Scott's original Edinburgh Life policy, number 406, of 1824, is preserved in the Aviva archives, NU3853, and is an example of this decorative document. Facsimiles of this particular policy were produced around 1900.

Chapter 5: 'The Athens' from Within

1 *The Times*, 3 May 1844, p. 3.
2 *Black's Picturesque Tourist*, fifth edition, p. 16.
3 Cockburn, *Life of Lord Jeffrey*, author's corrected proof copy, NLS. MS. 345, pp. 156, 157-58, 159.
4 *Memoir and Correspondence of Mrs Grant of Laggan*, second edition, I, pp. 235, 240, 256; II, p. 333.
5 Gillies, *Memoirs of a Literary Veteran*, I, pp. 343 and 263 referring to events of, respectively, 1812 and 1806.
6 *Ibid.*, p. 267.
7 Jenkins album of caricatures, NLS, Ry. II. b. 16, no. 85.
8 Brown, 'Erskine, David Steuart, 11th Earl of Buchan', in *Dictionary of British Collections and Collectors*.
9 NLS, MS. 3391, f. 37, endorsed on f. 40v: 'Lord Buchan's Prelude to his Breakfast'. The quotations are taken from pp. [3] and 4 of the printed pamphlet.
10 *Anonymous and Fugitive Essays of the Earl of Buchan*, I [sic: vol. I only published], p. 95. For the view that what Buchan wrote here reflected his own nature, see John Buchan [that is, the novelist and man of letters, later Lord Tweedsmuir], 'A Comic Chesterfield', p. 564.
11 *Ibid.*, pp. 301, 306; III, p. 127.
12 *NER*, p. 581.
13 Cockburn, *Memorials*, p. 277.
14 *Ibid.*, p. 277.
15 *Ibid.*, pp. 279-80, 277.
16 *Ibid.*, p. 279.
17 *Ibid.*, p. 433.
18 Zachs, *Without Regard to Good Manners*, p. 91.
19 Cockburn, *Memorials*, pp. 17-18.
20 Dalzel, *History of the University of Edinburgh*, I: *Memoir* [of Dalzell, by Cosmo Innes], pp. 234-35, Dalzell to Porson, 28 May 1804.
21 Edina/Athena, p. 62.
22 Gillies, *History of Greece*, I, [p. iii].
23 See Allan, 'The Age of Pericles in the Modern Athens', pp. 406, 409, 405, 410.
24 Cf. Alan Montgomery, *Classical Caledonia*, p. 192.
25 See Brown, '"A Faithless Truant to the Classic Page": Sir Walter Scott, Greek, Greece and the Greeks'.
26 *Letters of Sir Walter Scott*, XII, p. 74.
27 Alison 1823, pp. 140-41.
28 *Letters of Sir Walter Scott*, III, p. 84, Scott to the Revd Richard Polwhele, 29 February 1812.
29 *Ibid.*, III, p. 403, to the Revd Edward Berwick, 10 January 1814.
30 *Private Letter-Books of Sir Walter Scott*, p. 229, quoting Sophia Shedden to Scott, 24 January 1819.
31 Walter Scott, *The Visionary*, p. viii and facsimile p. 45.
32 Anon., 'Domestic Politics', p. 337.
33 *The Journal of Sir Walter Scott*, p. 98.
34 Scott, *Provincial Antiquities*, I, pp. 78-82, esp. pp. 81-82.
35 'Childe Harold's Pilgrimage, Canto III... By Lord Byron', p. 180.
36 *Ibid.*, p. 191.
37 'Childe Harold's Pilgrimage. Canto IV. By Lord Byron', p. 221.
38 *Miscellaneous Prose Works*, VI, 'Essay on the Drama', p. 220.

39 *Letters of Sir Walter Scott*, VI, p. 293, to Charles Scott, 14 Nov. 1820.

40 J. G. Lockhart, *Life of Sir Walter Scott*, VII, pp. 249-50.

41 On the Academy building see Watters, 'Καλοι κ΄αγαθοι', esp. pp. 285, 290-95 and Figs. 1 and 8. On the ethos of the new Academy and the place of Greek in the curriculum, see Miller, *Cockburn's Millennium*, p. 47.

42 *Some Letters of Lord Cockburn*, p. 20.

43 See Capital Collections, nos. 25854 and 25959.

44 Crombie, *Men of Modern Athens*, Introductory Notice.

45 Alison, *Autobiography*, I, p. 37.

46 Alison 1819 A, pp. 377, 381.

47 Cf. Rood, 'From Marathon to Waterloo', pp. 267-97.

48 Alison 1819 A, pp. 382, 383.

49 Alison 1819 B, p. 137.

50 *Ibid.*, pp. 139, 140.

51 *Ibid.*, p. 141.

52 *Ibid.*, p. 144.

53 *Ibid.*, pp. 144, 145.

54 'Traveller', pp. 99-105.

55 *Ibid.*, pp. 100-101, 103.

56 'OROP', p. 304.

57 *Ibid.*, p. 305.

58 NER, p. 556.

59 For Brougham's high-jinks see Cosh, *Edinburgh. The Golden Age*, p. 52; on Jessy Allan and New Town vandalism see Brown, *Elegance & Entertainment in the New Town of Edinburgh*, pp. 5-6. For Meadowbank's worries, see Mason, 'The Edinburgh School of Design', p. 86.

60 Cleghorn 1, p. 68.

61 Cleghorn 3, pp. 2-4, 6.

62 'OROP', pp. 305-6.

63 *Ibid.*, p. 306.

64 *Ibid.*, p. 308.

65 *Ibid.*, p. 308.

66 Williams, *Travels*, II, p. 377. For his part, John Galt had equivocated. Having confessed to being 'greatly vexed and disappointed by the dilapidation of the temple of Minerva', he assumed a more positive position, saying that he was 'consoled by the reflection, that the spoils are destined to ornament our own land, and that, if they had not been taken possession of by Lord Elgin, they would probably have been carried away by the French.' See *Letters from the Levant*, p. 112.

67 [W. R. Hamilton], *Memorandum on the Subject of the Earl of Elgin's Pursuits in Greece*, p. [29].

68 NLS, MS. 15937, ff. 12-13.

69 [Simpson], *Letters to Sir Walter Scott*, pp. 35, 58, 96. The verse quoted is from Felicia Hemans's 'Modern Greece'.

70 Stark, *Picture of Edinburgh*, third edition, p. 78. The section is inserted before Stark's description of the New Town and after the passage on the Calton Hill which appears in the previous edition of 1820.

71 Lockhart, *Life of Scott*, VII, p. 250.

72 NLS, Acc. 12668.

73 [Mudie], *Historical Account of His Majesty's Visit to Scotland*, p. 265.

74 Cohen, p. 331. Percy Smythe, sixth Viscount Strangford, had succeeded Sir Robert Liston as British Ambassador in Constantinople and was in post 1820-24.

75 *Letter to the Right Honourable the Lord Provost... By a Builder*, p. 7.

76 *Letter to the Right Honourable the Lord Provost ... By a Plain Honest Man*, p. 12.

77 M'Crie, *Life of Thomas M'Crie*, pp. 276-77, 279, 281.

78 Cf. Edina/Athena, pp. 50, 54. This is the meeting referred to incorrectly by Thomas Gordon, *History of the Greek Revolution*, II, p. 79 as having taken place on 21 August 1822. Edinburgh was then far too taken up with the King's visit to fit in such an event. But Gordon was right to credit this meeting with priority as the first in Britain in support of the Greek cause. Edward Masson, who was inspired to go to Greece by what he heard, says the same in the first number of his *Hellenic Banner* in June 1853, p. 46.

79 *Life of M'Crie*, Appendix IV. 'Speech at a Public Meeting in [*sic*] behalf of the Greeks', pp. 451-53. On the Massacre of Chios, and the shockwaves that spread across Europe as a result and which were reflected in literature and art, see Beaton, *The Greek Revolution of 1821*, pp. 33-37.

80 *Ibid.*, Appendix V, 'Speech at the Scottish Ladies' Society for Promoting Education in Greece', pp. 459-60.

81 Ritchie's portrait of M'Crie is listed as a bust, exhibited at the Royal Scottish Academy in 1836, but is now lost: see Roscoe, *Biographical Dictionary of Sculptors*, p. 1042.

82 *Antiquities of Athens*, III, Chapter VI, p. 43, tailpiece.

83 NLS, MS. 352, f. 168v.

84 On the Dundas column see Godard Desmarest, 'The Melville Monument', pp. 105-30.

85 Linning, *Memoranda Publica*, 'Melville Monument', p. 11.

86 *Ibid.*, 'National Monument of Scotland', pp. 57-58.

87 See Magnus Magnusson, *The Clacken and the Slate*, pp. 91, 283. The badge is illustrated in Edina-Athens, p. 21.

88 On the High School war-memorial inscription see McHaffie, *Greek Secrets Revealed*, pp. 93-95.

89 [William Hugh Logan], *The Edinburgh Rosciad for the Summer Season, 1834*, 'Imprinted At Modern Athens'.

90 *Letters to and from Charles Kirkpatrick Sharpe*, II, p. 172.

91 *Ibid.*, p. 214.

92 *Ibid.*, p. 179.

93 *Ibid.*, pp. 458-59, 462-63, 468, 485, 508, 544.

94 *Ibid.*, pp. 467, 474.

95 *Ibid.*, p. 509.

96 *Ibid.*, p. 164.

97 *Letter to the Right Honourable the Lord Provost of Edinburgh ... By a Plain Honest Man*, p. 17.

98 *Observations by Alexander Trotter ... in Illustration of his Modified Plan of a Communication*, p. 7.

99 Trotter, *Plan of Communication Between the New and the Old Town*, p. 6. Lowrey, ('Commerce and Conservation', p. 155) is confused by which Trotter proposed this scheme. It was, certainly, Alexander Trotter of Dreghorn; but he was neither a baronet nor a knight, nor yet was he Lord Provost of Edinburgh, 1825-27. That was William Trotter, of Ballindean.

100 *Private Letter-Books of Sir Walter Scott*, p. 310, Sharpe to Scott, 20 August 1824.

101 [Mudie], *Attic Fragments of Characters, Customs Opinions and Scenes*, pp. 97-98.

102 The West engraving has also been attributed to William Home Lizars and dated variously to 1828 and 1838 (see, for example, Fehlmann, 'A Striking Proof of Scotland's Pride', Fig. 6). However, a copy has now been located in an album in the 'Symbolae Scoticae' collection in EUL, Coll-10/1/163, a collection assembled by Adam White of the Department of Natural History in the British Museum. I am indebted to Dr Wilson Smith and Paul Fleming for pursuing what information I could furnish, and for finding, identifying and photographing this elusive and misunderstood image.

103 Gillies, *Memoirs of a Literary Veteran*, III, pp. 138, 127.

104 Hall, *Patchwork*, II, pp. 366-67.

105 NLS, MS. 638, f. 106v, Playfair to Cockerell, 23 October 1826.

106 NLS, MS. 638, f. 114, Williams to Cockerell, 22 January 1828.

107 On Henning's reproductions of the Parthenon frieze see *John Henning 1771-1851*, unpaginated. See also Boardman, *Parthenon and its Sculptures*, p. 252, where reference is made to Henning's 'small industry' devoted to 'producing miniature version of the frieze, in plaster, mounted in bound volumes.' On a very large scale, Henning's version of the Parthenon frieze ornaments, most appropriately, the exterior of the Athenaeum Club in Pall Mall, London.

108 Alison, 'British School of Architecture', pp. 237-38.

109 *Ibid.*, p. 238.

110 *Ibid.*, p. 238.

111 On Edinburgh's financial situation in this period, see Perman, *The Rise and Fall of The City of Money*, Chapter 18.

112 *Scotland Delineated in a Series of Views*, I, p. 119. This view was also drawn by Harding.

113 *Scotland Illustrated in Eighty Views* ... pp. 140-42. The plate and commentary are to be found in the edition of 1850, not in that of 1845.

114 Alison 1819 A, p. 384.

115 J. D. Harding in *Scotland Delineated* ... and G. M. Kemp in *Scotland Illustrated* ... both show the palisades as well: the words describing them are from the commentary in the latter publication, p. 142.

116 Rock, 'Robert Forrest (1789-1852) and his Exhibition on the Calton Hill'.

117 Macdonald, *Life Jottings of an Old Edinburgh Citizen*, pp. 199-200.

118 See Rock, 'Robert Forrest', p. 133.

119 *Edinburgh Dissected...*, pp. 26-27.

120 Batty, *Select Views of Some of the Principal Cities...*, unpaginated commentary on Plate 3.

121 *Picturesque Tourist*, first edition (1840), p. 25.

122 *Ibid.*, second edition (1842), pp. 27-28.

123 Cockburn, *Letter to the Lord Provost on the Best Ways of Spoiling the Beauty of Edinburgh*, p. 25.

124 *Lord Cockburn: Selected Letters*, p. 138.

125 Cockburn, *Letter to the Lord Provost*, p. 23.

126 *Ibid.*, p. 13.

127 *Lord Cockburn: Selected Letters*, p. 237. The term 'bitch' was a derogatory one in contemporary Scots usage, though actually applied to both men and women.

128 Begg, *How to Promote and Preserve the True Beauty of Edinburgh*, pp. 11, 15.

129 Wallace, *John Stuart Blackie*, pp. 235-36.

130 Cockburn, *Memorials*, p. 228.

131 James Ballantine, *Gaberlunzie's Wallet*, p. 96.

Chapter 6: New Athens from Without

1 Hogg, *Life of Percy Bysshe Shelley*, pp. 251, 253.
2 NLS, MS. 3108, f. 43.
3 *Peter's Letters*, I, p. 183, Letter XV, 'Mr Playfair'.
4 'C.', 'The Calton Hill', p. 145-46.
5 Nassau Senior's account of Edinburgh occurs in a travel journal in the possession of Messrs Bernard Quaritch. I am indebted to Theodore Hofmann for permission to quote from the unpublished manuscript.
6 *Diary of Frances Lady Shelley*, II, pp. 54, 57-58.
7 Southey, *Journal of a Tour in Scotland*, pp. 13, 15, 5.
8 *Diary of Benjamin Robert Haydon*, II (1960), pp. 294-95. For the suggestion that the artist had been rehearsing the 'dream of great genius' remark, see O'Keeffe, *A Genius for Failure*, p. 202.
9 *Collected Works of William Hazlitt*, 9, p. 324. Hazlitt used the term 'passing visitant' to describe the tourist in the city and the viewer of Williams's 1822 exhibition.
10 *Ibid.*, p. 324.
11 See *A Scots Grey at Waterloo*, p. 106. For doubts and reservations about the status of the manuscript, see the review by Iain Gordon Brown in *Scottish Archives*, 23 (2017), pp. 144-47.
12 *Memoir of Thomas Bewick*, pp. 182, 184.
13 NLS, Acc. 8801, 'Journal of a Tour in Scotland during the Long Vacation of the year 1823. By a Johnian Hog'. See also Brown, 'A Johnian Hog in Caledonia'.
14 *Hugh Miller's Memoir*. The actual *Memoir of Hugh Miller* occupies pp. 89-226 of this volume. Quotations are taken from pp. 198 and 207-8.
15 *The Scottish Tourist*, p. 11.
16 Cobbett, *Cobbett's Tour in Scotland*, pp. 74, 112.
17 Willis, *Pencillings by the Way*, III, pp. 128-30.
18 'The Second Voyage of Omai the Traveller'. A copy of this article, bearing a pencil note of the attribution to John Stark, is in NLS, shelfmark F.5. f.17(5). See also the earlier spoof, 'A Visit to the Great Island of Edinburgh, called Britain, by Eree Omai'. McCormick makes no mention of the *Blackwood's* spoof in his *Omai. Pacific Envoy*, where an otherwise informative chapter is to be found entitled 'Omai in Europe—the Literary Aftermath'.
19 'The King's Visit to Edinburgh. By a Londoner but no Cockney'.
20 *Ibid.*, p. 272.
21 *Ibid.*, pp. 272-73.
22 For a recent discussion of 'lions' (both animate and inanimate) and 'lion-hunters', see Brown, *Frolics in the Face of Europe*, pp. 72, 81, 87, 128-29, 170-71.
23 Nodier, *Promenade de Dieppe aux Montagnes d'Ecosse*; Idem, *Promenade from Dieppe to the Mountains of Scotland*.
24 Nodier, *Promenade*, English edition, pp. 76-77.
25 Simpson, *Letters to Sir Walter Scott*, p. 58 n.
26 Nodier, *Promenade*, pp. 80-81.
27 Nodier, *Promenade*, p. 111.
28 [Pichot], *Historical and Literary Tour of a Foreigner*, II, pp. 273, 276.
29 *Ibid.*, II, p. 286.
30 *Ibid.*, II, p. 309.
31 *Ibid.*, II, pp. 290-91.
32 *Ibid.*, II, p. 310.

33 Blanqui, *Voyage d'un Jeune Français en Angleterre et en Ècosse*, pp. 225, 226, 230-31, 239-40, 242, 244. *Les Puritains d'Écosse et le Nain mystérieux*, translated by Auguste-Jean-Baptiste Defauconpret, was the second Walter Scott novel to be published in France. It combined *The Black Dwarf* and *The Tale of Old Mortality*, which together had formed the four volumes of the first series of Scott's *Tales of my Landlord*.

34 Pernot, *Vues Pittoresque de'l Écosse*, pp. 17-18, 22.

35 *A French Sociologist Looks at Britain. Gustave d'Eichthal and British Society in 1828*, p. 74.

36 Buzonnière, *Le Touriste Écossais*, pp. 36-37.

37 Davie, *The Democratic Intellect*, p. 255.

38 See *Voyage à Reculons en Angleterre et en Écosse*. The translation by Janice Valls-Russell was published by W. & R. Chambers.

39 *Backwards to Britain*, p. 110; *Voyage à Reculons*, pp. 129-30.

40 *A Winter in Edinburgh; or, The Russian Brothers*, I, p. 117.

41 *From Charlotte Square to Fingal's Cave*, pp. 7-8.

42 'Naseweis', *Edinburgh and its Society*, pp. 7, 14-15.

43 *Bibliographical Antiquarian and Picturesque Tour*, II, pp. 478, 482, 583.

44 *Ibid.*, II, p. 592.

45 *Ibid.*, II, p. 596.

46 Brown, *Building for Books*, pp. 106-8.

47 *Bibliographical Antiquarian and Picturesque Tour*, II, pp. 632, 490-91.

48 *Ibid.*, II, pp. 590-91.

49 *Ibid.*, II, p. 667.

50 *Ibid.*, II, pp. 638, 960-61.

51 *The Times*, 28 July 1838, p. 4.

52 *The Times*, 24 October 1836, p. 4.

53 Raumer, *England in 1835*, III, pp. 166-67.

54 *The Times*, 3 September 1842, p. 3.

55 *Leaves from the Journal of Our Life in the Highlands*, p. 12.

56 Lauder, *Memorial of the Royal Progress in Scotland*, p. 83.

57 Cleghorn 3, pp. 8n, 34-35, 66; Cleghorn 4, pp. 126, 204.

58 Carus, *King of Saxony's Journey*, pp. 333, 336.

59 Kohl, *Travels in Scotland*, p. 35.

60 *Ibid.*, p. 36.

61 *Ibid.*, pp. 36, 38, 234.

62 Waagen, *Treasures of Art in Great Britain*, III, pp. 266-67

63 *Ibid.*, pp. 276-77.

64 *Ibid.*, pp. 277.

65 *Ibid.*, p. 267.

66 *Ibid.*, p. 271.

67 *Collected Works of Florence Nightingale, 7: European Travels*, p. 706.

Chapter 7: Athenian Edinburgh in British Satire

1 NLS, MS. 638, f. 114, Tyndall to Cockerell, 17 December 1827.

2 *Poems of William Wordsworth*, 3, p. 487.

3 [Johnstone], *The Saxon and the Gaël*, I, pp. 180-81.

4 *Edinburgh: a Satirical Novel*, I, Preface, p. vi and p. 192.

5 *Glenfell; or, Macdonalds and Campbells. An Edinburgh Tale of the Nineteenth Century*, pp. 1, 2, 52. The National Library of Scotland copy (pressmark

RB.s.39) is, apparently, unique. Gordon, *John Galt: the Life of a Writer*, p. 25 accepts it as a work of Galt of 1820.

6 *Letters of David Hume*, I, p. 436, to Hugh Blair, 26 April 1764.

7 *Glenfell*, pp. 160-63.

8 *Auld Reekie; or, a Mistake in Edinburgh*, in *Literary Life, and Miscellanies, of John Galt*, III. For the dating of this play, see Aberdein, *John Galt*, p. 96.

9 *Auld Reekie*, pp. 199, 218.

10 Galt, *The Last of the Lairds*, pp. 1, 8, 21, 64-65, 163.

11 *Glenfergus*, I, pp. 210, 153; II, pp. 179, 187.

12 [Combe], *The Tour of Doctor Prosody*.

13 Cockburn, *Memorials*, p. 38. See Brown, *The Hobby-Horsical Antiquary*, pp. 29, 43.

14 *The Tour of Dr Prosody*, pp. 38, 44.

15 *Ibid.*, pp. 48, 31.

16 *Ibid.*, pp. 63-64.

17 *Ibid.*, p. 83.

18 'Hogg's Royal Jubilee', p. 353.

19 [Wilson], 'Noctes Ambrosianae. No. VI', pp. 374, 377-78.

20 *Noctes Ambrosianae*, I, pp. 166-67.

21 *A Series of Original Portraits and Caricature Etchings*, II, p. 455.

22 *Noctes Ambrosianae*, IV, p. 89 (August 1830).

23 *Hermit in Edinburgh*, I, pp. 120, 15-16.

24 *Works of Thomas Love Peacock*, I, Preface, pp. xi-xii.

25 *Works of Peacock*, II, *Crotchet Castle*, p. 208.

26 *Ibid.*, pp. 193-95.

27 *Ibid.*, p. 212.

28 Christian Isobel Johnstone, *The Edinburgh Tales*. 'Mrs Mark Luke' occupies pp. 261-334 of the first volume (1845).

29 *Ibid.*, p. 261.

30 *Ibid.*, pp. 293-94.

31 *Things in General ...*, pp. 73-75.

32 *Noctes Ambrosianae*, II, pp. 239-40 (July 1826).

33 [Robert Mudie], *The Modern Athens*, p. 3.

34 *Ibid.*, p. 31.

35 *Ibid.*, pp. 160-61.

36 *Ibid.*, p. 162.

37 *Ibid.*, pp. 128-29.

38 *Ibid.*, pp. 129-30.

39 *Childe Harold's Pilgrimage*, Canto II, stanza xii. See St Clair, *Lord Elgin and the Marbles*, pp. 103 and 191; and Bracken, *Antiquities Acquired*, p. 35.

40 *The Modern Athens*, pp. 318-20.

Chapter 8: The Anti-Greeks of Modern Athens

1 'Decorations of Edinburgh'. No authorship is attributed in Strout, *Bibliography of Articles in Blackwood's Magazine*. The author may, however, just possibly be Allan Cunningham, who first worked as an apprentice stonemason, and who became a poet and, later, a biographer of the most eminent British painters, sculptors and architects. It does not seem possible that he can be Hugh Miller, despite the fact that Miller called himself a 'journeyman mason', and once intended to write a memoir under that name. Miller did not come to Edinburgh until 1824.

2 'Decorations of Edinburgh', pp. 76-77.

3 *Ibid.*, p. 78. By 'in the North Loch', the writer presumably meant the now drained and filled-in area at the lower end of The Mound, roughly where the Royal Institution would be constructed from 1822.

4 'Public Buildings of Edinburgh'. The quotations that follow are taken from every page of this article save the last.

5 Irwin, *Scottish Painters at Home and Abroad*, p. 96. See also Mason, 'The Edinburgh School of Design', p. 78; and, especially, Helen E. Smailes, 'A history of the Statue Gallery at the Trustees' Academy in Edinburgh ...', pp. 129-30 and 132-33; and, futher, Smailes, '"Uno Sfortunato Scultore Scozzese chiamato Campbell". The Correspondence of Thomas Campbell (1791-1858) and his Banking Maecenas, Gilbert Innes of Stow (1751-1832)', pp. 218, 220 and 225. See also Naik and Stewart, 'Hellenization of Edinburgh', p. 366 and note 4; and [Stewart], *The Edinburgh College of Art Cast Collection*, unpaginated [pp. 2-3].

6 [Thomas, Earl of Elgin] *Letter to the Editor of The Edinburgh Review*, p. 35. For Scott's opinion, see *Letters of Sir Walter Scott*, V, p. 103, Scott to Matthew Weld Hartstonge, 4 November 1818. For the tribute to the Earl, see C. H. Wilson, *Descriptive Catalogue of Casts from Antique Statues in the Trustees' Academy*, p. 5.

7 See Ian Jenkins, 'Acquisition and Supply of Casts of the Parthenon Sculptures by the British Museum, 1835-1939', p. 104. The casts were mostly moulded by the sculptor Richard Westmacott and the *formatore* Pietro Angelo Sarti. See also Naik and Stewart, 'Hellenization' of Edinburgh', p. 375 [Stewart], *Edinburgh College of Art Cast Collection*; and Stewart, 'Scenery and scenes: the plaster cast collection and its architecture at Edinburgh College of Art', pp 2-4. I am greatly indebted to Margaret Stewart for stimulating discussion of the history of Edinburgh's acquisition of its fine and important series of Parthenon casts.

8 The drawings are unmentioned by O'Keeffe in his treatment of the Edinburgh showing of *Jerusalem*: see *A Genius for Failure*, pp. 201, 203.

9 *Ibid.*, pp. 67, 69.

10 'Mr Haydon's Picture'.

11 O'Keeffe, *Genius for Failure*, p. 74. Campbell soon admitted his hasty misjudgment: '... they grew in my sight now I just adore them the Ease Elegance and execution is sublime ...'. See Smailes, '"Uno Sfortunato Scultore Scozzese chiamato Campbell"...', p. 243.

12 See *Diary of Benjamin Robert Haydon*, II, p. 293, n. 2 and pp. 40-41. For further references to the acquisition by Edinburgh of casts of the Parthenon marbles in 1816-17 see *Ibid.*, II, p. 41.

13 Basil Skinner first drew attention to Aikman's poem in his essay, 'Parthenon or Valhalla'. See also Gifford, pp. 50-54.

14 Aikman, *The Cenotaph*, Introduction, pp. xvi-xvii.

15 *Ibid.*, p. xx.

16 *Ibid.*, pp. xiii-xiv.

17 *Ibid.*, p. ix.

18 *Ibid.*, pp. 43, 46 and note on p. 73.

19 'Grecian Architecture—Lord Aberdeen', p. 705.

20 For a text of the *Atheniad*, see Galt's *Autobiography*, II, pp. 160-69.

21 'Grecian Architecture—Lord Aberdeen' p. 706. Aberdeen's *Inquiry* was published by John Murray in 1822. Galt quotes from p. 4 of this work.

22 Aberdeen, *Inquiry into the Principles of Beauty in Grecian Architecture*, pp. 2-3.

23 'Grecian Architecture—Lord Aberdeen', p. 706.

24 *Ibid.*, p.705.
25 McWilliam, *Scottish Townscape*, p. 116; Glendinning, MacInnes and MacKechnie, *History of Scottish Architecture*, p. 205.
26 Curl, *Georgian Architecture in the British Isles*, p. 341.
27 Cf. Kennedy, *Greek Revival America*, p. 5.
28 Cohen, *passim*.
29 Cohen, p. 328.
30 *Ibid.*, p. 329.
31 *Ibid.*, pp. 328-29.
32 *Ibid.*, p. 330.
33 *Ibid.*, p. 331.
34 NLS, MS. 638, f. 22, Williams to Cockerell, 29 December 1822.
35 Cleghorn 2, pp. 109-10. At a distance of fifteen years, Cleghorn confused in his mind the alleged topic of the *Quarterly* article with that of Archibald Alison's subsequent review in the *Edinburgh* of Lord Aberdeen's book on Greek architecture.
36 Cleghorn 2, pp. 141-42.
37 Dyce and Wilson, *Letter to Lord Meadowbank*, pp. 16, 20, 35.
38 Alison had recently suggested as much: see Alison 1823, pp. 135 and 140.
39 Cleghorn 1, pp. 100-101.
40 Cleghorn 2, pp. 55-59.
41 Hall, *Patchwork*, II, p. 366-67.
42 Stevenson, *Edinburgh. Picturesque Notes*, p. 4.
43 Cleghorn 2, pp. 94, 96.
44 *Ibid.*, pp. 96, 97n.
45 *Ibid.*, pp. 74-75.
46 *Ibid.*, p. 75.
47 Cleghorn 4, I, p. 168.
48 *Ibid.*, pp. 187, 190.
49 Scott, *Provincial Antiquities*, I, pp. [83]-84.
50 Stoddart, *Remarks on Local Scenery and Manners*, I, p. 86.
51 'Great Fire', p. 707.
52 *Letters from and to Charles Kirkpatrick Sharpe*, II, pp. 269-70.
53 *Ibid.*, II, 284.
54 *Ibid.*, II, pp. 371-74. Charles McKean (*Edinburgh*, p. 175), and following him Allan Massie (*Edinburgh*, p. 147), were surely incorrect to think this campaign was against a barrack building in the Castle itself. Sharpe's letter makes it clear that his concern was with the High Street and its surroundings, including the lowering of the level of the carriageway—the result of which public works one can indeed observe today in the Lawnmarket.
55 *Letters … Charles Kirkpatrick Sharpe*, II, p. 372.
56 *Ibid.*, II, p. 374.
57 *Ibid.*, II, pp. 375-76.
58 *Ibid.*, II, pp. 355-56.
59 *Ibid.*, II, p. 360.
60 *The Times*, 10 September 1825, p. 3.
61 *Letters … Charles Kirkpatrick Sharpe*, II, p. 361.
62 NLS, MS. 3521, ff. 118 and 120, Roberts to Hay, 18 and 28 May 1842; NLS, Acc. 12158, P. S. Fraser to Roberts, 17 February 1844.
63 Ruskin, *Lectures on Architecture and Painting, Delivered at Edinburgh*, p. 140.
64 Ruskin, *The Stones of Venice*, III, pp. 194-95.
65 *Modern Athens!*, p. 42.

66 Scott, *Provincial Antiquities*, I, p. 76.
67 Ruskin, *Lectures on Architecture*, pp. 7, 56.
68 Cockburn, *Memorials*, p. 275.
69 *Ibid.*, pp. 275-76. On Cockburn's views of the New Town, and on the relation of the New Town to the Old, see also Miller, *Cockburn's Millennium*, pp. 130-33.
70 Cockburn, *Memorials*, p. 277.
71 Scott, *Provincial Antiquities*, I, p. 76.
72 Ruskin, *Lectures on Architecture*, pp. 54-55.
73 *Ibid.*, p. 71.
74 *Ibid.*, pp. 76-77.
75 *Ibid.*, pp. 81-84.
76 *Ibid.*, pp. 133, 117.
77 *B o S Edinburgh*, pp. 170-1; Brown, *Rax Me That Buik*, p. 13.
78 Quoted in [Gourlay], *The Best Site for Trinity College Church*, pp. 16-18. The letter was originally published in the *Edinburgh Evening Post*, 19 April 1854.
79 *The Times*, 23 December 1856, p. 5.
80 *Edinburgh Dissected*, pp. 28, 26.
81 *Annals of the Fine Arts for MDCCCXVII*, Art. III, p. 31.
82 Fontane, *Beyond the Tweed*, pp. 71-72.
83 *Ibid.*, pp. 30, 71-72.
84 *Ibid.*, p. 73.

Chapter 9: Epilogue

1 Patterson, *On the National Character of the Athenians*, pp. 123-24.
2 *Edinburgh Dissected*, pp. 15, 28, 408.
3 *Ibid.*, p. 26.
4 *Ibid.*, p. 26.
5 White, *Four Short Letters ... on the Subject of an Open Museum*, p. 5.
6 Quoted in Morton, *Unionist Nationalism*, p. 187.
7 See Robert Crawford, *On Glasgow and Edinburgh*, pp. 27-28.
8 Kelly, *Scott-land: The Man Who Invented a Nation*, p. 39.
9 *SAHA*, nos. 253-54.
10 The Minute is quoted in Gow, 'Northern Athenian Temple of the Arts', p. 37.
11 Rowan, 'The Athens of the North Explored', p. 1055. The Trustees of Sir William Fettes (who included Playfair's great friend and supporter Andrew Rutherfurd, Lord Rutherfurd) had wanted the architect to design their proposed new school. It might well have been his last commission. Playfair's death, however, supervened. Would it, as has been speculated, have been a neoclassical building, or one in some more eclectic and flamboyant style such as was fixed upon by the eventual architect of Fettes College, David Bryce? (See Philp, *A Keen Wind Blows*, pp. 5-6.) Surely, much depends upon the site chosen. Where Fettes in fact stands, even a great building in a classical style—such as was associated with other Edinburgh schools of the 'Modern Athenian' age—might not have exploited the picturesque possibilities of the situation anything near so effectively as did Bryce with his remarkable confection.
12 *Autobiography*, I, p. 220.
13 Cleghorn 2, pp. v-vi.
14 Cleghorn 3, pp. 7-8, 10, 12. The maxim 'from [the size of] his foot, [we can measure] Hercules', is attributed to Pythagoras. It means that, from a part, one is in a position to estimate the whole. The phrases 'torpor and inactivity',

'disapprobation and indifference,' actually come from yet another publication by Cleghorn on his favourite topic: Cleghorn 5, pp. 88 and 85.

15 Cleghorn 3, p. 10; Cleghorn 4, I, p. 329. The latter comment was made in the context of the perceived prevailing mood of indecision in bringing sculptural projects to completion.

16 Cleghorn 2, p. 133. For Hosking see Colvin, pp. 544-45.

17 Cleghorn 4, I, p. 204.

18 Cleghorn 3, p. 12.

19 *Ibid.*, p. 8, n.

20 Cleghorn 2, p. 106.

21 Cleghorn 3, pp. 66, 34-35.

22 Cleghorn 4, I, p. 204.

23 Cleghorn 3, pp. 67-68.

24 Beattie, *Scotland Illustrated* (1838), pp. 117, 119; *The Danube...*, pp. 64-65.

25 Pevsner, *History of Building Types*, pp. 18-19. On the Walhalla see also Middleton and Watkin, *Neoclassical and 19th Century Architecture/ 1: The Enlightenment*, pp. 96-97, 101-3; also Bergdoll, *European Architecture 1750-1890*, pp. 149-51; and Philipp, 'Historicist and Romantic Architecture in Germany', pp. 186-90.

26 Cleghorn 3, pp. 5, 59.

27 *Ibid.*, pp. 84, 72.

28 Smith, *A Summer in Skye*, I, p. 9.

29 *Ibid.*, pp. 13-14.

30 *Ibid.*, pp. 24-26.

31 *Ibid.*, pp. 28-29.

32 Masson, *Memories of Two Cities*, p. 17. This is a posthumous collection of earlier writings.

33 See James Browne's text to Ewbank's *Picturesque Views of Edinburgh ...*, p. 210.

34 Masson, *Memories...*, p. 14.

35 Wilson, *Memorials of Edinburgh in the Olden Time*, II, pp. 151-52, 227-28. A second edition, in which the sentiments of the first are perpetuated, appeared in 1891.

36 Wilson, *Reminiscences of Old Edinburgh*, I, p. 3.

37 *The Modern Athenian*, no. 1, pp. 3-4, 7 with Club names from no. 2, p. 7. The Greek letter is *omega*, any significance in which is not apparent. For a concise discussion of the Academy in the context of other gymnasia and philosophical schools in Ancient Athens, see R. E. Wycherley, *The Stones of Athens*, pp. 220-21.

38 *The Times*, 30 December 1910, p. 9.

39 *The Times*, 23 December 1935, p. 9.

40 Stevenson, *Edinburgh. Picturesque Notes*, pp. 2, 28. The book was in fact issued late in 1878.

41 'Auld Reekie', *Pall Mall Gazette*, 21 January 1895. See Brown, 'Old Edinburgh Club Centenary Conference: President's Remarks', p. 12.

42 James Elmes, 'History of Architecture in Great Britain', pt. vi, p. 338.

43 [Henry Home, Lord Kames], *Elements of Criticism*, III, Chapter xxiv, 'Gardening and Architecture', p. 313.

44 Massie, *Edinburgh*, p. 133.

45 Murray's *Handbook for Travellers*, third edition, p. 58.

46 Grant, *Old and New Edinburgh*, II, p. 109.

47 Giles, *Across Western Waves and Home in a Royal Capital. America for Modern Athenians. Modern Athens for Americans*, pp. 185, 193, 296, 200.

48 On the search for a site for the Usher Hall, see McKenzie, King and Smith, *Public Sculpture of Edinburgh*, I, pp. 47-51, esp. p. 48.

49 Giles, *Across Western Waves*, p. 206.

50 Pevsner, *History of Building Types*, p. 23.

51 Linklater, *Edinburgh*, pp. 138-39.

52 Youngson, *Companion Guide to Edinburgh and the Border Country*, p. 165.

53 St Clair, *Lord Elgin and the Marbles*, p. 275.

54 *On Glasgow and Edinburgh*, p. 133.

55 Cleghorn 5, p. 103.

56 *Ibid.*, p. 112-13.

57 The Dick Peddie view is reproduced in Mitchell, p. iv. McKee, *Calton Hill*, pp. 152-53, reproduces a slightly later (1870) watercolour by Dick Peddie (with a different Waverley Station hotel scheme), in the background of which the National Monument is *not* completed. However, as McKee observes (p. 151), Dick Peddie contrives to omit or else erase from sight anything on the Calton that was Gothic or castellated—though, not, in fact, the Calton Gaol. In Chapter 7 of *Calton Hill*, McKee usefully reproduces drawings of many of the schemes for completion or adaptation of the unfinished National Monument.

58 *The Scotsman*, 3 February 1886.

59 The letter is quoted in Gifford, p. 77.

60 [A. S.], *The Scottish National Monument. A Plea for its Completion*. The NLS catalogue dates the copy there (5.5073) to *c.* 1905, though internal evidence indicates that George V had recently ascended the throne.

61 See https://library.nashville.org.blog/2019/10/nashville-athens.southbut-why.

62 Dinsmoor's still-standard *Architecture of Ancient Greece* had appeared in 1927.

63 See https://eidolon.pub/theheirs-of-athens-of-the-south-a8b730b84de3.

64 Lowenthal, *The Past is a Foreign Country*, pp. 291, 293 quoting Wilbur F. Creighton, *The Parthenon in Nashville*, privately printed (Nashville, TN, 1968).

65 *The Eastern Holiday of a Septuagenarian*, p. 216.

66 *Ibid.*, p. 243.

67 *Ibid.*, p. 243.

68 Mitchell, pp. 9-10.

69 *Ibid.*, pp. 1, 16, 17, 24.

70 'C.', 'The Calton Hill', p. 146.

71 Mitchell, p. 39.

72 Maxwell, *Scottish Gardens*, p. 54.

73 Geddes, *The Civic Survey of Edinburgh*, p. 551.

74 *Ibid.*, pp. 537-38.

75 *Ibid.*, p. 542.

76 *Ibid.*, p. 557.

77 Geddes, *Cities in Evolution*, p. 119.

78 Bolton, *Architecture of Robert & James Adam*, II, pp. 192-94.

79 Kennedy, *Greek Revival America*, p. 5.

80 *Works in Architecture of Robert and James Adam*, p. 42.

81 Watkin, *History of Western Architecture*, p. 463.

82 Watkin, 'Epilogue: The Impact of Stuart over Two Centuries', in *James 'Athenian' Stuart 1713-1788. The Rediscovery of Antiquity*, pp. 524-26.

83 Blaikie Murdoch, *Art Treasures of Edinburgh*, p. ccv.

84 Bone, *Perambulator in Edinburgh*, pp. 19-20, 35, 37.

85 *Ibid.*, p. 160.

86 *Ibid.*, p. 41.

87 Browne, 'Scheme for the Completion of the Scottish National Monument...'.

88 Browne, *Suggestion for the Completion of the Scottish National Monument ...*, [p. 2].

89 *The Times*, 22 August 1949, p. 4.

90 *The Times*, 26 August 1949, p. 8.

91 *The Times*, 21 July 1950, p. 7.

92 *The Times*, 19 August 1960, p. 6.

93 [William] Comyns Beaumont, *Britain—the Key to World History*, pp. 258-73 *passim*, esp. 264, 266.

94 *Letters of Mercurius*, p. 38. The attribution to Trevor-Roper, long surmised, has been confirmed since his death.

95 *The Times*, 22 August 1983, p. 8.

96 MacCaig 'Inward Bound', from *The White Bird* (1973). The poem is printed here by permission of Ewen McCaig [*sic*] as representative of the estate of the late Norman MacCaig.

97 'Edinburgh and the Calton Hill', pp. 19-20.

98 Massie, *Edinburgh*, p. 258.

99 Crawford, *On Glasgow and Edinburgh*, p. 113.

100 'Edinburgh as Athens', Fig. 1 and caption; McKenzie, et al, *Public Sculpture of Edinburgh*, I, pp. 76-81, esp. p. 78; Edina/Athena, p. 70.

101 Mitchell, p. 43, prints a facsimile letter of David Scott Moncrieff, 14 October 1906.

102 See Gifford, pp. 78-79.

103 Black, *All The First Minister's Men*, p. 40, cf. p.3.

104 *Ibid.*, pp. 89 and 117, and cf. p. 84.

105 *Private Eye*, no. 943 (6 February 1998), p. 9.

106 *The Times,* Saturday Supplement, 23 November 1991, p. 4.

107 *All The First Minister's Men*, pp. 84, 62.

108 *Ibid.*, p. 220.

109 Lindsay, *Georgian Edinburgh*, p. 17.

BIBLIOGRAPHY

References to manuscript sources cited are given in full in chapter endnotes

'A. S.', *The Scottish National Monument. A Plea for its Completion as a Memorial to Queen Victoria and the Heroes of Scotland* (Edinburgh n.d. [but 1910])

Adam, Robert and James, *The Works in Architecture of Robert and James Adam*, edited with an introduction by Robert Oresko (London and New York 1975)

Aberdeen, Earl of, see Gordon, George Hamilton-

Aberdein, Jennie W., *John Galt* (London 1936)

Aikman, James, *The Cenotaph, a Poem* (Edinburgh 1821)

Alexander, David, *A Biographical Dictionary of British and Irish Engravers 1714-1820* (London 2021)

[Alison, Archibald], 'On the Proposed National Monument at Edinburgh', *Blackwood's Edinburgh Magazine*, V, no. xxviii (July 1819), pp. 377-87

[—], 'Restoration of the Parthenon in the National Monument', *Blackwood's Edinburgh Magazine*, VI, no. xxxii (November 1819), pp. 137-48

[—], 'On the Proposed Monument for Lord Melville', *Blackwood's Edinburgh Magazine*, VI, no. xxxv (February 1820), pp. 562-67

[—], ['Restoration of the Parthenon'], Art. VI, *The Edinburgh Review*, XXXVII, no. lxxv (February 1823), pp. 126-44

[—], 'The British School of Architecture', *Blackwood's Magazine*, XL, no. ccxlix (August 1836), pp. 227-38

Alison, Archibald, *Some Account of my Life and Writings. An Autobiography*, edited by Lady [Jane R.] Alison, two vols (Edinburgh 1883)

Allan, David, 'The Age of Pericles in the Modern Athens', *The Historical Journal*, 44, no. 2 (2001), pp. 391-417

Allen, Nic, ed., *Scottish Pioneers of the Greek Revival* (Edinburgh 1984)

Andrew, Patricia R., 'St Bernard's Well, and the Water of Leith from the Stock Bridge to the Dean Bridge: A Cultural History', *The Book of the Old Edinburgh Club*, New Series, 9 (2012), pp. 1-32

Anon., *An Account of the Fair Intellectual-Club in Edinburgh: in a Letter to a [sic] Honourable Member of an Athenian Society there* (Edinburgh 1720)

—, *Memoirs of the House of Brandenburg. From the Earliest Accounts to the Death of Frederick I King of Prussia. By the Hand of a Master* (London 1751)

—, 'Cursory Remarks on Grecian & Gothic Architecture, Considered as an Object of Taste', *The Bee*, V (19 October 1791), p. 198

—, 'Additional Particulars touching the Communication to be formed from Princes Street to the Calton Hill by Wellington Bridge', *The Scots Magazine, and Edinburgh Literary Miscellany*, LXXVI (June 1814), pp. 403-6

—, *Report of the Proceedings of a Numerous and a Respectable Meeting of Nobleman and Gentlemen of Scotland held... with a View to the Erection of National Monument in the Metropolis of Scotland* (Edinburgh 1819)

—, *Edinburgh: a Satirical Novel*, three vols (London 1820)

—, 'On the Restoration of the Parthenon', *The Edinburgh Magazine, and Literary Miscellany; A New Series of the Scots Magazine*, VI (April 1820), pp. 304-12

—, 'Mr Haydon's Picture', *Blackwood's Edinburgh Magazine*, VII, no. xliv (November 1820), p. 219

—, 'Domestic Politics', *Blackwood's Edinburgh Magazine*, VIII, no. xlv (December 1820), pp. 329-37

—, 'On Mr Williams's Exhibition of Water-colour Drawings', *The Edinburgh Magazine, and Literary Miscellany; A New Series of the Scots Magazine*, X (February 1822), pp. 239-43

— [? John Stark], 'A Visit to the Great Island of Edinburgh, called Britain, by Eree Omai', of *Blackwood's Edinburgh Magazine*, XI, no. lxv (June 1822), pp. 709-15

— [? John Stark], 'The Second Voyage of Omai the Traveller', *Blackwood's Edinburgh Magazine*, XII, no. lxviii (September 1822), pp. 285-306

—, 'The King's Visit to Edinburgh. By a Londoner but no Cockney', *Blackwood's Edinburgh Magazine*, XII, no. lxviii (September 1822), pp. 268-84

— [? John Wilson], 'Hogg's Royal Jubilee', *Blackwood's Edinburgh Magazine*, XII, no. LXVIII (September 1822), pp. 344-54

—, '*Lectures on Architecture* .... By James Elmes', Art. XV, *New Edinburgh Review*, VIII (April 1823), pp. 554-603

—, '*Travels in Egypt and The Holy Land. By William Rae Wilson*', Art. VI, *The Edinburgh Review*, XXXVIII, no. lxxvi (May 1823), pp. 398-413

—, 'Great Fire', *Blackwood's Edinburgh Magazine*, XVI, no. xcv (December 1824), pp. 698-710

— [? Archibald Elliot], volume of engraved plans, elevations and perspectives, 'The Edinburgh Hotel, Tavern and Coffee House, Waterloo Place': NLS. R.251.d 2(2)

—, 'High School: New Academy of Edinburgh', extracted from an unnamed magazine and with page numbers double-printed: NLS, Ry.IV.e.4(19), p. 527* [*sic*]

—, *Edinburgh Dissected: Including Strictures on its Institutions, Legal, Clerical, Medical, Educational, &c, to which are Added, Confessions and Opinions of a Tory Country Gentleman: with a Variety of Anecdotal and Other Matter. In a Series of Letters Addressed to Roger Cutlar, Esquire, by his Nephew* (Edinburgh 1857)

Arnot, Hugo, *The History of Edinburgh* (Edinburgh and London 1779)

'Assistant Surgeon in the Royal Navy, An', 'Letters from the Mediterranean during the years 1829—1830—1831', *The Border Magazine, November 1831-December 1832*, 2 vols (Berwick 1833), II, pp. 203-15

Ballantine, James, *The Gaberlunzie's Wallet* (Edinburgh 1843)

Batty, Robert, *Select Views of Some of the Principal Cities of Europe from original paintings by Lieut Col Batty FRS* (London 1832)

Beaton, Roderick M., *The Greek Revolution of 1821 and its Global Significance* (Athens 2021)

Beattie, William, *Scotland Illustrated in a Series of Views Taken Expressly for this Work by Messrs T. Allom, W. H. Bartlett and H. McCulloch*, two vols (London 1838)

—, *The Danube: its History, Scenery, and Topography*, illustrated by W. H. Bartlett (London 1842)

Beaumont, [William] Comyns, *Britain—the Key to World History* (London 1949)

Begg, James, *How to Promote and Preserve the True Beauty of Edinburgh: Being a few Hints to The Hon Lord Cockburn on his Letter to the Lord Provost* (Edinburgh 1849)

Bergdoll, Barry, *European Architecture 1750-1890* (Oxford 2000)

Bewick, Thomas, *A Memoir of Thomas Bewick, written by Himself*, edited by Montague Weekley (London 1961)

Black, A[dam] & C[harles], *Black's Picturesque Tourist of Scotland* (Edinburgh 1840)

Black, David, *All the First Minister's Men. Uncovering the Truth Behind the Holyrood Scandal* (Edinburgh 2001)

Blackie, John Stuart, *The Letters of John Stuart Blackie to his Wife*, selected and edited by Archibald Stodart Walker (Edinburgh 1909)

Blanqui, Adolphe, *Voyage d'un Jeune Français en Angleterre et en Écosse* (Paris 1823)

Boardman, John with Finn, David, *The Parthenon and its Sculptures* (London 1985)

Bolton, Arthur T., *The Architecture of Robert & James Adam*, two vols (London 1922)

Bone, James, *The Perambulator in Edinburgh* (London 1926)

Bracken, C. P., *Antiquities Acquired. The Spoliation of Greece* (Newton Abbott 1975)

Brown, Iain Gordon, *The Hobby-Horsical Antiquary. A Scottish Character, 1640-1830* (Edinburgh 1980)

—, *Poet & Painter: Allan Ramsay, Father and Son, 1684-1784* (Edinburgh 1984)

—, 'The Pamphlets of Allan Ramsay the Younger', *The Book Collector*, 37, no. 1 (Spring 1988), pp. 55-85

—, *Building for Books: The Architectural Evolution of the Advocates' Library 1689-1925* (Aberdeen 1989)

—, 'David Hume's Tomb: A Roman mausoleum' by Robert Adam, *Proceedings of the Society of Antiquaries of Scotland*, 121 (1991), pp. 391-422

—, 'Robert Adam's Drawings: Edinburgh's Loss, London's Gain', *The Book of the Old Edinburgh Club*, New Series, 2 (1992), pp. 23-33

—, *Elegance & Entertainment in the New Town of Edinburgh. The Harden Drawings*, revised edition (Edinburgh 2002)

—, 'Intimacy and Immediacy: James Hall's Journals in Italy and Germany 1821-22', in *Britannia Italia Germania. Taste & Travel in the Nineteenth Century*, edited by Carol Richardson and Graham Smith (Edinburgh 2001), pp. 23-42

—, 'One City in its Time: Views of Edinburgh in the Age of Enlightenment', *Scottish Archives*, 14 (2008), pp. 102-11

—, 'Daniel Macintosh and the Repository of Arts', *The Book of the Old Edinburgh Club*, New Series, 7 (2008), pp. 171-75

—, 'Precarious Preferment in Apollo's Favourite Residence: London as Focus for Sir John Clerk's Political and Cultural Ambition', in *Scots in London in the Eighteenth Century*, edited by Stana Nenadic (Cranbury, NJ, 2010), pp. 49-72

—, *Rax Me That Buik. Highlights from the Collections of the National Library of Scotland* (London 2010)

—, 'The Old Edinburgh Club Centenary Conference: President's Remarks', *The Book of the Old Edinburgh Club*, New Series, 8 (2010), pp. 7-12

—, 'A Johnian Hog in Caledonia', *The Eagle* [St John's College, Cambridge], 93 (2011), pp. 53-60

—, '"A National Concern": but which Nation really gave birth to the Select Society of Edinburgh?', in *Scotland's Cultural Identity and Standing*, edited by Klaus Peter Müller, Bernhard Reitz and Sigrid Rieuwerts (Trier 2013), pp. 79-90

—, '"Tre Volte Terra Classica": La Spedizione Siciliana di James Hall', introduction to *James Hall, Diario Siciliano (Febbraio-Marzo 1822)*, edited by Rosario Portale (Lugano 2013), pp. 1-15

—, '"Spectator of the Busy Scene": a Visitor of 1793 Experiences Edinburgh Outside and In', *The Book of the Old Edinburgh Club*, New Series, 10 (2014), pp. 157-64

—, 'Edinburgh as Athens: New Evidence to Support a Topographical and Intellectual Idea Current in the Early Nineteenth Century', *The Book of the Old Edinburgh Club*, New Series, 15 (2019), pp. 1-12

—, *Frolics in the Face of Europe: Sir Walter Scott, Continental Travel and the Tradition of the Grand Tour* (Stroud 2020)

—, '"Gilded by the Rays of an Athenian Sun": Auld Reekie into Athens of the North', in *Edina/Athena 1821-2021 The Greek Revolution & The Athens of the North*, exhibition catalogue by Alasdair Grant, Niels Gaul, Iain Gordon Brown and Roderick Beaton, University of Edinburgh (Edinburgh 2021), p. 13

—, '"A Faithless Truant to the Classic Page": Sir Walter Scott, Greek, Greece and the Greeks', forthcoming in *The Greek Revolution of 1821: European Contexts, Scottish Connections*, edited by Roderick Beaton and Niels Gaul (Edinburgh 2023)

—, 'Erskine, David Steuart, 11th Earl of Buchan', forthcoming in *A Dictionary of British Collections and Collectors 1660-1939*, edited by Charles Sebag-Montefiore, online publication on the website of the National Gallery (London 2024)

Browne, George Washington, 'Scheme for the Completion of the Scottish National Monument, Calton Hill, Edinburgh, as a War Memorial', *The Builder*, CXV, no. 3938 (26 July 1918), p. 59 and plates following p. 60

—, *Suggestion for the Completion of the Scottish National Monument, Calton Hill, Edinburgh, as a War Memorial* [Edinburgh ?1918]

[Bruce, Thomas, 7th Earl of Elgin], *Letter to the Editor of The Edinburgh Review on the Subject of an Article in No. L of that Journal on 'The Remains of John Tweddell'* (Edinburgh 1815)

Brydall, Robert, *Art in Scotland* (Edinburgh 1889)

Buchan, Earl of, see Erskine, David Steuart

Buchan, James, *Capital of the Mind. How Edinburgh Changed the World* (London 2003)

Buchan, John, 'A Comic Chesterfield', *Blackwood's Magazine*, CLXVII (1900), pp. 557-68

'Builder, A.', *A Letter to the Right Honourable the Lord Provost on the Subject of the Proposed New Streets and Approaches to the City. By a Builder* (Edinburgh 1825)

Butchart, Robert, *Prints & Drawings of Edinburgh: a Descriptive Account of the Collection in the Edinburgh Room of the Central Public Library* (Edinburgh 1955)

—, 'Lost Opportunities: An Account of Some of Edinburgh's Unrealised Projects', *The Book of the Old Edinburgh Club*, XXX (1959), pp. 36-59

Buzonnière, Léon de, *Le Touriste Écossais, ou Itinéraire général de l'Écosse, ouvrage indispensable au voyageur* (Paris 1830)

Byrom, John, 'Edinburgh and the Calton Hill', *Proceedings of the Calton Conference*, 5 November 1983 (Edinburgh 1984), pp.18-24

Byron, Lord, *The Complete Poetical Works*, edited by Jerome J. McGann, seven vols (Oxford 1980-89)

'C.', 'The Calton Hill', in *The Republic of Letters, a Selection in Poetry and Prose ... with Many Original Pieces*, edited by Alexander Whitelaw, four vols (Glasgow 1833), IV, pp. 145-49

Camp, John M., *The Archaeology of Athens* (New Haven and London 2001)

Campbell, Alexander, *A Journey from Edinburgh through Parts of North Britain*, two vols (London 1802)

Carlyle, Nicholas, *A Topographical Dictionary of Scotland*, two vols (London 1813), II, *s.v.* 'Leith, South'

Carpenter, Rhys, *The Architects of the Parthenon* (Harmondsworth 1970)

Carr, John, *Caledonian Sketches, or a Tour through Scotland in 1807 ...* (London 1809)

Carus, C. G., *The King of Saxony's Journey through England and Scotland in the year 1844* (London 1846)

Chambers, Robert, *Walks in Edinburgh* (Edinburgh 1825)

Clarke, Edward Daniel, *Travels in Various Countries of Europe, Asia and Africa*, fourth edition, eight vols (London 1816-18)

Clarke, Edward Daniel, *The Life and Remains of Edward Daniel Clarke* [edited by William Otter] (London 1824)

[Clarke, William], *A Scots Grey at Waterloo: The Incredible Story of Troop Sergeant Major William Clarke*, edited by Gareth Glover (Barnsley 2017)

[Cleghorn, George], *Remarks on the Intended Restoration of the Parthenon of Athens as the National Monument of Scotland* (Edinburgh 1824)

|—, writing as 'An Amateur'], *Remarks on Ancient and Modern Art, in a Series of Essays By An Amateur* (Edinburgh 1837)

Cleghorn, George, *The Restoration of the Parthenon of Athens as the National Monument of Scotland* (Edinburgh 1846)

—, *Ancient and Modern Art, Historical and Critical*, second edition [*sic*] corrected and enlarged, two vols (Edinburgh 1848)

—, 'Essay on the National Monument of Scotland', *Transactions of the Architectural Institute of Scotland*, 2 (1851-52), pp. 81-120

Cobbett, William, *Cobbett's Tour in Scotland; and in the Four Northern Counties of England in the Autumn of the Year 1832* (London 1833)

Cockburn, Henry, Lord Cockburn, *A Letter to the Lord Provost on the Best Ways of Spoiling the Beauty of Edinburgh*, third edition (Edinburgh 1849)

—, *Life of Lord Jeffrey* (Edinburgh 1852)

—, *Memorials of his Time*, edited by Harry A. Cockburn (Edinburgh 1909)

—, *Some Letters of Lord Cockburn. With Pages Omitted from the Memorials of his Time*, edited by Harry A. Cockburn (Edinburgh 1932)

—, *Lord Cockburn: Selected Letters*, edited by Alan Bell (Edinburgh 2005)

[Francis Cohen, later Sir Francis Palgrave], ['Application of the Various Styles of Architecture'], Art. II, *The Quarterly Review*, XXVII, no. liv (July 1822), pp. 308-37

Colvin, Howard, *A Biographical Dictionary of British Architects 1600-1840*, fourth edition (New Haven and London 2008)

Cook, B. F., *The Elgin Marbles*, second edition (London 1997)

Cookson, J. E., 'Scotland's National Monument', *Scottish Tradition*, 24 (1999), pp. 3-12

[Combe, William], *The Tour of Doctor Prosody in Search of the Antique and Picturesque, through Scotland, the Hebrides, the Orkney and Shetland Isles* (London 1821)

Cosh, Mary, *Edinburgh. The Golden Age* (Edinburgh 2003)

Council of Europe, *The Age of Neo-Classicism*, exhibition catalogue, Royal Academy of Arts and Victoria & Albert Museum (London 1972)

Crawford, Robert, *On Glasgow and Edinburgh* (Cambridge, Mass., and London 2013)

Crichton-Browne, James, *Victorian Jottings from an Old Commonplace Book* (London 1926)

Cririe, James, *Scottish Scenery; or, Sketches in Verse, Descriptive of Scenes Chiefly in the Highlands of Scotland* (London 1803)

Crombie, Benjamin, and Hugh Paton, *Men of Modern Athens; Being Portraits of Eminent Personages (Existing or Supposed to Exist) in the Metropolis of Scotland* (Edinburgh 1839)

Crook, Joseph Mordaunt, *The Greek Revival*, RIBA Drawings Series (London 1968)

—, 'Broomhall, Fife', *Country Life*, 29 January 1970, pp. 242-46

—, *The Greek Revival. Neo-Classical Attitudes in British Architecture 1760-1870* (London 1972)

Cruft, Kitty and Andrew Fraser, *James Craig 1744-1795. "The Ingenious Architect of the New Town of Edinburgh"* (Edinburgh 1995)

Curl, James Stevens, *Georgian Architecture in the British Isles 1714-1830* (London 2011)

Cutmore, Jonathan, *Contributors to the Quarterly Review, 1809-25* (London 2008)

Daiches, David, *The Paradox of Scottish Culture: The Eighteenth-Century Experience* (London 1964)

—, *Edinburgh* (London 1978)

Dalzel, Andrew, *History of the University of Edinburgh from its Foundation*, two vols (Edinburgh 1862)

Davie, George Elder, *The Democratic Intellect. Scotland and her Universities in the Nineteenth Century* (Edinburgh 1964)

Dibdin, Thomas Frognall, *A Bibliographical Antiquarian and Picturesque Tour in the Northern Counties of England and in Scotland*, two vols (London 1838)

Dilettanti, Society of, *Ionian Antiquities* [the work of Richard Chandler, Nicholas Revett and William Pars] (London 1769)

Dinsmoor, William Bell, *The Architecture of Ancient Greece*, third, revised, edition (New York 1975)

Dodwell, Edward, *A Classical and Picturesque Tour through Greece during the years 1801, 1805 and 1806*, two vols (London 1819)

Duncan, Ian, *Scott's Shadow. The Novel in Romantic Edinburgh* (Princeton, NJ, and Woodstock, Oxon, 2007)

Dyce, William and Charles Heath Wilson, *Letter to Lord Meadowbank [Alexander Maconochie], and the Committee of the Honourable Board of Trustees for the Encouragement of Arts and Manufactures, on the Best Means of Ameliorating the Arts and Manufactures of Scotland in Point of Taste* (Edinburgh 1837)

Edina/Athena 1821-2021 The Greek Revolution & The Athens of the North, exhibition catalogue by Alasdair Grant, Niels Gaul, Iain Gordon Brown and Roderick Beaton (Edinburgh 2021)

Edinburgh Miscellany, The: Consisting of Original Poems, Translations, &c., by various hands, vol. 1 [all published] (Edinburgh 1720)

Edinburgh Town Council, *Address from the Town Council of Edinburgh on the subject of the New Buildings for the High School* (Edinburgh 1825)

Eichthal, Gustave d', *A French Sociologist Looks at Britain. Gustave d'Eichthal and British Society in 1828*, translated and edited by Barrie M. Ratcliffe and W. H. Chaloner (Manchester 1977)

Elgin, Earl of Elgin, see Bruce, Thomas

[Elliot, Sir Gilbert, of Minto], *Proposals for carrying on certain Public Works in the City of Edinburgh* (Edinburgh 1752)

Elmes, James, 'On the best Situation and most proper Mode of commemorating the great Victories of the late Wars by Sea and Land ...', *Annals of the Fine Arts for MDCCCXVII* (London 1818), Art. III, pp. 26-36

—, 'History of Architecture in Great Britain. A Brief Sketch or Epitome of the Rise and Progress of Architecture in Great Britain', pt. vi, *Civil Engineer and Architect's Journal, Scientific and Railway Gazette*, X, no. 122 (November 1847), pp. 337-41

Erskine, David Steuart, 11th Earl of Buchan, *The Four Repasts of the Day* (? Dryburgh, n.d.)

—, *The Anonymous and Fugitive Essays of the Earl of Buchan*, I [*sic*: vol. I only published], (Edinburgh 1812)

[Ewbank, J. W. and James Browne], *Picturesque Views of Edinburgh; The Drawings by J. Ewbank, Engraved by W. H. Lizars. To Which is Prefixed An Historical Sketch of Edinburgh by James Browne* (Edinburgh 1825)

Faujas de Saint-Fond, B., *Travels in England, Scotland and the Hebrides; Undertaken for the Purpose of Examining the State of the Arts, the Sciences, Natural History and Manners, in Great Britain*, two vols (London 1799)

Fehlmann, Marc, '"A Striking Proof of Scotland's Pride": Remarks on the Scottish National Monument on Calton Hill', *Journal of the Scottish Society for Art History*, 10 (2005), pp. 39-47

—, 'A Building from which Derived "All that is Good": Observations on the Intended Reconstruction of the Parthenon on Calton Hill', *Nineteenth-Century Art Worldwide*, 4, no. 3 (Autumn 2005) unpaginated http://www.19thc-artworldwide. org/autumn05/58-autumn05/autumn05article/207-a-building-from-which-derived-all-that-is-good-observations-on-the-intended-reconstruction-of-the-parthenon-on-calton-hill

—, 'As Greek as it Gets: British Attempts to Recreate the Parthenon', *Rethinking History*, 11, no. 3 (September 2007), pp. 353-77

Fergusson, James, *History of the Modern Styles of Architecture* (London 1862)

Finlayson, C. P. and S. M. Simpson, 'The History of the Library 1580-1710', in *Edinburgh University Library 1580-1980. A collection of historical essays*, edited by Jean R. Guild and Alexander Law (Edinburgh 1982), pp. 43-54

Fisher, Ian, 'Thomas Hamilton', in *Scottish Pioneers of the Greek Revival*, edited by Nic Allen (Edinburgh 1984), pp. 37-42

Fleming, John, *Robert Adam and his Circle in Edinburgh and Rome* (London 1962)

Fontane, Theodor, *Beyond the Tweed. A Tour of Scotland in 1858*, translated by Brian Battershaw (London 1998)

Forbes, The Hon. Mrs Atholl, *Curiosities of a Scots Charta Chest* (Edinburgh 1897)

Fraser Andrew G., *The Building of Old College. Adam, Playfair & the University of Edinburgh* (Edinburgh 1989)

—, 'A Reassessment of Craig's New Town Plans, 1766-1774', in *James Craig 1744-1795. "The Ingenious Architect of the New Town of Edinburgh"'*, edited by Kitty Cruft and Andrew Fraser (Edinburgh 1995), pp. 25-47

Fullarton, A, & Co. *The Topographical, Statistical, and Historical Gazetteer of Scotland*, two vols (Glasgow 1842)

Galloway, George, *The Loyal Albany Museum; or the Caledonian St Andrews Magazine*, third edition (Edinburgh 1817)

Galt, John, *Letters from the Levant; Containing Views of the State of Society, Manners, Opinions and Commerce in Greece, and Several of the Principal Islands of the Archipelago* (London 1813)

[—], *Atheniad*, in *The Autobiography of John Galt*, two vols (London 1833), II, pp. 160-69

[—], *Glenfell; or, Macdonalds and Campbells. An Edinburgh Tale of the Nineteenth Century* (London 1820)

[—, writing as 'Viator'], 'Grecian Architecture—Lord Aberdeen', *Blackwood's Edinburgh Magazine*, XI, no. lxv (June 1822), pp. 705-9

—, *The Last of the Lairds or The Life and Opinions of Malachi Mailings Esq. of Auldbiggings*, edited by Ian A. Gordon (Edinburgh 1976)

[—], *Auld Reekie; or, a Mistake in Edinburgh*, in *The Literary Life, and Miscellanies, of John Galt*, three vols (Edinburgh 1834)

—, *The Autobiography of John Galt*, two vols (London 1833)

Geddes, Patrick, with illustrations by Mears, F. C., *The Civic Survey of Edinburgh* (Edinburgh 1911): paper reprinted from *Transactions of the Town Planning Conference*, London 1910, pp. 537-74

—, *Cities in Evolution: An Introduction to the Town Planning Movement and to the Study of Civics* (London 1915)

Gibson, Patrick, *Select Views in Edinburgh: Consisting Chiefly of Prospects that have presented themselves, and Public Buildings that have been Erected in the Course of the recent Improvement of the City, Accompanied with Historical and Explanatory Notices* (Edinburgh 1818)

Gifford, John, McWilliam, Colin and Walker, David, *The Buildings of Scotland. Edinburgh*, reprinted with corrections (New Haven and London 2003)

Gifford, John, 'The National Monument of Scotland', *Architectural Heritage*, XXV (2014), pp. 43-83

Giles, Arthur, *Across Western Waves and Home in a Royal Capital. America for Modern Athenians. Modern Athens for Americans. A Personal Narrative in Tour and Time* (London 1898)

Gillies, John, *The History of Ancient Greece, its Colonies and Conquests*, two vols (London 1786)

Gillies, Robert Pearse, *Memoirs of a Literary Veteran*, three vols (London 1851)

Gilpin, William, *Observations, Relative Chiefly to Picturesque Beauty, Made in the Year 1776 on Several Parts of Great Britain; Particularly the High-Lands of Scotland*, two vols (London 1789)

Glendinning, Miles, Ranald MacInnes and Aonghus MacKechnie, *A History of Scottish Architecture* (Edinburgh 1996)

Glendinning, Miles, *The Architecture of Scottish Government* (Dundee 2004)

Godard Desmarest, Clarisse, 'The Melville Monument and the Shaping of the Scottish Metropolis', *Architectural History*, 61 (2018), pp. 105-30

—, ed., *The New Town of Edinburgh: An Architectural Celebration*, (Edinburgh 2019)

—, 'Princes Street, Edinburgh: a Street of Encounters', *The Book of the Old Edinburgh Club*, New Series, 15 (2019), pp. 13-27

Gomme, Andor and David Walker, *Architecture of Glasgow*, second, revised edition (London 1987)

Gordon, Alexander, *Itinerarium Septentrionale: or, a Journey Thro' most of the Counties of Scotland, and Those in the North of England* (London 1726)

Gordon, George Hamilton- , fourth Earl of Aberdeen, *Inquiry into the Principles of Beauty in Grecian Architecture; with an Historical View of the Rise and Progress of the Art in Greece* (London 1822)

Gordon, Ian A., *John Galt: the Life of a Writer* (Edinburgh 1972)

Gordon, Thomas, *History of the Greek Revolution*, two vols (Edinburgh and London 1832)

Gourlay, Robert Fleming, *The Mound Improvement, with A Plan and Elevations* (Edinburgh 1850)

[—], *The Best Site for Trinity College Church: with Ten Years Discussion on the Subject … Respectfully Submitted to His Royal Highness Prince Albert* (Edinburgh 1855)

Gow, Ian, 'William Henry Playfair', in *Scottish Pioneers of the Greek Revival*, edited by Nic Allen (Edinburgh 1984), pp. 43-55

—, 'C. R. Cockerell's Designs for the Northern Athenian Parthenon', *Architectural Heritage Society of Scotland Journal*, 16 (1989), pp. 20-25

—, 'The Northern Athenian Temple of the Arts', in Ian Gow and Timothy Clifford, *The National Gallery of Scotland. An Architectural and Decorative History* (Edinburgh 1989), pp. 11-44

—, 'Playfair: A Northern Athenian', *Royal Institute of British Architects Journal*, 79, no. 5 (May 1990), pp. 37-44

—, *Scotland's Lost Houses* (London 2006)

Graffman, C. S., and C. J. Billmark, *Skottska Vuer* (Stockholm 1831)

Grant, Anne, *Memoir and Correspondence of Mrs Grant of Laggan*, edited by John Peter Grant, three vols (London 1844); second edition (London 1845)

Grant, James, *Cassell's Old and New Edinburgh*, three vols (London 1882-87)

Groome, Francis, *Ordnance Gazetteer of Scotland*, six vols (Edinburgh 1882-85)

Hall, Basil, *Patchwork*, three vols, second edition (London 1841)

Hall, James, *Diario Siciliano (Febbraio-Marzo 1822)*, edited by Rosario Portale, with an Introduction by Iain Gordon Brown (Lugano 2013)

Hamilton, Thomas, *A Letter to the Right Hon. Lord John Russell MP, First Lord of Her Majesty's Treasury: On the Present Crisis Relative to the Fine Arts in Scotland; with Plans and Perspective Views of Proposed Galleries on the Mound* (Edinburgh 1850)

[Hamilton, William Richard], *Memorandum on the Subject of the Earl of Elgin's Pursuits in Greece* (Edinburgh 1811)

Harris, Eileen, with Nicholas Savage, *British Architectural Books and Writers 1556-1785* (Cambridge 1990)

Harris, John, 'C. R. Cockerell's "Ichnographica Domestica"', *Architectural History*, 14 (1971), pp. 5-29

Haydon, Benjamin Robert, *The Diary of Benjamin Robert Haydon*, edited by Willard Bissell Pope, five vols (Cambridge, Mass., 1960-63)

Haynes, D. E. L., *An Historical Guide to the Sculptures of the Parthenon* (London 1969)

—, *The Arundel Marbles* (Oxford 1975)

Haynes, Nick and Clive B. Fenton, *Building Knowledge. An Architectural History of the University of Edinburgh* (Edinburgh 2017)

Hazlitt, William, *The Collected Works of William Hazlitt*, edited by A. R. Waller and Arnold Glover, twelve vols (London 1902-6)

Herman, Arthur, *How the Scots invented the Modern World* (New York 2001); published in the UK as *The Scottish Enlightenment: The Scots' Invention of the Modern World* (London 2003)

Heron, Robert, *Observations Made in a Journey through the Western Counties of Scotland in the Autumn of MDCCXCII*, two vols (Perth 1793)

Hill, Ida Thallon, *The Ancient City of Athens: Its Topography and Monuments* (London 1953)

Hitchcock, Henry-Russell, *Architecture: Nineteenth and Twentieth Centuries*, fourth (integrated) edition (Harmondsworth 1977)

Hogg, Thomas Jefferson, *The Life of Percy Bysshe Shelley* (London 1906)

[Home, Henry, Lord Kames], *Elements of Criticism*, three vols (Edinburgh 1762)

Horn, D. B., *A Short History of the University of Edinburgh 1556-1889* (Edinburgh 1967)

Hume, David, *The Letters of David Hume*, edited by J. Y. T. Greig, two vols (Oxford 1932)

Irwin, David and Francina, *Scottish Painters at Home and Abroad 1700-1900* (London 1975)

Irwin, David, *Neoclassicism* (London 1997)

Isocrates, edited and translated by George Norlin, three vols (London and New York 1928-45)

Jenkins, Ian, 'Acquisition and Supply of Casts of the Parthenon Sculptures by the British Museum, 1835-1939', *The Annual of the British School at Athens*, 85 (1990), pp. 89-114

—, *Archaeologists & Aesthetes in the Sculpture Galleries of the British Museum 1800-1939* (London 1992)

Jenkins, John, assembled volume of 150 etched Caricature Portraits of Celebrities in Edinburgh: NLS, Ry. II. b. 16

John Henning 1771-1851: '... a very ingenious Modeller', exhibition catalogue by John Malden (Paisley 1977)

[Johnstone, Christian Isobel], *The Saxon and the Gaël; or, The Northern Metropolis: including a View of the Highland and Lowland Character*, four vols (London 1814)

[—], *The Edinburgh Tales, Conducted by Mrs Johnstone*, three vols (Edinburgh 1845-46)

'Journeyman Mason, A.', 'Decorations of Edinburgh', *Blackwood's Edinburgh Magazine*, V, no. xxxi (October 1819), pp. 76-78

—, 'Public Buildings of Edinburgh', *Blackwood's Edinburgh Magazine*, VI, no. xxxiv (January 1820), pp. 370-75

Joyce, Michael, *Edinburgh. The Golden Age* (London 1951)

Kay, John and Hugh Paton, *A Series of Original Portraits and Caricature Etchings, by the Late John Kay, Miniature Painter, Edinburgh; with Biographical Sketches and Illustrative Anecdotes*, two vols (Edinburgh 1837-38)

Kelly, Stuart, *Scott-land: The Man Who Invented a Nation* (Edinburgh 2010)

[Kelsall, Charles], *A Letter from Athens, Addressed to a Friend in England* (London 1812)

Kennedy, Roger G., *Greek Revival America* (New York 1989)

Kerr, Robert, *Memoirs of the Life, Writings, & Correspondence of William Smellie*, two vols, (Edinburgh 1811)

Knox, John, *A View of the British Empire, More Especially Scotland; with Some Proposals for the Improvement of that Country, the Extension of its Fisheries and the Relief of the People*, third edition, two vols (London 1785)

Kohl, J. G., *Travels in Scotland* (London 1844)

Lach-Szyrma, Krystyn, *From Charlotte Square to Fingal's Cave. Reminiscences of a Journey through Scotland 1820-1824 by Krystyn Lach-Szyrma*, edited by Mona Kedslie McLeod (East Linton 2004)

Lang, Andrew, *The Life and Letters of John Gibson Lockhart*, two vols (London 1897)

Lauder, Sir Thomas Dick, *Memorial of the Royal Progress in Scotland* (Edinburgh 1843)

Lawrence, A. W., revised by R. A. Tomlinson, *Greek Architecture*, fifth edition (New Haven and London 1996)

Leake, W. M., *The Topography of Athens, with Some Remarks on its Antiquities* (London 1821)

Lettice, I [John], *Letters on a Tour through various parts of Scotland in the Year 1792* (London 1794)

Lindsay, Ian G., *Georgian Edinburgh* (Edinburgh 1948); new expanded edition revised by David Walker (Edinburgh and London 1973)

Linklater, Eric, illustrated by Don Pottinger, *Edinburgh* (London 1960)

Linning, Michael, *Memoranda Publica* (Edinburgh 1834)

Lockhart, John Gibson, *Peter's Letters to His Kinsfolk*, three vols (Edinburgh 1819)

—, *The Life of Sir Walter Scott*, Edinburgh Edition, ten vols (Edinburgh 1902-3)

Lowenthal, David, *The Past is a Foreign Country* (Cambridge 1985)

Lowrey, John, 'Robert Adam and Edinburgh', *Rassegna*, 17, no. 64 (1995), pp. 26-33

—, 'From Caesarea to Athens. Greek Revival Edinburgh and the Question of Scottish Identity within the Unionist State', *The Journal of the Society of Architectural Historians*, 60, no. 2 (June 2001), pp. 136-57

—, 'Commerce and Conservation: Edinburgh New Town in the Early Twentieth Century', in *The New Town of Edinburgh: An Architectural Celebration*, edited by Clarisse Godard Desmarest, pp. 147-62

Macaulay, James, *The Classical Country House in Scotland 1660-1800* (London 1987)

MacCaig, Norman, *The White Bird* (1973)

McCall Smith, Alexander, *A Work of Beauty. Alexander McCall Smith's Edinburgh* (Edinburgh 2014)

McCormick, E. C., *Omai. Pacific Envoy* (Auckland 1977)

M'Crie, Thomas, *Life of Thomas M'Crie, DD* (Edinburgh 1840)

Macdonald, Angus J. 'The Athens of the North', *Rassegna*, 17, no. 64 (1995), pp. 35-39

Macdonald, Sir John A., *Life Jottings of an Old Edinburgh Citizen* (Edinburgh 1915)

[McDonough, Felix], *The Hermit in Edinburgh*, three vols (London 1824)

McElroy, Davis D., *Scotland's Age of Improvement: A Survey of Eighteenth-Century Literary Clubs and Societies* (Pullman, WA, 1969)

McHaffie, Ian, *Greek Secrets Revealed. Hidden Scottish History Uncovered. Greek inscriptions in Scotland, with a translation into English and some explanation of the background. Book 1—Edinburgh*, first edition (Edinburgh 2019), second, expanded edition (Edinburgh 2022)

McKean, Charles, 'The Athens of the North', *The Story of Scotland*, vol. 2, part 26 (1988), pp. 704-7

—, *Edinburgh: Portrait of a City* (London 1991)

—, *Edinburgh. An Illustrated Architectural Guide* (Edinburgh 1992)

McKee, Kirsten Carter, *Calton Hill and the Plans for Edinburgh's Third New Town* (Edinburgh 2018)

McKenzie, Ray, with Dianne King and Tracy Smith, *Public Sculpture of Edinburgh*, two vols (Liverpool 2018)

McMillan, Andrew A., Richard J. Gillanders, and John A. Fairhurst, *The Building Stones of Edinburgh*, second edition (Edinburgh 1999)

McMillan, Andrew A., 'The City of Edinburgh: Landscape and Building Stone', *The Book of the Old Edinburgh Club*, New Series, 9 (2012), pp. 129-35

[MacNeill, Hector], *Town Fashions, or Modern Manners Delineated, A Satirical Dialogue* (Edinburgh 1810)

McWilliam, Colin, *Scottish Townscape* (London 1975)

Magnusson, Magnus, *The Clacken and the Slate. The Story of the Edinburgh Academy 1824-1974* (London 1974)

Mason, John, 'The Edinburgh School of Design', *The Book of the Old Edinburgh Club*, 27 (1949), pp. 67-96

Massie, Allan, *Edinburgh* (London 1994)

Masson, David, *Memories of Two Cities. Edinburgh and Aberdeen* (Edinburgh 1911)

Mawman, Joseph, *An Excursion to the Highlands of Scotland and the English Lakes with Recollection, Descriptions, and References to Historical Facts* (London 1805)

Matthews, Henry, *The Diary of An Invalid: Being the Journal of a Tour in Pursuit of Health ...* (London 1820)

Maxwell, Sir Herbert, *Scottish Gardens* (London 1908)

Michaelis, Adolf, *Ancient Marbles in Great Britain* (Cambridge 1882)

Michie, Michael, *An Enlightenment Tory in Victorian Scotland. The Career of Sir Archibald Alison* (East Linton 1997)

Middleton, Robin and David Watkin, *Neoclassical and 19ᵗʰ Century Architecture/ 1: The Enlightenment in France and England* (London 1987)

Miller, Hugh, *Hugh Miller's Memoir: From Stonemason to Geologist*, edited by Michael Shortland (Edinburgh 1995)

Miller, Karl, *Cockburn's Millennium* (London 1975)

Mitchell, William, *The Eastern Holiday of a Septuagenarian* (Edinburgh 1906)

—, *The National Monument to be Completed for the Scottish National Gallery on the Model of the Parthenon at Athens. An Appeal to the Scottish People* (London 1907)

Modern Athenian, The (Edinburgh 1875-78)

Montgomery, Alan, *Classical Caledonia. Roman History and Myth in Eighteenth-century Scotland* (Edinburgh 2020)

Morton, Graeme, *Unionist Nationalism. Governing Urban Scotland, 1830-1860* (East Linton 1999)

[Mudie, Robert], *Glenfergus*, three vols (Edinburgh 1820)

[Mudie, Robert], *A Historical Account of His Majesty's Visit to Scotland*, third edition (Edinburgh 1822)

[—, writing as 'Lawrence Longshank'], *Things in General; Being Delineations of Persons, Places, Scenes, Circumstances, Situations and Occurrences, in the Metropolis and Other Parts of Britain, with an Autobiographic Sketch in Limine, and a Notice Touching Edinburgh* (London 1824)

[—], *The Modern Athens: A Dissection and Demonstration of Men and Things in the Scotch Capital. By a Modern Greek* (London 1825)

[—], *Attic Fragments of Characters, Customs Opinions and Scenes* (London 1825)

Murdoch, W. G. Blaikie, *The Art Treasures of Edinburgh* (Edinburgh 1924)

Mure, William, of Caldwell, *Journal of a Tour in Greece and the Ionian Islands*, two vols (Edinburgh 1842)

Murray John, *Handbook for Travellers in Scotland*, third and thoroughly revised edition (London 1873)

Naik, Anuradha S., and Margaret C. H. Stewart, 'The Hellenization of Edinburgh: Cityscape, Architecture and the Athenian Cast Collection', *The Journal of the Society of Architectural Historians*, 66, no. 3 (September 2007), pp. 366-89

'Naseweis, Sebaldus', *Edinburgh and its Society in 1838* (Edinburgh 1838)

Necker de Saussure, Louis Albert, *Travels in Scotland; Descriptive of the State of Manners, Literature and Science* (London 1821)

New Picture of Edinburgh for 1818 (Edinburgh 1818)

[Nightingale, Florence] *The Collected Works of Florence Nightingale*, sixteen vols, 7, *Florence Nightingale's European Travels*, edited by Lynn McDonald (Waterloo, Ontario, 2007)

Nisbet, Thomas, Auctioneer, *Catalogue of the Valuable Cabinet of Pictures & Engravings of the late W. H. Playfair, Esq., Architect ... also the Valuable and Interesting Collection of Drawings in Water Colours, by H. W. Williams ... the property of the late Aeneas MacBean, Esquire* (Edinburgh 1858)

Nodier, Charles, *Promenade de Dieppe aux Montagnes d'Ecosse* (Paris 1821)

—, *Promenade from Dieppe to the Mountains of Scotland* (Edinburgh and London 1822)

O'Keeffe, Paul, *A Genius for Failure. The Life of Benjamin Robert Haydon* (London 2009)

Patterson, John Brown, *On the National Character of the Athenians and the Causes of those Peculiarities by which it was Distinguished. An Essay which Gained the Prize of One Hundred Guineas Proposed to the Students of the University of Edinburgh by His Majesty's Commissioners for Visiting the Universities and Colleges of Scotland* (Edinburgh 1828)

Peacham, Henry, *The Compleat Gentleman* (London 1634)

Peacock, Thomas Love, *The Works of Thomas Love Peacock*, edited by Henry Cole, with a Preface by the Rt Hon. Lord Houghton, three vols (London 1875)

Perman, Ray, *The Rise and Fall of The City of Money. A Financial History of Edinburgh* (Edinburgh 2019)

Pernot, F. A., *Vues Pittoresque de'l Écosse* (Paris 1826)

Pevsner, Nikolaus, *A History of Building Types* (London 1976)

Philp, Robert, *A Keen Wind Blows. The Story of Fettes College*, second edition (London 2008)

Philipp, Klaus Jan, 'Historicist and Romantic Architecture in Germany', in Rolf Toman, ed., *Neoclassicism and Romanticism. Architecture, Sculpture, Painting, Drawings 1750-1848* (Cologne 2000)

[Pichot, Amédée], *Historical and Literary Tour of a Foreigner in England and Scotland*, two vols (London 1825)

'Plain Honest Man, A.', *A Letter to the Right Honourable the Lord Provost of Edinburgh on the Subject of the Proposed New Streets and Approaches to the City. By a Plain Honest Man* (Edinburgh 1825)

Prebble, John, *The King's Jaunt. George IV in Scotland, August 1822. 'One and twenty daft days'* (London 1988)

'R.', 'Restoration of the Parthenon for the National Monument', *Blackwood's Edinburgh Magazine*, V, no. xxix (August 1819), pp. 509-12

Ramsay, Allan, *Poems* (Edinburgh 1721)

—, *The Poems of Allan Ramsay*, new edition, two vols (London 1800)

—, *The Works of Allan Ramsay*, Scottish Text Society, six vols (1951-74), IV, edited by Alexander M. Kinghorn and Alexander Law (Edinburgh 1970)

Raumer, Frederick [*sic*] von, *England in 1835: Being a Series of Letters Written to Friends in Germany During a Residence in London and Excursions into the Provinces*, translated by H. E. Lloyd, three vols (London 1836)

Richardson, A. E., *Monumental Classic Architecture in Great Britain and Ireland in the Eighteenth & Nineteenth Centuries* (London and New York [1914])

[Robertson, Andrew], *National Monument to be Erected at Edinburgh, to the Memory of Robert Burns* ([London] 1819)

—, *The Parthenon, Adapted to the Purpose of a National Monument, to Commemorate the Victories of the Late War; Proposed to be Erected in Trafalgar Square, or Hyde Park* (London 1838)

Robertson, Emily, *Letters and Papers of Andrew Robertson, A.M.* (London 1895)

Rock, Joe, *Thomas Hamilton Architect 1784-1858* (Edinburgh 1984)

—, 'Hugh William Williams ('Grecian' Williams) 1773-1829', *The Book of the Old Edinburgh Club*, New Series, 5 (2002), pp. 83-91

—, http://sites.google.com/site/hughwilliamwilliams

—, 'Robert Forrest (1789-1852) and his Exhibition on the Calton Hill', *The Book of the Old Edinburgh Club*, New Series, 7 (2008), pp. 127-38

Rood, Timothy, 'From Marathon to Waterloo. Byron, Battle Monuments, and the Persian Wars', in *Cultural Responses to the Persian Wars. Antiquity to the Third Millennium*, edited by Emma Bridges, Edith Hall and P. J. Rhodes (Oxford 2007), pp. 267-97

Roscoe, Ingrid, with Emma Hardy and M. G. Sullivan, *A Biographical Dictionary of Sculptors in Britain 1660-1851* (New Haven and London 2009)

'Roundrobin, Roger' [? Patrick Gibson], *A Letter to the Directors and Members of the Institution for the Encouragement of the Fine Arts in Scotland, By Roger Roundrobin, Esq.* (Edinburgh 1826)

Rowan, Alistair, 'Bicentenary of a Classical City. Georgian Edinburgh—I', *Country Life*, 19 October 1967, pp. 956-59

—, 'The Athens of the North Explored. Georgian Edinburgh—II', *Country Life*, 26 October 1967, pp. 1052-55

Royle, Trevor, *The Mainstream Companion to Scottish Literature* (Edinburgh 1993)

Ruskin, John, *The Stones of Venice*, three vols (London 1851-53)

—, *Lectures on Architecture and Painting, Delivered at Edinburgh in November 1853* (London 1854)

St Clair, William, *Lord Elgin and the Marbles*, third revised edition (Oxford 1998)

St John, John, *Mary, Queen of Scots* (London 1789)

Schinkel, Karl Friedrich, *The English Journey*, edited by David Bindman and Gottfried Riemann (New Haven and London 1993)

Scotland Delineated in a Series of Views, lithographed John Duffield Harding, and with Historical, Antiquarian and Descriptive letterpress by John Parker Lawson, two vols (London 1847)

Scotland Illustrated in a Series of Eighty Views from Drawings by John C. Brown, William Brown, Andrew Donaldson ... and Other Scottish Artists, with Letter-Press Descriptions (London, Dublin and Edinburgh 1850)

'Scotus', *A Letter to the Lord Provost on the Mischievous Tendency of a Scheme for Abolishing the High School of Edinburgh* (Edinburgh 1822)

Scott, Honoria, *A Winter in Edinburgh; or, The Russian Brothers; a Novel*, three vols (London 1810)

[Scott, Walter], 'Childe Harold's Pilgrimage, Canto III... By Lord Byron', *Quarterly Review*, XVI, no xxxi (October 1816), Art. IX, pp. 172-208

[—], 'Childe Harold's Pilgrimage. Canto IV. By Lord Byron', *Quarterly Review*, XIX, no xxxvii (April 1818), Art. IX, pp. 215-32

[—], *The Visionary. Nos. I. II. III.* [1819], edited and with an introduction by Peter Garside (Cardiff 1984)

Scott, Walter, *Provincial Antiquities and Picturesque Scenery of Scotland, with Descriptive Illustrations*, two vols (London 1826)

—, *Miscellaneous Prose Works of Sir Walter Scott*, twenty-eight vols (Edinburgh 1834-36), VI, 'Essay on the Drama', pp. 219-395

—, *The Private Letter-Books of Sir Walter Scott*, edited by Wilfred Partington (London 1930)

—, *The Letters of Sir Walter Scott*, edited by H. J. C. Grierson assisted by Davidson Cook and W. M. Parker, twelve volumes (London 1932-37)

—, *The Journal of Sir Walter Scott*, edited by W. E. K. Anderson (Oxford 1972)

Scottish Architects at Home and Abroad, exhibition catalogue by Alastair Cherry and Iain Gordon Brown (Edinburgh 1978)

Scottish Tourist, and Itinerary, The: or, a Guide to the Scenery and Antiquities of Scotland and the Western Islands, second edition (Edinburgh 1827)

Sharpe, Charles Kirkpatrick, *Letters to and from Charles Kirkpatrick Sharpe, Esq.*, edited by Alexander Allardyce, two vols (Edinburgh 1888)

Shelley, Frances, *The Diary of Frances Lady Shelley*, edited by Richard Edgcumbe, two vols (London 1913)

Shepherd, Thomas Hosmer and James Elmes, *Metropolitan Improvements; or, London in the Nineteenth Century: Displayed in a Series of Engravings of the New and Most Interesting Objects in the British Metropolis & its Vicinity* (London 1827)

Shepherd, Thomas Hosmer and John Britton, *Modern Athens! Displayed in a Series of Views: Or, Edinburgh in the Nineteenth Century* (London 1829)

Sher, Richard B., *The Enlightenment & the Book. Scottish Authors & Their Publishers in Eighteenth-Century Britain, Ireland, & America* (Chicago & London 2006)

—, *Church and University in the Scottish Enlightenment*, Classic Edition (Edinburgh 2015)

Shine, Hill and Shine, Helen Chadwick, *The Quarterly Review Under Gifford: Identification of Contributors* (Chapel Hill, NC, 1949)

[Simond, Louis], *Journal of Tour and Residence in Great Britain during the Years 1810 and 1811 by a French Traveller*, two vols (Edinburgh 1815)

[James Simpson], *Letters to Sir Walter Scott, Bart. On the Moral and Political Character and Effects of the Visit to Scotland in August 1822, of His Majesty King George IV* (Edinburgh 1822)

Sinclair, John, 'Address to the Citizens of Edinburgh, and to the Inhabitants of North Britain in General, on His Majesty's Expected Visit to Scotland. By the Rt Hon Sir J. Sinclair, Bt', *The Morning Post*, 20 November 1821

Skinner, Basil, 'Parthenon or Valhalla', *Proceedings of the Calton Conference*, 5 November 1983 (Edinburgh 1984), pp. 3-7

Skrine, Henry, *Three Successive Tours in the North of England, and a Great Part of Scotland* (London 1795)

Smailes, Helen E., 'A history of the Statue Gallery at the Trustees' Academy in Edinburgh and the acquisition of the Albacini casts in 1838', *Journal of the History of Collections*, 3, No 2 (1991), pp. 125-43

—, '"Uno Sfortunato Scultore Scozzese chiamato Campbell". The Correspondence of Thomas Campbell (1791-1858) and his Banking Maecenas, Gilbert Innes of Stow (1751-1832)', *The Walpole Society*, LXXI (2009), pp. 217-323

Smart, Alastair, *Allan Ramsay: Painter, Essayist and Man of the Enlightenment* (New Haven and London 1992)

Smith, Alexander, *A Summer in Skye*, two vols (London 1865)

Smith, A. H., 'Lord Elgin and his Collection', *Journal of Hellenic Studies*, 36 (1919), pp. 163-372

Southey, Robert, *Journal of a Tour in Scotland in 1819*, with an introduction and notes by C. H. Herford (London 1929)

Spawforth, Tony, *The Complete Greek Temples* (London 2006)

Stamp, Gavin, 'Should auld acquaintance be forgot?', *The Times,* Saturday Supplement, 23 November 1991, p. 4

Stark, John, *Picture of Edinburgh; Containing a History and Description of the City* (Edinburgh 1806)

—, *The Picture of Edinburgh: Containing a Description of the City and Its Environs* (Edinburgh 1820)

—, *The Picture of Edinburgh*, third edition, improved (Edinburgh 1823)

—, *The Statistical Account of Scotland, Drawn up from the Communications of the Ministers of the Various Parishes,* Vol. 1 (Linlithgowshire), [edited by Sir John Sinclair] (Edinburgh 1791)

Stevenson, Robert Louis, *Edinburgh. Picturesque Notes* (London 1879)

Stewart, Dugald, *Dissertation, Part Second*, edited by Sir William Hamilton, second edition (Edinburgh 1854)

[Stewart, Margaret C. H.], *The Edinburgh College of Art Cast Collection and Architecture* (Edinburgh 2009)

—, 'Scenery and scenes: the plaster cast collection and its architecture at Edinburgh College of Art', unpublished paper (Edinburgh 2009)

Stillman, Damie, *English Neo-classical Architecture*, two vols (London 1988)

Stoddart, Anna M., *John Stuart Blackie*, two vols (Edinburgh 1895)

Stoddart, John, *Remarks on Local Scenery and Manners in Scotland during the Years 1799 and 1800*, two vols (London 1801)

Storer, J. and H. S., *Views in Edinburgh and its Vicinity; Drawn and Engraved by J. & H. S. Storer*, two vols (Edinburgh and London 1820)

Stranger's Guide to Edinburgh, The, Containing a History and Description of the City..., sixth edition (Edinburgh 1817)

Strout, Alan Lang, *A Bibliography of Articles in Blackwood's Magazine, 1817-1825* (Lubbock, Texas, 1959)

Stuart, James and Nicholas Revett, *The Antiquities of Athens. Measured and Delineated. Volume the First* (London 1762 [1763]); vol. II (London 1787 [1790]), vol. 3 (London 1794), vol. IV (London 1816)
Szatkowski, Sheila, *Enlightenment Edinburgh. A Guide* (Edinburgh 2017)

Thomson, Alexander, 'Art and Architecture: A Course of Four Lectures', no. III, pts I and II, *The British Architect: a National Record of the Aesthetic and Constructive Arts; and the Business Journal of the Building Community*, II (1874), nos 30 (24 July 1874) and 32 (7 August 1874,) pp. 50-52 and 82-84
—, *The Light of Truth and Beauty. The Lectures of Alexander 'Greek' Thomson 1817-1875*, edited and with an introduction by Gavin Stamp (Glasgow 1999)
Thomson, Katrina, *Turner and Sir Walter Scott. The Provincial Antiquities and Picturesque Scenery of Scotland* (Edinburgh 1999)
'Traveller, A', 'Restoration of the Parthenon. [Letter] To the Right Honourable the Lord Advocate of Scotland, Convener of the Committee on the National Monument', *The Edinburgh Magazine, and Literary Miscellany: A New Series of the Scots Magazine*, VI (February 1820), pp. 99-105
[Trevor-Roper, Hugh], *The Letters of Mercurius* (London 1970)
Trotter, Alexander, of Dreghorn, *A Plan of Communication Between the New and the Old Town of Edinburgh in the Line of the Earthen Mound*, second edition, greatly enlarged, with Additional Plates (Edinburgh 1829)
—, *Observations by Alexander Trotter, Esq, of Dreghorn, in Illustration of his Modified Plan of a Communication Between the Old and New Town of Edinburgh* (Edinburgh and London 1836)

Verne, Jules, *Voyage a Reculons en Angleterre et en Écosse* (Paris 1989)
—, *Backwards to Britain*, translated by Janice Valls-Russell (Edinburgh 1992)
Victoria, H M Queen, *Leaves from the Journal of Our Life in the Highlands from 1848 to 1861, To Which are Prefixed and Added Extracts from the Same Journal Giving an Account of Earlier Visits to Scotland...*, edited by Arthur Helps (London 1868)

Waagen, G. F., *Treasures of Art in Great Britain*, three vols (London 1854)
Walker, David, 'William Burn' in *Scottish Pioneers of the Greek Revival*, edited by Nic Allen (Edinburgh 1984), pp. 3-35
Wallace, Stuart, *John Stuart Blackie: Scottish Scholar and Patriot* (Edinburgh 2006)
Watkin, David, *A History of Western Architecture*, fourth edition (London 2005)
—, 'Epilogue: The Impact of Stuart over Two Centuries', in *James 'Athenian' Stuart 1713-1788. The Rediscovery of Antiquity*, edited by Susan Weber Soros (New Haven and London 2007), pp. 515-48
Watters, Diane, 'Καλοι κ'αγαθοι (The Beautiful and the Good): Classical School Architecture and Educational Elitism in Early Nineteenth-Century Edinburgh', *Architectural History*, 57 (2014), pp. 277-321
White, Adam, *Four Short Letters... on the Subject of an Open Museum in the Scottish Capital* (Edinburgh [1850])
Williams, Hugh William, *Travels in Italy, Greece, and the Ionian Islands. In a Series of Letters Descriptive of Manners, Scenery, and the Fine Arts*, two vols (Edinburgh 1820)
—, *Catalogue of Views in Greece, Italy, Sicily, [and] the Ionian Islands [etc., etc.] by Hugh William Williams, Painted in Water Colours ...* (Edinburgh 1822 and 1826)
—, *Select Views in Greece with Classical Illustrations*, two vols (London and Edinburgh 1829)
Willis, Nathaniel Parker, *Pencillings by the Way*, three vols (London 1835)
Wilson, C[harles] H[eath], *Descriptive Catalogue of Casts from Antique Statues in the Trustees' Academy* (Edinburgh 1837)
Wilson, Daniel, *Memorials of Edinburgh in the Olden Time*, two vols (Edinburgh 1848); second edition (Edinburgh 1891)

—, *Reminiscences of Old Edinburgh*, two vols (Edinburgh 1878)

[Wilson, John], 'Noctes Ambrosianae. No. VI', *Blackwood's Edinburgh Magazine*, XII, no. LXVIII (September 1822), pp. 369-91

[—], *Noctes Ambrosianae by the Late John Wilson*, edited by R. Shelton Mackenzie, four vols (New York 1863)

Wordsworth, William, *The Poems of William Wordsworth, Collected Reading Texts from The Cornell Wordsworth*, edited by Jared Curtis, three vols (Ithaca, NY 2009)

Wycherley, R. E., *How the Greeks Built Cities*, second edition, revised (London 1967)

—, *The Stones of Athens* (Princeton, NJ 1978)

Xenophon, *Memorabilia*, translated and annotated at Amy L. Bonnette (Ithaca, NY 1994)

Youngson, A. J., *The Making of Classical Edinburgh* (Edinburgh 1966)

—, *The Companion Guide to Edinburgh and the Border Country* (London 1993)

Zaccarini, Matteo, 'The Athens of the North? Scotland and the National Struggle for the Parthenon, its Marbles and its Identity', *Aevum. Rassegna di Scienze Storiche Linguistiche e Filologiche*, 92, fasc. 1 (2018), pp. 179-95

Zachs, William, *Without Regard to Good Manners: a Biography of Gilbert Stuart, 1743-1786* (Edinburgh 1992)

INDEX

Locations and institutions in Edinburgh are listed separately, e.g. 'County Hall'. There are no entries for Edinburgh as 'the Athens of the North', 'the Modern Athens' or 'Edinburgh as Athens'. References to images, their captions, or both, are printed in italic.